Social-Science Commentary
on the Book of Acts

Social-Science Commentary
on the
Book of Acts

BRUCE J. MALINA

JOHN J. PILCH

Fortress Press

MINNEAPOLIS

SOCIAL-SCIENCE COMMENTARY ON THE BOOK OF ACTS

Cover design: Douglas Schmitz

Cover photo: Fragments of a leaf from P^{38}, a papyrus codex from c. 200 c.e., bearing Acts 18:27–19:6, 12-16 (P.Mich. 138, Inv. 1571). Digitally reproduced with the Permission of the Papyrology Collection, Graduate Library, The University of Michigan.

Interior photos: Photos on pp. 32, 47, 63, 72, 94, 102, 134, 151, 163 are © Erich Lessing/Art Resource, N.Y.; photo on p. 8 is © The Pierpont Morgan Library, N.Y./Art Resource, N.Y.; photos on pp. 25 and 102 are © Scala/Art Resource, N.Y.; photo on p. 119 is © Alinari/Art Resource, N.Y.; photo on p. 189 is © Art Resource, N.Y.; photo on p. 214 is © Vanni/Art Resource, N.Y.; all are used by permission. Photos on pp. 127, 128, 131, 141, 192, 199, 212, 220, 236 are from Cities of Paul © 2004 The President and Fellows of Harvard College. Map on pp. 12–13 by Lucidity Information Design.

Library of Congress Cataloging-in-Publication Data

Malina, Bruce J.
   Social-science commentary on the book of Acts / Bruce J. Malina and John J. Pilch.
     p. cm. — (Social-science commentary)
   ISBN 978-0-8006-3845-0 (alk. paper)
    1. Bible. N.T. Acts—Commentaries. 2. Bible. N.T. Acts—Social scientific criticism. I. Pilch, John J. II. Title.

   BS2625.53.M34 2008
   226.6'07—dc22

                                              2007044120

Manufactured in the U.S.A.
12   11   10   09   08   1   2   3   4   5   6   7   8   9   10

For S. Scott Bartchy
Friend, Colleague, and Intrepid Acts Researcher

Contents

Introduction

The name of the anonymous work entitled the "Acts of the Apostles" comes from a transliteration of the Latin: *Acta apostolorum* (Greek: *pragmata apostolōn*). The Latin word *acta* (like the Greek *pragmata*) means deeds and activities along with the events surrounding those deeds and activities. The prologue to Acts indicates that it is the second of a two-volume work. The first volume is called the Gospel of Luke, a work that might equally be called the "Acts of Jesus." The title "gospel" for the "Acts of Jesus" comes from Mark 1:1: "The beginning of the *gospel* of Jesus Christ, the Son of God." The ascription of the work to a person named Luke comes from later tradition (based on the presumed but unfounded identification of the writer of this work with the Luke of Philemon 24, the post-Pauline "beloved physician" of Col 4:14, and the statement in 2 Tim 4:11 that "Luke alone is with me").

We intend this book to be a social-scientific commentary on the book of Acts. We would like to understand how a first-century Israelite audience, the minority group located in the majority non-Israelite city of Ephesus, understood the narratives written by Luke (we use the traditional name for the writer). To get to this first-century audience living in the capital of the Roman province of Asia, we have to travel through two thousand years of historical interpretation of Luke's work. That journey has revealed a landscape littered with a layer of intellectual debris that makes the understanding of first-century Jesus groups rather daunting. Much of this debris is due to the sloppy work of modern historians who have allowed anachronism to reign supreme in their explanation of these documents.

The Problems of Anachronism

For example, all historians know that the separation of church and state and of bank and state is an eighteenth-century phenomenon. In more abstract terms, that means that the separation of religion from politics and economics from politics dates to the eighteenth century. Before that time, there were no formal social institutions called religion and economics. Rather religion and economics were substantial social institutions that were embedded in politics, resulting in political religion and political economy. The same was true of the focal social institution of the past, namely, kinship. There was kinship religion and kinship economy—but no religion

1

as a freestanding, unembedded institution as we know it today. To be historically accurate, then, Jesus' project was an enterprise in political religion; the Jesus groups that emerged from his communication of the innovation of a forthcoming Israelite political theocracy (that is, his preaching of a kingdom of heaven/God, or the reign of God) were domestic religious groups awaiting this new Israelite theocracy.

Historians also know that all forms of the Jewish religion today are rooted in that fifth-century rabbinic (Pharisaic) compilation known as the Talmud. Yet too often they fail to distinguish between contemporary and ancient Judaism. To retroject fifth-century talmudic perspectives to first-century Israel is, of course, anachronistic. To speak of "Jewish religion" in first-century Israel is doubly anachronistic for the reasons mentioned in the previous paragraph.

Finally, historians know that the form of Judaism best known in the modern world is culturally very different from either first- or fifth-century Judaism. Most Jews today, including the vast majority of Jews living in the State of Israel (which was created, by appropriation of Palestinian land, only in 1948), are "Ashkenazi" Jews, the descendants of migrations into eastern Europe going back for centuries (as described already by the twelfth-century Jewish writer Judah Ha-Levi). Much of the language, liturgy, and culture of Ashkenazi Judaism are the result of a distinctive history.

The point is that historians and Bible readers cannot retroject their experiences of contemporary Jews (or Christians, for that matter, as we shall see) to the first century. Furthermore, first-century Israelite society across the Mediterranean was far more variegated and complicated than the division into Pharisees, Sadducees, Herodians, and Essenes. Moreover, it would have been difficult at first glance to distinguish a Mediterranean Judean from a Mediterranean non-Israelite. As Jewish historian Shaye Cohen observes: "Jews and gentiles were corporeally, visually, linguistically, and socially indistinguishable" (Cohen 1999:37). And further: "If, then, circumcision was neither an infallible nor a usable marker of Jewishness; if there were no genealogical records that would have proven who was a Jew and who was not; and if the Jews of antiquity looked like everyone else, spoke like everyone else, were named like everyone else, and supported themselves like everyone else, how did you know a Jew in antiquity when you saw one?" (Cohen 1999:53). Aside from his confusing and anachronistic translations of *Ioudaios* as "Jew" instead of Judean, Cohen's description of Israelites in the world of Acts is quite on target.

Similarly, historians know that

> It is common knowledge that Christianity is different from the religion of the Old Testament, but some are still unaware that Judaism (sometimes referred to as Rabbinic Judaism, as opposed to the religion or the Judaism practiced during biblical times) is a different religion from that of the Hebrew Bible. What is different about it? Nearly everything: its liturgy, its forms of worship, its codes of laws and its theologies. (Reuven Firestone, in *The Jewish Journal of Greater Los Angeles*, December 14, 2001)

The point of all this is that there was no Jew or Jewishness as known today in the Israelite society of the first-century Mediteranean. The Greek word for the inhabitants of the region of Judea (not "Jewish land") is *Ioudaioi*, best translated "Judeans" so as not to confuse them with modern Jews, with whom they have little in common. With a little historical awareness, one can understand that Judean peoples and customs are quite different from contemporary Jewish peoples and customs. To refer to the Judeans described by Luke as "Jews" is, once more, quite anachronistic.

But so are a number of other words to which so many modern readers have become inured: foremost among them, *Christian*, but also *Greece* (as a national region), *state, nation, Old Testament, pagan, paganism, eschatology, apocalyptic, economics, religion, religious sect, countercultural, city, supernatural, miracle, author,* and the like. All these words refer to realities that are well known in subsequent centuries and common coin among contemporaries living in the twenty-first century but were totally *unknown* to first-century peoples in their Hellenistic societies.

Should we couple such obvious anachronisms with the ethnocentric perspectives of modern Bible readers, deriving from commonly shared Enlightenment and Romantic values, the problem of a fair interpretation of Acts simply grows exponentially. The United States is a country founded on Enlightenment principles, including the separation of church and state. The eighteenth-century Enlightenment focused on the objectively real, on nature and regularity, and on authority based on reason. Enlightenment approaches laid great stress on the generality and uniformity of human experience, so useful to a legalistic "true" or "false" approach and to a scientific approach especially when applied in technology. The distinction between fact and fiction in history dates back only to the close of the eighteenth century (Prickett 1996:45).

The nineteenth century witnessed a reaction to the arid rationalism and presumed objectivity of the Enlightenment. The constellations of persons, perspectives, and events that emerged in response to the Enlightenment has been called the Romantic movement or Romanticism. The term comes from the French and German words for the literary form called the novel, *le roman,* or *der Roman.* Romanticism focused on the subjective, on the individual person and idiosyncrasy, and on the affirmation of feeling ("sensibility"), with stress on an individual's particularity and even uniqueness. For the Romantics, human living unfolds as a story in novel form, with its characterization, plot, progression, even dramatic conclusion.

This radical shift in understanding human living in novelistic terms led to a radical shift in reading the Bible as though it were a story (a salvation story, salvation history). Its narratives came to be treated as those of a novel, peopled by characters with recognizable psychological motivations and feelings. The only difference is that these are not, of course, fictional characters but presumably real ones, described for us by the only truly omniscient Author. As Stephen Prickett has noted, "the idea of the Bible as presenting a novel-like narrative, with character, motivation and plot is, like the modern novel itself, no older than the 18th century" (Prickett 1996:265).

For the medieval Scholastics, a principle of metaphysics was that "whatever is received is received according to the dispositions and capabilities of the receiver" (*quidquid recipitur, recipitur modo recipientis*). The Romantics carried this principle over to the cognitive realm and coined the term *appropriation* for the process by which a person (for example, a reader) takes an alien concept from another cultural context and so assimilates it as to render it a part of his or her own personal world. This process of the Romantic "appropriation" of the Bible is now called "contextualization," or even "inculturation." The process is little concerned with what a concept might have meant to the people who originally expressed and lived it. The main concern is to demonstrate its contemporary relevance.

A number of scholars have demonstrated how before the nineteenth century there was no sense of history as we use the term today. Today people believe the past was different from the present, and hence people today need not be bound to the past. Before the nineteenth century, it was generally believed that people in the past were just as we are in all significant dimensions. The purpose of history was to present slices of living that illustrate unchanging truths about human nature and God's judgment through a series of transparent instances of timeless truths, as a process of verifiable and meaningful change. History before the nineteenth century presented the past as similar to our own day, thus offering a living source of legitimation of life as it is. The appropriated and contextualized Bible does much the same.

The first intimations of a radical, step-level change in the assessment of the Bible took place between about 1760 and 1790, with the focus on characterization and personal motivation (as distinct from literary style). By the early nineteenth century, the new "sentimental" and novelistic way of reading the Bible became the accepted norm among elites. "The problem is whether the new way of reading was, as has been generally assumed, fundamentally 'historical,' and concerned first and foremost with questions of narrative veracity, or whether it involved something that at first glance looked very like this, but was in fact much more concerned with seeing the biblical protagonists as individual characters of the kind made familiar through the new literary genre of the novel and possessed of a quite new kind of inner consciousness" (Prickett 1996:131). Subjectivism became the Romantic norm. "Whether in religion, literature, gardening or sexual relations, he stresses personal response over convention, private association over traditional typology, feeling over meaning" (Prickett 1996:150).

While people still continued to proclaim the contemporary relevance of the Bible, among educated elite by the mid-nineteenth century neither millenarian nor historically based positions seemed capable of giving the Scriptures an immediate relevance, since the literal meaning of biblical documents demonstrated their historical remoteness and essentially unrepeatable quality. The outcome of this awareness gave rise to the contemporary concern for the Bible as literature, a concern deriving from Romanticism. For the church fathers (for example, Ambrose, Augustine, Jerome, Origen), in contrast, biblical documents were almost totally devoid of any kind of aesthetic appeal. Yet a host of scholars today deal with biblical "literature" and delve into all sorts of dimensions considered aesthetically pleasing. This is as true of university theology departments as of English departments.

With Romanticism, there was a palpable shift from a collective to an individualistic religious sensibility, like the parallel movement from an externalized to an internalized apprehension of feelings. Before the eighteenth century, nothing in the Bible was considered dramatic; there was no dramatic reading of the Bible in the sense of "dramatic" as a story whose plot unfolds in surprising or mysterious ways. This is a new meaning of the word "drama" that coincides with the introduction of the theatrical metaphors of "scene" and "scenery" to describe landscape. Such narrative suspense in the pre-eighteenth-century world would be quite anachronistic. To read the Bible as univocal, linear, and successive scenes from a play or chapters of a novel is a Romantic invention. Likewise, the word *revolution* changes meaning from one turn in a cycle to a clean break with the immediate political (or social, aesthetic, philosophical) past. This perception undergirds the new sense of history and its awareness of dissimilarity from the past.

The developed Enlightenment understanding of the scientific heliocentric worldview led to the loss of the divinely guaranteed world order as recorded in the Bible. Romantics, in turn, sought to root a new religious synthesis in the subjectivity of individual experience, especially through the balanced yet total development of every individual's powers. A fundamental view of European Romantics is the concept of "literature" as possessing inherent value in itself over and above its ostensible subject. Literature was the mediator of reality. By the end of the eighteenth century, scholars in England, France, and Germany responded to the Bible similarly: a quest for wholeness, a literary form that permitted discussion of the human condition in all its cultural, intellectual, social, and religious complexity, the gradual recognition of the essential subjectivity of human experience. All these features placed an increasing premium on the literary and poetic qualities of the Scriptures, the Scripture as aesthetic ideal, a metatype offering a universal and absolute category giving meaning and shape to the rest of literature.

The Protestant reading of the Bible as novel-like narrative became widespread in Britain and Germany by the end of the eighteenth century. The result was a new kind of reader–text relationship that consisted of a solitary experience (unlike the theater) with more unpredictable consequences. This solitary way of reading the Bible was affirmed by the Romantic view of the personal and singular quality of all experience. What counted was moments of special intuition or grace of unmediated spiritual experience. This modern form of the medieval *lectio divina* results in a personal remystification of "text."

The outcome of this process of biblical novelization can be found in contemporary fundamentalism, with its attachment to the literal "historical truth" of the narrative stories themselves instead of the traditional idea of divinely inspired meaning in the Bible. It is no longer the inspired documents but the inspired readers that count. It is all part of the sense of self as a philosophical and moral foundation that in presently popularized forms is essentially a nineteenth-century Romantic experience: firsthand experience rather than accepting someone else's judgment, a stress on personal immediacy. A recent Barna poll (2002) found that more than 70 percent of Americans believe they have no need of any information to understand the Bible aside from their own reading of the English translation.

Noteworthy for historians and biblical scholars of early Jesus-group documents such as Acts is the Romantic flurry of novels about "early Christianity" through which European Protestants and Catholics debated their respective ecclesiastical positions: *Hypatia, Last Days of Pompeii, Zenobia, Valerius, Callista*. What is significant is that most people today who read and hear Acts have their images of early Jesus groups from such novels (and later movie and television adaptations). All of these, of course, emphasize individualistic protagonists, with a sense of self that is unique and different, who "convert" from "paganism to Christianity" thanks to their individual identity and private judgment. There is nothing Mediterranean about them at all!

In sum, most interpretations of Acts read that document with the anachronistic lenses polished with eighteenth-century Enlightenment beliefs, such as separation of church and state, of bank and state, eighteenth- and nineteenth-century sense of history and history writing, a Romantic sense of individualism and story, and the values of the Industrial Revolution and twentieth-century principles of science in the service of technology. The cultural chasm between antiquity and modernity, between Acts and the modern reader, is far greater than the changes in technology and economics.

Luke-Acts as History

The fact that the Gospel of Luke and the Acts of the Apostles have prologues of the sort that preface Hellenistic histories indicates that Luke's documents were intended to be first-century history. "In terms of classical historiography, moreover, Luke's work, executed in reasonably polished Greek, could be reckoned nonfictional, useful and complying with conventional canons of history-writing" (Trompf 1979:322). G. W. Trompf's excellent study of Luke as ancient historian underscores the great differences separating the purpose and significance of "history" in antiquity from contemporary standards.

The book of Acts tells of the foundation and expansion of Jesus groups after the death and resurrection of Jesus and his final appearance among his core group of disciples. According to the writer of this story, the personage exclusively responsible for the foundation and expansion of Jesus groups in the post-Jesus period is the God of Israel. The activity of the God of Israel is described in terms of God's power personified, that is, the Holy Spirit. For Luke, the founder of "Christianity"—and the one responsible for "Christian" expansion—is solely the God of Israel. Such history writing causes many moderns to consider Luke a theologian rather than a historian. However, this kind of anachronistic judgment is based on a worldview that distinguishes natural from supernatural, the imperceptible realm of God from the concrete and measurable realm of human beings. In antiquity, there was no such distinction until Origen. It was quite natural for God (and gods) to interact with humans, and vice versa. The objective world was full of humans as well as demons, angels, spirits, and deities. Although ordinary people experienced that objective world, there were some persons experienced in interacting with nonhuman personages. These persons were holy men and women.

Luke's works were written for first-century Israelites. Just as Luke's Gospel story explains the significance "for us" first-century Jesus group members of what the God of Israel was up to in the activity, death, and resurrection of Jesus, Acts in turn continues the story by describing the significance "for us" fourth-generation Jesus group members of what the God of Israel was up to in the activity of the foundation and expansion of Jesus groups up to "our own day." The concern of Luke-Acts is totally focused on Israel. There is little if any indication that Luke was a non-Israelite or that he was writing for non-Israelites (although many modern historians gratuitously assert this—as the adage puts it, *gratis asseritur, gratis negatur,* what is gratuitously asserted can be gratuitously denied). The protagonists of the story are witnesses to what the God of Israel has done in and to Jesus of Nazareth, Israel's Messiah to come. *Messiah* is an exclusively Israelite social role. Even a satirist such as Lucian notes the characteristics of true history: the events the writer describes must have been seen by the writer himself or heard from someone else with a reputation for truthfulness; he must write about things he has seen or had to do with or learned from others (see preface to Lucian's *A True Story* [trans. A. M. Harmon; LCL 1:247-49]). The witnesses upon whom Luke bases his history are the reliable witnesses who had seen events, had had to do with those events, and who Luke believed had a reputation for truthfulness.

Luke's citation of Israel's Scriptures as proof, his style of writing patterned after Israel's Sacred Scripture (the Septuagint), his notice from opening to close of the forthcoming kingdom of God (Israelite theocracy), as well as his description of the activities of the God of Israel would only make sense to and win the credibility of an Israelite. All significant interactions take place within Israelite groups and are about Israelite groups, including the incident of God's sending Cornelius to Peter. Cornelius is, in fact, peripheral to the argument that takes place among Israelites, on Israelite terms, and in favor of Israelite interests.

God's selection of Cornelius becomes a test case for how Jesus groups might expand among non-Israelites. Because of the ancient Mediterranean appreciation of stereotypes about generation, gender, and geography, it was believed that general knowledge about any population always yields accurate and specific knowledge of individuals belonging to that population and vice versa. As Virgil said of the devious Greek Sinon, "Learn about them all from this one instance" (*Ab uno disce omnes* [*Aen.* 2.65 LCL]). Luke portrays the various Jesus groups as considering it important to know how God dealt with a single person and thus he generalizes: one non-Israelite joining the group leads to the conclusion "Gentiles have joined." Furthermore, it is quite common for people who do not belong to a particular group (in this case to "Gentiles" or non-Israelites) to generally perceive that outgroup to be less diverse than group members assume (Krueger 2001:21, 142).

For Luke, the ritual dipping that brings a person into a Jesus group was dipping in the spirit. John's dipping was in water; the dipping of Jesus' group was in God's spirit. Whoever has been dipped in the spirit thus is a member of the group, whether group members are aware of it or not. After all, the God of Israel is in charge of the expansion of these Jesus groups.

Many modern scholars consider Luke-Acts to be a narrative in travel-story form, and so it is. The focus of the travel, however, is not from place to place, but from population to population. The mention of places is important only because in antiquity, populations and their characteristics derive from the places they inhabit,

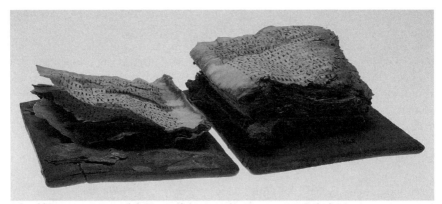

This fifth-century copy of the Acts of the Apostles is written in Sahidic Coptic.
MS M. 910. The Pierpont Morgan Library, New York, N.Y. Photo: © The Pierpont
Morgan Library, New York / Art Resource, N.Y. Used by permission.

the air they breathe, and the water they drink. This feature was clearly set forth in
the *Hippocratic Corpus.* The value of airs, waters, and places for ethnic qualities
became common knowledge among elites, and points of honor among non-elites as
well (Hippocrates, *Airs, Waters, Places*; Strabo, *Geography*; see Aujac 1966:270-73).
And just as ethnic groups have their own geographical location, they likewise
evidence geographically rooted ethnic stereotypes by which other groups might
assess them. For example, Cicero observes how the Carthaginians are fraudulent
and liars because of their ports being visited by too many merchants. Then there
are the Campanians, who are so arrogant because of the fertility and beauty of
their land. And the Ligurians are hard and wild because they are just like all
other people who struggle to make mountain soil productive (*Agrarian Laws* 2.95;
LCL 6:470-75). Josephus, in turn, notes how Tiberians have "a passion for war"
(Josephus, *Life* §352; LCL 1:131); Scythians "delight in murdering people and are
little better than wild beasts" (Josephus, *Against Apion* §269; LCL 1:401); "Cretans
are always liars, evil beasts, lazy gluttons" (Titus 1:12); in "the seamanship of its
people . . . the Phoenicians in general have been superior to all peoples of all times"
(Strabo, *Geography* 16.2.23; trans. Jones, LCL 7:269); "this is a trait common to all
the Arabian kings" that they do "not care much about public affairs and particularly
military affairs" (Strabo, *Geography* 16.4.24; LCL 7:357). "These are the marks of
the little-minded man. He is small limbed, small and round, dry, with small eyes
and a small face, like a Corinthian or Leucadian" (Ps. Aristotle, *Physiognomics*
808a, 30-33; trans. Hett, LCL 14:103).

However Luke's interest in places in the expansion of Jesus groups is not in
the local population but in the Israelites resident in those places. These Israelites,
whom he calls "Judeans," will differ from the locals since they will be marked by
Judean characteristics. What is characteristic of Judeans? In Luke-Acts, we find
such characteristics as contentiousness, stiff-neckedness (meaning being incapable
of obeying God properly), envy, greed, and violence, all in the name of Torah and
temple (persons in the Mishnah and Talmud; see Rubenstein 2003).

The Story in Acts

The main sections of Acts are based on two commands of the resurrected Jesus: the first command to the Eleven (soon to be Twelve) (Acts 1:8), and the second command to Saul/Paul (Acts 9:15). The Twelve are to witness to the resurrected Jesus in Judea and Samaria up to the boundary of the land of Israel. Paul, on the other hand, is to witness before a few kings and many sons of Israel living in non-Israelite territory. In the opening chapters of the work, we learn the events or information to which these persons are to bear witness and the significance of this witness to Israelites. This witness invariably leads to conflict with fellow Israelites. Some Israelites accept the witness; others do not and are aggrieved, as evidenced in the reaction of dispute described in the story. The dispute usually develops into conflict, and conflict resolution of one sort or another leads to the unfolding of the incidents in question.

The story of Acts unfolds while underscoring the expansion of Jesus groups. The central personage featured in the second part of Luke's story is Paul, and the last place Paul visits before departing for Jerusalem is Ephesus. This feature has led some scholars to the conclusion that Ephesus, the goal of Luke's story in expanding Jesus groups, was Luke's hometown. As a fourth-generation Jesus group member, he tells the story about the founding of the Jesus group in Ephesus for his fourth-generation members. It was among Israelite Jesus group members in Ephesus that the book of Acts saw the light of day. It was for those Israelite Jesus group members in Ephesus that Luke-Acts was written.

In the description of the fulfillment of the commands of Jesus, the book of Acts breaks down into two major sections: activities among Judeans living in the traditional Israelite lands and nearby regions with an Israelite majority population (for example, Antioch), and activities among Judeans living in non-Israelite regions, where Israelites are a distinct minority. This matches the two major sections that structure the Gospel of Luke: Jesus among Galileans and Jesus among Judeans.

General Social Dimensions of Acts: Some Presuppositions

There are several general social dimensions of Acts that emerge in the course of our book. In the writing of this social-scientific commentary, we presume that Acts is a high-context document presuming a number of things. We hope that our stating these high-context perspectives will prove useful for understanding the work.

First, the focus of Luke-Acts is the Jesus ingroup. Luke is a retelling of the well-known story of Jesus, to which Acts adds another generally known story of the development of a specific Jesus group in specific circumstances. In other words, Luke-Acts is meant not for outsiders but for members of a specific Jesus group, hence for insiders.

Second, the two-volume Luke-Acts is an occasional writing. Given the fact that it was written for a specific Jesus group in specific circumstances, Luke-Acts is occasional, written at a certain time to realize certain purposes (especially certainty), thus working to keep the ingroup intact. In other words, Luke-Acts was not written for all people of all times.

Third, Luke-Acts is not concerned about the outgroup. This means that these volumes are not documents for outsiders. They were not composed to be shared with non–Jesus group members to read, so that they might become Jesus group members. On the contrary, they are documents to be read within specific groups to maintain those groups in their loyalty to the God of Israel as revealed in the experience of Jesus and those change agents commissioned by him. The themes that they emphasize are themes that the writer and his audience believed the ingroup would find relevant to hear at a certain time and in a given situation. Luke's Holy Spirit is one such specific theme evidenced in these writings. In other words, Luke-Acts was not written for missionizing or proselytizing.

Fourth, Luke-Acts is not theological in content, purpose, or scope. That is, it is not explicitly concerned with articulating, expressing, unfolding, or explaining a doctrine of God, the nature of God, or ideas or definitions of God, as theology is. The God of Israel enters the story from beginning to end because God is part and parcel of daily life. First-century Mediterraneans, including Israelites, had no explicit religion. Rather, people of the time had domestic religion and political religion. Luke-Acts articulates Jesus' political religion (Gospel) for an audience now devoted to a domestic religion, that of Israelite brothers (and sisters) in Christ (Acts). In other words, Luke's first volume tells of Jesus' activity within a framework of Israelite politics: Jesus' program was one of proclaiming theocracy (kingdom of heaven/God) with God as Patron (father); Jesus was crucified as a political agitator. Those who were held by these Gospel stories eventually formed fictive kin groups, as Acts describes in some detail. These were domestic religious groups with a political-religious agenda (kingdom of heaven/God) to be shared with fellow Israelites. Group members were Israelite "brothers and sisters" looking forward to a forthcoming Israelite theocracy

Fifth, the stories of Jesus and Jesus group members told in Luke-Acts are essentially meant to be narratives that might make sense of the experience of those hearing the story. They are narratives with a beginning, middle, and end describing group development. Narratives generally begin with an equilibrium, followed by a disturbance of that equilibrium, and conclude with a restored equilibrium in the end. The presumption is that hearers of the story, various Jesus ingroups, lived in a situation of disturbed equilibrium. The story of Luke-Acts is meant in the end to restore their equilibrium of life, their collectivistic life story. The story is to carry Jesus group members and help them make sense of their experiences, thus providing them with a framework for their fictive kin group religion and offering them pegs on which to hang all of their experiences. In other words, Luke-Acts is only indirectly concerned with making sense of the experience of Jesus.

Sixth, abstractly considered, the stories of Jesus and the Jesus group in Luke-Acts are each, in their own way, focused on what the God of Israel gives to faithful Israelites by means of Jesus with the help of the apostles, while being opposed by Israelite elites. In other words, the audiences of these stories, as faithful Israelites, identified with what God did to/for Israel through Jesus. Their main social opposition came from Israelite Jesus-deniers.

Seventh, and most specifically, Luke-Acts was written by and for fourth-generation Jesus group members (third Pauline generation) who wished to know about the first-generation experience that accounted for their fictive kinship groups deriving from Paul and rooted in Jesus. Luke tells of what Jesus said and did with a view to its consequences in the story of the Jesus group concluding with Paul. The story develops in a way relevant to third-generation Pauline groups (hence fourth-generation Jesus group members). Documents that tell the story of a central personage located at the origins of some movement group are usually third-generation documents. And this is what the Gospels of Mark and Matthew are, two of the "many" who have told the story of Jesus that Luke knows. In other words, from a social-scientific point of view, Luke's prologue (Luke 1:1-4) accurately describes the well-known third-generation principle: in a situation of radical and irreversible change, grandchildren wish to remember what children wished to forget of the experience of first-generation parents, and this is what "the many" did. Acts, with the telling of the life of Paul, sets Luke-Acts a generation later.

Materials Provided in This Book

Two types of materials are provided in this book. First, by way of clarification, we offer short **Notes** commenting on Acts. These draw the reader's attention to the encoding of the social system in the language of the document. The **Notes** provide a kind of social-science commentary that can supplement the countless and valuable traditional studies available on Acts.

Second, we provide a collection of **Reading Scenarios** drawn from anthropological studies of the Mediterranean social system. This is the social system that has been encoded in the language of Acts in ways that are not always obvious to modern readers. Since most of the reading scenarios apply throughout Acts, however, we have duly referenced them in the commentary for the convenience of the reader. Together with the **Notes** the **Reading Scenarios** offer clues for filling in the unwritten elements of the writing as a Mediterranean reader might have done and thereby help the modern reader develop a considerate posture toward the ancient writer. An index of reading scenarios is provided at the close of the book.

Finally, the illustrations, maps, and diagrams included are intended to serve as a reminder that in reading the New Testament we are indeed in a different world. The scenarios that these and our written comments evoke, and which we ask the reader to understand, come from a time and place that for all of us remain on the far side of the eighteenth- and nineteenth-century contexts that have shaped our modern world. It is unlike anything we are likely to imagine from our experience in the modern West. It is a world we invite you to enter as a thoughtful and considerate reader.

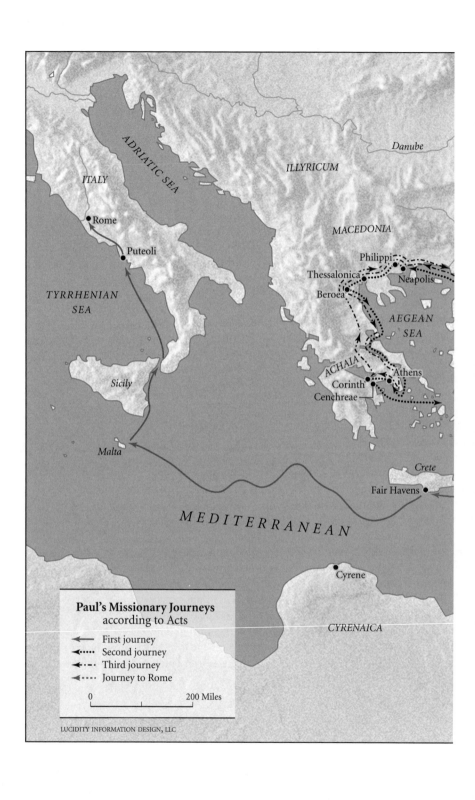

Danube

ILLYRICUM

ITALY

ADRIATIC SEA

MACEDONIA

● Rome

Puteoli ●

Philippi ●

Thessalonica ●

Neapolis

*TYRRHENIAN
SEA*

Beroea ●

*AEGEAN
SEA*

ACHAIA

Athens ●

Corinth ●

Sicily

Cenchreae ●

Malta

Crete

Fair Havens ●

MEDITERRANEAN

Cyrene ●

Paul's Missionary Journeys
according to Acts

◄─── First journey
◄····· Second journey
◄─·─· Third journey
◄···· Journey to Rome

CYRENAICA

0   200 Miles

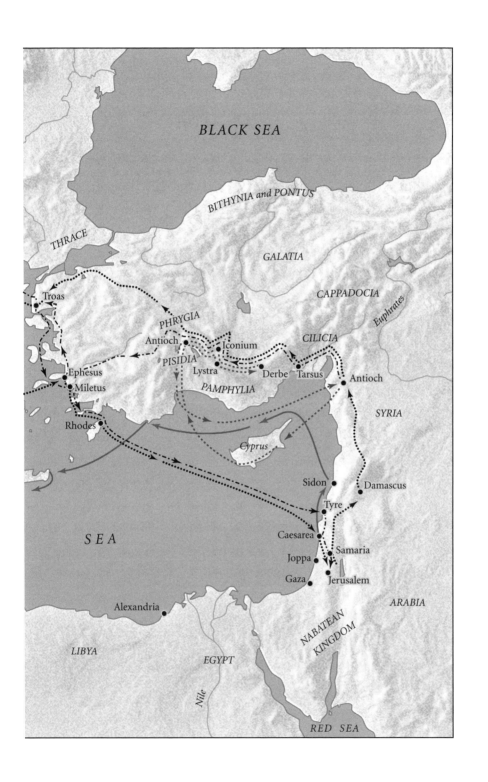

Acts of the Apostles

Acts 5:13-42
Witnessing in Jerusalem and Subsequent Elite Reactions: A Dispute in the Temple
5:13-18   Introductory Summary: Healing Successes
5:19-26   Reaction of Temple Elites and God's Intervention
5:27-33   Witnessing in Jerusalem a Fourth Time
5:34-40   Reaction of the Councilor Gamaliel and Its Outcome
5:41-42   Conclusion: Dishonored but Honored

Acts 6:1–8:4
Witnessing in Jerusalem: The Story of the Greek Deacon Stephen
6:1-7   Introduction: How Does Stephen Fit In
6:8-15   Greeks Challenge Stephen in Jerusalem
7:1-53   Stephen's Riposte to the Challenge
7:54-60   Greeks Take Satisfaction: Stephen's Death
8:1-4   Appendix: Introducing Saul

Acts 8:5-40
Witnessing in Samaria: The Story of the Greek Deacon Philip
8:5-13   Philip in Samaria
8:14-25   Interlude: Peter and John in Samaria
8:26-38   Philip on the Gaza Road
8:39-40   Philip from Azotus to Caesarea

Acts 9:1-30
The Story of Why/How Paul Was Baptized: From Damascus to Jerusalem
9:1-9   Part 1: Paul's ASC Experience near Damascus
9:10-19a   Part 2: With Ananias the Prophet in Damascus
9:19b-30   Part 3: Why/How Paul Returned to Jerusalem

Acts 9:31–11:18
Witnessing at Land's End: Peter's Travels
9:31-35   Healing Aeneas
9:36-43   Healing Tabitha
10:1-8   Cornelius the Centurion: His ASC Vision and Its Outcome
10:9-23   Peter's Parallel Vision and Its Outcome
10:24-48   Peter Witnesses to Cornelius
             10:24-33   Introduction
                          10:24-29 Peter Meets Cornelius
                          10:30-33 Cornelius Explains to Peter
             10:34-43   Peter's Attestation
             10:44-48   Outcome: The Spirit and Baptism
11:1-18   Peter Explains His Vision Once More

Introduction to Acts for Luke's Patron Acts 1:1-3

1:1 In the first book, Theophilus, I wrote about all that Jesus did and taught from the beginning 2 until the day when he was taken up to heaven, after giving instructions through the Holy Spirit to the apostles whom he had chosen. 3 After his suffering he presented himself alive to them by many convincing proofs, appearing to them during forty days and speaking about the kingdom of God.

Textual Notes: Acts 1:1-3

1:1-2: These opening verses of Acts are a summary of the writer's *bios* (life) of Jesus set out in the Gospel of Luke. The anonymous writer is traditionally called "Luke," a practice we shall follow. Right after this introduction, the final part of that Gospel is restated in greater detail. Luke notes that Acts is the second of the two-volume work. Luke-Acts form a diptych, that is a work made up of two sets of matching scenes. We shall point them out as we proceed and list those scenes in an appendix. The first matching scene is the dedication of each book (Luke and Acts) to Theophilus (Luke 1:1-14 and Acts 1:1-3).

The "Theophilus" mentioned here is given the honorific title of "most excellent" in Luke 1:3, and this is the language of patronage (cf. Josephus, *Life* 430; *Against Apion* 1.1). Luke thus continues to write for a benefactor whom he considers his social superior and may in fact be challenging him to continue his support for the community of which Luke is an insider. **Patronage.**

At the opening of the Gospel, Luke states his purpose: "so that you may know with certainty the things which you have been taught" (Luke 1:4; RSV/NRSV have "truth" for the Greek *asphaleia*, certainty). This goal likewise undergirds the book of Acts. The certainty will derive from witnesses, a word-field of great prominence in Acts.

1:2: Luke's Gospel ends with Jesus being taken up into the sky (Luke 24:51). The passive voice verb "was taken up" indicates that God is the doer. The word heaven is better translated "sky." The problem for us is that the "sky" is endless space, while for first-century Israelites there was no perception of "space." Instead, the sky was bounded by a "firmament" and served as the locus of stars and planets, which were affixed to the uppermost level of the sky beyond which was the realm of God. Thus the sky encompassed the round earth at the center of God's creation. The learned believed that only one-fourth of this round earth was knowable by human beings, since the desert to the south and the seas to the west and east blocked off access to the rest of the earth. For all practical purposes, this one-fourth of the round earth formed the *oikoumenē*, the known world. This known world consisted of three parts: Europe, Asia, and Libya ("Africa"), focused on the circum-Mediterranean. For Israel, the center of the known world was Jerusalem in general, the temple specifically. The God of Israel was presumed to be beyond the uppermost reaches of the sky, notably over the Jerusalem temple, and could be accessed through an opening in the sky found above Jerusalem. Jesus' trip, orchestrated by the God of Israel, would take him through that opening into God's realm. In a later chapter, Stephen gets to peer through that opening (Luke 7:55-56). **Opening in the Sky.**

1:2: The resurrected Jesus instructed his apostles "through the Holy Spirit." The description here refers to the apostles' experience of Jesus in an alternate state of consciousness (ASC) involving a group trance or vision. **Alternate States of Consciousness (= ASC).** The apostles in question are specifically those chosen by Jesus (soon to be listed vv. 13-14), and not others who appear later in the story with that title.

1:3: Luke refers to Jesus' crucifixion and death as "his suffering." He mentions Jesus' crucifixion only three times, and this in Peter's discourses to Jerusalemites. However, Luke's point here is that Jesus presented himself alive to the apostles by many convincing proofs. It is the apostles who are essentially the witnesses who provide the certitude about which Theophilus is concerned. The topic of Jesus' instruction in this forty-day (from Easter to Pentecost) postresurrection period is the forthcoming Israelite theocracy, the kingdom of God. **Kingdom of God.** The mentions of the kingdom here as a topic of interest of first-generation Jesus group members and at the conclusion of Acts (28:31) for second-generation Paul serve as an inclusion and perhaps point up the difference in interests between those generations and Luke's fourth-generation Jesus group. **Generational Differences.** After the divinely willed destruction of Jerusalem by the Romans in 70 C.E., interest in a forthcoming Israelite theocracy wanes.

Part I: Jesus' First Command: To the Eleven (Twelve)—Their Activities among Israelite Majority Populations (Acts 1:4—12:24)

Acts 1:4-26 The First Command of the Resurrected Lord and Its Setting

Just as Luke's story of Jesus, his Gospel, has two main sections (Jesus in Galilee, Jesus in Judea/Jerusalem), so too the book of Acts has two main sections. The sections in Acts are marked by commands given by the resurrected Jesus. The first command is directed to the core group of disciples who were with Jesus from the beginning, the Eleven soon be to Twelve again. **The Twelve.** The second command is directed to Paul (Acts 13:2). According to these commands, the Twelve confine their activities to Israelites living in territories where Israelites are the majority. Paul, on the other hand, goes to Israelites living in territories where Israelites are a minority. The purpose of the commands is to have the apostles continue Jesus' prophetic task: to proclaim the forthcoming kingdom or theocracy in Israel. To this end, the apostles are to bear witness to what the God of Israel has done by raising Jesus from the dead, constituting him Lord and Israel's forthcoming Messiah, and this with a view to establishing a theocracy in Israel. All Israelites need to know about this.

Group Trance Experience with a Vision of the Risen Jesus Being Taken to the Realm of God Acts 1:4-11

1:4 While staying with them, he ordered them not to leave Jerusalem, but to wait there for the promise of the Father. "This," he said, "is what you have heard from me; 5 for John baptized with water, but you will be baptized with the Holy Spirit not many days from now."

6 So when they had come together, they asked him, "Lord, is this the time when you will restore the kingdom to Israel?" 7 He replied, "It is not for you to know the times or periods that the Father has set by his own authority. 8 But you will receive power when the Holy Spirit has come upon you; and you will be my witnesses in Jerusalem, in all Judea and Samaria, and to the ends of the earth." 9 When he had said this, as they were watching, he was lifted up, and a cloud took him out of their sight. 10 While he was going and they were gazing up toward heaven, suddenly two men in white robes stood by them. 11 They said, "Men of Galilee, why do you stand looking up toward heaven? This Jesus, who has been taken up from you into heaven, will come in the same way as you saw him go into heaven."

Textual Notes: Acts 1:4-11

1:4-5: The resurrected Jesus commands his apostles to remain in Jerusalem to experience the realization of the promise of the Father (restating Luke 24:49). The reference to God as Father intimates an understanding of the God of Israel as the patron who bestows favors on his clients. **Patronage.** The theme of God as patron runs through the Synoptic story of Jesus and seems to have been a distinctive theological position of Jesus. The patronage favor that Jesus' followers will now receive from their patron comes through a distinctive baptismal experience. As Jesus explains, the apostles need to be baptized with the Holy Spirit, "clothed with power from on high" (Luke 24:49). **Baptism.** It is important to note that the personage doing the baptism here is the very God of Israel (passive voice indicates God as doer of the action).

1:6: The sole concern of Jesus' core group is Israel's forthcoming theocracy—the focus of Jesus' activity in Luke's first book. The apostles wish to know how soon this political religious institution will be realized. Their question with a present tense verb (literally: "are you restoring") indicates the expectation of a quick realization.

Note that for the first time in Acts, Jesus is given his new title as resurrected personage, the title of "Lord." It is true that in the Gospel, Jesus is addressed as "Lord" countless times (forty-three, to be exact). This usage is a term of respect for a socially superior personage. The same word is used of the God of Israel, for the most part as a substitute for the word *God* (in Luke twenty-seven times in the infancy stories alone, and twelve times in the rest of the story). However, here in Acts, in a postresurrection setting, the word *lord* takes on another meaning. As Peter testifies in Acts 2:36: "God has made him both Lord and Messiah, this Jesus whom you crucified." "Lord" is now more than an interpersonal title of respect; it is a title that refers to the new status ascribed to Jesus by the God of Israel. *Lord* (Greek: *kyrios*; Latin: *dominus*; Semitic: *ʾadon* or *baal*) is a Hellenistic word referring to a person having the most complete power over persons and things. The lord is the absolute owner of all persons and things in his domain. He is a person who has the power to dispose of persons and things as he likes and who holds this power by a title recognized as valid (either by ad hoc force, custom, or law). This power is lordship (Greek: *kyriotēs*; Latin: *dominium*). The lord was entitled to use any thing or person that was his, to enjoy all their products or properties, and to consume entirely whatever was capable of consumption. Given the perception that Jesus was raised by the God of Israel and was soon to take up his position in the sky, to call Jesus "lord" meant that he wielded supreme cosmic dominion, after God.

In addition, given the fact that Jesus' proclamation was ultimately about a forthcoming Israelite theocracy, it is noteworthy that Roman emperors during the period described in Acts and later likewise bore the title "Lord." The underlying clash of political religious ideologies is not far below the surface of social interactions. **Kingdom of God.** Talk of a forthcoming Israelite theocracy with the resurrected Jesus as living lord could be interpreted by outsiders only as a political challenge to Roman power.

1:7-8: Here in his final words to his core group, the resurrected Lord does not give an answer to their question because the Father alone has that information (as in Jesus' final words in Matt 24:36). **Final Words.** Yet he does know what their forthcoming baptism entails. Their task and role are to serve as witnesses to what the God of Israel has done to Jesus on Israel's behalf (Acts 2:32; 3:15; 5:32; 10:39, 41; 13:31). A witness is a person who can attest to a fact or an event and thus ascertain the truth of a matter. **Witness and Witnessing.** Witnesses offer firsthand authentication of a fact. It is important to note that witnesses have no successors—there cannot be successors to the Eleven/Twelve apostles, whose task and role are to serve as firsthand witnesses.

The resurrected Jesus further tells them that they are to bear this witness "in Jerusalem, in all Judea and Samaria, and to the ends of the earth." Jerusalem, Judea, and Samaria are places of majority Israelite populations. In point of fact, in Acts one or another of the Eleven/Twelve do travel around Jerusalem, through Judea and Samaria. However, none of the Eleven/Twelve travels "to the ends of the earth"—if we take this phrase, as many scholars do, to refer to Rome. In this way, these scholars would claim that this sequence of regional names served as the outline of the travels described in Luke's work, with Paul ending up in Rome. The problem is that Paul is not part of this first command; he receives his own command, noted three times in the second half of the work (see Acts 9:15; 22:14; 26:16).

A few scholars, basing themselves on the literal Greek, translate the phrase "to the end of the land." Does "land" mean land as territory (for example, the land of Israel) or land as opposed to the sea. It is doubtful whether "land" meant "land of Israel," since it would be redundant here, and the category "land of Israel" belongs to Israel's biblical story (and modern Zionist propaganda). It is not a geographical designation used in the New Testament aside from Matthew 2. So we take the phrase "ends of the land" to mean "land's end," that is, the Mediterranean seashore: Gaza, Azotus, Joppa, Caesarea. Peter and the managerial assistant (deacon) Philip do bring their witness to these places at land's end.

The first part of Acts describes the activities of these witnesses in the order listed: in 2:1-13 they are baptized with the Spirit; in 2:14—8:3 they witness in Jerusalem and the surrounds; in 8:4-25 they witness in Samaria thanks to Philip, who moves on to "land's end": Gaza (8:26), Azotus (8:40), and Caesarea (8:40), with Peter eventually in Joppa (9:36) and Caesarea (10:24).

1:9-11: After the previous command and clarification, the Eleven see Jesus taken up (by God, passive voice) and vanish from their sight into a cloud. In Acts, the verb in v. 10 translated "gaze" (Greek *atenizō*) belongs to the vocabulary of ASC (= **Alternate States of Consciousness**) vision experiences (see Acts 3:4; 7:55; 10:4; 11:6; 13:9; 14:9; but perhaps not in Acts 3:12; 6:15; 23:1). As they gazed into the sky, two sky beings ("white robes" is an indication that they were sky beings or God's messengers) come with further information for them in their ASC. Since they are in an ASC, they need not be calmed by the celestial visitors (usually with a "Don't be afraid"); instead they are addressed in terms of their place of origin, "men of Galilee," a point that will be significant in the reaction to Peter's opening discourse to outsiders (Acts 2:7) and of relevance to their witness (13:31). The message the two sky beings deliver is that the resurrected Jesus, who was taken by God to the other side of the vault of the sky through the access point over Jerusalem will return through that access point. **Opening in the Sky.**

The List of Witnesses: A Short Summary Acts 1:12-14

1:12 Then they returned to Jerusalem from the mount called Olivet, which is near Jerusalem, a sabbath day's journey away. 13 When they had entered the city, they went to the room upstairs where they were staying, Peter, and John, and James, and Andrew, Philip and Thomas, Bartholomew and Matthew, James son of Alphaeus, and Simon the Zealot, and Judas son of James. 14 All these were constantly devoting themselves to prayer, together with certain women, including Mary the mother of Jesus, as well as his brothers.

Textual Notes: Acts 1:12-14

The Eleven are now back in ordinary or consensual reality as they return to the upper room where they were lodging. Luke tells us this in a summary. A summary is the name given to a short passage usually offering general biographical and/or geographical information. Such summaries are usually used in the Synoptics and Acts to connect longer accounts. Here this summary connects the opening ASC account (1:3-11) with the following incident (1:16-26). It briefly marks the movement of the apostles from the scene of Jesus' being taken up on the Mount of Olives to the upper room in Jerusalem. It also describes the cast of characters for the subsequent scenes in Jerusalem.

1:12: Mount Olivet, also known as the Mount of Olives, is a hill located to the east of Jerusalem. It overlooked the city, with its western slope separated from the city by the Kedron Wadi. Atop the hill, more or less, was the village of Bethany (Luke 24:50). Since the western hillside overlooked Jerusalem, it offered an excellent view of the Golden Gate in the Jerusalem wall, through which Israel's Messiah was supposed to enter the city when he arrived at midnight on Passover night (see the ancient Book of Memorials cited in TgEx 12). According to Luke's story, Jesus and his disciples went to the Mount of Olives after the Passover meal—undoubtedly to await the Messiah along with many Jerusalemites. It would have been because of the crowds there that some person had to point Jesus out to the temple police (and it was Judas, see Luke 22:39-53).

A Sabbath's day journey was the distance a person was allowed to walk on a Sabbath, about a half-mile.

1:13: The list of apostles here is the same as in Luke 6:14-16, minus Judas.

1:14: Interestingly, Luke notes that in the upper room, the disciples joined some women (who followed Jesus from Galilee [Luke 23:49]) as well as members of Jesus' family—his mother and brothers. Jesus' brother, James, will play a prominent role in the further development of the Jerusalemite Jesus group.

The matching scene (see Textual Notes Acts 1:1-2) for Acts 1:14, 24 (the disciples praying) is Luke 3:21 (Jesus praying at his baptism).

Peter the Moral Entrepreneur: Reconstituting the Jesus Group Acts 1:15-26

1:15 In those days Peter stood up among the believers (together the crowd numbered about one hundred twenty persons) and said, 16 "Friends, the scripture had to be fulfilled, which the Holy Spirit through David foretold concerning Judas, who became guide for those who arrested Jesus—17 for he was numbered among us and was allotted his share in this ministry." 18 (Now this man acquired a field with the reward of his wickedness; and falling headlong, he burst open in the middle and all his bowels gushed out. 19 This became known to all the residents of Jerusalem, so that the field was called in their language Hakeldama, that is, Field of Blood.) 20 "For it is written in the book of Psalms,

'Let his homestead become desolate,
and let there be no one to live
in it';

and

'Let another take his position of
overseer.'

21 So one of the men who have accompanied us during all the time that the Lord Jesus went in and out among us, 22 beginning from the baptism of John until the day when he was taken up from us—one of these must become a witness with us to his resurrection." 23 So they proposed two, Joseph called Barsabbas, who was also known as Justus, and Matthias. 24 Then they prayed and said, "Lord, you know everyone's heart. Show us which one of these two you have chosen 25 to take the place in this ministry and apostleship from which Judas turned aside to go to his own place." 26 And they cast lots for them, and the lot fell on Matthias; and he was added to the eleven apostles.

Textual Notes: Acts 1:15-26

The story of the Jesus faction in the Gospel of Luke went through the usual phases of small group development: forming, storming, norming, performing, and adjourning. **Group Development.** Yet the opening ASC experience in Acts reports

Eucharist banquet of seven disciples. Early Christian fresco, third century C.E. *Location: Catacomb of S. Callisto, Rome, Italy. Photo © Scala / Art Resource, N.Y.*

that Jesus would have the faction form again, this time under the aegis of God's spirit rather than as a Jesus faction of Twelve. As Jesus' recruits, this core group had as its task to proclaim the forthcoming kingdom to Israel, to heal and to exorcise. The group formed an action group. The reconstituted group of Acts, on the other hand, would be formed as a group of Twelve core witnesses, specifically attesting to all that Jesus said and did until God raised Jesus and took him to the sky.

1:15: The passage opens by situating Peter among the "brothers" (*adelphoi*), and addressing them as "men, brothers." The NRSV takes out these words in favor of a gender neutral "believers," and "friends." While the goal of gender inclusiveness in twenty-first-century U.S. and northern European society is most laudable, such translations do detract from what is going on in the first-century, eastern Mediterranean scene described by Luke. The first numeral in the story to be mentioned after 12 is noted in here: 120 "names" ("names" = persons). The note that there were 120 "names" (NRSV: persons) present would have each of the Twelve affiliated with ten males, ten being the requisite number for an Israelite prayer group (Hebrew *minyan* = number).

1:15: Peter takes the lead in the re-forming process. Luke does not explain either who Peter is or why he might act in this way. The explanation, of course, lies in the Gospel of Luke. In the Gospel and here as well, Peter plays the social role of moral entrepreneur. **Moral Entrepreneur.** An entrepreneur is a person who organizes, manages, and assumes the risks of an enterprise, defined as a project that is difficult, complicated, or risky. A moral entrepreneur is an entrepreneur whose risky and complicated project is one of supporting social values and persons who embody those values. The value bearer in this instance is Jesus. In the story of what Jesus said and did, Peter takes the initiative and the risk of acknowledging

Jesus as Israel's Messiah and publicly supporting Jesus' project of proclaiming the forthcoming theocracy in Israel. All the Synoptics record this point (Mark 8:27-30; Matt 16:13-20; Luke 9:18-20). After the initial ASC experience, the group returns to culturally normal or consensual reality and has to deal with the first item on the agenda, reconstituting the group by filling Judas's place. This agenda item is obviously rooted in the need to have twelve authentic witnesses in the core group. **Numbers in Acts.** The Synoptic tradition is emphatic in noting that Jesus chose twelve: Luke 6:13: "And when it was day, he called his disciples, and chose from them twelve, whom he named apostles," to whom he ascribed a role in the forthcoming kingdom: 'You are those who have continued with me in my trials; and I assign to you, as my Father assigned to me, a kingdom, that you may eat and drink at my table in my kingdom, and sit on thrones judging the twelve tribes of Israel'" (Luke 22:28-30). The first passage from Luke's Gospel indicates that there were more than the twelve core group members with Jesus, and Acts here intimates that some of them were with Jesus from the beginning up to the resurrection, but only one more will be allowed to form the functional and symbolic Twelve. **The Twelve.**

1:16-20: These verses form a chiasm in which Peter uses passages from the Psalms to explain the Judas incident and its aftermath. He cleverly speaks first of Judas's role in the group and then explains that and how he died. He proceeds by citing Ps 69:26, which is to explain Judas's death, and finally Ps 109:8, which explains why his role needs to be filled now. Judas was a core group member, one of the Twelve, allotted the role of apostle. Yet he was the guide for those who arrested Jesus, as previously noted.

1:18: Luke does not elaborate on how Judas "acquired a field" (as does Matt 27:3-10). The point is that he died by "falling headlong" and bursting "open in the middle and all his bowels gushed out," and the field is called in Aramaic transliteration *Hakeldama*, that is, "Field of Blood." This event is duly clarified by Ps 69:26, which the writer or his tradition modifies from plural to singular to fit the case of Judas. The Hebrew refers to empty tents; Luke's Greek has homestead (*epaulis*) that becomes desolate, "with no one to live in it." The allusion is to the normal human dwelling of the body; the gushing bowels indicate the vacating of the dwelling in death—and thus the psalm described Judas's death. Even the subsequent name of the place, "Field of Blood," points to a burial place, desolate of living human beings.

1:20: The citation of Ps 109:8 is more forthright. The passage indicates that it is God's will that another take over his core group position, here labeled "overseer" (Greek: *episkopē*).

1:21-22: As moral entrepreneur, Peter now sets out the conditions required of a Judas substitute: to have accompanied Jesus during his career as prophet and holy man to the moment when he was taken up, and specifically, to be a witness to Jesus' being raised by God. What is significant here is that Luke believed there was a pool of men among the 120 Galilean "names" with sufficient qualifications to belong to the core group. After meeting these qualifications, what is further necessary is selection by the Lord through the drawing of lots.

1:23-26: As the prayer indicates, God was behind the selection of core group members. Selection took place by lot. A lot is an object used as a counter in determining a question by chance. To select by lot may include rolling dice or picking straws and the like. The prevailing wisdom was that "the lot is cast into the lap, but the decision is the Lord's alone" (Prov 16:33). The point is that God was behind the apparent randomness of the lot. For example, Saul was chosen the first king of mythical Israel by lot (1 Sam 10:20-23); later in the story, unverifiable guilt was ascribed by lot (1 Sam 14:41-42: the devices for casting lots here are called Urim and Thummim).

With Matthias added to the eleven apostles, the Twelve is reconstituted. The group can now continue its proper activities.

Acts 2:1-47 The Promise of the Resurrected Lord Is Realized, Witnessing in Jerusalem Begins

Chapter 2 opens with the fulfillment of the promise of the resurrected Lord: God's spirit is poured out on the Jerusalem Jesus group. The outcome is the initial realization of the task laid upon group members to bear witness to what God had done by raising Jesus from the dead (2:14-41). This initial witness is followed by further witnessing in Jerusalem and first elite reactions after two days in the Jerusalem temple (3:1—5:12); and finally witnessing in Jerusalem is marked by subsequent Israelite elite reactions with a dispute in the temple (5:13-42). The account of Jerusalem witnessing closes with the story of the witness of the Greek deacon Stephen (Acts 6:1—8:1-4). The witness in Jerusalem is thus set forth to both Hebrews (devoted Judeans) and Hellenists (civilized Israelites) resident in the city.

In the opening ASC of the book, the Lord commanded the Eleven to remain in Jerusalem until they were baptized with the Spirit. The word "baptism" means dipping in some liquid. To appreciate the image, the reader must realize that in the cultural perception of the period, water, wind, oil, and fire were all liquids that could be poured out on persons and things. The word translated "spirit" means wind, winds of all sorts (tornado, breeze, etc.). Since the wind is invisible yet perceptible in its effects, the term was applied to God as acting among humans; it was also applied to human beings as living, as alive. The opening scene of this chapter describes how the reconstituted Twelve, now joined with all Jesus believers in Jerusalem, are baptized with God's spirit along with the results of this event.

This scene (Acts 2:1-13: the Spirit "falls" on the disciples) has its match in the scene of Jesus' baptism and the descent of the Spirit upon him in physical form (Luke 3:22).

Group Trance Experience of the Promised Spirit of God Acts 2:1-4

2:1 When the day of Pentecost had come, they were all together in one place. 2 And suddenly from heaven there came a sound like the rush of a violent wind, and it filled the entire house where they were sit= ting. 3 Divided tongues, as of fire, appeared among them, and a tongue rested on each of them. 4 All of them were filled with the Holy Spirit and began to speak in other languages, as the Spirit gave them ability.

Textual Notes: Acts 2:1-4

2:1: Pentecost was an Israelite feast occurring fifty days after Passover (Lev 23:15-21), when new grain was to be offered to God. In Israelite lore, it also marked the day of the giving of the Torah to Moses (fifty days after the exodus from Egypt). **Pentecosts.**

2:2-3: The ASC experience here begins with a sound from the sky, like a violent wind, and all see "divided tongues as of fire" among them, that is, a flame over each one there. The sound of the wind and sight of the flame introduce the experience of God's spirit, demonstrated by their speaking in other languages. **Three Zones of Personality.** The spirit always stands for action, activity, doing. It is activity and effect that demonstrate that the spirit is or has been actually present. Here Luke reports that the spirit-filled group speaks in a range of foreign languages (Greek: *xenoglossia*; to be distinguished from *glossolalia*, ecstatic speech, as in 1 Cor 12:10, 18, 30; 14:1, 4-6, 9; Acts 10:46; 19:6).

As for *glossolalia*, the noted researcher in contemporary ecstatic speech Felicitas Goodman has written:

> [S]peaking in tongues is an act of vocalization, of uttering sounds while the person is in the religious trance. The syllables uttered are empty of semantic content, although Pentecostals believe that what they say is a language that could be understood if someone who spoke it was present. This theory is called xenoglossia. However, the syllables produced do not conform to the characteristics of a natural language as defined by modern linguistics. The confusion dissolves if we define speaking in tongues not as language but as communication. In this sense, it is communication between the Holy Spirit and the speaker, and between the speaker and the congregation. (Goodman 2001:8-9)

Esler (1992:141), basing himself on Goodman's research earlier than that just cited, argues that Luke has either misunderstood the ASC experience or has intentionally exaggerated for effect. It is implausible that these (or any) spirit-filled people were speaking foreign languages.

Public Reaction to the Group Trance Experience Acts 2:5-13

2:5 Now there were devout Jews from every nation under heaven living in Jerusalem. 6 And at this sound the crowd gathered and was bewildered, because each one heard them speaking in the native language of each. 7 Amazed and astonished, they asked, "Are not all these who are speaking Galileans? 8 And how is it that we hear, each of us, in our own native language? 9 Parthians, Medes, Elamites, and residents of Mesopotamia, Judea and Cappadocia, Pontus and Asia, 10 Phrygia and Pamphylia, Egypt and the parts of Libya belonging to Cyrene, and visitors from Rome, both Jews and proselytes, 11 Cretans and Arabs—in our own languages we hear them speaking about God's deeds of power." 12 All were amazed and perplexed, saying to one another, "What does this mean?" 13 But others sneered and said, "They are filled with new wine."

Textual Notes: Acts 2:5-13

2:5-11: The NRSV, like most English Bible translations, demonstrates inconsistency with the Greek words *Ioudaios* and *Ioudaia*. The first word is translated "Jew," and the second "Judea"—and not "Jewland" as one would expect. This passage provides an excellent indication of the meaning of *Ioudaios* in the book of Acts. The opening statement literally states: "Now there were housed in Jerusalem *Judeans*, pious men, from among all the non-Israelites (Gentiles) under the sky." The verse refers to Judeans resident among non-Israelites (Gentiles) now in Jerusalem for the feast. As noted in the introduction, the word *Judean* in outgroup (that is, non-Israelite) Hellenistic usage referred to any person with presumed ancestral origins traceable to Judea. The word refers to genealogy, not ideology. Ingroup Israelite usage would refer to such "Judean" people as Israelites. Luke thus employs Greco-Roman usage, perhaps in vogue in Ephesus, where he presumably composed his work. The passage then lists these Judeans according to where they lived among non-Israelites: Judean Parthians, Judean Medes, Judean Elamites, Judean Mesopotamians, Judean Judeans, Judean Cappadocians, Judean Pontians, Judean Asians, Judean Romans along with some outsiders who came to join Judean groups, Judean Cretans and Judean Arabs. Of course we should include the Twelve and their group, Judean Galileans.

In this usage, the word *Judean* means "of or pertaining to Judea." It was used as a generic label that embraced all persons of Israelite origin resident among various non-Israelite majority populations. It is to such Judeans that Paul will later go to "teach all the Judeans who are among the Gentiles" (Acts 21:21). "Gentile" is the Israelite designation for all non-Israelites. To distinguish civilized Judeans from barbarian Judeans, Luke uses the terms *Hellenists* and *Hebrews* respectively. This usage is quite different from Paul's. Paul adopts an Israelite ingroup perspective that divides the world's population between non-Israelites (Gentiles) and Israelites. Israelites, in turn, are divided into Greeks (Hellenists = civilized) and Judeans (uncivilized, followers of the customs of Judea). (The only instance of "Gentiles and Jews" in the New Testament is in Acts 14:5, describing the groups hostile to Paul and Barnabas, yet the members of the Judean synagogue consisted of Judeans and Greeks—both Israelites [Acts 14:1].)

2:5: Luke's sampling of peoples among whom Judeans lived covers "every nation under heaven." To list the range of esoteric peoples conquered by the Romans gave honor to Roman emperors and their armies. Perhaps this list was to give honor to the God of Israel, whose covenanted worshipers were to be found among "every nation under heaven."

2:7: This motley crowd knows that the speakers are Galileans. The crowd perceives these Galileans as speaking of God's deeds of power in their trance state (v. 11). Thus as they speak "in foreign tongues," there is communication between the speakers and the crowd of Judeans.

2:10: The NRSV does not translate the word *prosēlytos*, but rather transliterates it as proselyte. This word means "stranger, foreigner, an outsider who comes [to us]." The LXX uses *prosēlytos* to translate the Hebrew *gēr*, the resident alien or outsider who lives in an Israelite town or city. The verb *prosēlyteuō* means to live in a place as a stranger, for example, "in Israel" (Ezek 14:7 LXX), and the noun *prosēlyteusis* means residence as a stranger. Thus a "proselyte" was an outsider who lived in an Israelite quarter of a Greco-Roman city. The "respectful" outsider (Acts 13:43) was one who showed respect for local Israelites and their traditions. They would be supportive of a forthcoming Israelite theocracy. Hence the visitors from Rome were Judeans and outsiders resident in the Israelite section of the city. Whether these outsiders followed the customs of Judea is not specified.

2:12-13: Some hearers are amazed and perplexed, others sneer, attributing the phenomenon to drinking new wine. The reference to new wine (Greek *gleukos*) may be an allusion to one of three fifty-day (Pentecost) celebrations in first-century Judea. Among the Dead Sea scrolls, a document known as the *Temple Scroll* mentions the Feast of Weeks (New Grain), which corresponds to the Pentecost of Leviticus, as well as a Feast of New Wine and a Feast of New Oil (11QTemple 18:1-13; 19:11-14; 21:12-16). **Pentecosts.** It seems that some in the pilgrimage crowd of Judeans resident among non-Israelites have their calendar mixed up. This is not surprising, since there was really no way Israelites resident among majority non-Israelites could keep up with developing customs of Judea. And if, in fact, the pilgrims came to Jerusalem from the distant places listed here, pilgrimage to Jerusalem would not be a frequent event at all. For non-elites it might have been a once-in-a-lifetime trip.

2:13: In any event, ascribing the Jesus group's experience of the Spirit of the God of Israel to wine—and this with a mocking sneer—is a challenge both to God who sends the Spirit and to the Jesus group. Such a challenge requires a riposte, which Peter provides, taking the opportunity to bear witness to the resurrected Lord Jesus.

Initial Witnessing in Jerusalem Acts 2:14-41

2:14 But Peter, standing with the eleven, raised his voice and addressed them, "Men of Judea and all who live in Jerusalem, let this be known to you, and listen to what I say. 15 Indeed, these are not drunk, as you suppose, for it is only nine o'clock in the morning. 16 No, this is what was spoken through the prophet Joel:
17 'In the last days it will be, God declares,
that I will pour out my Spirit upon all flesh,
and your sons and your daughters shall prophesy,
and your young men shall see visions,
and your old men shall dream dreams.
18 Even upon my slaves, both men and women,
in those days I will pour out my Spirit;
and they shall prophesy.
19 And I will show portents in the heaven above
and signs on the earth below,
blood, and fire, and smoky mist.
20 The sun shall be turned to darkness
and the moon to blood,
before the coming of the Lord's great and glorious day.
21 Then everyone who calls on the name of the Lord shall be saved.'
22 You that are Israelites, listen to what I have to say: Jesus of Nazareth, a man attested to you by God with deeds of power, wonders,

and signs that God did through him among you, as you yourselves know—23 this man, handed over to you according to the definite plan and foreknowledge of God, you crucified and killed by the hands of those outside the law. 24 But God raised him up, having freed him from death, because it was impossible for him to be held in its power. 25 For David says concerning him,

'I saw the Lord always before me,
    for he is at my right hand so that I
      will not be shaken;
26 therefore my heart was glad, and
    my tongue rejoiced;
    moreover my flesh will live in hope.
27 For you will not abandon my soul
    to Hades,
    or let your Holy One experience
      corruption.
28 You have made known to me the
    ways of life;
    you will make me full of gladness
      with your presence.'

29 Fellow Israelites, I may say to you confidently of our ancestor David that he both died and was buried, and his tomb is with us to this day. 30 Since he was a prophet, he knew that God had sworn with an oath to him that he would put one of his descendants on his throne. 31 Foreseeing this, David spoke of the resurrection of the Messiah, saying,

'He was not abandoned to Hades,
    nor did his flesh experience
      corruption.'

32 This Jesus God raised up, and of that all of us are witnesses. 33 Being therefore exalted at the right hand of God, and having received from the Father the promise of the Holy Spirit, he has poured out this that you both see and hear. 34 For David did not ascend into the heavens, but he himself says,

'The Lord said to my Lord,
"Sit at my right hand,
    35 until I make your enemies your
      footstool."'

36 Therefore let the entire house of Israel know with certainty that God has made him both Lord and Messiah, this Jesus whom you crucified."

37 Now when they heard this, they were cut to the heart and said to Peter and to the other apostles, "Brothers, what should we do?" 38 Peter said to them, "Repent, and be baptized every one of you in the name of Jesus Christ so that your sins may be forgiven; and you will receive the gift of the Holy Spirit. 39 For the promise is for you, for your children, and for all who are far away, everyone whom the Lord our God calls to him." 40 And he testified with many other arguments and exhorted them, saying, "Save yourselves from this corrupt generation." 41 So those who welcomed his message were baptized, and that day about three thousand persons were added.

Textual Notes: Acts 2:14-41

This passage is the first of five discourses in Acts in which Peter witnesses to Jesus' life and resurrection by God (Acts 2:14-39; 3:12-26; 4:8-12; 5:29-32; 10:34-43). The common pattern in all of these declarations proclaimed before Israelite audiences is that (1) Judeans [and more specifically Jerusalemite authorities] crucified Jesus, (2) the God of Israel raised Jesus from the dead; (3) the Twelve can personally witness to this; (4) the God of Israel exalted this crucified and resurrected Jesus. All of these attestations conclude with an appeal to these Israelites to get their affairs in order (that is, repent), since the foregoing events indicate God's willingness to waive any forthcoming satisfaction for behaviors that dishonored God (that is, remission of sin). In Acts 13:16-41, Paul likewise proclaims a similar declaration, basing himself on the witness of the Twelve.

Each of these attestations here is bolstered by various clarifications or proofs deriving from Israel's sacred writings, and each emphasizes some dimensions of Jesus' present role as Lord and forthcoming role as Israel's Messiah.

This declaration has the following structure:

Introduction 2:14-15
Scriptural Citation to Explain the Situation 2:16-21
Attestation 2:22-24
Scriptural Citation to Explain the Attestation 2:25-31
Attestation 2:32-33
Scriptural Citation to Explain the Attestation 2:34-35
Conclusion 2:36
Call to Repentance 2:38-39

Modern model of Jerusalem at the time of the Herodian Temple (c. 50 B.C.E.).
Location: Holy Land Hotel, Jerusalem, Israel. Photo © Erich Lessing /
Art Resource, N.Y.

This scene (Acts 2:14-40) with a sermon giving a theme for what follows, fulfillment of prophecy and rejection of Jesus, has its matching scene in the Gospel with the same content (Luke 4:16-30).

2:14-15: *Introduction.* Peter and the Eleven bear witness together. Peter speaks, as moral entrepreneur. Given the provenance of the members of his audience previously mentioned, Peter addresses them as Judeans and Jerusalemites. His first task is to defend the honor of the group by denying the insulting allegation that their experience of the Spirit derives from new wine.

2:16-21: *Scriptural Citation to Explain the Situation.* The citation of the prophet Joel is to explain what just happened (citing LXX Joel 2:28-32; see Hebrew 3:1-5) with slight alterations. Peter explains that these are the last days before the coming of God's kingdom. God has poured his Spirit on the Jesus group, standing for all of Israel. The outcomes are evidence of the presence of God's spirit: children prophesy, young men see visions, old men see dreams, and all devoted to God (namely, his "slaves") will prophesy. The noise and effects marking the coming of the Spirit are identified with Joel's predicted portents in the sky, signs on earth, with sun darkened and moon red.

All who call upon the person of the Lord will be saved by God. The word *Lord* probably means Jesus rather than God (see Acts 1:15, where "name" means person). On the other hand, "to be saved" is passive voice, and as usual in the New Testament, verbs with an unnamed subject in the passive voice always imply that God is the agent or doer. "They will be saved" means God will save them.

"To be saved" means to be rescued from a difficult situation. In context, the difficult situation must be the prevailing social corruption: greed, injustice, maltreatment, abuse (see v. 40, where contemporary society is described as corrupt).

2:22-24: *Attestation.* Peter now gets to witnessing to the resurrected Jesus. He begins with the ingroup designation: "Men, Israelites," meaning "fellow Israelites" (not "you that are Israelites," as the NRSV has it, as though there were non-Israelites present). Luke does not share a perspective of Jesus as preexistent. Peter's witness to Jesus begins with his attestation concerning Jesus' activity, which indicates both that God himself attests to Jesus and what God himself effects through Jesus. Since Jesus was in fact handed over to his Judean enemies and crucified and killed by non-Israelite outsiders, this must have happened "according to the definite plan and foreknowledge of God." This is a judgment of after-the-fact predestination; God's plan can be definitely known by humans after that plan has been effected. Humans simply cannot know the future (see Acts 1:7).

And just as God acted through Jesus, so now God raised Jesus up and "freed him from the pains of death" (the NRSV omits "pains of"). The pains of death afflict a person during the dissolution of the cadaver during the death process, which lasts at least a year in ancient Israelite thinking. Jesus passed directly from death to life; hence he was freed by God from the pains of death. **Pains of Death.** Since God in fact raised Jesus, one may conclude after the fact that it was impossible for Jesus to be held in death's power. The following scriptural citation will explain this point.

2:25-31: *Scriptural Citation to Explain the Attestation.* David was generally believed to be the author of the book of Psalms in the Bible. In the first century, he was considered a prophet (as here in v. 30; and in the Qumran writings, 11QPs^a 27:2-11; Josephus, *Ant.* 6.8.2 §166); hence the psalms were considered prophetic. Peter cites Ps 16:8-11 (concluding with v. 10; note how the psalm sets out the **Three Zones of Personality**). His point is that since David died and had a tomb right in Jerusalem as everyone knew, the psalm verse about rescue from Hades and the corruption death entails could not refer to David. **Pains of Death.** David had to be speaking of someone else, specifically a descendant of David (see 2 Sam 7:11-14)— that is, the Messiah—who would be raised and spared corruption.

2:29: The word translated "confidently" (Greek: *parrhēsia*) is often translated "boldly." In first-century Hellenism, *parrhēsia* describes the behavior of a lower-status person speaking shamelessly in the face of higher-status people, without regard for the status honor of the higher-status person. Proper response by higher-status persons might include punishment or even death. *Parrhēsia* speaking is simply dishonoring to the higher-status person. It cannot be taken as a challenge to elite honor since the speaker is of lower status and culturally incapable of challenging a superior. To avoid negative reaction from elites, *parrhēsia* speakers often provide an excuse, for example, Israel's Scriptures require it, God said it, the Spirit moves me to say, and so on. The word (noun and verb forms) is used frequently by Luke to characterize the speaking of Jesus group members (Acts 4:13, 29, 31; 9:27, 28; 13:46; 14:3; 18:20, 26; 19:8; 26:26).

2:32-33: *Attestation.* Now speaking on behalf of the Twelve, Peter attests that God raised Jesus and exalted him to God's right hand—a position of cosmic power. In that position Jesus can now dispense the power of the Holy Spirit of God, as God promised. It is the coming of the Spirit that the crowd of Judeans have experienced, coming from the Father through Jesus. They have seen it and heard it, but not yet experienced it. **Three Zones of Personality.**

2:34-35: *Scriptural Citation to Explain the Attestation.* Citing Ps 110:1 in a context of power dispensed from the sky, Peter argues that David was speaking not of himself but of his Lord to whom God said: "Sit at my right hand, until I make your enemies your footstool."

2:36: *Conclusion.* Peter now emphatically concludes his witness. The whole house of Israel (the ingroup name of Israelites from Judea, Perea, Galilee, and the Diaspora) must know with certainty that this Jesus whom the house of Israel crucified has been made both Lord and Messiah by the God of Israel. Of course this all occurred after Jesus' death and resurrection. As previously noted, the title "Lord" points to his role of cosmic domination, while the title "Messiah" points to his role as God's vice-gerent on Israel's behalf.

2:37-39: *Call for Repentance.* The heart is the zone of persons where judgments are made and conscience is formed. **Three Zones of Personality.** Discourses in Acts are often interrupted when the climactic point is reached (for example, Acts 10:44; 17:32; 22:22). NRSV "Brothers," translates the Greek "men, brothers" equivalent to "fellow Israelites," indicating ingroup belonging.

A call for repentance is part and parcel of Peter's attestations to what God did to Jesus on Israel's behalf. The word "repent" translates the Greek *metanoēsate* (a favorite Lukan word, along with the noun form *metanoia*: Acts 3:19; 8:22; 17:30; 26:20 for the verb; Acts 5:31; 11:18; 13:24; 19:4; 20:21; 26:20 for the noun). It is often explained to mean "have a change of heart, of mind." However, since in the culture an internal state requires a corresponding external action to be adequately labeled, *metanoia* does not simply mean an internal state. It requires corresponding external action. Hence translations such as "get your affairs in order," "reform your lives," are on target. Without discernible "fruits of repentance," there is no repentance to speak about. Along with getting one's affairs in order, Peter urges *baptism*. The Greek term is not translated, but transliterated (put into another alphabet, the Roman alphabet). Previously the Twelve and those with them were "baptized" or "immersed" in the liquid called the Holy Spirit. Here the presumption is that Peter urges his audience to be "immersed" in water, in Jesus' name or person. **Baptism.** This sort of immersion is a symbolic or ritual action. What is to follow is God's pardoning of the ones baptized for their actions that shamed or dishonored God (that is what sin is). God's waiving satisfaction for the dishonor is demonstrated by a following experience of God's power, the Holy Spirit.

The promise in question is the promise of God's Spirit or power (see Acts 2:33 above). The promise is for all Israelites, both in Judea and in the Diaspora called by the God of Israel. In Luke's perspective, the founder of the Jesus group is the God of Israel. God works on Israel's behalf through Jesus and calls Israelites to join Jesus groups. God is always in charge.

2:40-41: Luke notes that his account of Peter's witnessing is selective. His general exhortation is for his fellow Israelites to "be saved" (the verb is passive; the NRSV translates it as middle or reflexive). God does the saving, a rescue from "this corrupt generation." Jesus passed a similar judgment on his fellows (see Luke 9:41). Luke concludes with a statement of the phenomenal response to Peter's witness; about three thousand persons were baptized. **Numbers in Acts.**

A Scene of Jesus Group Activity: Another Summary Acts 2:42-47

2:42 They devoted themselves to the apostles' teaching and fellowship, to the breaking of bread and the prayers.

43 Awe came upon everyone, because many wonders and signs were being done by the apostles. 44 All who believed were together and had all things in common; 45 they would sell their possessions and goods and distribute the proceeds to all, as any had need. 46 Day by day, as they spent much time together in the temple, they broke bread at home and ate their food with glad and generous hearts, 47 praising God and having the goodwill of all the people. And day by day the Lord added to their number those who were being saved.

Textual Notes: Acts 2:42-47

What did people do upon joining Jesus groups? The following summary explains. As previously noted, a summary is the name given to a short passage usually offering general biographical and/or geographical information. Such summaries are usually used in the Synoptics and Acts to connect longer accounts. Here this summary connects Peter's initial witness declaration in Jerusalem (Acts 2:14-41) with a description of Peter as holy man with healing power (Acts 3:1-11). The summary briefly tells of the way of life of the growing Jerusalemite Jesus group.

The whole passage of Acts 2:14—12:17 is a text segment that sounds the theme of fulfillment illustrated by examples of prophesying and wonders. Persecutions illustrate the note of unbelief. Its matching scene is Luke 4:31—8:46, which sounds the same themes: fulfillment (Luke 4:16-30) illustrated by examples of preaching and healing. Conflicts illustrate the note of rejection.

2:42-43: In the Lukan story line (Gospel), Jesus recruited a number of persons to assist him in his task of proclaiming the forthcoming kingdom of God. A group recruited by a person or persons for the recruiter's purpose for a given time is called a faction. A faction is a type of coalition or temporary grouping. **Coalitions/Factions.** The reconstituted Jesus group of Acts as described here is likewise a faction, this time formed about Jesus' previous core group, the Twelve, for their purpose, to attest to what the God of Israel has done through and to Jesus of Nazareth. Group members have been recruited by the Twelve for the purpose of "being saved" (v. 47), presumably within a reasonable time. An indication of this is the fact that they pooled their resources (v. 45).

2:42: The teaching of the apostles refers to further instructions beyond the common proclamation. Fellowship (Greek: *koinōnia*; Latin: *societas*) may mean spending time together as in a social club. However, given the fact that group members did pool their resources, the word would mean that Luke is referring to the mutual obligations of partnership or association between one person and one or more other people with regard to a particular action, thing, or person. It is a type of informal partnership contract. Partners were obliged to support the project of the group from their resources. **Fellowship.** The faction is developing into an Israelite political religious party.

2:43-45: Group members are described as "those who believed," presumably they believed the witness of the apostles, supported by many wonders and signs. That they had all things in common points to the partnership arrangement just mentioned and further described in v. 45. On the other hand, even in a partnership context, those who sold off what they had might act as patrons by bestowing favor on those in the group who had need. This interaction left the clients with a debt of gratitude to those who supported them and not to the group as a whole. In any event, that they sell what they own points to expectations of this arrangement coming to an end soon (just as Jesus proclaimed the coming of a theocracy soon).

2:46-47: A coalition never forms the general social structure of a whole society. Rather, the coalition exists as a social form in some broader social structure. A coalition is embedded, encysted or encapsulated in that broader social structure. Here we are told that Jesus group members participated in the larger political religion of the temple as well as in their own kin groups.

2:47: Another notice of the growing numbers of Jesus group members prepares the reader for the problems growing numbers pose for a coalition. **Coalitions/Factions.**

Acts 3:1—5:12 Witnessing in Jerusalem and First Elite Reactions: Two Days in the Jerusalem Temple

This section telling of the Jesus group's witnessing in Jerusalem switches scenes from the place where the group gathered to the city's famed temple. Peter, the group's moral entrepreneur, accompanied by another group member (John, son of Zebedee), call the attention of the temple elites to themselves—hence to their witness. They end up spending two days in the temple. Upon their rejoining the group, the author of Acts describes how the group sustained itself thanks to the reciprocal support of its members.

Day 1 in the Temple Acts 3:1—4:4

Luke's presentation of Peter and John's first day in the temple opens with Peter acting as an Israelite Holy Man. **Holy Man.** His success in healing leads to an opportunity to bear witness before Israelites gathered in the temple, as well as before Israel's temple elites. The elites react to this witness and arrest the two for the night; thus ends the first day in the temple.

Peter as Holy Man Acts 3:1-11

3:1 One day Peter and John were going up to the temple at the hour of prayer, at three o'clock in the afternoon. 2 And a man lame from birth was being carried in. People would lay him daily at the gate of the temple called the Beautiful Gate so that he could ask for alms from those entering the temple. 3 When he saw Peter and John about to go into the temple, he asked them for alms. 4 Peter looked intently at him, as did John, and said, "Look at us." 5 And he fixed his attention on them, expecting to receive something from them. 6 But Peter said, "I have no silver or gold, but what I have I give you; in the name of Jesus Christ of Nazareth, stand up and walk." 7 And he took him by the right hand and raised him up; and immediately his feet and ankles were made strong. 8 Jumping up, he stood and began to walk, and he entered the temple with them, walking and leaping and praising God. 9 All the people saw him walking and praising God, 10 and they recognized him as the one who used to sit and ask for alms at the Beautiful Gate of the temple; and they were filled with wonder and amazement at what had happened to him. 11 While he clung to Peter and John, all the people ran together to them in the portico called Solomon's Portico, utterly astonished.

Textual Notes: Acts 3:1-11

Peter has been presented as moral entrepreneur of the Jesus group and witness, along with the Eleven, to what the God of Israel had done in the career and resurrection of Jesus of Nazareth. In Luke's first volume, we learned that the Twelve had the power of healing, just like Jesus, who was presented as holy man and prophet. With this healing scene, Peter is likewise described as a holy man. **Holy Man.** In this role he has contact with the realm of God and can be of benefit to his fellows, notably by healing. The healing is described in the usual pattern of problem, solution, proof. Yet in a more culturally specific way, the healing involves the three zones of personality: eyes-heart (gazing, seeing), mouth-ears (speaking), hands-feet (touching). **Three Zones of Personality.**

This text segment (Acts 3:1-10), which relates the healing of a lame man in the name of Jesus, has its matching scene in the Gospel's account of a similar healing (Luke 5:17-26).

3:1-3: In the previous summary, Luke tells of the Jesus group's frequenting the Jerusalem temple. One of those times, Peter and John go to the temple during the ninth hour offering (NRSV three o'clock), at which the daily Tamid sacrifice was presented on behalf of all Israel. **Sacrifice.** The location of the Beautiful Gate is disputed, but if it is the gate facing the Mount of Olives, it was believed that Israel's Messiah would eventually enter the city through that gate to redeem Israel (this was the gate faced by Jesus, his disciples, and a Jerusalemite crowd on Passover night as they awaited the Messiah). A man born crippled (the problem) used to collect alms there.

3:4: "To look intently" (gaze, stare, Greek: *atenizō*) is a word that belongs to the vocabulary of holy man procedure **Holy Man** and ASC behavior **Alternate States of Consciousness** (see Acts 1:10; 7:55 [Stephen]; 10:4 [Peter]; 11:6 [Peter]; 13:9 and 14:9 [Paul healing]; but not 3:12; 6:15; 23:1). Peter looked intently at him, as did John, and said, "Look at us."

3:6: Peter speaks a word of power, healing in the person ("name") of Jesus Messiah of Nazareth.

3:7-8: Then he physically grabs the crippled man and raises him up. The former crippled man proceeds to demonstrate his new state of being (he is *not* restored since he never could walk).

3:10: The healed person praises God (not Jesus or the healer), while those who recognized him are filled with wonder and amazement—proper reactions to witnessing such a healing. The mention of the Beautiful Gate here serves as an inclusion to close the scene (see Acts 3:2).

3:11: This verse presents a change of scene in the temple, to Solomon's Portico (mentioned only in John 10:23 as a place where Jesus was threatened). Here the people gather, and Peter once more assumes the role of witness to the resurrection.

Witnessing in Jerusalem a Second Time Acts 3:12-26

3:12 When Peter saw it, he addressed the people, "You Israelites, why do you wonder at this, or why do you stare at us, as though by our own power or piety we had made him walk? 13 The God of Abraham, the God of Isaac, and the God of Jacob, the God of our ancestors has glorified his servant Jesus, whom you handed over and rejected in the presence of Pilate, though he had decided to release him. 14 But you rejected the Holy and Righteous One and asked to have a murderer given to you, 15 and you killed the Author of life, whom God raised from the dead. To this we are witnesses. 16 And by faith in his name, his name itself has made this man strong, whom you see and know; and the faith that is through Jesus has given him this perfect health in the presence of all of you.

17 And now, friends, I know that you acted in ignorance, as did also your rulers. 18 In this way God fulfilled what he had foretold through all the prophets, that his Messiah would suffer. 19 Repent therefore,

and turn to God so that your sins may be wiped out, 20 so that times of refreshing may come from the presence of the Lord, and that he may send the Messiah appointed for you, that is, Jesus, 21 who must remain in heaven until the time of universal restoration that God announced long ago through his holy prophets. 22 Moses said, 'The Lord your God will raise up for you from your own people a prophet like me. You must listen to whatever he tells you. 23 And it will be that everyone who does not listen to that prophet will be utterly rooted out of the people.' 24 And all the prophets, as many as have spoken, from Samuel and those after him, also predicted these days. 25 You are the descendants of the prophets and of the covenant that God gave to your ancestors, saying to Abraham, 'And in your descendants all the families of the earth shall be blessed.' 26 When God raised up his servant, he sent him first to you, to bless you by turning each of you from your wicked ways."

Textual Notes: Acts 3:12-26

The healing at the gate of the temple triggers a gathering of people that provides Peter with another occasion to witness to what God had done through Jesus' career and resurrection.

This attestation of Peter's has the following structure:

Introduction 3:12a
Ascription of the Holy Man's Healing Ability to the God of Israel 3:12b
Attestation 3:13-15
Ascription of the Holy Man's Healing Ability to the God of Israel 3:16
Call to Repentance 3:17-20a
Attestation 3:20b-21
Scriptural Citation to Explain the Attestation 3:22-24
Conclusion 3:25-26

3:12a: *Introduction.* Peter once more addresses the crowd as "men, Israelites," better translated as previously: "fellow Israelites " (Acts 2:22). His witness is directed to the same people that Jesus unsuccessfully sought to influence, the people of Israel in Jerusalem who turned against him (Acts 3:13).

3:12b: *Ascription of the Holy Man's Healing Ability to the God of Israel.* Before launching into a statement of witness, Peter first denies deserving any credit for the healing just performed. He here implies and then specifies that the astounding and astonishing results they witness are due entirely to the God of Israel.

3:13-15: *Attestation.* Peter's witness opens with an ascription of Jesus' glorification to the God of Israel's ancestors. **Ancestor Reverence.** The highly honored status given to Jesus by God is clarified in terms of a number of titles: God's Servant, God's Holy Man, the Righteous One of God, the Author (Source) of Life. Although the Jerusalemites rejected this presently exalted Jesus and handed him over to the Roman procurator Pilate, God raised him from the dead.

3:16: *Ascription of the Holy Man's Healing Ability to the God of Israel.* Now Peter ascribes the healing of the crippled man to the person ("name") of the resurrected and glorified Jesus, just called "Author of Life." The required approach for healing is faith focused on Jesus, "faith in the resurrected and glorified Jesus" (= "in his name"). Faith refers to the social value of placing one's complete trust in another person's reliability, the person in whom one has faith. The value is ascribed to persons as well as to objects and qualities. Relative to persons, faith is one's belief in another's reliability in interpersonal relations; it thus takes on the value of enduring personal trust in another's personal faithfulness. The nouns "faith," "belief," "fidelity," and "faithfulness," as well as the verbs "to have faith" and "to believe," refer to the social glue of trust that binds one person to another, trusted person.

3:17-20a: *Call to Repentance.* Here the expected call to repentance is rooted in the fact that these Jerusalemites as well as their rulers were ignorant of what they were doing. They unwittingly cooperated with what God expected to happen: his Messiah would suffer. Given their ignorance, if they get their affairs in order (repent) and turn to God, God will waive the expected satisfaction required by their having shamed God (their sins).

3:20b-21: *Attestation.* This statement presents another dimension of Peter's witness. It answers the question: What will now happen given that God raised Jesus from the dead and exalted him as Lord? It is a clarification of the question posed at the beginning of the story of Acts: "Lord, is this the time when you will restore the kingdom to Israel?" (1:6). The Israelite theocracy to come is described as a period characterized by joy ("refreshing" or consolation) and marked by times of the redoing or remodeling of everything ("universal restoration"). At that time, Jesus will finally come as Israel's Messiah. This significant statement means that Jesus group members, like other Israelites, expect the coming of a Messiah, but Jesus group members know his name, his function as Lord of the cosmos, and his present location with God in the sky. All this was foretold by God himself of old through his prophets.

3:22-24: *Scriptural Citation to Explain the Attestation.* The citation from Deut 18:15, 19, along with reference to the prophet Samuel and unnamed other, has spoken of the prophet to come and what would happen at his coming.

3:25-26: *Conclusion.* In conclusion, Peter reminds his audience of who they are: sons (NRSV: "descendants") of the prophets who spoke of what God did through and to Jesus, as well as sons of the covenant—notably that struck by God with Abraham. In this covenant with Abraham, God promised that in Abraham's seed (singular; NRSV: descendants) all the tribes (Greek: *patria*, groups of people deriving from a common father) of the land (Greek: *gē*; NRSV: earth) would receive benefactions from God. Usually this statement from Gen 22:18 is read in a universalizing way, to include "all the nations of the earth"; however, there is little warrant for such a version in the language itself. Abraham's blessing is a high-context statement. It obviously looks to the peoples deriving from his offspring to be found in the land given to him by God—that is, the ancient Israelites. Peter concludes with the observation that when God raised Jesus (here called God's servant; Greek: *pais*) he came first to "you"—again obviously to Jerusalemites, as in the command of Acts 1:8. The purpose behind their receiving the witness of the Twelve is to have these people change their way of living and comply with what God has in store for them.

Elite Reaction in the Temple Acts 4:1-4

4:1 While Peter and John were speaking to the people, the priests, the captain of the temple, and the Sadducees came to them, 2 much annoyed because they were teaching the people and proclaiming that in Jesus there is the resurrection of the dead. 3 So they arrested them and put them in custody until the next day, for it was already evening. 4 But many of those who heard the word believed; and they numbered about five thousand.

Textual Notes: Acts 4:1-4

The scene in Acts 4:1—8:3 reports conflicts with religious leaders and has its matching scene in Luke 5:29—6:11, where Jesus experiences the same.

4:1: Mention of "the priests, the captain of the temple, and the Sadducees" without further explanation once more indicates that Luke's audience knew of such Israelite institutional roles and parties. In context, the priests were temple personnel who performed temple rituals (notably sacrifice **Sacrifice**) for the people Israel under the chief priests and high priest, while the captain of the temple was a priest in charge of maintaining order. **Temple Personnel.** The Sadducees were a political religious party consisting of priestly elites and wellborn laymen. The personages who came to Peter and John were representative of the ruling political religious elite of Judea. This elite was in control of two of the three central political religious symbols of Israel—the temple and the land. The third central symbol of Israel, the Torah, was to have been controlled by priests as well (as it was among the Essene party of Qumran; see Lev 10:11, where priests are official teachers of Torah), but the Pharisaic party consisting largely of laymen contended for the total priestly control of the Torah with their own Torah experts, called *sopherim* (Hebrew). The term is translated *grammateus* in Greek, "scribes." (In the Gospel, Luke uses *nomikos*, "lawyer," rather than "scribe"; see Luke 7:30; 10:25; 11:45, 46, 52; 14:3; but in Acts he uses *grammateus*.) The emerging Jesus group party had its own take on Torah, as the story in Acts intimates. Furthermore, Sadducee partisans did not share the popular Pharisee belief in the resurrection of the dead, adopted by Judean Torah experts from the Persians. Peter and John now successfully witnessed to their recently experienced reality of that belief, a witness that brought out the temple elite.

These elite persons occupied the top rungs of Judean hierarchical society. The word *hierarchy* means sacred rule, a form of political religion in which priests appointed by God ruled according to God's revealed will. Ideally, such appointments derived from birth and lineage (like royalty). In the social order, elites were the takers (less than 2 percent) and the rest of the population were the givers. Elite rule was one of extortion and control. Why non-elites acquiesced in elite control is based on the fact that non-elites sought security both as provided by the deity for the cosmos and by the elite military for their society. Barbaric extortion and vicious means of control were a by-product of hierarchy that non-elites learned to put up with.

That Jerusalem elites should be concerned with the holy man activity of such low-status persons as Peter and John indicates the threat such holy men posed to the hierarchs, perhaps because of the possibility of social disorder in the temple area. Such disorder was something intolerable to the Roman procurator, whose support the elites needed to maintain the status quo. Thus Peter and John were put in custody, to be dealt with the next day.

4:4: The round number here underscores Peter and John's success, and the basis for elite concerns. In Hellenistic tradition, about five thousand is the proper size of an ideal city (see Plato, *Republic* V: "The number of our citizens shall be 5040—this will be a convenient number; and these shall be owners of the land and protectors of the allotment." See Mark 6:44//Matt 14:21//Luke 9:14//John 6:10.

Day 2 in the Temple Acts 4:5-35

Witnessing in Jerusalem a Third Time Acts 4:5-12

4:5 The next day their rulers, elders, and scribes assembled in Jerusalem, 6 with Annas the high priest, Caiaphas, John, and Alexander, and all who were of the high-priestly family. 7 When they had made the prisoners stand in their midst, they inquired, "By what power or by what name did you do this?" 8 Then Peter, filled with the Holy Spirit, said to them, "Rulers of the people and elders, 9 if we are questioned today because of a good deed done to someone who was sick and are asked how this man has been healed, 10 let it be known to all of you, and to all the people of Israel, that this man is standing before you in good health by the name of Jesus Christ of Nazareth, whom you crucified, whom God raised from the dead. 11 This Jesus is

'the stone that was rejected by you, the builders;
it has become the cornerstone.'

12 There is salvation in no one else, for there is no other name under heaven given among mortals by which we must be saved."

Textual Notes: Acts 4:5-12

4:5-6: On their second day in the temple, Peter and John are provided with a third opportunity for a Jerusalem witness to what the God of Israel did to Jesus. Once more, Luke presumes that his readers know what a Jerusalem assembly of Israel's "rulers, elders, and scribes" means. The high-context reference is to the Sanhedrin, Israel's political religious authority. The rulers (Greek: *archontes*) are noted in the next sentence: the high priest Annas (high priests have lifetime appointments; they are priests forever), and the current high priest, Caiaphas, and others from the same social rank. What Luke intimates is that the whole political religious assembly of Jerusalem met to deal with the case of Peter and John's doings. Of course, such concern implies great honor for the Jesus group and its Jerusalem activity. Since the Jesus group was in fact rather insignificant, if we wish to give this event any verisimilitude, the Sanhedrin's problem will have to have been concern for Roman intervention for disturbances of public order.

4:7: As is usual in most of the Gospel narratives, groups or categories of people are made to speak as individuals, whether crowds, or opponents, or, as here, the whole assembly. When "they" speak, the writers provide us with the presumed and stereotypical concerns of the speakers. Here the question put to Peter and John is about the basis or source of their action. The questioners presume that the source is some person since effects that count are always caused by some person. Throughout

Acts, when referring to a person, the word *name* does in fact mean "person" (clearly in Acts 1:15; 3:16; there is no Greek word for "person" in our usage). This passage is punctuated with the word *name* (vv. 7, 10, 12, 17, 18), and it always means "person." The question thus means "Who is behind what you are doing?"

4:8-9: Significantly, in Luke 12:11-12, Jesus tells his core group that when they have to stand before Israel's authorities, they should not be anxious about how to answer since "the Holy Spirit will teach you in that very hour what you ought to say." Thus Peter gets to witness before the very political religious elite of Israel, at the center of Israel's political religion, the temple, and this thanks to God at work with his Spirit. Peter's witness is a sort of alternate state of consciousness (ASC) experience, inspired by the Spirit. He opens his statement with reference to his holy man action of healing, since that in fact was the question put by the Sanhedrin (v. 9).

4:10-12: Peter directs his testimony to the Sanhedrin and to all Israel, for whom they stand. He attests that the person behind his activity is Jesus of Nazareth, Israel's Messiah, a person whom the Sanhedrin crucified, yet whom the God of Israel raised from the dead. He characterizes Jesus with a statement from the Psalms (Ps 118:22) applied to members of the Sanhedrin. There is no other person who can offer Israel salvation. Luke uses "salvation" as a high-context, Jesus group buzzword. As previously noted, salvation means rescue from a difficult situation. Paul characterizes the difficult situation as "sin," meaning a culture of willingness to dishonor God that leads to God's wrath or act of restoring his divine honor among human beings. In context, of course, the crippled man is saved from his illness through the person of Jesus.

Disputing with Temple Elites Acts 4:13-22

4:13 Now when they saw the boldness of Peter and John and realized that they were uneducated and ordinary men, they were amazed and recognized them as companions of Jesus. 14 When they saw the man who had been cured standing beside them, they had nothing to say in opposition. 15 So they ordered them to leave the council while they discussed the matter with one another. 16 They said, "What will we do with them? For it is obvious to all who live in Jerusalem that a notable sign has been done through them; we cannot deny it. 17 But to keep it from spreading further among the people, let us warn them to speak no more to anyone in this name." 18 So they called them and ordered them not to speak or teach at all in the name of Jesus. 19 But Peter and John answered them, "Whether it is right in God's sight to listen to you rather than to God, you must judge; 20 for we cannot keep from speaking about what we have seen and heard." 21 After threatening them again, they let them go, finding no way to punish them because of the people, for all of them praised God for what had happened. 22 For the man on whom this sign of healing had been performed was more than forty years old.

Textual Notes: Acts 4:13-22

These verses spell out the reaction of the members of the Sanhedrin. First they were amazed at the boldness of Peter and John, given their low social status. In the end, they had nothing to say to Peter in face of the healing, so they ordered all three to leave the Sanhedrin meeting. Luke notes two things: the Sanhedrin recognized Peter and John as Jesus' followers, and they acknowledged the crippled man as healed.

4:13-15: Of course, the way Peter speaks before Israel's elite is totally inappropriate. This is what the word "boldness" (Greek *parrhēsia*, translated "confidently" in Acts 2:29) connotes. In first-century Hellenism, teaching or speaking to high-status people "boldly" (*parrhēsia*) describes the behavior of a lower-status person speaking to higher-status persons without regard for their honor status. Such speech is dishonoring to elites. To avoid any negative assessment of Peter, the writer of Acts ascribes his use of language to God's spirit. The phrase "to speak boldly" (noun and verb forms) is used frequently by Luke to characterize the style of speaking and teaching of Jesus group members (Acts 2:29; 4:13, 29, 31; 9:27, 28; 13:46; 14:3; 18:26; 19:8; 26:26; 28:31).

4:16-17: The Sanhedrin discussion notes that God has accomplished a notable sign. That God is the doer is indicated by the passive voice of the verb. Their problem now is to keep "it" from spreading; here the "it" relates to the testimony of Peter and John, since more than five thousand in the city have already witnessed the healing. So the members of the Sanhedrin seek to curtail the witnessing: no more speaking on behalf of the person of the resurrected Jesus.

4:18-19: In the face of the Sanhedrin's decision to muzzle them, Peter (and John) answer that they must listen to God's command given by the resurrected Jesus, specifically to be witnesses to Jesus in Jerusalem. Of course, Peter and John speaking at the same time is the stereotyped way of describing the viewpoint of those in the role of the Twelve.

4:21: Peter and John leave without harm because people recognized that God was behind the healing. Successful Israelite holy men, like Jesus and Peter, have their effect thanks to the God of Israel, who deserves the honor recognition.

4:22: In conclusion, Luke notes once more that the healing was a sign, and this on a forty-year-old man crippled from birth (Acts 3:2), a healing that only God could effect.

Praying Together: ASC Experience Acts 4:23-31

4:23 After they were released, they went to their friends and reported what the chief priests and the elders had said to them. 24 When they heard it, they raised their voices together to God and said, "Sovereign Lord, who made the heaven and the earth, the sea, and everything in them, 25 it is you who said by the Holy Spirit through our ancestor David, your servant:

'Why did the Gentiles rage,
    and the peoples imagine vain
        things?
26 The kings of the earth took their
        stand,
    and the rulers have gathered
        together
    against the Lord and against his
        Messiah.'

27 For in this city, in fact, both Herod and Pontius Pilate, with the Gentiles and the peoples of Israel, gathered together against your holy servant Jesus, whom you anointed, 28 to do whatever your hand and your plan had predestined to take place. 29 And now, Lord, look at their threats, and grant to your servants to speak your word with all boldness, 30 while you stretch out your hand to heal, and signs and wonders are performed through the name of your holy servant Jesus." 31 When they had prayed, the place in which they were gathered together was shaken; and they were all filled with the Holy Spirit and spoke the word of God with boldness.

Textual Notes: Acts 4:23-31

4:23-25: Peter and John now return to "their own" kind (NRSV: their friends) as opposed to the elites. The Jesus group response to their report is a spontaneous prayer that acknowledges God's activity on their behalf. Of course, this group response "in unison" is the work of some Jesus group scribe articulating the group's viewpoint.

Reference to ancestors is rather frequent in Acts. Ancestor reverence is a replication of kinship structures in which father and son form a focal dyad or twosome. Such kinship structures likewise put heavy emphasis on tradition, especially tradition of the elders. **Ancestor Reverence.**

4:25-27: The prayer is essentially an interpretation of Ps 2:1-2, seen as applying to Roman and Israelite rulers versus Jesus and his circle. The contrast is between the stance of both non-Israelites (Gentiles) and "peoples" (here a reference to Israelites), with non-Israelite kings and Israelite rulers gathering against God ("the Lord") and his Messiah. This is spelled out in v. 27 noting that Herod and Pontius Pilate, the peoples of Israel and non-Israelites (Gentiles) gathered against God's servant Jesus whom God anointed, that is, made the Anointed One or Messiah.

4:28-30: These verses describe a theological interpretation of events as early Jesus group members perceived what the God of Israel was doing. First he anointed Jesus by sending the Spirit ("hand" or the "hand of God" refers to God acting, God's power, designated as God's spirit, **Three Zones of Personality**). Then everything that has taken place is exactly what God intended. Finally, while God continues to act in healings, signs, and wonders done in the person of Jesus, those praying ask to "speak God's word with boldness." Those praying call themselves God's slaves (*douloi*), a significant term in the slave-based agricultural economy of the Roman Empire. A slave was a person whose freedom and actions were totally controlled by the slave owner. In the Lukan story, it is significant that all of this occurs "in this city," that is, in Jerusalem.

4:31: People in antiquity believed earthquakes were caused by some deity from the sky (see, for example, Dio Cassius, *Roman History* 68.24-25 for a description of an earthquake at Antioch during the time of Emperor Trajan). Here the earthquake marked the coming of God's Spirit, enabling the Jesus group members to speak freely and fearlessly even to higher-status persons.

Concluding Summary: A Scene of Jesus Group Reciprocity
Acts 4:32–5:12

Jesus Group Activity Acts 4:32-35

4:32 Now the whole group of those who believed were of one heart and soul, and no one claimed private ownership of any possessions, but everything they owned was held in common. 33 With great power the apostles gave their testimony to the resurrection of the Lord Jesus, and great grace was upon them all. 34 There was not a needy person among them, for as many as owned lands or houses sold them and brought the proceeds of what was sold. 35 They laid it at the apostles' feet, and it was distributed to each as any had need.

Textual Notes: Acts 4:32-35

This summary concludes the section dealing with the apostles' (Peter and John) witnessing in Jerusalem and the first reactions of Israel's temple elites. The writer turns from outgroup interactions in the temple to a scene depicting the inside of the Jerusalemite Jesus group. The scene depicts a fictive kin group in great harmony and unity, qualities greatly valued in the Greco-Roman world. That they held things in common indicates that they felt obligated to pool resources for the benefit of those in need, for the sake of the group's goal of awaiting the coming of God's kingdom. Such obligatory pooling of resources for group goals was called *koinōnia* in Greek (in Latin: *societas*) and translated "fellowship." Why would such obligatory sharing be required?

Paul (2 Cor 8:1-24) witnesses to the fact that the Jerusalemite Jesus group could not support itself. The underlying problems would derive from the fact that group members were displaced in Jerusalem as they awaited the forthcoming kingdom of God—as promised by Jesus. Paul himself mentioned the Galileans to be found in Jerusalem: Peter, John, James, and perhaps others along with Judeans from the countryside. In Jerusalem they would have no means of support, hence were dependent on help from outside. The social context of first- and second-generation Jesus group members in Jerusalem unable to support themselves seems to be where Paul's collection on their behalf fits in. Further, the appended example of Barnabas along with that of Ananias and Sapphira are instances of what was necessary as Jesus groups clustered in Jerusalem. Paul's collections taken from among Jesus group members located in non-Israelite cities served to alleviate the situation. Of course, once Jerusalem fell to the Romans and Israelites were dispersed (c. 70 C.E.), Jesus group members in Judea would have to go elsewhere to await the forthcoming kingdom of God.

The central emphasis in this summary underscores the quality characteristic of the apostles' activity of witness to the resurrection of the Lord Jesus—it is performed with great effectiveness (v. 33). At the same time, great "grace" (Greek: *charis*) was upon the whole Jesus group. The word translated "grace" means the favor of a patron on behalf of his or her clients. Favors were goods or services that people needed and could not get on their own at a specific time. The favors here are those given by God. Patrons are the usual dispensers of favor, thereby setting up relations of generalized reciprocity. **Patronage.** But family members and friends do endless "favors" within their social groups. And the God of Israel, like a patron, dispenses favors on his people, most notably through the death and resurrection of Israel's Messiah, Jesus. The first witnesses to this divine benefaction were to be found in the Jerusalem Jesus groups, from whom the gospel of God was transmitted.

Verse 35, in contrast to Acts 2:42-47, tells that the goods were placed at the feet of the apostles, that is, that the apostles disposed of them, not the owner of the goods. This radically transforms the reciprocal interaction, since by having the apostles distribute the goods, the original owner could not act as patron who would make others beholden as clients. In other words, in the context of the

Modern model of the Herodian Temple and Jerusalem at the time of the Temple (c. 50 B.C.E.). Location: Holy Land Hotel, Jerusalem, Israel. Photo © Erich Lessing / Art Resource, N.Y.

reciprocal relations typical of small-scale, face-to-face social groups (for example, villages or neighborhoods in cities), giving to one in need followed the back-and-forth exchanges that frequently followed the pattern of open sharing, but always implying the expectation of some obligatory returned assistance left indefinite and open-ended. In order to dispense with the obligation of return to the giver, donations were given to the apostles, to distribute as needed. In this way gifts could not be used to reciprocally oblige another.

The writer now offers two examples of reciprocity characteristic of life in the early Jerusalem Jesus group.

Examples of Reciprocity Acts 4:36–5:12

The Case of Barnabas Acts 4:36-37

4:36 There was a Levite, a native of Cyprus, Joseph, to whom the apostles gave the name Barnabas (which means "son of encouragement"). 37 He sold a field that belonged to him, then brought the money, and laid it at the apostles' feet.

Textual Notes: Acts 4:36-37

Joseph Barnabas later figures prominently in the Acts story of Paul, whom Barnabas introduced to the apostles in Jerusalem (Acts 9:27). He was a Levite, a person born into the class of people whose task it was to serve the temple and who were to be supported by tithing since they were not given any land in the tribal distribution described in Israel's story. But Barnabas was not born into the temple system of Israel. Rather, he was an Israelite resident in a majority non-Israelite region. A native of Cyprus, he owned land there. He is an exemplary person in the story since he contributes to the support of the needy in Jerusalem by having the apostles distribute funds.

The next story, not as exemplary, does make an example of Ananias and Sapphira.

The Case of Ananias and Sapphira Acts 5:1-12

5:1 But a man named Ananias, with the consent of his wife Sapphira, sold a piece of property; 2 with his wife's knowledge, he kept back some of the proceeds, and brought only a part and laid it at the apostles' feet. 3 "Ananias," Peter asked, "why has Satan filled your heart to lie to the Holy Spirit and to keep back part of the proceeds of the land? 4 While it remained unsold, did it not remain your own? And after it was sold, were not the proceeds at your disposal? How is it that you have contrived this deed in your heart? You did not lie to us but to God!" 5 Now when Ananias heard these words, he fell down and died. And great fear seized all who heard of it. 6 The young men came and wrapped up his body, then carried him out and buried him.

7 After an interval of about three hours his wife came in, not knowing what had happened. 8 Peter said to her, "Tell me whether you and your husband sold the land for such and such a price." And she said, "Yes, that was the price." 9 Then Peter said to her, "How is it that you have agreed together to put the Spirit of the Lord to the test? Look, the feet of those who have buried your husband are at the door, and they will carry you out." 10 Immediately she fell down at his feet and died. When the young men came in they found her dead, so they carried her out and buried her beside her husband. 11 And great fear seized the whole church and all who heard of these things. 12 Now many signs and wonders were done among the people through the apostles. And they were all together in Solomon's Portico.

Textual Notes: Acts 5:1-12

This is a high-context story that presupposes that Ananias and Sapphira had promised or vowed to God to give the proceeds of the sale of their land to the Jerusalem Jesus group. Vows are promises to God with a view to obtaining something from the deity in return. The story presupposes some such vow, so that by not giving all of the proceeds to the Jerusalem Jesus group, the couple dishonors God by lying to God, by promising and then reneging (v. 3).

Peter is featured in the story once more as a holy man who knows the realm of God and the ways of human beings with God. He knows that the couple have withheld some of their property after promising to give all of it. And he ascribes their choice to the work of Satan.

Satan (Greek: *diabolos*; English: devil), in the first century C.E., was a cosmic personage whose name ("Satan") comes from Persian, where it designated the role of a secret service agent who worked undercover testing people's loyalty to the king. This role was borrowed by analogy to describe the origin of tests of loyalty to God in Israel, for example Job 1. In Job, Satan is still part of God's council, but about the third-century B.C.E., Satan was ascribed an anti-God role. He was a rogue secret service agent who recruited anti-God persons on his own behalf. His temptations became both a testing and a recruiting device. Such deceptive secret police tactics were known in the first century. Consider the offhand remark of Epictetus, a first-century Stoic philosopher: "When someone gives us the impression of having talked to us frankly about his personal affairs, somehow or other we are likewise led to tell him our own secrets . . . In this fashion the rash are ensnared by the soldiers in Rome. A soldier, dressed like a civilian, sits down by your side, and begins to speak ill of Caesar, and then you too, just as though you had received from him some guarantee of good faith in the fact that he began the abuse, tell likewise everything you think. And the next thing is—you are led off to prison in chains" (*Discourses* IV, 13, 1.5 LCL).

Satan's loyalty test is described as his "filling their heart," and they succumb. They "lie to the Holy Spirit" (Acts 5:3); they did not "lie to us but to God" (5:4). It was culturally permissible to lie to some outgroup person, that is, to any person whose honor one may challenge. But it was dishonoring to lie to ingroup members, and a fortiori, to lie to God. Lying to God dishonors God. By their lying, Ananias and Sapphira "put the Spirit of the Lord to the test" (5:9). This explains why Ananias and Sapphira died. To test God publicly is to challenge God's honor publicly. In order for God to maintain his honor, God must get satisfaction—if only to demonstrate that God is trustworthy. For a person of honor, such satisfaction is "nothing personal," a sort of "natural" consequence of dishonoring behavior.

Burial on the day of death (vv. 6 and 10) was Israelite custom.

The result of these events among Jesus group members was "fear," meaning even greater reverence for God (vv. 5 and 11).

5:12: "Signs and wonders" refer to the significant acts and wonderful events done by God among the Jerusalemites through the apostles. In context, these signs and wonders are healings.

Acts 5:13-42 Witnessing in Jerusalem and Subsequent Elite Reactions: A Dispute in the Temple

Introductory Summary: Healing Successes Acts 5:13-18

5:13 None of the rest dared to join them, but the people held them in high esteem. 14 Yet more than ever believers were added to the Lord, great numbers of both men and women, 15 so that they even carried out the sick into the streets, and laid them on cots and mats, in order that Peter's shadow might fall on some of them as he came by. 16 A great number of people would also gather from the towns around Jerusalem, bringing the sick and those tormented by unclean spirits, and they were all cured.

17 Then the high priest took action; he and all who were with him (that is, the sect of the Sadducees), being filled with jealousy, 18 arrested the apostles and put them in the public prison.

Textual Notes: Acts 5:13-18

This summary statement serves to link the previous set of episodes with what follows. Once again, it highlights the success of God acting through the apostles as well as through the activity of Peter as holy man of God.

5:14 and 16 indicate Luke's interest in highlighting the increasing number of Israelites who believe in God's raising Jesus from the dead, intimating their hope in the forthcoming kingdom of God.

5:15: This verse underscores Peter's roles as holy man and healer, healing through his shadow alone. "The shadow is a person's or animal's soul, life force, doppelganger, or alter ego. One can do harm to another by doing violence to his shadow. And it can be dangerous or helpful to touch the shadow of certain people or animals. Shadows and life force are identical to such an extent that many feared the noon hour because then the shadow shrinks. And the shadow disappears when a person dies. Many magical practices are based upon these beliefs" (Van der Horst 1979:27-28). For example, in the RSV Num 14:9, "Only do not rebel against the Lord; and do not fear the people of the land, for they are bread for us; their protection is removed from them"; literally the passage states: "their shadow is removed from them" (that is, power). Similarly, "to overshadow" in the LXX and in Luke means "to exert power on behalf of" (Deut 33:12 LXX; Luke 1:35).

5:16: The healings are not ascribed to the mediation of any specific apostle here; the context would favor Peter. Yet the agency for all the healings is God working through the agents chosen by Jesus.

5:17: Luke assigns the high priest and his temple entourage to the party of the Sadducees. The Sadducees were largely Israelite elites, the wellborn aristocracy in control of the political religious establishment and the main intermediaries between the Roman imperial presence and Judeans. The writer calls them a *hairesis*, that is, a political party or coalition (NRSV: sect).

Their motive for taking action against Peter and the apostles is *zēlos* (in Greek; NRSV: jealousy). The difficulty is that the word *zēlos* can mean "zeal" or "jealousy" or "envy." Following John H. Elliott (Salamanca, Context Group Meeting, 2006), we describe each as follows:

1. Zeal is the intensity of feeling a person or group has toward another person or group, object, or cause involving enthusiasm, earnest concern, serious commitment or devotion. Zeal is not about possessing, as are jealousy and envy. It may be positive or negative according to the situation.

2. Jealousy arises in a social situation of perceived rivalry between two persons or groups, with the jealous person or group feeling pain over the possible loss of something possessed as a result of the suspected machinations of a rival; it is the intense concern for protecting one's possessions from the encroachment of perceived rivals. It may be positive or negative according to the situation. Jealousy is triadic involving two parties and some third entity (person or object). (See also Hagedorn and Neyrey 1998.)

3. Envy is the grief or pain of a person or group at the sight of valued goods possessed and enjoyed by a perceived rival, accompanied by the wish that the rival be dispossessed of the goods causing happiness. It is pain over perceived inferiority resulting from comparison of self with some "advantaged" others fed by the belief that gain of others occurs only at the cost of loss to oneself, resulting in the wish that the "advantaged" person or group be deprived of the good fortune. Envy is always opposed to change in the status quo. It is socially divisive, never positive, hence always negative. Envy causes persons or groups to dispossess rivals. Envy is dyadic, involving a twosome with one begrudging another. And the "self" involved is always a collective self, that is, a person embedded in some larger ingroup, never a stand-alone self.

Given these three sets of meanings for the word *zēlos*, the one that fits the situation best here is "envy." The high priest and his party stand in opposition to Peter and the Jesus core group, begrudging them their successes among the Jerusalemite population. This is a dyadic conflict, with the high priest and his party aggrieved at the Jesus group's growing popularity. Mark 15:10 ascribes the same motive to Jesus' opponents, recognized by the Roman observer, Pilate (Hagedorn and Neyrey 1998).

5:17-18: The high priest and party take action and imprison all the apostles (not just Peter and John as previously).

Reaction of Temple Elites and God's Intervention Acts 5:19-26

19 But during the night an angel of the Lord opened the prison doors, brought them out, and said, 20 "Go, stand in the temple and tell the people the whole message about this life." 21 When they heard this, they entered the temple at daybreak and went on with their teaching.

When the high priest and those with him arrived, they called together the council and the whole body of the elders of Israel, and sent to the prison to have them brought. 22 But when the temple police went there, they did not find them in the prison; so they returned and reported, 23 "We found the prison securely locked and the guards standing at the doors, but when we opened them, we found no one inside." 24 Now when the captain of the temple and the chief priests heard these words, they were perplexed about them, wondering what might be going on. 25 Then someone arrived and announced, "Look, the men whom you put in prison are standing in the temple and teaching the people!" 26 Then the captain went with the temple police and brought them, but without violence, for they were afraid of being stoned by the people.

Textual Notes: Acts 5:19-26

For the second time in the story (see Acts 3:1—4:31), Peter's successful holy man healing abilities lead to an arrest by the political religious authorities. Only this time not just Peter and John, but all the apostles were arrested. The problem for the political religious elite is the growing numbers of people following the apostles; the authorities were afraid of the people. Why? People healed by folk healers are healed free of charge. In a limited good culture, however, there are really no free gifts. **Limited Good.** Those healed and their families incur a debt of gratitude toward the healer. This is a form of generalized reciprocity in which the debtor-healer can call in the debt by having those indebted comply with his or her wishes. A healer interested in social change might easily provoke his indebted following to take action against the political religious authorities (see the important essay Hollenbach 1982).

5:19: The passage vv. 19-21a describes a group altered or alternate state of consciousness experience. **Alternate States of Consciousness.** An unspecified angel of the Lord releases the group from prison and gives them a command (see also Luke 1:11; 2:9 and 8:26; 12:7; 12:23). The angel of the Lord is one of the chief angels in God's celestial realm (Michael, Gabriel, Raphael, and Uriel are best known), appearing to make known God's will with a command in a specific situation (see Pilch 2004:52-54).

5:20-21a: God commands that they are to continue informing Israelites in the temple about the gospel of God: the God of Israel raised Jesus from the dead, and Jesus would come as Israel's Messiah and inaugurate God's kingdom soon. This viewpoint and the way of living it further are called "the life" (Greek: *hē zōē*, meaningful living, as opposed to *bios*, simply being alive) an early Jesus group self-designation. The apostles immediately obey the command.

5:21b-24: These verses form a sort of diptych describing simultaneous activity of the two groups in question. While the apostles taught in the temple, the temple authorities gathered to discuss the problem raised by Jesus group activity and summoned the apostles. But they were no longer in prison, even though everything there was in order. This left the temple police and the chief priests perplexed.

5:24-25: Upon hearing where the apostles were and what they were up to, the temple police apprehended them again to lead them to the council, but peaceably for fear of the people.

Witnessing in Jerusalem a Fourth Time Acts 5:27-33

5:27 When they had brought them, they had them stand before the council. The high priest questioned them, 28 saying, "We gave you strict orders not to teach in this name, yet here you have filled Jerusalem with your teaching and you are determined to bring this man's blood on us." 29 But Peter and the apostles answered, "We must obey God rather than any human authority. 30 The God of our ancestors raised up Jesus, whom you had killed by hanging him on a tree. 31 God exalted him at his right hand as Leader and Savior that he might give repentance to Israel and forgiveness of sins. 32 And we are witnesses to these things, and so is the Holy Spirit whom God has given to those who obey him."

33 When they heard this, they were enraged and wanted to kill them.

Textual Notes: Acts 5:27-33

5:27-28: Before the council again, the high priest makes his accusation that the apostles spread their gospel to all of Jerusalem as well as the accusation that the council was responsible for the death of Jesus. This they did "in this name," that is, as representatives of Jesus.

5:29-32: In response to this accusation of disobedience to Israel's political religious authority, Peter claims that the Jesus group had a command from God, the God "of our ancestors." **Ancestor Reverence.** And once more Peter proclaims to the council that it is they who were responsible for the death of Jesus, whom the God of Israel raised from the dead and exalted to God's right hand as Israel's leader and savior. Thanks to Jesus, the God of Israel now allows Israel the occasion to get their affairs in order (repentance) and waives any satisfaction for Israel's dishonoring behavior (sin). Peter states this to the council on behalf of all the apostles who are witnesses to Jesus' being raised by the God of Israel. Further proof of repentance and forgiveness comes from their experience of the Holy Spirit, which is further witness to what Peter says.

5:33: Of course, the council's reaction is one of being enraged at the impertinence and lack of respect shown by Peter and the apostles. If Peter and group were cited before the council it was because they did something wrong—otherwise they would not be cited before the council. By defending their patent disobedience, Peter and group proved incorrigible and worthy of death. Hence when the council members heard this, they were enraged and wanted to kill them.

Reaction of the Councilor Gamaliel and Its Outcome Acts 5:34-40

5:34 But a Pharisee in the council named Gamaliel, a teacher of the law, respected by all the people, stood up and ordered the men to be put outside for a short time. 35 Then he said to them, "Fellow Israelites, consider carefully what you propose to do to these men. 36 For some time ago Theudas rose up, claiming to be somebody, and a number of men, about four hundred, joined him; but he was killed, and all who followed him were dispersed and disappeared. 37 After him Judas the Galilean rose up at the time of the census and got people to follow him; he also perished, and all who followed him were scattered. 38 So in the present case, I tell you, keep away from these men and let them alone; because if this plan or this undertaking is of human origin, it will fail; 39 but if it is of God, you will not be able to overthrow them—in that case you may even be found fighting against God!"

They were convinced by him, 40 and when they had called in the apostles, they had them flogged. Then they ordered them not to speak in the name of Jesus, and let them go.

Textual Notes: Acts 5:34-40

5:34: Here we learn that the council in Jerusalem had Pharisee members as well. Luke mentions a noted Pharisee Torah expert, Gamaliel, and his judgment in regard to the expanding Jesus group movement. Gamaliel is explicitly mentioned here presumably because Paul claims to have been associated with him (Acts 23:3). Paul in fact was a Pharisee who joined the Jesus group, even if not on his own.

5:35-39: This passage sets out Gamaliel's argument in favor of leaving the Jerusalem Jesus group alone. If the Jesus movement was not from God, it will inevitably fail as all knew from the cases of a certain Theudas (v. 36) and Judas the Galilean (v. 37). Luke presumes everyone knows the cases of these two persons, although he writes some two generations after the events. Our only source of information about the two is the Judean apologist Flavius Josephus, writing toward the turn of the first century (for Judas, c. 6 C.E.: *War* 2.433 and *Ant.* 18.1-10; 18.23; and Luke 2:2 for the census; for Theudas, c. 46 C.E. *Ant.* 20.97-98). Obviously Gamaliel thinks Peter and his associates are behind their "plan or undertaking"

(v. 38). What links Theudas, Judas, and Peter together is activities with a view to a new political religious situation. They sought to overturn the prevailing Israelite theocracy. The reader of Acts may then presume that Paul, who studied at the feet of Gamaliel (Acts 23:3), believed the same things about Peter and the Jesus group as his teacher did.

5:40: Luke notes that the council was convinced by Gamaliel's words and had the apostles flogged (as a warning and for public temple disturbance, presumably). The council once more orders them to cease and desist their task of witnessing to the resurrected Jesus! Of course, Jesus' command countervails anything the council will have to say.

Conclusion: Dishonored but Honored Acts 5:41-42

5:41 As they left the council, they rejoiced that they were considered worthy to suffer dishonor for the sake of the name. 42 And every day in the temple and at home they did not cease to teach and proclaim Jesus as the Messiah.

Textual Notes: Acts 5:41-42

This concluding statement underscores the values of the Jesus group. A value is a quality and direction of behavior. Values are contentless in themselves; their contents come from the group that espouses the value. In Mediterranean society, honor is a value. Honor means a claim to worth and the public's acknowledgment of the worth. Hence, what is worthy of honor depends on what the group considers valuable, of worth. In this statement, we learn that Jerusalemites considered it honorable to punish and demean Jesus and Jesus' followers. Like Jesus, Jesus' followers were criminals, public sinners worthy of death, as was Jesus himself. This is the assessment of Jerusalemites in general and temple officials in particular.

Jesus group members, on the other hand, redefined what was honorable in their group. Suffering for the sake of the name (that is, person) of Jesus was honorable. Suffering for upholding the word (that is, the gospel of God about Jesus' resurrection) and for believing that Jesus is Israel's Messiah to come soon is honorable. For Jesus group members in comparison with the values of the council, it is the opposite that is dishonorable.

They thus continued in their honorable behavior, "every day" all over Jerusalem.

Acts 6:1—8:4 Witnessing in Jerusalem: The Story of the Greek Deacon Stephen

The whole passage running from Acts 6:1 to 8:4 is about a new personage in the story, the "deacon" Stephen. It would seem that Luke dedicates so much of his story to Stephen because he was of great significance to the early Jerusalemite community of Jesus believers. First of all, he is the first Jesus group member who is killed because a circle of Jerusalemites were aggrieved by Stephen's Jesus group affiliation. Further, he was a Hellenist, a Greek Israelite, civilized in language and custom in the ways of Hellenism. The dispute that Stephen provokes arises from a grievance that his fellow Israelite Hellenists nurture against him, specifically due to his views about the temple of Jerusalem and an interpretation of Torah deriving from Jesus. While he belongs within the ingroup of Israel, he falls into the outgroup of Jerusalemites because he was a Hellenist, not a "Hebrew." **Conflict Resolution.**

Introduction: How Does Stephen Fit in? Acts 6:1-7

6:1 Now during those days, when the disciples were increasing in number, the Hellenists complained against the Hebrews because their widows were being neglected in the daily distribution of food. 2 And the twelve called together the whole community of the disciples and said, "It is not right that we should neglect the word of God in order to wait on tables. 3 Therefore, friends, select from among yourselves seven men of good standing, full of the Spirit and of wisdom, whom we may appoint to this task, 4 while we, for our part, will devote ourselves to prayer and to serving the word." 5 What they said pleased the whole community, and they chose Stephen, a man full of faith and the Holy Spirit, together with Philip, Prochorus, Nicanor, Timon, Parmenas, and Nicolaus, a proselyte of Antioch. 6 They had these men stand before the apostles, who prayed and laid their hands on them.

7 The word of God continued to spread; the number of the disciples increased greatly in Jerusalem, and a great many of the priests became obedient to the faith.

Textual Notes: Acts 6:1-7

This passage serves as an introduction to the story of Stephen. Verses 1 and 7 serve as an inclusion or bracket to mark off the passage by the repetition of the notice of the increasing number of Jerusalemite Jesus group members.

6:1: This verse is full of information. First of all, we are informed that the Jerusalem Jesus group took care of group members who were widows with some sort of daily care. The Greek text simply says daily *diakonia*; the NRSV translates this word "distribution of food," perhaps because the next verse speaks of *diakonein* at table (NRSV: to wait on tables). The difficulty with this translation is that the Greek term for the person doing such activity is *diakonos* (not translated in the English versions, only transliterated as *deacon*). In the Hellenistic world, the word *diakonos* normally referred to a person who functioned as an agent of a higher-ranking person, either as an intermediary in commercial transactions or as a messenger or a diplomat. Here these "deacons" soon to be appointed were persons in the service of the supervising managers of the Jerusalemite Jesus group, the Twelve. (It might be useful to note here that words such as *apostle, bishop, deacon,* and *prophet* are not translated but are left by English translators in transliterated form so as to give these words the meanings they had and continue to have in the churches for whom these translations were made.)

No mention is made of where this daily activity might have taken place. Ancient Middle Eastern laws always mentioned the obligation of the polity to show special care for the truly helpless, that is widows and orphans (see, for example, Deut 14:29; 16:11, 14; 24:17; 26:12-13). Unlike the problem in 1 Tim 5:14-16 that classifies widows by age and by available sources of support (the "real" widow was older without children), here the problem is a grievance between "Hellenist" widows and "Hebrew" widows (in Paul's terminology: Greeks and Judeans). The Hellenists were Israelites inculturated in Greek values, language, and customs, while the Hebrews were Israelites fully devoted to the piety and customs of Judea. Given the fact that the Jesus group described here was Jerusalemite, in the heart of Judean culture and values, the "Hebrews" would be right at home, while the "Hellenists" would be outsiders of sorts (just the opposite from the Pauline Jesus groups).

6:2-4: The grievance was resolved by the Twelve, who served as supervising managers of the Jerusalem Jesus group. This is the only time in Acts that the core group of witnesses is called "the Twelve" (unlike in the Gospel of Luke 8:1; 9:1, 12; 18:31; 22:3, 4). The solution of the Twelve was to have the group choose seven men of good standing (honorable to outsiders) and full of Spirit and wisdom (respected by insiders) as their agents in the task of caring for widows. **Numbers in Acts.** Such care obviously was the responsibility of the Twelve. As previously noted, an agent of a superior supervising manager was a *diakonos*. The Twelve would be devoted to "the word of God," a reference in Acts to the task of proclaiming the events to which the Twelve uniquely were witnesses. After all, their task is to witness (see Acts 1:8). As witnesses, they have no successors or substitutes, since one must have experienced events in order to be witness to those events—here called the word of God.

6:5: The listing of these seven agents of the Twelve begins with Stephen, the central personage of the following story. All the names are Hellenistic names or names of Hellenists, since it was to the needs of Hellenistic widows that they were assigned. The last of the series, a certain Nicolaus, is said to be an Antiochean proselyte. The last word, again, is not translated but transliterated. As a Greek word, it means a person coming to the group from outside, a foreigner. In this sense it indicates that, unlike the other six who were Jerusalemites, Nicolaus was a native not of Jerusalem but of Antioch (see Acts 2:10).

6:6: The laying on of hands was a rite of assigning a person to a task (in Latin: assigning a person to a task or job is called *ordinatio*). The hands stand for activity, action, doing, performance. **Three Zones of Personality.**

6:7: The concluding inclusion about the growth of the group likewise notes that many priests joined Jesus groups. Any male born of a priest was a priest, with the entitlements of priests to be supported by temple tithes and to serve in the temple (usually one week per year, like Zechariah in Luke 1). The high-status priests were usually Sadducees.

Greeks Challenge Stephen in Jerusalem Acts 6:8-15

6:8 Stephen, full of grace and power, did great wonders and signs among the people. 9 Then some of those who belonged to the synagogue of the Freedmen (as it was called), Cyrenians, Alexandrians, and others of those from Cilicia and Asia, stood up and argued with Stephen. 10 But they could not withstand the wisdom and the Spirit with which he spoke. 11 Then they secretly instigated some men to say, "We have heard him speak blasphemous words against Moses and God." 12 They stirred up the people as well as the elders and the scribes; then they suddenly confronted him, seized him, and brought him before the council. 13 They set up false witnesses who said, "This man never stops saying things against this holy place and the law; 14 for we have heard him say that this Jesus of Nazareth will destroy this place and will change the customs that Moses handed on to us." 15 And all who sat in the council looked intently at him, and they saw that his face was like the face of an angel.

Textual Notes: Acts 6:8-15

This scene depicts Stephen in discussion with other Hellenists hostile to the Jerusalemite Jesus groups. The hostile Hellenists get the worst of it, hence are dishonored. But instead of riposting with counterarguments, they resort to violence by taking the required steps to have Stephen physically removed. By the rules of honor-shame challenge, these Hellenists lose because they resorted to violence, and Stephen gains honor.

6:8-10: Once more we find wonders and signs done among the Jerusalemites through God's favor and power, this time by God's agent Stephen—himself an agent of the Twelve. His activity is perceived as a challenge by members of a Hellenistic synagogue (with Greek members from Cyrene, Alexandria, Cilicia, and Asia). Presumably the challenge is to the honor of the God of Israel, whose honor these Hellenists feel obligated to defend. Yet the challenge, in the form of a dispute, is riposted by Stephen, as Luke notes, thanks to God's Spirit and wisdom.

6:11-12: To get even for their being dishonored by losing the challenge, the Hellenists spread lies about Stephen among the people, the council elders, and Torah experts in the city. The gist of it was that Stephen spoke disparagingly about the prophet Moses and his revelations and about the God of Israel. This is what blasphemy meant. Again the word is not translated, but transliteration from the Greek *blasphēmia*. The word means to insult or injure the honor of another by words.

6:13-14: These dishonored Hellenists continue their smear campaign with more lies, by having some of their allies state that Stephen continued his blasphemy ("saying things against"), this time against "this holy place," that is, the temple, as well as against God's Torah. Stephen's blasphemy was supposed to have consisted in his saying that "Jesus of Nazareth will destroy this place and will change the customs that Moses handed on to us." Luke, it seems, sets out charges commonly put against Hellenistic Jesus group members by their fellow Israelites in Luke's society.

6:15: When Stephen was brought before the council, Luke notes that all the council members there "looked intently at him." "To look intently" (Greek: *atenizō*) is most often a technical term in Acts that refers to gazing or staring connected with an ASC experience (like rapture, holy man healing, vision; for example, Acts 1:10; 3:4; 7:55; 10:4; 11:6; 13:9; 14:9; 23:1). **Alternate States of Consciousness.** Stephen looked like a person transformed. The council members were enraptured at the sight of him. They would surely pay attention to his speech.

Stephen's Riposte to the Challenge Acts 7:1-53

7:1 Then the high priest asked him, "Are these things so?" 2 And Stephen replied: "Brothers and fathers, listen to me. The God of glory appeared to our ancestor Abraham when he was in Mesopotamia, before he lived in Haran, 3 and said to him, 'Leave your country and your relatives and go to the land that I will show you.' 4 Then he left the country of the Chaldeans and settled in Haran. After his father died, God had him move from there to this country in which you are now living. 5 He did not give him any of it as a heritage, not even a foot's length, but promised to give it to him as his possession and to his descendants after him, even though he had no child. 6 And God spoke in these terms, that his descendants would be resident aliens in a country belonging to others, who would enslave them and mistreat them during four hundred years. 7 'But I will judge the nation that they serve,' said God, 'and after that they shall come out and worship me in this place.' 8 Then he gave him the covenant of circumcision. And so Abraham became the father of Isaac and circumcised him on the eighth day; and Isaac became the father of Jacob, and Jacob of the twelve patriarchs.

9 The patriarchs, jealous of Joseph, sold him into Egypt; but God was with him, 10 and rescued him from all his afflictions, and enabled him to win favor and to show wisdom when he stood before Pharaoh, king of Egypt, who appointed him ruler over Egypt and over all his household. 11 Now there came a famine throughout Egypt and Canaan, and great suffering, and our ancestors could find no food. 12 But when Jacob heard that there was grain in Egypt, he sent our ancestors there on their first visit. 13 On the second visit Joseph made himself known to his brothers, and Joseph's family became known to Pharaoh. 14 Then Joseph sent and invited his father Jacob and all his relatives to come to him, seventy-five in all; 15 so Jacob went down to Egypt. He himself died there as well as our ancestors, 16 and their bodies were brought back to Shechem and laid in the tomb that Abraham had bought for a sum of silver from the sons of Hamor in Shechem.

17 But as the time drew near for the fulfillment of the promise that God had made to Abraham, our people in Egypt increased and multiplied 18 until another king who had not known Joseph ruled over Egypt. 19 He dealt craftily with our race and forced our ancestors to abandon their infants so that they would die. 20 At this time Moses was born, and he was beautiful before God. For three months he was brought up in his father's house; 21 and when he was abandoned, Pharaoh's daughter adopted him and brought him up as her own son. 22 So Moses was instructed in all the wisdom of the Egyptians and was powerful in his words and deeds.

23 When he was forty years old, it came into his heart to visit his relatives, the Israelites. 24 When he saw one of them being wronged, he defended the oppressed man and avenged him by striking down the Egyptian. 25 He supposed that his kinsfolk would understand that God through him was rescuing them, but they did not understand. 26 The next day he came to some of them as they were quarreling and tried to reconcile them, saying, 'Men, you are brothers; why do you wrong each other?' 27 But the man who was wronging his neighbor pushed Moses aside, saying, 'Who made you a ruler and a judge over us? 28 Do you want to kill me as you killed the Egyptian yesterday?' 29 When he heard this, Moses fled and became a resident alien in the land of Midian. There he became the father of two sons. 30 Now when forty years had passed, an angel appeared to him in the wilderness of Mount Sinai, in the flame of a burning bush. 31 When Moses saw it, he was amazed at the sight; and as he approached to look, there came the voice of the Lord: 32 'I am the God of your ancestors, the God of Abraham, Isaac, and Jacob.' Moses began to tremble and did not dare to look. 33 Then the Lord said to him, 'Take off the sandals from your feet, for the place where you are standing is holy ground. 34 I have surely seen the mistreatment of my people who are in Egypt and have heard their groaning, and I have come down to rescue them. Come now, I will send you to Egypt.'

35 It was this Moses whom they rejected when they said, 'Who made you a ruler and a judge?' and whom God now sent as both ruler and liberator through the angel who appeared to him in the bush. 36 He led them out, having performed wonders and signs in Egypt, at the Red Sea, and in the wilderness for forty years. 37 This is the Moses who said to the Israelites, 'God will raise up a prophet for you from your own people as he raised me up.' 38 He is the one who was in the congregation in the wilderness with the angel who spoke to him at Mount Sinai, and with our ancestors; and he received living oracles to give to us. 39 Our ancestors were unwilling to obey him; instead, they pushed him aside, and in their hearts they turned back to Egypt, 40 saying to Aaron, 'Make gods for us who will lead the way for us; as for this Moses who led us out from the land of Egypt, we do not know what has happened to him.' 41 At that time they made a calf, offered a sacrifice to the idol, and reveled in the works of their hands. 42 But God turned away from them and handed them over to worship the host of heaven, as it is written in the book of the prophets:

'Did you offer to me slain victims and
    sacrifices
    forty years in the wilderness, O
      house of Israel?
43 No; you took along the tent of
    Moloch,
    and the star of your god Rephan,

    the images that you made to
      worship;
    so I will remove you beyond Babylon.'

44 Our ancestors had the tent of testimony in the wilderness, as God directed when he spoke to Moses, ordering him to make it according to the pattern he had seen. 45 Our ancestors in turn brought it in with Joshua when they dispossessed the nations that God drove out before our ancestors. And it was there until the time of David, 46 who found favor with God and asked that he might find a dwelling place for the house of Jacob. 47 But it was Solomon who built a house for him. 48 Yet the Most High does not dwell in houses made with human hands; as the prophet says,

49 'Heaven is my throne,
    and the earth is my footstool.
What kind of house will you build for
    me, says the Lord,
    or what is the place of my rest?
50 Did not my hand make all these
    things?'

51 You stiff-necked people, uncircumcised in heart and ears, you are forever opposing the Holy Spirit, just as your ancestors used to do. 52 Which of the prophets did your ancestors not persecute? They killed those who foretold the coming of the Righteous One, and now you have become his betrayers and murderers. 53 You are the ones that received the law as ordained by angels, and yet you have not kept it."

Textual Notes: Acts 7:1-53

Stephen now takes up the challenge to his honor (and the honor of Jesus and the Jesus group—these are all collectively related). He stands accused of dishonoring the temple and the Torah because he said that Jesus would destroy the Temple and make alterations to Mosaic custom. The high-context omission here is that these actions by Jesus would occur with the coming of a new theocratic political religious system soon, the kingdom of God.

Stephen does not deny the allegation of the false witnesses. What makes them "false" is that they were not around when Stephen said what he did. Instead he opens by adopting two cultural perspectives in his defense. First of all, he underscores the perspective of the cultural adage, "The son is like the father!" (Acts 7:51; see Matt 11:27; Sir 30:1; Deut 23:2; Isa 57:3; Hos 1:2). The point is that those "brothers and fathers" who oppose his witness to the God of Israel who raised Jesus from the dead are no different than their forefathers who killed prophets (Acts 7:51-53). This passage makes repeated mention of the "fathers" (NRSV: "ancestors") from Abraham, through Isaac, Jacob, and his sons in Egypt. After God intervened in Egypt (a much-repeated, hence emphasized, word), and through Moses liberated the offspring of the founding patriarchs, the wilderness generation revolted against God with Israel's original sin, making an image (NRSV "idol") of a calf and attempting to control God, who was to appear over the calf placed on a steerable pedestal. (Note that in Israel's tradition, God is later enthroned above the ark over two winged bulls, the "cherubim," like the calf here; see Heb 9:5.) And after being ensconced in the land promised by God to Abraham's offspring, the settlement generation rejected the worship place revealed by God to Moses, the tent of meeting, in favor of a temple built by human craft. Further, Moses promised that the God of the Fathers would provide his people with prophets, but previous generations consistently killed the prophets of God. Stephen accuses his fellow Jerusalemites of acting like their fathers. Like their fathers, they continue in the sin of the wilderness generation, and in the sin of the settlement generation, and in their custom of killing God's prophets.

Second, he insists on the perspective that although something new may have happened with God's raising Jesus from the dead, it is fully in line with the old. This "old" is the traditional story of Israel, from Abraham to the present. Jesus fits into this story in multiple ways: he is of the lineage of Abraham, a prophet like those foretold by Moses, and killed as prophet since this is in line with Israel's tradition of disobeying God and killing prophets.

Stephen's explanation of Israel's history and how Jesus fits into it is too much for his opponents. They feel obliged to kill him for his blasphemy. The mention of the presence of the young man Saul with the Israelite Hellenists explains how he fits into the story and what he specifically finds objectionable in Jesus group members so that he later volunteers to bring them to trial in the city.

Greeks Take Satisfaction: Stephen's Death Acts 7:54-60

7:54 When they heard these things, they became enraged and ground their teeth at Stephen. 55 But filled with the Holy Spirit, he gazed into heaven and saw the glory of God and Jesus standing at the right hand of God. 56 "Look," he said, "I see the heavens opened and the Son of Man standing at the right hand of God!" 57 But they covered their ears, and with a loud shout all rushed together against him. 58 Then they dragged him out of the city and began to stone him; and the witnesses laid their coats at the feet of a young man named Saul. 59 While they were stoning Stephen, he prayed, "Lord Jesus, receive my spirit." 60 Then he knelt down and cried out in a loud voice, "Lord, do not hold this sin against them." When he had said this, he died.

Textual Notes: Acts 7:54-60

7:54: Stephen's opponents realize that they lost the challenge-riposte interaction by resorting to violence. **Establishment Violence.** They presumably are so dishonored that they are enraged and feel obliged to get satisfaction by killing Stephen.

7:55-56: Meanwhile Stephen falls into an alternate state of consciousness. The clue to this state, again, is Luke's use of the verb "gaze." Stephen has a vision and sees the sky (NRSV: heavens) open. **Opening in the Sky.** Through the opening, he sees God's glory, or exalted and brilliant presence, along with Jesus standing at God's right hand. The standing posture is that of one who intercedes or mediates before the throne. In the next verse Stephen identifies Jesus as "the Son of man."

Several things are curious here. First of all, in the Gospels only Jesus uses the name "Son of man." There Jesus uses this title to describe three roles: a forthcoming personage (not himself); a person soon to suffer, die, and be raised (himself); and a present personage (himself) in the story. This is the first instance in which someone other than Jesus uses the title for Jesus, although it seems that third-generation Jesus group members did refer to Jesus as "the Son of man," as can be see in third-generation Gospel statements that put the title in Jesus' mouth. The vision explains what the ascended Lord Jesus is doing for Jesus group members at present, before his proximate coming as Son of man. He stands before God interceding for his own.

7:57-58a: The covering of the ears is a denial of the veracity of what Stephen now witnesses to. Instead of heeding him, the crowd takes him outside the holy city to kill him there rather than in the city. This shows their respect for the purity of the city.

7:58b: The mention of Saul here situates him in the city at the murder of the first murdered Jesus group member, and ready to be more fully presented in the story that follows (see Acts 8:1-4).

7:59: What is significant here is that as Stephen is being killed, he commends himself to the Lord Jesus (as Jesus once did to God [Luke 23:46]). Presumably Jesus will serve as mediator upon Stephen's appearance before God.

7:60: The word translated "sin" is the Greek *hamartia*. The word means grave dishonor, an act of shaming another that requires the total annihilation of the "sinner" as satisfaction. Stephen's prayer now is directed to God, since the behavior of the Jerusalemite crowd is a serious act of dishonoring God, to whom Stephen has borne witness. His attitude of forgiveness or waiving the need for satisfaction matches that of Jesus (Luke 23:34).

Appendix: Introducing Saul Acts 8:1-4

8:1 And Saul approved of their killing him. That day a severe persecution began against the church in Jerusalem, and all except the apostles were scattered throughout the countryside of Judea and Samaria. 2 Devout men buried Stephen and made loud lamentation over him. 3 But Saul was ravaging the church by entering house after house; dragging off both men and women, he committed them to prison.

4 Now those who were scattered went from place to place, proclaiming the word.

Textual Notes: Acts 8:1-4

This summary statement is composed as a bracket: (A) Saul (B) Stephen (A') Saul and conclusion.

8:1: This verse introduces Saul, the youth of Acts 7:58b in a context of conflict with Jesus group members, as the establishment violence of Jerusalemites widens its scope. **Establishment Violence.** Why and how the apostles (presumably the Twelve) could remain in the city is not noted. These Jesus group members spread through Judea and Samaria, which provided them with the opportunity of proclaiming the good news of the "word," that is, that the God of Israel raised Jesus of Nazareth from the dead, as Lord and Messiah, to inaugurate the Israelite kingdom of God soon.

8:2: Stephen's burial by devout Israelites is accompanied by great lamentation. Such lamentation entailed striking the breast, tearing one's garment, and loud ululation; these acts of mourning proclaimed the evil of the deed performed by the Jerusalemites.

8:3: Now back to Saul, who joins in the establishment violence against the Jesus group in Jerusalem. His behavior is described stereotypically: persecuted people are forcibly dragged from their houses and committed to prison to be held for punishment. It is important to note that people brought to trial are presumed guilty and simply appear for their punishment. If they were not guilty, they would not be on trial! The crime of Jesus group members that Paul knows about is that they believe "this Jesus of Nazareth will destroy this place and will change the customs that Moses handed on to us" (Acts 6:14). Temple and Torah were the linchpins of extant forms of Israelite political religious ideology. To proclaim their demise was blasphemous, insulting to the God of Israel who established them.

Acts 8:5-40 Witnessing in Samaria:
The Story of the Greek Deacon Philip

Philip in Samaria Acts 8:5-13

8:5 Philip went down to the city of Samaria and proclaimed the Messiah to them. 6 The crowds with one accord listened eagerly to what was said by Philip, hearing and seeing the signs that he did, 7 for unclean spirits, crying with loud shrieks, came out of many who were possessed; and many others who were paralyzed or lame were cured. 8 So there was great joy in that city.

9 Now a certain man named Simon had previously practiced magic in the city and amazed the people of Samaria, saying that he was someone great. 10 All of them, from the least to the greatest, listened to him eagerly, saying, "This man is the power of God that is called Great." 11 And they listened eagerly to him because for a long time he had amazed them with his magic. 12 But when they believed Philip, who was proclaiming the good news about the kingdom of God and the name of Jesus Christ, they were baptized, both men and women. 13 Even Simon himself believed. After being baptized, he stayed constantly with Philip and was amazed when he saw the signs and great miracles that took place.

Textual Notes: Acts 8:5-13

8:5: This passage offers an instance of what went on when Jerusalemite Jesus group members were forced out of the city. Here the example is provided by Philip, an agent of the apostles (a deacon) noted in Acts 6:5 right after Stephen. Philip went "down" to the city of Samaria (Sebaste = Augustus, built by Herod the Great) because all roads from Jerusalem go "down." What he does is what Luke stated in his summary. He proclaimed the word: Jesus is Israel's Messiah soon to come. From

The Roman aqueduct of Caesarea, Israel. 30–10 B.C.E. *Caesarea was the Roman administrative center of Judea and a place where Paul was judged. Location: Caesarea, Israel. Photo © Erich Lessing / Art Resource, N.Y.*

the viewpoint of Israel's normative story, the Samaritans were bastard Israelites who lost their pedigree through intermarriage with Assyrians during the Assyrian invasion that destroyed the kingdom of Israel. The Samaritans claimed to be older than the upstart Persian settlement of Yehud (Judea) with its Persian-funded temple in Jerusalem. Samaritans followed the Torah and undoubtedly claimed to be true Israel. That the resurrected Jesus commanded his witnesses to witness in Samaria is quite significant (compare this with the pre-resurrected Jesus' command in Matt 10:5). Now all Israel will be united in the forthcoming kingdom, even the Samaritans.

8:6-8: Like the first adopters of the word in Jerusalem, the Samaritans of Sebaste welcomed Philip's proclamation, supported as it was by deeds of power: exorcisms and healings. The result was that this Samaritan group of believers was purified of unclean spirits and made whole—thus ready for baptism (to follow in Acts 8:12). The outcome was great joy—while Jesus group members in Jerusalem underwent great suffering.

8:9-13: This passage presents a Samaritan named Simon, a successful magician or sorcerer and self-proclaimed great one. He practiced his magic arts for the good of the people since they believed in him as "the great power of God." (The NRSV is misleading: it is the power that is great). And it is precisely such power that Philip exerts on behalf of the possessed and crippled Samaritans of Sebaste. Magic was the ability to use various techniques and incantations to exert control over God, gods, demons, and humans as well as over the celestial bodies impacting humans. **Magi-Magician.**

Simon, too, believed the gospel proclaimed by Philip and was baptized. And, Luke notes, he stayed glued to Philip, undoubtedly to learn his technique in effecting the signs and "great powers" (see Simon's nickname in v. 10) that took place. However, nowhere in this passage does Luke mention how in fact Philip did perform these signs and great powers. The reader is expected to recall that such events were effected "in the name of Jesus."

Interlude: Peter and John in Samaria Acts 8:14-25

8:14 Now when the apostles at Jerusalem heard that Samaria had accepted the word of God, they sent Peter and John to them. 15 The two went down and prayed for them that they might receive the Holy Spirit 16 (for as yet the Spirit had not come upon any of them; they had only been baptized in the name of the Lord Jesus). 17 Then Peter and John laid their hands on them, and they received the Holy Spirit. 18 Now when Simon saw that the Spirit was given through the laying on of the apostles' hands, he offered them money, 19 saying, "Give me also this power so that anyone on whom I lay my hands may receive the Holy Spirit." 20 But Peter said to him, "May your silver perish with you, because you thought you could obtain God's gift with money! 21 You have no part or share in this, for your heart is not right before God. 22 Repent therefore of this wickedness of yours, and pray to the Lord that, if possible, the intent of your heart may be forgiven you. 23 For I see that you are in the gall of bitterness and the chains of wickedness." 24 Simon answered, "Pray for me to the Lord, that nothing of what you have said may happen to me."

25 Now after Peter and John had testified and spoken the word of the Lord, they returned to Jerusalem, proclaiming the good news to many villages of the Samaritans.

Textual Notes: Acts 8:14-25

8:14-17: In the first part of Acts, Peter and John are the main agents. Here we learn that the board of the Twelve send Peter and John once more, this time to Samaria, or more specifically, to the city of Samaria, Sebaste. The purpose of their task is to impart the Spirit of God, God's power. It would seem that in Luke's communities, third-generation groups after Paul, baptism alone did not result in manifestations of the Spirit. A special apostolic procedure known as the "laying on of hands" was required. **Holy Spirit** (see **Three Zones of Personality**).

8:18: Such a procedure had all the characteristics of a magic technique. Hence it obviously caught the interest of Simon, who specialized in such techniques. So he sought to buy the ability to apply the technique from the Jerusalem apostles, much as magicians purchased techniques from other magicians.

8:20-21: Peter's rebuff seems misguided, since how would Simon know that the presence of the Spirit was a gift of God and not a human technique? Peter ascribes Simon's obtuseness to his heart (that is, his attitudes, intellect, will, intentions, desires, conscience, personality thrust all in one **Three Zones of Personality**).

8:22-24: Simon's attitude, Peter states, is offensive to God, who freely gives the Spirit. Hence he urges Simon to pray for forgiveness, lest God take satisfaction on him for this offense. How did Peter know of Simon's ill intentions? From his profession, Peter says that Simon is "in the gall of bitterness." This phrase from Deut 29:17 LXX refers metaphorically to "bitter gall," a plant that is harmful to others; Simon with his sorcerer's attitudes is a person who is harmful to others, bound up with the wickedness typical of the magician's profession. Simon is remorseful and asks for Peter's intercession before God (or Jesus).

8:25: Here we learn that only some in the city of Samaria, Sebaste, accepted the word of God, since Peter and John proclaimed that word to "many villages of the Samaritans" on their way back to Jerusalem.

Philip on the Gaza Road Acts 8:26-38

8:26 Then an angel of the Lord said to Philip, "Get up and go toward the south to the road that goes down from Jerusalem to Gaza." (This is a wilderness road.) 27 So he got up and went. Now there was an Ethiopian eunuch, a court official of the Candace, queen of the Ethiopians, in charge of her entire treasury. He had come to Jerusalem to worship 28 and was returning home; seated in his chariot, he was reading the prophet Isaiah. 29 Then the Spirit said to Philip, "Go over to this chariot and join it." 30 So Philip ran up to it and heard him reading the prophet Isaiah. He asked, "Do you understand what you are reading?" 31 He replied, "How can I, unless someone guides me?" And he invited Philip to get in and sit beside him. 32 Now the passage of the scripture that he was reading was this:
"Like a sheep he was led to the
    slaughter,
and like a lamb silent before its
    shearer,
  so he does not open his mouth.
33 In his humiliation justice was
    denied him.
  Who can describe his generation?
  For his life is taken away from
    the earth."
34 The eunuch asked Philip, "About whom, may I ask you, does the prophet say this, about himself or about someone else?" 35 Then Philip began to speak, and starting with this scripture, he proclaimed to him the good news about Jesus. 36 As they were going along the road, they came to some water; and the eunuch said, "Look, here is water! What is to prevent me from being baptized?" 38 He commanded the chariot to stop, and both of them, Philip and the eunuch, went down into the water, and Philip baptized him.

Textual Notes: Acts 8:26-38

Meanwhile Philip's travels, directed by an angel of the Lord in an alternate state of consciousness, take him now toward Gaza, then to Azotus, and finally to Caesarea. All these locations are along the Mediterranean coast (land's end), with Caesarea right on the coast.

8:27: On the road, Philip has a providential encounter with an Ethiopian eunuch, an official of the court of an Ethiopian queen. This Ethiopian was the treasurer, in charge of the royal treasury (Greek: *gaza*), on his way to Gaza. The pun has the signs of a developing tale.

Further, Luke (or some scribe) adds that they were on a wilderness road. A wilderness was a place where there were no houses or settlements, often a place of residence of various spirits and wild animals. The Ethiopian will eventually be baptized in the wilderness (recalling in Luke-Acts the activity of John the Baptist in the wilderness [Luke 3; 7:24]).

The Ethiopian's coming to Jerusalem to worship and his ability to read indicate that he was a Hellenistic Israelite; the first presumably non-Israelite to join the Jesus group in this story will be Cornelius in Caesarea (Acts 10), yet even his status as non-Israelite might be dubious.

8:28: On his way back to Ethiopia, certainly with some entourage, he was seated in a riding chariot, reading aloud from a scroll of Isaiah. That he had such a scroll at all is surprising, a sign of his wealth. The man has the characteristics of an Ethiopian wellborn elite.

8:29-33: Again, Philip's actions are under the direction of the Spirit, urging him to go to the chariot and engage the treasurer in conversation about what he is reading. The Ethiopian is aware that he needs help in understanding what he is reading, and he is willing to get this help from Philip. The passage in question was from Isa 53:7-8 LXX: "Like a sheep he was led to the slaughter, and like a lamb silent before its shearer, so he does not open his mouth. In his humiliation justice was denied him. Who can describe his generation? For his life is taken away from the earth."

8:34-35: To the Ethiopian's question about to whom the passage referred, Philip began with the passage to demonstrate that it ultimately was about Jesus. He proceeded to give him the good news about God's raising Jesus, making him Messiah and Lord, and about the forthcoming Israelite theocracy.

8:36-38: The Ethiopian indicated his belief in the God of Israel and what he had done to Jesus by asking to be baptized. Philip obliged.

Philip from Azotus to Caesarea Acts 8:39-40

8:39 When they came up out of the water, the Spirit of the Lord snatched Philip away; the eunuch saw him no more, and went on his way rejoicing. 40 But Philip found himself at Azotus, and as he was passing through the region, he proclaimed the good news to all the towns until he came to Caesarea.

Textual Notes: Acts 8:39-40

The Philip tradition comes to an abrupt end at the close of the eunuch's baptism, with Philip snatched by the Spirit of the Lord, another alternate state of consciousness experience. **Alternate States of Consciousness.** While the eunuch proceeds on his way, Philip finds himself at Azotus, then proclaiming the word in towns along the way to Caesarea. This is where his story ends, with Caesarea picked up again in the story of Cornelius the centurion (Acts 10). The Caesarea connection is interrupted by another travel story, this time from Damascus to Jerusalem. That travel story is to explain why and how Saul/Paul was baptized and thus entered the Jesus group.

Acts 9:1-30 The Story of Why/How Paul Was Baptized: From Damascus to Jerusalem

---

Part 1: Paul's ASC Experience near Damascus Acts 9:1-9

9:1 Meanwhile Saul, still breathing threats and murder against the disciples of the Lord, went to the high priest 2 and asked him for letters to the synagogues at Damascus, so that if he found any who belonged to the Way, men or women, he might bring them bound to Jerusalem. 3 Now as he was going along and approaching Damascus, suddenly a light from heaven flashed around him. 4 He fell to the ground and heard a voice saying to him, "Saul, Saul, why do you persecute me?" 5 He asked, "Who are you, Lord?" The reply came, "I am Jesus, whom you are persecuting. 6 But get up and enter the city, and you will be told what you are to do." 7 The men who were traveling with him stood speechless because they heard the voice but saw no one. 8 Saul got up from the ground, and though his eyes were open, he could see nothing; so they led him by the hand and brought him into Damascus. 9 For three days he was without sight, and neither ate nor drank.

Textual Notes: Acts 9:1-9

9:1-2: Luke now links up with his story of Saul. He left off with Saul and others in conflict with Jerusalem Jesus group members, driven by establishment violence against these disciples of the Lord for their alleged blasphemy against the temple and Torah. Knowledge of the presence of these disciples in Damascus must have reached Jerusalem, where Saul received an official letter of recommendation from the Jerusalem high priest to members of the Damascus synagogues to pursue his task.

It is significant here that the name of the Jerusalem Jesus group was the Way (see also Acts 19:9, 23; 22:4; 24:14, 22). The term refers to their way of life in Christ characterized by relationships and aspirations focused on the forthcoming kingdom of God in Jerusalem.

9:3-7: This passage describes Saul's alternate state of consciousness experience on the road to Damascus. **Alternate States of Consciousness.** The event does not describe Saul's conversion (to what?), and there is no call here either. Rather, the event tells about how Saul found out that the Jesus group members he persecuted were indeed connected with an actual cosmic Lord Jesus—something he knew they claimed, but which he himself did not believe. In sum, the event is a revelation of who Jesus group members really were. It is a significant event in the story of Luke's understanding of Saul's career, since descriptions of the event are repeated two more times (Acts 22:1-21; 26:2-23).

Luke describes a pattern of a personal encounter in an alternate state of consciousness (see Pilch 2004:69-78). The sudden light from the sky points to such an experience. Saul sees nothing yet knows some entity is there since he is addressed by name and then enters into a conversation with that entity. Presumably he loses his eyesight when the sudden light from the sky flashes around him (v. 4). The pattern, in three movements, goes as follows (after Lohfink 1965; 1966; who calls this a "dialogue with apparition"; but there is no apparition here, only an alternate state of consciousness auditory experience):

A1	Introductory formula	. . . saying to him,	Acts 9:4; 22:7; 26:14
A2	Double vocative	"Saul, Saul!	
A3	Question of the Lord	Why do you persecute me?"	
B1	Introductory formula	But he answered/I said,	Acts 9:5; 22:8; 26:15
B2	Question of Paul	"Who are you, Lord?"	

C1 Introductory formula   And he said . . .   Acts 9:5; 22:8; 26:15
C2 Self-presentation of Jesus "I am Jesus, the one whom
                              you are persecuting . . .
C3 Command   "But rise . . ."   Acts 9:15; 22:14; 26:16

It is important to note that this description is not simply a literary form or story pattern. Rather it belongs to the genre of alternate state of consciousness reports, a predictable Mediterranean cultural behavior pattern commonly known from cultural experience. Literary genres derive from the social system and are not part of the language or linguistic system. Since the social system specifies appropriate and meaningful behavior, it is quite plausible that people having alternate state of consciousness auditory experiences did perceive things very much as the stereotypical pattern indicates for Saul and others.

9:5: This verse sets out the core of what is revealed to Saul: that the Jesus groups he persecutes are "Jesus whom you are persecuting" (much like Paul identified the Corinthian Jesus groups as the corporate body of Christ [1 Cor 12:27]). Thus Jesus groups form a single, corporate ingroup that includes the exalted Lord Jesus and actually is the exalted Lord Jesus as present in Israelite society.

9:6: The command to the blinded Saul is to enter the city of Damascus to find out what the exalted Lord has in store for him.

9:7-9: Interestingly, the men traveling with Saul heard the voice but saw no one—just as Saul experienced. Since they heard the command, they too comply by leading the blinded Saul to Damascus. In spite of his open eyes, Saul saw nothing. So he fasted for three days, a sign of mourning and self-humiliation in Israelite society.

For first-century Mediterraneans, sight consisted of light emanating from the eyes of living beings and rooted in the heart. Just as the main human-controlled source of light is fire, so too it is because the eyes emanate light constituted of fire that humans can see. As Jesus says, "The eye is the lamp of the body" (Matt 6:22). Aristotle observed: "Is it because in shame the eyes are chilled (for shame resides in the eyes), so that they cannot face one?" (*Problems* 31.957b); "Sight (is made) from fire and hearing from air" (960a); "[V]ision is fire" (959b). Saul's unseeing open eyes indicate that something is going on in his heart. **Three Zones of Personality.**

Part 2: With Ananias the Prophet in Damascus Acts 9:10-19a

9:10 Now there was a disciple in Damascus named Ananias. The Lord said to him in a vision, "Ananias." He answered, "Here I am, Lord." 11 The Lord said to him, "Get up and go to the street called Straight, and at the house of Judas look for a man of Tarsus named Saul. At this moment he is praying, 12 and he has seen in a vision a man named Ananias come in and lay his hands on him so that he might regain his sight." 13 But Ananias answered, "Lord, I have heard from many about this man, how much evil he has done to your saints in Jerusalem; 14 and here he has authority from the chief priests to bind all who invoke your name." 15 But the Lord said to him, "Go, for he is an instrument whom I have chosen to bring my name before Gentiles and kings and before the people of Israel; 16 I myself will show him how much he must suffer for the sake of my name." 17 So Ananias went and entered the house. He laid his hands on Saul and said, "Brother Saul, the Lord Jesus, who appeared to you on your way here, has sent me so that you may regain your sight and be filled with the Holy Spirit." 18 And immediately something like scales fell from his eyes, and his sight was restored. Then he got up and was baptized, 19a and after taking some food, he regained his strength.

Textual Notes: Acts 9:10-19a

This passage explains the role of the Lord in restoring Saul's sight. It implies fire poured in along with God's Holy Spirit (v. 17). Once more we have a person having an alternate state of consciousness auditory experience. Ananias, as we learn in Acts 22:12, was a devout, Torah-observing Judean, a man greatly respected and living in the Israelite quarter of Damascus. He acts very much like a prophet, accustomed to having alternate state of consciousness experiences.

Now he hears the Lord and enters into dialogue:

A1 Introductory formula: The Lord said to him in a vision,
A2 Vocative: "Ananias."
A3 Response: "Here I am, Lord."
A4 Command: "Get up and go to the street called Straight, and at the house of Judas look for a man of Tarsus named Saul. At this moment he is praying, and he has seen in a vision a man named Ananias come in and lay his hands on him so that he might regain his sight."

9:11-12: Ananias is given a command of the Lord, from which we learn that Saul is staying at the house of Judas, presumably a Jesus group disciple living on Straight Street in Damascus. We also learn that Saul is from Tarsus (something never mentioned at all in any of Paul's letters). Finally, Ananias is told that Saul is having a vision of him, that he is the one who will lay hands on Saul that he might regain sight. Luke describes similar simultaneous visions relative to Peter and Cornelius shortly after this event (Acts 10:1-16).

B1 Introductory formula: But Ananias answered,
B2 Demurer: "Lord, I have heard from many about this man, how much evil he has done to your saints in Jerusalem; (9:13) and here he has authority from the chief priests to bind all who invoke your name" (9:14).
B3 Introductory formula: But the Lord said to him,
B4 Second Command: "Go, for he is an instrument whom I have chosen to bring my name among Gentiles, both kings and sons of Israel (9:15); I myself will show him how much he must suffer for the sake of my name" (9:16).

9:13-14: Here we have a recap of the information we know about Saul. Jesus group members in Jerusalem are set apart for/in the Lord; they are an ingroup over against other Israelites. Further, the clue to being a member of this ingroup is invoking the name of the Lord, that is, the person of Jesus, Israel's forthcoming Messiah.

9:15-16: This second command to Ananias underscores why he must go to Saul. The resurrected Lord Jesus has chosen Saul for a task: he will be of service to the Lord by proclaiming him among non-Israelites, both before royalty and before fellow Israelites resident in non-Israelite regions (see Luke 21:12 for Jesus' words to the Twelve mentioning kings and governors, but not non-Israelite lands. The NRSV is inaccurate; the Greek states: "before/among Gentiles, both kings and sons of Israel").

Ananias then fulfills the command of the Lord and performs a prophetic symbolic action. When described in writing, a symbolic prophetic action consists of the description of some symbolic undertaking (commanded by God) performed by a prophet, followed by words that clarify the meaning of the action. Such symbolic actions convey meaning and feeling and invariably effect what they symbolize. For example, in Ezekiel 5 God commands the prophet to cut off and divide some of the hair on his head and face. The fate of this hair will be the fate of the Jerusalemites. "Thus says the Lord God: This is Jerusalem" (Ezek 5:5). The outcome of that prophetic action is then described. Thus:

C1 Fulfillment of command Acts 9:17	So Ananias went and entered the house.
C2 Prophetic symbolic action:	He laid his hands on Saul
C3 Introductory formula:	and said
C4 Explanation of the action:	"Brother Saul, the Lord Jesus, who appeared to you on your way here, has sent me so that you may regain your sight and be filled with the Holy Spirit."
C5 Outcome 1:	And immediately something like scales fell from his eyes, and his sight was restored
C6 Outcome 2:	Then he got up and was baptized (Acts 9:18),
Conclusion Acts 9:19	and after taking some food, he regained his strength.

9:17: Ananias performs the prophetic symbolic action as commanded by the Lord. It consists of laying on of hands. **Three Zones of Personality.** Hands symbolize power, effectiveness. This is shown by Ananias's words describing the significance of the action: to regain sight and to be filled with the Holy Spirit.

9:18: The outcome of the prophetic symbolic action is effectively demonstrated in that Saul sees and is baptized. He is now an ingroup member, in the Lord. Since the whole passage is really about Paul's joining the Jesus group, the purpose of this whole incident is to describe how Saul got to be a Jesus ingroup member.

Part 3: Why/How Paul Returned to Jerusalem Acts 9:19b-30

9:19b For several days he was with the disciples in Damascus, 20 and immediately he began to proclaim Jesus in the synagogues, saying, "He is the Son of God." 21 All who heard him were amazed and said, "Is not this the man who made havoc in Jerusalem among those who invoked this name? And has he not come here for the purpose of bringing them bound before the chief priests?" 22 Saul became increasingly more powerful and confounded the Jews who lived in Damascus by proving that Jesus was the Messiah.

23 After some time had passed, the Jews plotted to kill him, 24 but their plot became known to Saul. They were watching the gates day and night so that they might kill him; 25 but his disciples took him by night and let him down through an opening in the wall, lowering him in a basket.

26 When he had come to Jerusalem, he attempted to join the disciples; and they were all afraid of him, for they did not believe that he was a disciple. 27 But Barnabas took him, brought him to the apostles, and described for them how on the road he had seen the Lord, who had spoken to him, and how in Damascus he had spoken boldly in the name of Jesus. 28 So he went in and out among them in Jerusalem, speaking boldly in the name of the Lord. 29 He spoke and argued with the Hellenists; but they were attempting to kill him. 30 When the believers learned of it, they brought him down to Caesarea and sent him off to Tarsus.

Textual Notes: Acts 9:19b-30

9:19b-20: The effect of Saul's baptism is that he enters some Damascus synagogues where he proclaims Jesus as "Son of God." This is Saul's first proclamation since receiving the Spirit. Such a proclamation would make sense to Paul, since only a deity of sorts would be behind the celestial experience he had had. Further, the word "god" did not bear an exclusive, monotheistic (only-one-God-ism) significance in the first-century Mediterranean. Paul could write in 1 Cor 8:5, "Indeed there are many gods and many lords."

What would it mean to proclaim Jesus as "son of God"? First of all, the title was commonly applied to Roman emperors. For example, there were inscriptions to "Tiberius Caesar, the August God, the son of the God Augustus, emperor, most great high priest, and so on" (Dittenberger OGI 583) or "Tiberius Caesar, the son of the God Augustus, the grandson of the God Julius, August personage, most great high priest, and so on" (Dittenberger OGI 471). This made perfect sense, since, as the dictum had it: "The king is the last of the gods as a whole, but the first of human beings" (A. D. Nock and A.-J. Festugière, *Corpus Hermeticum* [Paris: Belles Lettres, 1945-54], 3:53, frag. XXIV, 3). Then, too, non-kings might also be recognized as gods. Consider later in Acts 14:11-12: "And when the crowds saw what Paul had done, they lifted up their voices, saying in Lycaonian, 'The gods have come down to us in the likeness of men!' Barnabas they called Zeus, and Paul, because he was the chief speaker, they called Hermes."

To determine the meaning of the title "Son of God," it seems best to begin with a linguistic observation fitting the Semitic cultures of the time. A phrase such as "son of X" means "having the qualities of X." Thus "son of man" would mean having the qualities of man, hence human. "Son of the day" means having the quality of the day, hence full of light, morally upright. And "son of hair" means hairy or hoary. In this vein, "Son of God" would mean "having the quality of God or a god,"

Old road to Damascus over the Golan Heights, Israel. This road was probably already used by Paul. The Golan Heights were densely populated until the Jewish revolt of 352 C.E. against Emperor Gallus. Location: Golan Heights, Israel. Photo © Erich Lessing / Art Resource, N.Y.

hence divine, divine-like. In an Israelite context, even among Hellenistic Israelites in Damascus, it is important to note that Son of God could hardly mean "having the essence of the Most High God."

Further, among Hellenistic Israelite elites of this period, God's power is of two chief kinds: creativity and control. Philo calls God's creative power *dynamis poietikē* (power to make/do) and his controlling power *dynamis basilikē* (power to rule as king). God's creative power includes goodness, beneficence, kindness, and creativity itself. It is through this power that God "creates and operates the universe" (Philo, *Quest. Gen.* 4.2). God's controlling power includes sovereignty, authority, jurisdiction, retribution, and ruling. "By this power God rules what has come into being" (ibid.). These two powers, therefore, represent the complete and fundamental aspects of the deity. Thus any person, invisible (such as angels in Gen 6:1-4; Job 1) or visible (such as kings), who evidences creativity and control over other beings to a significant degree will be considered "divine," hence "Son of God." To experience Jesus the Lord in an alternate state of consciousness experience with light flashing from the sky, restoring sight after blindness, is enough to qualify Jesus as "son of God."

9:21: For the third and emphatic time, the reader is alerted to Paul's original purpose in coming to Damascus (see Acts 9:2, 14). Saul's purpose was well known in the Israelite community.

9:22-24: As with Stephen previously, Saul too has success in challenging local Judeans with his demonstration of why Jesus is Israel's forthcoming Messiah. The result is that those challenged feel aggrieved and dishonored, hence plot to kill him. The motive is the same establishment violence that previously motivated Saul. **Establishment Violence.**

9:25: The phrase "his disciples" is difficult here—in what contexts did Paul have the opportunity to form a group of his own disciples during his short stay in Damascus? Furthermore, the pronoun "him" is not in the text. Literally, the Greek has: "His disciples taking at night. . . ." Some manuscripts read: "Disciples taking him at night. . . ." These disciples would be some of his new Jesus group fellow believers. Be that as it may, Saul leaves Damascus at night in a basket through an opening in the city wall.

9:26-27: Saul somehow gets to Jerusalem, where Jesus group members treat him like a spy. But Barnabas brings him to the Twelve, the apostles, and explains what happened to Saul. In Barnabas's explanation, Paul is now said to have seen the Lord, although that is not mentioned in the previous account of Paul's alternate state of consciousness experience. If anything, he was blinded by the Lord, who then spoke to him. In Damascus, Paul spoke boldly in the name of Jesus. "Boldly," as previously noted, describes the behavior of a lower-status person speaking shamelessly in the face of higher-status people, without regard for the status honor of the higher-status person. Proper response by higher-status persons might include punishment or even death. To equals, such speech was a challenge. Saul spoke boldly in Damascus and had to run for his life from his fellow Israelites.

9:28-29: Now in Jerusalem, Saul likewise speaks boldly in the name of the Lord, stirring up the Hellenistic Israelites there to attempt to kill him, as they previously did to Stephen.

9:30: So as in Damascus, his fellow believers assist him in escaping, this time to Caesarea, at land's end, from where they send him off by ship to Tarsus, Saul's place of origin.

Acts 9:31—11:18 Witnessing at Land's End: Peter's Travels

Healing Aeneas 9:31-35

9:31 Meanwhile the church throughout Judea, Galilee, and Samaria had peace and was built up. Living in the fear of the Lord and in the comfort of the Holy Spirit, it increased in numbers. 32 Now as Peter went here and there among all the believers, he came down also to the saints living in Lydda. 33 There he found a man named Aeneas, who had been bedridden for eight years, for he was paralyzed. 34 Peter said to him, "Aeneas, Jesus Christ heals you; get up and make your bed!" And immediately he got up. 35 And all the residents of Lydda and Sharon saw him and turned to the Lord.

Textual Notes: Acts 9:31-35

With the previous mention of Saul in Caesarea at land's end, Luke presents a summary statement about the well-being and growth of Israelite Jesus groups (v. 31) and then picks up the story of Peter in Lydda, not far away from Caesarea.

9:32-35: Peter once more acts like a holy man, with the ability to heal. In Lydda he encounters a person, one Aeneas, bedridden for eight years, and brings him to health using the formula, "Jesus Christ heals you." The presence of the healed Aeneas in Lydda leads still others in Lydda and nearby Sharon (Luke refers to "all the residents") to belief in Jesus and to membership in Jesus groups.

Healing Tabitha Acts 9:36-43

9:36 Now in Joppa there was a disciple whose name was Tabitha, which in Greek is Dorcas. She was devoted to good works and acts of charity. 37 At that time she became ill and died. When they had washed her, they laid her in a room upstairs. 38 Since Lydda was near Joppa, the disciples, who heard that Peter was there, sent two men to him with the request, "Please come to us without delay." 39 So Peter got up and went with them; and when he arrived, they took him to the room upstairs. All the widows stood beside him, weeping and showing tunics and other clothing that Dorcas had made while she was with them. 40 Peter put all of them outside, and then he knelt down and prayed. He turned to the body and said, "Tabitha, get up." Then she opened her eyes, and seeing Peter, she sat up. 41 He gave her his hand and helped her up. Then calling the saints and widows, he showed her to be alive. 42 This became known throughout Joppa, and many believed in the Lord. 43 Meanwhile he stayed in Joppa for some time with a certain Simon, a tanner.

Textual Notes: Acts 9:36-43

9:36-38: This passage opens with a description of the passing of Tabitha (Greek: Dorcas—the name means "gazelle"), an Israelite Jesus group member who lived not far from Lydda, in Joppa at land's end. She was known, we are told, for her good works in the Jesus group. Her fellow believers contacted Peter, who was in the vicinity healing as a holy man does, as we learned in the previous episode. This passage (Acts 9:36-43) concerning widows and a resurrection has its matching scene in Luke 7:11-17 (a widow and the raising of her son).

9:39: Widows performed the role of funeral mourners, and they showed objects of Dorcas's handiwork, of the type which she gave those in need.

9:40-42: This description is much like Jesus' healing/raising of Jairus's daughter in Luke 8:41-56. Peter sends the mourners away (as Jesus presumably did in Luke 8:51). He then turns to the body and says in Aramaic (he uses the woman's Aramaic name), "Tabitha, get up," gives her his hand and calls in the Jesus group members. (Perhaps the commands of power to heal like Jesus were Aramaic ones, noted by Mark 5:41: "Talitha qumi"). Following Ananias's usage in 9:13 (the "saints of Jerusalem") Peter here calls Jesus group members "saints." This designation is frequent in the Psalms for faithful Israelites. Paul likewise uses it frequently for the Jesus group members belonging to the groups he founded. The term refers to persons set apart, devoted exclusively to God. The term aptly described Jesus group members. Once more, the healing in Jesus' name results in further growth in the number of those who believed in the Lord Jesus, this time in Joppa.

9:43: Luke prepares for the next episode by situating Peter, as a house guest of one Simon the Tanner, in Joppa, at land's end, like relatively nearby Caesarea in the next episode. **Hospitality.**

Cornelius the Centurion: His ASC Vision and Its Outcome Acts 10:1-8

10:1 In Caesarea there was a man named Cornelius, a centurion of the Italian Cohort, as it was called. 2 He was a devout man who feared God with all his household; he gave alms generously to the people and prayed constantly to God. 3 One afternoon at about three o'clock he had a vision in which he clearly saw an angel of God coming in and saying to him, "Cornelius." 4 He stared at him in terror and said, "What is it, Lord?" He answered, "Your prayers and your alms have ascended as a memorial before God. 5 Now send men to Joppa for a certain Simon who is called Peter; 6 he is lodging with Simon, a tanner, whose house is by the seaside." 7 When the angel who spoke to him had left, he called two of his slaves and a devout soldier from the ranks of those who served him, 8 and after telling them everything, he sent them to Joppa.

Textual Notes: Acts 10:1-8

The report about Cornelius, a Roman centurion (Acts 10:1-8) has its matching scene in Luke 7:1-10, where a centurion, well regarded by Israelites, sends men to Jesus to ask him to come to his house.

10:1-2: The story moves along land's end to Caesarea. The central figure now is Cornelius, a Roman centurion, described as a devout man who feared God with all his household. The God in question was the God of Israel. To fear God means to reverence the God of Israel by proper worship. The problem for interpreters is to determine where Cornelius is to be situated in the categories by which Judeans pigeon-holed people. The facts that Cornelius has a Roman name and is a Roman centurion may not be very useful. After all, the famous governor of Alexandria (and later Palestine) Tiberius Julius Alexander, was the nephew of the equally well known Judean of Alexandria Philo, and a significant Roman political figure in his own right (see Josephus, *War* 2.487ff.). One would never deduce Tiberius's Israelite genealogy from his name, occupation, or social rank. It would seem that the category of God-fearer (Greek: *phoboumenos ton theon*) referred to persons of Israelite origin who showed respect and reverence for the God of Israel to varying degrees but were too assimilated to Hellenistic ways to bother about the niceties of Judean customs and Torah practice. Thus, even if Cornelius is not an Israelite, as a "God-fearer" he is not very different from totally assimilated Hellenistic Israelites.

10:3-8: While Peter is in Joppa, Cornelius has an alternate state of consciousness experience, a vision of an angel of the God of Israel. **Alternate States of Consciousness.** The experience is described in the usual pattern:

A1	Introductory formula:	The angel of God comes in and says
A2	Vocative:	"Cornelius"
A3	Response with terror:	"What is it, Lord"
A4	Command (prefaced with reason for the command):	"Your prayers and your alms have ascended as a memorial before God. Now send men to Joppa for a certain Simon who is called Peter; he is lodging with Simon, a tanner, whose house is by the seaside."
A5	Fulfillment of command:	When the angel who spoke to him had left, he called two of his slaves and a devout soldier from the ranks of those who served him, and after telling them everything, he sent them to Joppa.

Peter's Parallel Vision and Its Outcome Acts 10:9-23

10:9 About noon the next day, as they were on their journey and approaching the city, Peter went up on the roof to pray. 10 He became hungry and wanted something to eat; and while it was being prepared, he fell into a trance. 11 He saw the heaven opened and something like a large sheet coming down, being lowered to the ground by its four corners. 12 In it were all kinds of four-footed creatures and reptiles and birds of the air. 13 Then he heard a voice saying, "Get up, Peter; kill and eat." 14 But Peter said, "By no means, Lord; for I have never eaten anything that is profane or unclean." 15 The voice said to him again, a second time, "What God has made clean, you must not call profane." 16 This happened three times, and the thing was suddenly taken up to heaven.

17 Now while Peter was greatly puzzled about what to make of the vision that he had seen, suddenly the men sent by Cornelius appeared. They were asking for Simon's house and were standing by the gate. 18 They called out to ask whether Simon, who was called Peter, was staying there. 19 While Peter was still thinking about the vision, the Spirit said to him, "Look, three men are searching for you. 20 Now get up, go down, and go with them without hesitation; for I have sent them." 21 So Peter went down to the men and said, "I am the one you are looking for; what is the reason for your coming?" 22 They answered, "Cornelius, a centurion, an upright and God-fearing man, who is well spoken of by the whole Jewish nation, was directed by a holy angel to send for you to come to his house and to hear what you have to say." 23 So Peter invited them in and gave them lodging.

The next day he got up and went with them, and some of the believers from Joppa accompanied him.

Textual Notes: Acts 10:9-23

In this text segment, we find Peter having an alternate state of consciousness experience at the same time that Cornelius had his vision. Peter's vision prepares this holy man for an encounter with Cornelius and family.

The whole passage has the shape of a vision, a command, and fulfillment of the command directed to Peter at Joppa.

Vision: A three-time vision to Peter
Command: to Peter
Fulfillment of command: prefaced with reason for the command, then fulfillment of the command.

10:9-16: Peter's vision is about food as he falls into an alternate state of consciousness at the time he was hungry. The sky opens (as frequently in ASCs), and from the realm of God comes a sheet with all kinds of edible, animate entities. God commands Peter to kill any of the creatures and eat it, but Peter protests that he has always followed God's Torah and never eaten anything "profane or unclean." Of course, the reference is to Israel's Torah rules of prohibited foods (Leviticus 11). But the sky voice insists that it is the God of Israel who determines what is clean and unclean, sacred or profane, not some Torah interpreters. If God calls everything clean, then no one is entitled to determine otherwise.

This strong statement disavowing Israel's food laws about what foods are appropriate was repeated three times. Of course the question is: Is this about food or about something else? It must be about something other than food since in what follows the question is about profane and unclean people, not food. On the other hand, Israel's purity rules concerning food replicate its rules concerning people (see Malina 2001:161-80).

10:17-20: Command to Peter: obviously Peter is puzzled by the vision since Israel's God would not reverse the food regulations so meticulously laid out in the Torah. Meanwhile Cornelius's men arrive. With their arrival, Peter receives a command from God's Spirit: to accompany the men without hesitation since God has sent them.

10:21-23: Peter goes on to fulfill the command. The reference to "the whole *nation* of Judeans" in v. 22 is the way Hellenists would describe Israelites. Before he does so, however, he is given a reason for obeying: Cornelius, a foreigner, or member of an outgroup, was upright and God-fearing; Judeans hold him in high esteem; and God's angel directed him to Peter to hear what Peter had to say. After offering the messengers hospitality, the next day Peter with entourage goes with them as commanded. **Hospitality.**

Peter Witnesses to Cornelius Acts 10:24-48

Introduction Acts 10:24-33

The introductory segment to Peter's encounter with Cornelius consists of two passages setting up the situation so Peter can tell Cornelius "what Peter had to say" (Acts 10:22). The first passage describes the meeting of Cornelius and Peter (Acts 10:24-29), and the second has Cornelius explaining to Peter why he was summoned (Acts 10:30-33).

Peter Meets Cornelius 10:24-29

10:24 The following day they came to Caesarea. Cornelius was expecting them and had called together his relatives and close friends. 25 On Peter's arrival Cornelius met him, and falling at his feet, worshiped him. 26 But Peter made him get up, saying, "Stand up; I am only a mortal." 27 And as he talked with him, he went in and found that many had assembled; 28 and he said to them, "You yourselves know that it is unlawful for a Jew to associate with or to visit a Gentile; but God has shown me that I should not call anyone profane or unclean. 29 So when I was sent for, I came without objection. Now may I ask why you sent for me?"

Textual Notes: Acts 10:24-29

10:24-26: Cornelius awaits Peter's arrival with relatives and close friends. When Peter appears, Cornelius greets him like some celestial entity. Peter insists that he is but a human being (Greek: *anthrōpos*; NRSV "mortal" is inaccurate).

10:28a: Peter now enunciates the custom to which his food vision actually pertains, that is, the custom of relating to different people. The NRSV is, again, inaccurate in its translation. What Peter says is that Cornelius, versed in the customs of Judea, knows that it is not permitted (Greek: *athemiton*) for a Judean to associate with or approach a foreigner (Greek: *allophylos*, a person of another tribe, a non-Israelite; this is not the usual word for "Gentile").

10:28b-29: Now we come to the real significance of Peter's vision: "God has shown me that I should not call anyone profane or unclean." So this much is clear to Peter—human beings are not to be considered profane or unclean. But Peter questions why he is there at all.

Cornelius Explains to Peter 10:30-33

10:30 Cornelius replied, "Four days ago at this very hour, at three o'clock, I was praying in my house when suddenly a man in dazzling clothes stood before me. 31 He said, 'Cornelius, your prayer has been heard and your alms have been remembered before God. 32 Send therefore to Joppa and ask for Simon, who is called Peter; he is staying in the home of Simon, a tanner, by the sea.' 33 Therefore I sent for you immediately, and you have been kind enough to come. So now all of us are here in the presence of God to listen to all that the Lord has commanded you to say."

Textual Notes: Acts 10:30-33

10:30-32: Cornelius now explains to Peter why he was summoned. He sets out the circumstances and content of his alternate state of consciousness experience: a vision of a celestial being (that is what "dazzling clothes" indicates). Thanks to his prayer and almsgiving, the God of Israel decided that Peter should come to his house and that the Lord would command Peter what to tell Cornelius and family. Thus Peter's words will be those of the Lord, as one might expect from a holy man.

10:33: The gathering is not a simple hospitality welcome. Rather, as Cornelius notes, they are "in the presence of God," presumably the God of Israel, whom Cornelius venerates. What Peter has to say comes from the Lord and is not his own. The meeting is a sacred meeting in which divinely commanded information will be imparted by a divinely sanctioned holy man to a divinely chosen audience. The God of Israel alone is responsible for Cornelius's "conversion."

Peter's Attestation Acts 10:34-43

10:34 Then Peter began to speak to them: "I truly understand that God shows no partiality, 35 but in every nation anyone who fears him and does what is right is acceptable to him. 36 You know the message he sent to the people of Israel, preaching peace by Jesus Christ—he is Lord of all. 37 That message spread throughout Judea, beginning in Galilee after the baptism that John announced: 38 how God anointed Jesus of Nazareth with the Holy Spirit and with power; how he went about doing good and healing all who were oppressed by the devil, for God was with him. 39 We are witnesses to all that he did both in Judea and in Jerusalem. They put him to death by hanging him on a tree; 40 but God raised him on the third day and allowed him to appear, 41 not to all the people but to us who were chosen by God as witnesses, and who ate and drank with him after he rose from the dead. 42 He commanded us to preach to the people and to testify that he is the one ordained by God as judge of the living and the dead. 43 All the prophets testify about him that everyone who believes in him receives forgiveness of sins through his name."

Textual Notes: Acts 10:34-43

10:34-35: Peter opens with a principle well known in Israel: "God shows no partiality" (Deut 10:17-18; Sir 35:15-16; Rom 2:11). What the phrase means is that God cannot be bribed, by a person's status, by a gift, or by anything else. In the Israelite tradition, the principle was applied to God's dealings with Israel, his people. What Peter learns from his vision is that the principle applies to God's dealings with all human beings, not just Israel. That is rather remarkable in an Israelite context: the God of Israel is open to all peoples who show reverence for the God of Israel and do what is right. To fear God means to honor God, ascribing God prominence and precedence over all other gods ("You shall have no other gods before me"). What it might mean to do "what is right" (Greek: *dikaiosynē*, righteousness) is not specified, but it presumably means treating others as one would have others treat oneself. The remarkable point is that such persons are accepted (Greek: *dektos*; not NRSV "acceptable") by the God of Israel.

10:36: Peter now begins a proclamation of the word, the gospel. He opens with the fact, obvious to Israelites, that the God of Israel sent his word, proclaimed by Jesus to the "sons of Israel" (Greek), and no one else.

10:37: He continues with a rhetorical "you all know" and proceeds to tell the story of Jesus of Nazareth. Since Peter is presumably speaking with a non-Israelite, he refers to the land of Israel as Judea, as was non-Israelite usage and perhaps also the usage of assimilated Israelites. Thus "that message spread throughout Judea, beginning in Galilee" (v. 37). He continues telling of Jesus' activity from Galilee, where God anointed him with Spirit and power. Because the God of Israel was with him, he could confront the devil, who oppressed so many. Peter and colleagues likewise witnessed to what Jesus did in Judea and Jerusalem, where he was killed "on a tree" but raised by the God of Israel on the third day. This God of Israel allowed Jesus to appear to the Eleven chosen by God to be witnesses. And they ate and drank with him after he was raised.

10:42-43: The resurrected Jesus commanded the Eleven to proclaim and attest to the people Israel (Greek: *tō laō*) that Jesus was designated by the God of Israel as judge of the living and the dead. Furthermore, all of Israel's prophets testify that everyone who believes in him receives from God, through the person of Jesus, forgiveness of sins committed against God.

Outcome: The Spirit and Baptism Acts 10:44-48

10:44 While Peter was still speaking, the Holy Spirit fell upon all who heard the word. 45 The circumcised believers who had come with Peter were astounded that the gift of the Holy Spirit had been poured out even on the Gentiles, 46 for they heard them speaking in tongues and extolling God. Then Peter said, 47 "Can anyone withhold the water for baptizing these people who have received the Holy Spirit just as we have?"48 So he ordered them to be baptized in the name of Jesus Christ. Then they invited him to stay for several days.

Textual Notes: Acts 10:44-48

10:44-45: To the astonishment of the Israelite Jesus group members who accompanied Peter, even as he spoke the word, God's Spirit fell upon all present even though they were non-Israelites.

10:46: Proof that they had the Spirit working in them was that they spoke in tongues and extolled the God of Israel.

10:47-48: Peter concluded that since they had the Spirit, they should be included in the Jesus group through the rite of baptism in the name of Jesus.

The most significant feature of chapter 10 is that it was the God of Israel, at work through his Spirit, who was responsible for having non-Israelites join the Jesus group, and this the Jesus group in Judea. The whole story, thus far, indicates how Luke believes that the founder of the growing Jesus group, the "church," was the God of Israel.

Peter Explains His Vision Once More Acts 11:1-18

11:1 Now the apostles and the believers who were in Judea heard that the Gentiles had also accepted the word of God. 2 So when Peter went up to Jerusalem, the circumcised believers criticized him, 3 saying, "Why did you go to uncircumcised men and eat with them?" 4 Then Peter began to explain it to them, step by step, saying, 5 "I was in the city of Joppa praying, and in a trance I saw a vision. There was something like a large sheet coming down from heaven, being lowered by its four corners; and it came close to me. 6 As I looked at it closely I saw four-footed animals, beasts of prey, reptiles, and birds of the air. 7 I also heard a voice saying to me, 'Get up, Peter; kill and eat.' 8 But I replied, 'By no means, Lord; for nothing profane or unclean has ever entered my mouth.' 9 But a second time the voice answered from heaven, 'What God has made clean, you must not call profane.' 10 This happened three times; then everything was pulled up again to heaven. 11 At that very moment three men, sent to me from Caesarea, arrived at the house where we were. 12 The Spirit told me to go with them and not to make a distinction between them and us. These six brothers also accompanied me, and we entered the man's house. 13 He told us how he had seen the angel standing in his house and saying, 'Send to Joppa and bring Simon, who is called Peter; 14 he will give you a message by which you and your entire household will be saved.' 15 And as I began to speak, the Holy Spirit fell upon them just as it had upon us at the beginning. 16 And I remembered the word of the Lord, how he had said, 'John baptized with water, but you will be baptized with the Holy Spirit.' 17 If then God gave them the same gift that he gave us when we believed in the Lord Jesus Christ, who was I that I could hinder God?" 18 When they heard this, they were silenced. And they praised God, saying, "Then God has given even to the Gentiles the repentance that leads to life."

Textual Notes: Acts 11:1-18

The scenario here (Acts 11:1-18) in which the Pharisee party criticizes Peter for associating with non-Israelites has its matching scenario in Luke 7:36-50, where Pharisees criticized Jesus for being touched by the wrong kind of woman.

11:1-3: Through the gossip network, the apostles and other Judean Jesus group members heard all about Peter's activities in Caesarea, when non-Israelites accepted the word of the God of Israel (see Rohrbaugh 2001). When confronted by Judean Jesus group members with the fact of his eating with non-Israelites, Peter recounts the whole story of his vision and its consequence, in answer to the question and accusation: "Why did you go to uncircumcised men and eat with them?"

11:4-17: In his explanation, Peter repeats all that had previously occurred in his encounter with Cornelius.

11:12: We learn that Peter's entourage consisted of six Jesus group members. Further, the point of his vision as indicated by the Spirit is that Peter and entourage were "not to make a distinction between them and us."

11:16-17: Not noted in the previous account is that Peter says he remembered the word of the Lord, how he had said, "John baptized with water, but you will be baptized with the Holy Spirit" (see Luke 3:16). The passive voice here means God will baptize you with the Holy Spirit. The Spirit is God's gift—and that is precisely what happened to Cornelius and friends. The point is that God did it, and who is Peter to hinder God?

11:18: In the end, the Jerusalemite Jesus group had to conclude that the God of Israel has given even to devoted and righteous non-Israelites "the repentance that leads to life." This repentance that leads to life refers to getting one's life in order with a view to the forthcoming kingdom of God and Israelite theocracy. For a non-Israelite, such repentance truly entails a social conversion of sorts. Yet nothing is mentioned about following Israelite kosher rules to make one fitting before the God of Israel.

Acts 11:19-29 Events among Judeans in Antioch

Barnabas and Greeks Acts 11:19-24

11:19 Now those who were scattered because of the persecution that took place over Stephen traveled as far as Phoenicia, Cyprus, and Antioch, and they spoke the word to no one except Jews. 20 But among them were some men of Cyprus and Cyrene who, on coming to Antioch, spoke to the Hellenists also, proclaiming the Lord Jesus. 21 The hand of the Lord was with them, and a great number became believers and turned to the Lord. 22 News of this came to the ears of the church in Jerusalem, and they sent Barnabas to Antioch. 23 When he came and saw the grace of God, he rejoiced, and he exhorted them all to remain faithful to the Lord with steadfast devotion; 24 for he was a good man, full of the Holy Spirit and of faith. And a great many people were brought to the Lord.

Textual Notes: Acts 11:19-24

11:19: Mention of Stephen, a Hellenist, links up the following incident to what preceded. The persecution that followed the Stephen incident drove many to land's end and the nearby island of Cyprus. Luke notes that Jesus group members from Jerusalem spoke only to Judeans, that is, those attached to the customs and behaviors of Judea.

11:20-21: The new feature noted here is that some Jesus group members from Cyprus and Cyrene (North Africa) likewise proclaimed Jesus Messiah to Israelites who were Hellenized, that is, inculturated in the language and behaviors of Hellenistic values, therefore civilized. In this they were like Stephen. Many of these Hellenists had the hand of the Lord upon them, that is, the Spirit—hence they became believers.

11:22-23: Again, the gossip network reached the Jerusalem Jesus group, and it sent Barnabas to Antioch. Barnabas confirmed what had been said about God's favor in Antioch, and he exhorted the group. (On gossip, see Rohrbaugh 2001.)

11:24: Luke now takes the opportunity to characterize Barnabas, who would figure prominently in what follows. He previously noted that Barnabas was a Levite from Cyprus (4:36). Now he notes that he was "a good man, full of the Holy Spirit and of faith." Such characterization seems quite stereotypical to us, but was fully sufficient in antiquity. Finally, another note about the continued growth of the Jesus movement groups, now among Israelite Judeans and Hellenists in Antioch.

Jesus Group Members Called Messianists Acts 11:25-26

11:25 Then Barnabas went to Tarsus to look for Saul, 26 and when he had found him, he brought him to Antioch. So it was that for an entire year they met with the church and taught a great many people, and it was in Antioch that the disciples were first called "Christians."

Textual Notes: Acts 11:25-26

11:25-26a: Barnabas was the person who introduced Saul to the apostles in Jerusalem (Acts 9:37). His trip to Tarsus marks the first time in the story that anyone goes beyond Israel's land's end. Yet Barnabas goes not to proclaim the word but to fetch Saul. Together they stayed a year in Antioch, teaching a great many. No indication is given about what they taught or how they taught.

11:26b: This note is significant for later Jesus groups. Luke notes that it was in Antioch that outsiders called Jesus group members "Messianists," or "Messiah followers" (NRSV does not translate, but transliterates "Christians"). This label obviously derived from Jesus group belief that Jesus would be the Messiah with power inaugurating the forthcoming kingdom of God. And to some outsiders in Antioch, it was this messianic belief that characterized Jesus group members.

Agabus the Prophet and Famine Acts 11:27-29

11:27 At that time prophets came down from Jerusalem to Antioch. 28 One of them named Agabus stood up and predicted by the Spirit that there would be a severe famine over all the world; and this took place during the reign of Claudius. 29 The disciples determined that according to their ability, each would send relief to the believers living in Judea.

Textual Notes: Acts 11:27-29

11:27-28: Agabus, presumably a Jesus group prophet, comes "down" from Jerusalem with a group of prophets to Antioch during the reign of Claudius to tell of a forthcoming famine.

11:29: While this famine was to occur "over all the world," we find out that it was Jesus group members in Judea who were particularly affected. The response of Jesus group members in Antioch was to assist their brothers in Judea according to their ability. This was the same behavior noted previously about the Jerusalemite group itself. It indicates the expanding quality of the ingroup consisting of those who believe the word.

Acts 11:30—12:24 Events among Judeans in Jerusalem

Introduction: While Barnabas and Saul Are Bringing Assistance from Antioch

King Herod Kills James and Imprisons Peter Acts 11:30—12:4

11:30 This they did, sending it to the elders by Barnabas and Saul. 12:1 About that time King Herod laid violent hands upon some who belonged to the church.

2 He had James, the brother of John, killed with the sword. 3 After he saw that it pleased the Jews, he proceeded to arrest Peter also. (This was during the festival of Unleavened Bread.) 4 When he had seized him, he put him in prison and handed him over to four squads of soldiers to guard him, intending to bring him out to the people after the Passover.

Textual Notes: Acts 11:30—12:4

11:30: During this Judean famine, Barnabas and Saul travel together with assistance to be delivered to the elders in Jerusalem. Obviously, the assistance was in terms of coins or precious metal of some sort since it was portable. Meanwhile, in that city King Herod, king of Galilee, began killing Jesus group members because "it pleased the Judeans." He must have done this with the collusion of the Roman procurator, who was to maintain order in Judea.

12:1-4: The scenario in this passage very much matches what happened in the case of Jesus (Luke 21:1-7; 23:7-15). In this case Jesus' disciple and one of the Twelve, James son of Zebedee, is killed by Herod during the Feast of Unleavened Bread. Right after that, because it pleased the Judeans, Herod seized Peter, to bring him out to the people right after the Passover.

12:4: To this end Herod has four squads of soldiers arrest and take guard of Peter.

Peter Escapes from Prison in an ASC Experience Acts 12:5-11

12:5 While Peter was kept in prison, the church prayed fervently to God for him.

6 The very night before Herod was going to bring him out, Peter, bound with two chains, was sleeping between two soldiers, while guards in front of the door were keeping watch over the prison. 7 Suddenly an angel of the Lord appeared and a light shone in the cell. He tapped Peter on the side and woke him, saying, "Get up quickly." And the chains fell off his wrists. 8 The angel said to him, "Fasten your belt and put on your sandals." He did so. Then he said to him, "Wrap your cloak around you and fol-low me." 9 Peter went out and followed him; he did not realize that what was happening with the angel's help was real; he thought he was seeing a vision. 10 After they had passed the first and the second guard, they came before the iron gate leading into the city. It opened for them of its own accord, and they went outside and walked along a lane, when suddenly the angel left him. 11 Then Peter came to himself and said, "Now I am sure that the Lord has sent his angel and rescued me from the hands of Herod and from all that the Jewish people were expecting."

Textual Notes: Acts 12:5-11

12:5: While Peter was kept in prison, the church prayed fervently to God for him.

12:6-9: The very night before Herod was going to bring him out, Peter, bound with two chains, was sleeping between two soldiers, while guards in front of the door were keeping watch over the prison. Suddenly an angel of the Lord appeared and a light shone in the cell. He tapped Peter on the side and woke him, saying,

Command:	"Get up quickly."
Result:	And the chains fell off his wrists.

The angel said to him,

Command: "Fasten your belt and put on your sandals."
Fulfillment: He did so.

   Then he said to him,

Command: "Wrap your cloak around you and follow me."
Fulfillment: Peter went out and followed him;
ASC quality: he did not realize that what was happening with the angel's help
                  was real;

he thought he was seeing a vision (see Pilch 2004:99-101).

12:10: After they had passed the first and the second guard, they came before the iron gate leading into the city. It opened for them of its own accord, and they went outside and walked along a lane, when suddenly the angel left him.

12:11: Then Peter came to himself and said, "Now I am sure that the Lord has sent his angel and rescued me from the hands of Herod and from all that the Judeans were expecting."

Peter at Mary's House in Jerusalem Acts 12:12-17

12:12 As soon as he realized this, he went to the house of Mary, the mother of John whose other name was Mark, where many had gathered and were praying. 13 When he knocked at the outer gate, a maid named Rhoda came to answer. 14 On recognizing Peter's voice, she was so overjoyed that, instead of opening the gate, she ran in and announced that Peter was standing at the gate. 15 They said to her, "You are out of your mind!" But she insisted that it was so. They said, "It is his angel." 16 Meanwhile Peter continued knocking; and when they opened the gate, they saw him and were amazed. 17 He motioned to them with his hand to be silent, and described for them how the Lord had brought him out of the prison. And he added, "Tell this to James and to the believers." Then he left and went to another place.

Textual Notes: Acts 12:12-17

12:12: John Mark's mother's house was a gathering place for Jesus group members. He has the usual two names of Hellenists, John being an Israelite name and Mark a Roman one. His mother owned a two-story, gated house in Jerusalem and had a maid and house large enough for such a gathering. These are qualities of first adopters of the gospel of God. **Communication of Innovation.**

12:13-14: Rhoda's behavior, both the surprised absentmindedness and the running, are considered humorous. Her announcement of Peter's presence was greeted with incredulity.

12:15: The explanation, "It is his angel," points to the popular Mediterranean belief that individuals had guardian angels (or demons among Greeks, or genii among Romans).

12:16-17: Peter describes his ASC experience in which "the Lord had brought him out of the prison." He concludes with a message to James.

   In the story, we now learn that there was a significant person named "James" in the Jerusalem Jesus group. Obviously this is not James the son of Zebedee who has just been murdered. Rather, this James is the brother of the Lord, who ends up in charge of the Jerusalem Jesus group. Paul mentions him in 1 Cor 15:7 as the only one of Jesus' relatives specifically experiencing a vision of the resurrected Jesus, and in Galatians 1:9; 2:9, 12 as a person of significance in the Jerusalem gathering. This supports Luke's assessment of James's central role in the Jerusalem decision-making group (see Acts 12:17; 15:13; 21:18). It seems that the Jerusalem Jesus group considered it a matter of course that this brother of Jesus (noted in Mark 6:3) should preside over the Jerusalem assembly.

The Death of Herod Acts 12:18-23

12:18 When morning came, there was no small commotion among the soldiers over what had become of Peter. 19 When Herod had searched for him and could not find him, he examined the guards and ordered them to be put to death. Then Peter went down from Judea to Caesarea and stayed there. 20 Now Herod was angry with the people of Tyre and Sidon. So they came to him in a body; and after winning over Blastus, the king's chamberlain, they asked for a reconciliation, because their country depended on the king's country for food. 21 On an appointed day Herod put on his royal robes, took his seat on the platform, and delivered a public address to them. 22 The people kept shouting, "The voice of a god, and not of a mortal!" 23 And immediately, because he had not given the glory to God, an angel of the Lord struck him down, and he was eaten by worms and died.

Textual Notes: Acts 12:18-23

12:18-19a: The presumption of the outgroup was that Peter's escape happened because of the carelessness of the soldiers. Herod has them put to death for their negligence in the line of duty.

12:19b: Peter in turn went down from Jerusalem to Caesarea, where he stayed. With this mention of Peter, the writer concludes his "Peter cycle," at land's end. While Peter does emerge in Acts 15:7 to attest to his experience with Cornelius, his main witness concludes at Caesarea. This episode likewise marks the close of the description of the resurrected Jesus' command to the Eleven at the beginning of the book. The command that set in motion the activities of the first part of the book has been fulfilled.

12:20-21: This passage describes what God does to those who attempt to harm those who are faithful to him. The cities of Tyre and Sidon were in conflict with Herod. They sought to defuse the conflict because they needed to trade with Herod for food. To this end, they used the king's chamberlain, Blastus, as broker. In that way they got an appointed day when the king would hold an official reception. Indications of this are the king's garb and his being seated on a raised platform. Herod spoke to the representatives of Tyre and Sidon and gathered dignitaries, who duly expressed fawning adulation: Herod's was the voice of a god, not a man. It was such adulation, along with gifts, that led to the "acceptance of persons." Yet it was on this occasion of conflict resolution with Tyre and Sidon that Herod died, "eaten by worms," we are told.

Conclusion: Continued Expansion of the Jesus Group Movement Acts 12:24

24 But the word of God continued to
advance and gain.

Textual Notes: Acts 12:24
12:24: This short summary continues to remind the audience of the continued growth of the Jesus group. **Numbers in Acts.** It also reminds readers of the successful outcome of the fulfillment of the Lord Jesus' command to the Eleven to bear witness from Jerusalem to land's end.

Part II: Jesus' Second Command: To Saul/Paul—His Activities among Israelite Minority Populations (Acts 12:25—28:31)

In Acts 1–12 (Part I) the activities of Peter and his associates dominate. This is readily noticeable by the fact that while Peter's name occurs sixty-two times in Acts, except for one occurrence in Acts 15, these instances are located in Acts 1–12. Peter now yields center stage to Paul and his associates, whose proclamation activities will dominate the remaining chapters of Acts (Part II). Paul was introduced in Acts 7:58 at the martyrdom of Stephen and presented as a persecutor of those who believed in Jesus Messiah (Acts 8:3). Then in an ASC experience **Alternate States of Consciousness**, Paul learned that the Jesus group members he persecuted were indeed connected with an actual cosmic Lord Jesus. He turned his zeal to proclaiming the resurrected Lord Jesus, but his preaching met with skepticism and attempts on his life by fellow Israelites (9:23), including the Greek-speaking ones (9:29). Israelites sympathetic to Paul's proclamation sent him off to Tarsus in order to save his life.

Acts 12:25–15:35 Proclaiming the Resurrected Lord in the Mediterranean World

Because Luke does not distinguish three discrete journeys for Paul, as modern commentators are in the habit of doing, we treat these journeys from a perspective suggested by an *inclusio* in Luke's text. The mention of "all that God had done" (Acts 14:27) and the repetition of "the things that God had done" (Acts 21:19) signal one unit that can then be divided into two segments: a Mediterranean expedition (13:1—15:35) and an Aegean expedition (15:36—21:36).

Commissioning by the Spirit in Antioch Acts 12:25–13:3

12:25 Then after completing their mission Barnabas and Saul returned to Jerusalem and brought with them John, whose other name was Mark.

13:1 Now in the church at Antioch there were prophets and teachers: Barnabas, Simeon who was called Niger, Lucius of Cyrene, Manaen a member of the court of Herod the ruler, and Saul. 2 While they were worshiping the Lord and fasting, the Holy Spirit said, "Set apart for me Barnabas and Saul for the work to which I have called them." 3 Then after fasting and praying they laid their hands on them and sent them off.

Textual Notes: Acts 12:25–13:3

12:25: Scholars identify this verse as a Lukan suture connecting the narrative that follows with 11:30. At that point, Barnabas and Saul were entrusted with a collection taken up in Antioch to be delivered to Jerusalem for use in famine relief. The manuscript evidence for this verse (Acts 12:25) indicates that many scribes had difficulty with the phrase "returned to Jerusalem." Since the whole passage deals with a significant event in Antioch, persons responsible for a number of very ancient manuscripts (for example, Papyrus 74) wrote: "returned from Jerusalem," or "returned from Jerusalem to Antioch."

The point is that in this text segment, Barnabas and Saul are in Antioch. For this reason, it seems that Luke's intended sense (contrary to the NRSV but respecting the best evidence) is that Barnabas and Saul returned to Antioch, having completed their work in Jerusalem (see preferable reading in RSV: from). They bring with them John Mark, whose home is in Jerusalem.

The scene painted by Luke in Acts 13–20, wherein he traces the journeys of Paul, has its matching scene in Luke 12:1-12, which describes the mission of the seventy.

13:1: In Antioch, five males are identified as opinion leaders (prophets and teachers) in the Jesus group at Antioch. **Communication of Innovation.** They bear Greek forms of Hebrew names, indicating their Hellenistic inculturation, as one might expect of Israelite opinion leaders in Antioch.

13:2-3: These men are very likely in a larger Jesus group engaged in a worship service. During this service, the men have a communal trance experience. **Alternate States of Consciousness.** In this group experience, the Holy Spirit verbally instructs them to serve as the Spirit's agents and to commission Barnabas and Saul for a specific divinely determined task. Prayer and fasting prepare them for their task. Note that prayer, fasting, and ritual are proven techniques for inducing ASCs.

These verses thus reflect a "mediated agency commissioning" form that consists of two parts: an introduction specifying the agency (v. 2, command from the Spirit) and the actual commissioning (v. 3). The commission is formal. Barnabas and Saul are set apart as agents for the Holy Spirit ("the task to which I have called them"). The laying on of hands is frequent in this story, indicating the imparting of power (earlier, 6:6; 8:17-19; 9:12; and later, 19:6; 28:8). Hands, like God's Spirit, are about effective power. **Three Zones of Personality.**

This commissioning is the fulfillment of what the resurrected Jesus told the prophet Ananias in the account of Paul's vision (9:15-16). The Holy Spirit thus is the Spirit of Jesus, an agent acting in Jesus' name. Paul's task previously announced by the resurrected Jesus to the prophet Ananias is that Paul will be of service to the Lord by proclaiming Jesus among non-Israelites, both before royalty and before fellow Israelites resident in non-Israelite regions. (See Luke 21:12 for Jesus' words to the Twelve mentioning kings and governors, but not non-Israelite lands. The NRSV version of Acts 9:15-16 is inaccurate; the Greek states: "before/among Gentiles, both kings and sons of Israel.") This is a sort of outline of Paul's activity described in Acts, but in reverse order: first to Israelites, then to royalty.

Paul's activity of "bringing the Lord's name" to Israelites living among non-Israelite majorities is always marked by the presence of one or more other Jesus group members. Here Paul's commissioning is shared by Barnabas, a Jesus group member long before Paul and Paul's original sponsor. Paul will later evidence the qualities of an Israelite holy man and prophet. Perhaps it was Barnabas who initiated him into this role. **Holy Man.**

Winning a Challenge to Honor in Cyprus Acts 13:4-12

13:4 So, being sent out by the Holy Spirit, they went down to Seleucia; and from there they sailed to Cyprus. 5 When they arrived at Salamis, they proclaimed the word of God in the synagogues of the Jews. And they had John also to assist them. 6 When they had gone through the whole island as far as Paphos, they met a certain magician, a Jewish false prophet, named Bar-Jesus. 7 He was with the proconsul, Sergius Paulus, an intelligent man, who summoned Barnabas and Saul and wanted to hear the word of God. 8 But the magician Elymas (for that is the translation of his name) opposed them and tried to turn the proconsul away from the faith. 9 But Saul, also known as Paul, filled with the Holy Spirit, looked intently at him 10 and said, "You son of the devil, you enemy of all righteousness, full of all deceit and villainy, will you not stop making crooked the straight paths of the Lord? 11 And now listen—the hand of the Lord is against you, and you will be blind for a while, unable to see the sun." Immediately mist and darkness came over him, and he went about groping for someone to lead him by the hand. 12 When the proconsul saw what had happened, he believed, for he was astonished at the teaching about the Lord.

Textual Notes: Acts 13:4-12

13:4-6: The commissioned agents traverse the island of Cyprus in a southwesterly direction beginning at Salamis and ending at Paphos, its Roman capital.

Cyprus would not be a difficult region for the three, since Barnabas was from the island and had land (hence relatives) there (Acts 4:36). He would know where the Judeans assembled in Salamis. The word *synagogē* meant a gathering or meeting (see LXX Exod 12:3). By extension it was applied to the places of meeting, actually social centers or clubs used for multiple purposes. For this reason the phrase "synagogues of the Judeans" is not a tautology. Other groups had their own gatherings, and Israelite ethnocentrism would have Luke's audience believe all other peoples called their gatherings and places of assembly "synagogues."

13:5: Assisted by John Mark, the two divinely commissioned agents from Antioch make their proclamation of the word of God to their fellow Israelites. This "word of God" was about what the God of Israel had done through the death and resurrection of Jesus, Lord and Israel's Messiah to come, and about the forthcoming theocracy for Israel.

13:6: Bar-Jesus (identified in v. 8 as Elymas) is described by Luke as a Judean magician (Greek: *magos*) and false prophet. In the Hellenistic period, the word *magos* had two meanings that existed side by side: Persian fire-priests (the original "magi" who professed Zoroastrianism, which in Israel was adopted and adapted by the Pharisees), and Chaldean magicians or sorcerers. **Magi-Magician.** In the Hellenistic world, a magician was a person who claimed to have and to have demonstrated extraordinary power or influence. Such persons specialized in the use of charms, spells, and rituals in seeking or pretending to cause or control events or to govern certain extraordinary forces, invisible and visible. As becomes clear in v. 10, both Elymas and Saul recognized a clash of powers in their encounter. Elymas is already designated a Judean prophet and magician, and now Saul acts like an Israelite holy man. **Holy Man.** Saul's power, like that of Jesus and Israel's holy men of old, derived from God's Spirit (see Acts 10:38; compare Luke 5:17); Elymas's power came from the devil.

Elymas is also called a "false" prophet, a phrase and judgment introduced by the Septuagint. The Hebrew Bible has no equivalent phrase. "Prophet" is a social role in which some person claims to speak for and communicate the will of God for the present time (see the title of Hananiah in the Hebrew text of Jer 28:1 [NRSV/RSV]). By Luke's day, the distinction of "true" and "false" prophet, introduced by the Septuagint, was common coin, so that Luke informs his Israelite readers of Elymas's true nature at the very beginning of his report.

13:7: The prophet and magician Elymas is ready to face off with the prophet and holy man Paul. The important witness to this showdown is the Roman provincial governor ("proconsul"), Sergius Paulus, "a discerning man" (NRSV: "intelligent"/RSV: "man of intelligence"). Since Elymas was in his service, it is quite plausible that Sergius knew much about Judaism and that Elymas exerted influence on him. Hence, Sergius invited the Judean visitors to present "the word of God." Given Elymas's response to the situation (v. 8), Sergius appears to have found their message appealing, perhaps convincing.

13:9: From this point on in the story, Saul is referred to by the Hellenistic name of "Paul" (except in Acts 22:7, 13; 26:14). This verse does not support the common belief that Paul underwent a change of name from Saul to Paul. It was common for members of the house of Israel to have two names: a Hebrew one for insiders, a Greek or Latin name for outsiders. Thus, *Saulos* is the Greek form of a Hebrew name: *Sa'ul* (meaning "[the child] asked for"), while *Paulos* is a Hellenistic name. The connotation of the Greek adjective *saulos* ("loose, wanton"), which described the peculiar walking style of courtesans and effeminate males, might have prompted Luke (and Paul) to prefer to use "Paul."

The Greek word translated "looked intently" (NRSV/RSV) literally means "gazed" or "stared" at. Of its fourteen occurrences in the New Testament, Luke records it twelve times (Acts 1:10; 3:4, 12; 6:15; 7:55; 10:4; 11:6; 13:9; 14:9; 23:1; see also Luke 4:20; 22:56). In the majority of instances, this word signals that the subject has slipped into trance **Alternate States of Consciousness**. Of course, the preceding notice that Paul was "filled with the Holy Spirit" has already indicated that he is in trance; gazing or staring indicates and confirms that fact. Thus, it is in trance that Paul gains insight to the true nature of Elymas (son of the devil; enemy of all righteousness; full of deceit and villainy), the source of his power (the devil), and his deeds requiring repentance (making crooked the straight paths of the lord; see Prov 10:9; Hos 14:9 NRSV [v. 10 in Hebrew]).

Elymas and Paul each put their honor on the line as well as the honor of their respective sources of power. By successfully blinding Elymas, Paul and God, Paul's source of power, win the honor contest. Such divine intervention echoes the way in which Peter dealt with Ananias and Sapphira and their attempted deception (Acts 5:1-11). Sergius is duly impressed not only by the event that just took place but especially by the teaching of the Lord. What exactly does Luke mean when he says that Sergius became a believer? Scholars are divided, with some saying he is Paul's first convert and others saying he was simply impressed by Paul's presentation and its accompanying confirmation in deed. The latter seems more probable, since Paul, like Jesus, was concerned with God's kingdom, that is, God's refashioning the Israel of his day. Like Jesus, Paul was not establishing a new organization and seeking new recruits. Sergius is not said to have joined any group; hence he behaves as described, namely, as an intelligent and discerning person. The upshot of this episode is that in Acts, the abilities of the Jesus group change agents **Change Agent** and the power they wielded was far stronger than that of successful and well-placed magi-magicians. **Communication of Innovation.** There can be little doubt that in the eyes of contemporaries, those who effectively proclaimed the word of the God of Israel belonged to the same category as magi-magicians (see Acts 14:11).

Proclaiming the Word of God to Israelites in Pisidia Acts 13:13-43

13:13 Then Paul and his companions set sail from Paphos and came to Perga in Pamphylia. John, however, left them and returned to Jerusalem; 14 but they went on from Perga and came to Antioch in Pisidia. And on the sabbath day they went into the synagogue and sat down. 15 After the reading of the law and the prophets, the officials of the synagogue sent them a message, saying, "Brothers, if you have any word of exhortation for the people, give it." 16 So Paul stood up and with a gesture began to speak:

"You Israelites, and others who fear God, listen. 17 The God of this people Israel chose our ancestors and made the people great during their stay in the land of Egypt, and with uplifted arm he led them out of it. 18 For about forty years he put up with them in the wilderness. 19 After he had destroyed seven nations in the land of Canaan, he gave them their land as an inheritance 20 for about four hundred fifty years. After that he gave them judges until the time of the prophet Samuel. 21 Then they asked for a king; and God gave them Saul son of Kish, a man of the tribe of Benjamin, who reigned for forty years. 22 When he had removed him, he made David their king. In his testimony about him he said, 'I have found David, son of Jesse, to be a man after my heart, who will carry out all my wishes.' 23 Of this man's posterity God has brought to Israel a Savior, Jesus, as he promised; 24 before his coming John had already proclaimed a baptism of repentance to all the people of Israel. 25 And as John was finishing his work, he said, 'What do you suppose that I am? I am not he. No, but one is coming after me; I am not worthy to untie the thong of the sandals on his feet.'

26 My brothers, you descendants of Abraham's family, and others who fear God, to us the message of this salvation has been sent. 27 Because the residents of Jerusalem and their leaders did not recognize him or understand the words of the prophets that are read every sabbath, they fulfilled those words by condemning him. 28 Even though they found no cause for a sentence of death, they asked Pilate to have him killed. 29 When they had carried out everything that was written about him, they took him down from the tree and laid him in a tomb. 30 But God raised him from the dead; 31 and for many days he appeared to those who came up with him from Galilee to Jerusalem, and they are now his witnesses to the people. 32 And we bring you the good news that what God promised to our ancestors 33 he has fulfilled for us, their children, by raising Jesus; as also it is written in the second psalm,

'You are my Son;
today I have begotten you.'

34 As to his raising him from the dead, no more to return to corruption, he has spoken in this way,

'I will give you the holy promises made to David.'

35 Therefore he has also said in another psalm,

'You will not let your Holy One experience corruption.'

36 For David, after he had served the purpose of God in his own generation, died, was laid beside his ancestors, and experienced corruption; 37 but he whom God raised up experienced no corruption. 38 Let it be known to you therefore, my brothers, that through this man forgiveness of sins is proclaimed to you; 39 by this Jesus everyone who believes is set free from all those sins from which you could not be freed by the law of Moses. 40 Beware, therefore, that what the prophets said does not happen to you:

41 'Look, you scoffers!
Be amazed and perish,
for in your days I am doing a work,
a work that you will never believe,
even if someone tells you.'"

42 As Paul and Barnabas were going out, the people urged them to speak about these things again the next sabbath. 43 When the meeting of the synagogue broke up, many Jews and devout converts to Judaism followed Paul and Barnabas, who spoke to them and urged them to continue in the grace of God.

Textual Notes: Acts 13:13-43

13:13: After describing Paul's initiative and success in confronting Satan's agent in the previous story, Luke henceforth tends to put Paul's name first and to focus the story on him.

13:14: On a Sabbath after arriving in Pisidian Antioch, Paul and his companions seek out the Judean community center or men's social club (synagogue). They sat down to listen to the "reading" from the Torah and the Prophets. Even though the temple was still standing and sacrifice was still being offered, it was already customary in the first century for Israelites outside Jerusalem to gather on the Sabbath to "read" and discuss a portion of the Torah and a selection from the Prophets. Given that less than one-half of one percent of this population was literate, it is preferable to understand the Greek word *read* (*anaginōskō*) in its primary sense as "knowing again" perhaps "recalling." The "reader" would actually be "reciting" from memory something that was familiar to everyone in this essentially oral culture.

A proposed reconstruction of how this meeting was organized suggests that it began with the recitation of the Shema (Deut 6:4-9; 11:13-21; and Num 15:37-41), Israel's profession of faith that Pharisees urged be recited morning, noon, and night. Then followed a recitation of Eighteen Blessings followed by a priestly blessing, if the personnel were present. At this point, someone recited a selection from the Torah and then from the Prophets. A relevant reflection followed the reading or recitation.

13:15: The officers of the gathering invite the visiting strangers to offer some words of exhortation at the point where the reflection would take place. Paul obliges.

13:16b-41: This is Paul's first major address to fellow Israelites in Acts. It is mainly a Lukan composition, of course, reflecting the speeches he crafted for Peter in Jerusalem (especially Acts 2:14-36). It is important to note that this is a speech and not a sermon. Paul is communicating a new idea to his fellow Israelites. **Communication of Innovation.** Luke has divided the speech into three parts signaled by the repeated interpersonal phrases: "you Israelites" (v. 16; literally, "Israelite men" or "men of Israel," as in RSV), "brethren" (v. 26), and "my brothers" (v. 38; in the latter two references literally "men brothers," that is, men who share beliefs to such an extent as to be considered kin). Paul's designations for his fellow Israelites expresses the warmth of ingroup feeling. Since only males were present in these community gatherings, these designations are not inclusive nor should they be rendered as such in reading (or in preaching).

Part 1 of the speech (vv. 16b-25) is a selective recital of events from Israel's past. It is intended to prepare the audience to understand that the innovation to be announced next is quite in harmony with the past. The main point of these verses is that God lovingly guided Israel from its election to the point of providing it with a savior, Jesus, from the line of David. This, of course, introduces the new idea.

Part 2 (vv. 26-37) explains the new thing that God has done for the "descendants of Abraham's family" (v. 26). While inhabitants of Jerusalem (Judeans, not Jews) and their leaders condemned fellow Israelite Jesus of the Davidic line and had Pilate put him to death, God raised him from the dead. The proof is that the risen Jesus appeared to his associates from Galilee who are now witnesses to God's deed. This is the innovation Paul shares, and he supports this position with references from Israel's sacred writings (Isa 55:3 LXX in v. 34; and Ps 16:10 LXX in v. 35). Thus did God fulfill promises made to the ancestors.

In part 3 (vv. 38-41), Paul tells what this means for them and how they should respond. In Messiah Jesus, Israelites receive forgiveness of sin. Everyone who pledges loyalty to ("believes," v. 39) Messiah Jesus will be made right with God, which could not happen under the law of Moses. He concludes with a warning about the penalty for ignoring this information, adapting words of the prophet Habakkuk (1:5 LXX) directed against Chaldeans (608–598 B.C.E.). It would be foolhardy not to heed Paul's proclamation.

13:16: Though traditional scholarship has identified "those who fear God" ("God-fearers"; see Acts 10:22, 35; 13:16, 26) as non-Israelites sympathetic to Judaism who were not circumcised nor obeyed the entire Torah, we relate the phrase to the one that the Septuagint regularly applies to Israelites, namely, a segment of Israelites "who fear the Lord" (see Pss 115:11 [LXX 113:19]; 118:4; 135:20). Paul is addressing Israelites exclusively, the only ones who would be allowed into the club or community center ("synagogue"). The phrases would refer to sophisticated, practicing Israelites

Synagogue in Paphos, traditionally thought to be a place where Paul preached. Location: New Paphos, Cyprus. Photo © Erich Lessing / Art Resource, N.Y.

who would be fully cognizant of the traditions Paul cites, and other Israelites less sophisticated and familiar with the traditions. Certainly no non-Israelite could appreciate Paul's masterful use of Israelite traditions, that is, Scripture.

13:20: God guided the people of Israel with judges (that is, military leaders) and a prophet, Samuel (1 Sam 3:20).

13:22: Though God appointed Saul to be king over the people, Saul's disobedience caused God to regret the choice (1 Sam 15:11-35; 16:1) and removed him (1 Sam 13:13-14). In his place, God appointed David, "a man after my heart" (see 1 Sam 13:14 LXX). David earned this compliment from God because like Cyrus, who is also called a messiah (Isa 45:1), he performed all that God desired of him (Isa 44:28 LXX).

13:23: According to Paul, God's promise in the oracle of Nathan (1 Sam 7:12, 16) has finally been implemented in Jesus, born of Davidic lineage. He is Israel's savior.

13:30: Mention that God raised Jesus from the dead (three times in this speech: vv. 30, 33, 37) contrasts with what fellow Israelites did to him.

13:31: Paul refers to the multiple experiences of the risen Jesus by disciples in alternate states of consciousness (see Acts 1:3). These are now witnesses to his risen status (see Acts 1:8; 2:32; 3:15; 5:32; 10:39, 41).

13:32-33: Paul identifies himself and Barnabas as communicators of the new understanding of Jesus Messiah, raised by God from the dead to be savior of Israel. To confirm his point, he once again draws on the sacred traditions (Ps 2:7 LXX).

13:34: Paul cites another passage from Israel's tradition (Isa 55:3 LXX) to further bolster his message, that the covenant blessings promised to David are now realized in the risen Messiah.

13:35: Jesus did not decay in the tomb (see Ps 16:10 LXX)—the same argument that Peter used in his speech (Acts 2:27b). **Pains of Death.**

13:38-39: In this third part of the speech, Paul draws important conclusions. His "word of exhortation" (v. 15) is that the death and resurrection of Jesus brought "forgiveness of sins." The second effect of the Messiah's death and resurrection is that sinners are acquitted ("set free from all those sins"). This means God will not take vengeance on those who dishonor him by their continued, insulting behavior.

13:40-41: Paul the change agent would be a failure if he only announced a new idea. **Change Agent.** Change agents desire that hearers of the message actually implement the lifestyle required by the new idea. Hence, to motivate such implementation, Paul concludes with a threat drawn from the prophet Habakkuk (1:5 LXX). Listeners ridicule or worse yet dismiss Paul's message only at their own peril.

13:42-43: The immediate response to Paul's speech is a desire to know more, hence an invitation to return next week for further enlightenment. Meanwhile, Paul exhorts these listeners to "continue in the grace of God." The Greek word for grace is *charis*, meaning the favor of a patron. Such favor refers to goods and services that a person either cannot acquire or cannot acquire at a given time and place. Here that divine favor refers to Paul's proclamation and the divine guidance and assistance of which Paul spoke.

Luke mentions another category of people in the assembly that Paul just addressed. They are called *sebomenoi prosēlytai* (NRSV has "devout converts to Judaism"; the word *Judaism* does not appear in the text but is an interpretative comment, rather frequent in the NRSV). The Greek word *sebomenos* means "respectful, reverent, respected." And *prosēlytēs* means "one who comes over, foreigner, alien, stranger." The NRSV translates the phrase "devout converts." Of course, the problem is whether it is possible for an outsider to "convert" to first-century Judaism. As Paul properly explains in this presentation, the house of Israel consists of descendants of Abraham, Isaac, and Jacob, just as the God of Israel was the ancestral God of Abraham, Isaac, and Jacob. People become Israelites by birth. **Ancestor Reverence.** Obviously one cannot "convert" to a group held together by the exclusivity deriving from common ancestry. In antiquity, ancestry-based, political religious "conversion" was not a psychological process entailing movement from one ideology to another ideology when a focal feature of the ideology was requisite birth.

The Septuagint uses *prosēlytos* to translate the Hebrew *gēr*, the resident alien or outsider who lives in an Israelite town or city. Here in Pisidian Antioch, the resident alien would be a non-Israelite resident in the Israelite quarter of the city. The "respectful" outsider is one who shows respect for local Israelites and their traditions. The audience that was moved by Paul's message included Israelites and respectful outsiders, who wanted the best for their Israelite neighbors. They would stand in awe of the God of Israel's raising Jesus from the dead and would be supportive of a forthcoming Israelite theocracy.

Response to Rejection Acts 13:44-52

13:44 The next sabbath almost the whole city gathered to hear the word of the Lord. 45 But when the Jews saw the crowds, they were filled with jealousy; and blaspheming, they contradicted what was spoken by Paul. 46 Then both Paul and Barnabas spoke out boldly, saying, "It was necessary that the word of God should be spoken first to you. Since you reject it and judge yourselves to be unworthy of eternal life, we are now turning to the Gentiles. 47 For so the Lord has commanded us, saying,

'I have set you to be a light for the
        Gentiles,

so that you may bring salvation to
        the ends of the earth.'"

48 When the Gentiles heard this, they were glad and praised the word of the Lord; and as many as had been destined for eternal life became believers. 49 Thus the word of the Lord spread throughout the region. 50 But the Jews incited the devout women of high standing and the leading men of the city, and stirred up persecution against Paul and Barnabas, and drove them out of their region. 51 So they shook the dust off their feet in protest against them, and went to Iconium. 52 And the disciples were filled with joy and with the Holy Spirit.

Textual Notes: Acts 13:44-52

13:44: A full week later, there is a gathering of "almost the whole city," to be understood as "almost the entire Israelite minority population in this city." As the next verse indicates, Israelite skeptics who might not have been present the preceding Sabbath now joined the gathering.

13:45: The Greek word translated by the NRSV/RSV as "jealousy" is better translated as "envy" (see the explanation at Acts 5:17). Jealousy as a Middle Eastern value is attachment to or concern for what is exclusively one's own. In contrast, envy as a Middle Eastern value begrudges another the possession of some singular quality, object, or relationship. When fellow Israelites saw the crowds that Paul and Barnabas had attracted in their second appearance at the community center, they begrudged them this popularity, recognition, admiration, and the like. Envy is rooted in the experience of limited good. People who prosper do so at the expense of others. **Limited Good.** If the popularity of Paul and his associates has increased, that means it has decreased for others. Life in this social setting is a zero sum game.

"To blaspheme" means to dishonor or outrage a person verbally. Luke specifies the dishonor: they were speaking against Paul, countering what he had said. This is yet another instance of a challenge to the reputation of Paul and his associates. It requires a forceful response, or Paul would lose face.

13:46-49: These verses form a block, a sort of stereotypical explanation of and response to rejection in Israelite communities. It has a unified structure, focusing on the Isaiah quotation:

> **A** word of God . . . eonic life (v. 46)
>   **B** to non-Israelites (v. 46)
>   **C** Isaiah citation (v. 47)
>   **B'** non-Israelites (v. 48)
> **A'** word of the Lord . . . life eonic (v. 48)
> Conclusion: word of the Lord (v. 49)

13:46-47: Although Paul delivered the previous proclamation, the attack of the Judeans is presumed to be against both Paul and Barnabas. The result is that both of them replied with boldness. As previously noted, in first-century Hellenism, "boldness" (Greek *parrhēsia*) describes the behavior of a lower-status person speaking shamelessly in the face of higher-status people, without regard for the status honor of the higher-status person. Proper response by higher-status persons might include physical punishment or even death (see 13:50). The gist of the reply by Paul and Barnabas is that God providently directed them first of all to this Israelite community. They proclaimed the word of God to them, but they (or properly, some of them) rejected it thus rendering themselves unfit for "eternal life" (NRSV; the Greek has "eonic life," Israelite shorthand for a meaningful life in the forthcoming theocracy, in the eon or age to come). It is life in the forthcoming theocracy that marks "salvation" for Israelites. Consequently, they turn to other non-Israelite cities with minority Israelite populations. This is what "we are now turning to the Gentiles" means in Israelite ingroup dialogue. To make their point, they cite Isa 49:6 as a command of the Lord directed to them (although it is in the singular); we offer our own translation, which differs from the NRSV: "I have set you (sing.)

for a light among non-Israelites, for you (sing.) to be for salvation to the end of the earth."

In context, their expressed decision to turn to the Gentiles means that they will now go to the many other places where Israelites are a veritable minority. Their task is to be a light among non-Israelites (genitive of direction). Ethnocentric people of antiquity actually had no interest in "other peoples." They were interested in their own who might be living among "other peoples." This is Paul's ethnocentric view as well. That is the thrust of his assignment from God: "bring my name before/among Gentiles, both to kings and to the children of Israel" (Acts 9:15; NRSV is not accurate).

13:48: When they heard Paul and Barnabas's statement, non-Israelites who were present at this altercation rejoiced and praised "the word of the Lord" presented by Paul. They thus give a grant of honor to the two. Further, as many as had been destined for eternal life among the Israelites became believers. And the Israelite innovation proclaimed by Paul and Barnabas got to be known in the region of Pisidian Antioch.

13:50: As expected, the blaspheming Judeans whose honor was dragged through the mud get their satisfaction. They incite well-to-do (therefore, connected) women among them as well as elites in the city to harass Paul and Barnabas. These latter two now suffer the same fate as Peter and John earlier (Acts 4). These influential people ride Paul and Barnabas out of town on a rail.

13:51: Not to be outdone by these elite personages, Paul and Barnabas shake the dust off their feet in protest, obeying the advice of Jesus (see Luke 9:5; 10:11). This is a symbolic act of total repudiation.

13:52: Luke then reports that "the disciples were filled with joy and with the Holy Spirit." It is difficult to determine who "the disciples" might be. In context the word refers to Paul and Barnabas.

Proclaiming in the Lycaonian Region Acts 14:1-20

Iconium, Success and Resistance Acts 14:1-7

14:1 The same thing occurred in Iconium, where Paul and Barnabas went into the Jewish synagogue and spoke in such a way that a great number of both Jews and Greeks became believers. 2 But the unbelieving Jews stirred up the Gentiles and poisoned their minds against the brothers. 3 So they remained for a long time, speaking boldly for the Lord, who testified to the word of his grace by granting signs and wonders to be done through them. 4 But the residents of the city were divided; some sided with the Jews, and some with the apostles. 5 And when an attempt was made by both Gentiles and Jews, with their rulers, to mistreat them and to stone them, 6 the apostles learned of it and fled to Lystra and Derbe, cities of Lycaonia, and to the surrounding country; 7 and there they continued proclaiming the good news.

Textual Notes: Acts 14:1-7

14:1-7: The "same thing" refers to a stereotypical pattern that Luke uses to describe what occurs in each city visited by Paul and Barnabas:

1. Arrival in some city

2. Proceeding to the local Israelite gathering (synagogue)

3. Proclamation of the "word of the Lord"

4. A number of Israelites, both Judean and Greek, accept

5. A presumably larger number reject and are aggrieved

5b. Addition: Paul heals plus reaction

6. Those who reject the message harass Paul and companion, with the assistance of localite non-Israelites

7. Paul and companion must leave (or barely make it out)

14:1: Arriving in Iconium in south central Asia Minor (Konya in modern Turkey), Paul and Barnabas continue their task of proclaiming the word of the Lord among fellow [male] Israelites gathered in their community center (synagogue). They meet with mixed results similar to those experienced in Pisidian Antioch.

Once more we come upon the confusing set of names applied to Israelites. The general outgroup name for Israelites used by non-Israelites was "Judeans." To non-Israelites, all Israelites were Judeans. In ingroup Israel of the Diaspora, "Judeans" were those Israelites who followed the customs and behaviors of Judea rather closely, while "Greeks" were those Israelites who followed the "civilized" usages of Hellenistic culture. For those used to the terminology, of course, there would be little confusion.

Paul and Barnabas have success with a goodly number of their fellow Israelites who accepted their proclamation about Jesus Messiah and the forthcoming kingdom. These included both those who observed Judean customs (erroneously translated Jews) and those who followed Hellenistic customs, considered "civilized" practices (erroneously translated as Greeks, since Greece did not exist in the first century).

14:2: Fellow Israelites whom the two did not persuade or convince with their proclamation incited others, non-Israelites, against those who did believe what Paul and Barnabas had to say. It is important to appreciate this as an intensely local matter. The Israelites, who often considered themselves resident aliens ("the dispersion") may well be concerned about their continuing well-being in Iconium as a minority group; hence they persuade local citizens to apply pressure against their fellow Israelites persuaded by Paul and Barnabas.

The term *brother(s)* is commonly used throughout Acts to describe fellow believers (Acts 1:16; 9:30; 10:23b; 11:1, 12, 29; 12:17; 14:2; 15:3, 22, 32, 33, 40; 17:6, 10, 14; 18:18, 27; 21:7, 17, 20; 28:14, 15). It is an appropriate appellation for those who formed a fictive-kin group by reason of their common Israelite faith in Jesus Messiah raised by the God of Israel from the dead (Mark 3:31-35).

14:3: Paul and Barnabas were undeterred; they spoke "boldly," undoubtedly offending the honor of elites. This they did "for a long time." God authenticated their witness "to the word of his favor" by "granting signs and wonders to be done by them." The "word of his favor" describes the innovation proclaimed by Paul and Barnabas, namely, how the God of Israel demonstrated his patronal favor in what he did in Christ Jesus. That is the innovation they are presenting to their fellow Israelites. God authenticated their innovation with deeds performed literally "by their hands." This may point to deeds of healing in the same way that Peter taught that God authenticated the teaching of Jesus with signs and wonders (see Acts 2:22).

14:4: Only here and in v. 14 does Luke call Paul (and Barnabas) an apostle. Luke probably neglected to "correct" his source to agree with his criteria for apostleship (see Acts 1:21-22), which neither Paul nor Barnabas met. Rather, Paul is presented as prophet and holy man; as prophet he proclaims the word of the Lord, as holy man he performs signs and wonders. Once more, Luke notes the mixed reaction of what people heard and saw. Leaders of the unbelieving Judeans convince local non-Israelites to dishonor or insult (NRSV mistreat) and even to stone these "apostles."

14:6-7: When they learn of it, Paul and Barnabas move on to Lystra (about twenty-four miles south-southwest of Iconium) and then to Derbe (about fifty-eight miles southeast of Lystra), and obviously through the surrounding countryside where they continued to proclaim the good news.

In Lystra, Paul in an ASC Heals a Paralytic Acts 14:8-20

14:8 In Lystra there was a man sitting who could not use his feet and had never walked, for he had been crippled from birth. 9 He listened to Paul as he was speaking. And Paul, looking at him intently and seeing that he had faith to be healed, 10 said in a loud voice, "Stand upright on your feet." And the man sprang up and began to walk. 11 When the crowds saw what Paul had done, they shouted in the Lycaonian language, "The gods have come down to us in human form!" 12 Barnabas they called Zeus, and Paul they called Hermes, because he was the chief speaker. 13 The priest of Zeus, whose temple was just outside the city, brought oxen and garlands to the gates; he and the crowds wanted to offer sacrifice. 14 When the apostles Barnabas and Paul heard of it, they tore their clothes and rushed out into the crowd, shouting, 15 "Friends, why are you doing this? We are mortals just like you, and we bring you good news, that you should turn from these worthless things to the living God, who made the heaven and the earth and the sea and all that is in them. 16 In past generations he allowed all the nations to follow their own ways; 17 yet he has not left himself without a witness in doing good—giving you rains from heaven and fruitful seasons, and filling you with food and your hearts with joy." 18 Even with these words, they scarcely restrained the crowds from offering sacrifice to them.

19 But Jews came there from Antioch and Iconium and won over the crowds. Then they stoned Paul and dragged him out of the city, supposing that he was dead. 20 But when the disciples surrounded him, he got up and went into the city. The next day he went on with Barnabas to Derbe.

Textual Notes: Acts 14:8-20

14:8-10: This first healing attributed to Paul is obviously patterned after the healing effected by Peter earlier (Acts 3; "literary form"). Both sick men are described in similar terms: "a man lame from birth" (Acts 3:2) and "a man . . . who could not use his feet and had never walked, for he had been crippled from birth"

(Acts 14:2). Peter and Paul "looked intently" (literally, "stared") at the man (Acts 3:4; 14:9). Both confirm their restoration to mobility: "Jumping up, he stood and began to walk, he entered the temple with them, walking and leaping" (Acts 3:8) and "the man sprang up and began to walk" (Acts 14:10). Both events occurred near temple gates (Acts 3:2, Beautiful Gate in Jerusalem; Acts 14:13 temple of Zeus). The literary form is: exposition (v. 8), healer's word and gesture (vv. 9-10), proof of healing (v. 10), and the effect on bystanders (vv. 11-13).

14:9: The place where Paul is speaking is not specified. Presumably it is at a gathering of Israelites, since Paul's word of the Lord is Israelite specific. The lame man listens to Paul's prophetic proclamation of the risen Lord. Yet as a holy man (see Acts 13:9 and 52, "filled with the Holy Spirit") empowered by the "living God" (Acts 14:9), he slips into trance ("looking at him intently"). **Holy Man.** As indicated above (note at Acts 1:9-11), this word ("stare, gaze, look intently") indicates that the subject is in an alternate state of consciousness. In this state, he sees that the man has "faith [loyalty] to be healed" and restores mobility to the man. The healing takes place in trance.

14:10: Speaking in a "loud voice" is yet another indication that a person might be in trance. This manner of speech is a characteristic of holy men across cultures. It is also typical in glossolalia experiences, which take place in alternate states of consciousness. Thus, Luke mentions a loud voice when he describes those who are praising God (for example, Luke 1:42), who are also very likely in trance, a state of intense emotion. Moreover, in the ancient world, a holy person who spoke with a loud voice was a sign that God was present to or in him (see Virgil, *Aeneid* 6.65-83). Paul in trance—that is, empowered by God—commands the man to stand up, and he does.

What exactly happened here? There is little reason to doubt that this is a factual report of an extraordinary restoration of a lame man to mobility. It is reported in terms of the consensual reality shared by first-century Mediterraneans. Such reports in the New Testament are called *emic* reports, reports described in terms shared by people of the culture area of that time and place. However, in terms of twenty-first-century consensual reality, contemporary science offers an alternative interpretation. This interpretation is called an *etic* explanation, an explanation by a foreigner from another culture area situated in another time and place. According to this view, the man's condition was caused by a repressed idea or repressed emotion. This they call a conversion disorder. The subject "converts" a mental or emotional problem into a physical manifestation. A person who inspires confidence in such a person to release the cause of his psychological or emotional problem causes an abreaction. The result is that the subject is made whole again by the abreactive treatment of the healer. Which one of these interpretations is correct? To the healed person, it did not and does not matter.

14:11-12: The loud voice associated with the gods and the effective healing convince the crowd that the gods are present in Paul and Barnabas. After all, the presence of the gods is known by what they actually do for people. Specifically, they identify Barnabas as Zeus and Paul as Hermes.

Colossal head of Zeus, from
Otricoli. Hellenistic, first century
B.C.E. Location: Museo Pio
Clementino, Vatican Museums,
Vatican State. Photo © Scala /
Art Resource, N.Y.

Hermes, bearded head. Marble
fence bust, second century C.E.
Roman copy of a Greek original
of the fifth century B.C.E., found
near the Mazaeus-Mithridates
gate in Ephesus, Turkey.
Location: Kunsthistorisches
Museum, Vienna, Austria.
Photo © Erich Lessing / Art
Resource, N.Y.

14:13-14: Predictably, the priest from the nearby temple of Zeus (Zeus-outside-the-Walls) wants to offer sacrifice and honor (garlands) to the gods for their benefaction. **Sacrifice.** It was a common belief among first-century Mediterraneans that the gods might visit people disguised as human beings (examples in Ovid, *Metamorphoses* 1.125-244; 8.618-724; in Israel, angels act like these visiting deities, for example, in Gen 18:1-16). They can be recognized by their benefactions. The behavior of the priest moves Paul and Barnabas to tear their garments at such an abomination, from an Israelite perspective. "Tearing garments" is a sign of protest against some social evil (for example, see Gen 37:29). The two thus seek to stop this response to healing.

14:15-18: Paul now makes a brief presentation to the non-Israelite crowd. This sort of "good news" is what non-Israelites can understand and perhaps stands as a model of what Jesus group members in predominantly non-Israelite cities can tell their non-Israelite neighbors.

Paul speaks of "the living God," as opposed to the deities worshiped by non-Israelites, which he calls "vain or empty things." This living God is creator of everything and is providently good, as indicated by his "giving you rains from heaven and fruitful seasons, and filling you with food and your hearts with joy." *What is noteworthy about Paul's message is that it says nothing of Jesus, or God's raising Jesus from the dead, or about the forthcoming theocracy in Israel. All these features are Israelite specific, of little or no consequence to non-Israelites.* Still, it was difficult to restrain the crowds from continuing to consider them as gods.

14:19-20: While in the previous scene hostile Judeans oppose Paul and Barnabas because of their successes resulting from their proclamation to local Israelites, now these hostile Judeans from Antioch and Iconium track Paul down. **Establishment Violence.** In the face of their positive, if overzealous, reception by non-Israelites in Lystra, these Judean opponents persuade the locals to change their views about Paul and Barnabas. Again, presumably impelled by the envy that seeks to destroy what is envied, the Judean resident aliens and the local crowd stoned Paul and left him for dead outside of town. Lystrans who believed the word of the Lord ("his disciples") revived him, and Paul reentered the town. The next day he and Barnabas continued to Derbe.

Retracing Steps to Syrian Antioch Acts 14:21-28

14:21 After they had proclaimed the good news to that city and had made many disciples, they returned to Lystra, then on to Iconium and Antioch. 22 There they strengthened the souls of the disciples and encouraged them to continue in the faith, saying, "It is through many persecutions that we must enter the kingdom of God." 23 And after they had appointed elders for them in each church, with prayer and fasting they entrusted them to the Lord in whom they had come to believe.

24 Then they passed through Pisidia and came to Pamphylia. 25 When they had spoken the word in Perga, they went down to Attalia. 26 From there they sailed back to Antioch, where they had been commended to the grace of God for the work that they had completed. 27 When they arrived, they called the church together and related all that God had done with them, and how he had opened a door of faith for the Gentiles. 28 And they stayed there with the disciples for some time.

Textual Notes: Acts 14:21-28

14:22: In retracing their steps, Paul and Barnabas encourage those who accepted their message to remain steadfast in the new lifestyle adopted in response to their proclamation. Faith here concerns practice rather than content. The word translated "persecutions" is the Greek *thlipsis*, which means distress, anxiety. Distress implies an external and usually temporary cause of great physical or mental strain and stress, while anxiety refers to feelings of uncertainty in the face of impending harm. Those Israelites who accepted the gospel of the Lord normally experienced distress resulting from adopting the innovation in the face of those who rejected it in their Israelite communities and refused to believe what the God of Israel had recently done in Jerusalem. These opposing Israelites, perhaps a local majority, were aggrieved because these new Jesus group members discontinued their customary Israelite behavior and often split with the local Israelite group. Grievance quickly leads to conflict, and this is what distress entailed. **Conflict Resolution.** Entering the kingdom here means preparing for life in the theocracy soon to be established by the God of Israel, with the resurrected Jesus as Messiah and cosmic Lord.

14:23: Appointing elders in each congregation indicates that the group is in the forming stage. **Group Formation.** The word *elders* occurs in Acts 4:5, 8, 23; 6:12; 14:23; 15:2, 4, 6, 22, 23; 16:4; 20:17; 21:18; 23:14; 24:1; 25:15. Curiously, the word appears nowhere in the undisputed Pauline letters. Since the word appears in the Pastorals (1 Tim 5:17, 19; Titus 1:5), written in the third generation after Paul, scholars conjecture that Luke may have associated the word anachronistically with Paul and Barnabas in Acts. No doubt the two would recognize local leaders among the first adopters of the innovation they proclaimed, but these leaders quite likely had no special title. In their letters, Paul and his collaborators speak of those "who have charge of you in the Lord" (1 Thess 5:12) and "bishops and deacons" (Phil 1:1 NRSV; a better word for bishops is "supervisors"). They are essentially individuals who are able to hold the allegiance of all community members and look to attracting new members to the group. They do not stand in for Paul (or Peter, or anyone else).

14:23: Prayer and fasting are two techniques for inducing alternate states of consciousness. In this instance, the techniques serve to enhance and intensify their communication with the risen Lord whose protection they seek for the communities they have established.

14:27: Upon their return to Antioch, from where they had embarked on their journey (Acts 13:2-3), the duo summon the community to hear their report of all that God accomplished with them. They also explain how God "opened a door of faith among the Gentiles" (NRSV). Once more, this translation is inaccurate—given what chapter 14 has just reported. Actually God opened a door of faith to Israelite minority populations living among "Gentiles," that is, living among non-Israelite majority populations.

Jerusalem Elites Evaluate the Activity of Paul and Barnabas Acts 15:1–35

The activity of Paul and Barnabas had not only been stirring violent opposition along the way. It also stirred up internal controversy among Judean (as opposed to Greek) members of the house of Israel who had accepted Jesus as Messiah and cosmic lord and hoped for the forthcoming kingdom of God. In this section of Acts, Luke explains how the disagreement was resolved before Paul and Barnabas began their next expedition, in the Aegean area (Acts 15:36).

The Convocation: Peter's View Acts 15:1-12

15:1 Then certain individuals came down from Judea and were teaching the brothers, "Unless you are circumcised according to the custom of Moses, you cannot be saved." 2 And after Paul and Barnabas had no small dissension and debate with them, Paul and Barnabas and some of the others were appointed to go up to Jerusalem to discuss this question with the apostles and the elders. 3 So they were sent on their way by the church, and as they passed through both Phoenicia and Samaria, they reported the conversion of the Gentiles, and brought great joy to all the believers. 4 When they came to Jerusalem, they were welcomed by the church and the apostles and the elders, and they reported all that God had done with them. 5 But some believers who belonged to the sect of the Pharisees stood up and said, "It is necessary for them to be circumcised and ordered to keep the law of Moses."

6 The apostles and the elders met together to consider this matter. 7 After there had been much debate, Peter stood up and said to them, "My brothers, you know that in the early days God made a choice among you, that I should be the one through whom the Gentiles would hear the message of the good news and become believers. 8 And God, who knows the human heart, testified to them by giving them the Holy Spirit, just as he did to us; 9 and in cleansing their hearts by faith he has made no distinction between them and us. 10 Now therefore why are you putting God to the test by placing on the neck of the disciples a yoke that neither our ancestors nor we have been able to bear? 11 On the contrary, we believe that we will be saved through the grace of the Lord Jesus, just as they will."

12 The whole assembly kept silence, and listened to Barnabas and Paul as they told of all the signs and wonders that God had done through them among the Gentiles.

Textual Notes: Acts 15:1-12

Chapter 15 conflates two different concerns in Antioch and a discrete solution for each concern: one by Peter, and one by James. Peter, the apostles, and elders dealt with the question of circumcision and the Mosaic law (vv. 3-12). On another occasion, James and the elders wrote a letter instructing about diet and marriages, the so-called Jerusalem decree.

Moreover, the background that Luke presents to the controversy caused by the activity of Paul and Barnabas contrasts with Paul's report in Gal 2:1-10, but essentially Acts and Galatians agree in substance. We leave the question of historical sources aside and focus on Acts 15 demonstrating what social science contributes to interpreting the text as it stands.

15:1: Members of the Jesus group in Jerusalem come down from Judea to Antioch and insist on the necessity of circumcision for salvation (see Lev 13:2). As we noted in our commentary on the authentic letters of Paul (Malina and Pilch 2006), infant genital mutilation as a Judean marker was rather late in Palestine (c. 150 B.C.E.), and perhaps several centuries later, if at all, among Israelite Yahweh worshipers living far from Judea. (In this period, Judea proper was almost identifiable with the territory of the city of Jerusalem.) Samaria and Galilee were outside it. Antioch was very far outside of Judea. Throughout his story, Luke never defines salvation or what being saved consists in. Presumably, for Jesus group members, it means entering the forthcoming theocracy.

Furthermore, two issues are conflated here: circumcision (related in the Scriptures to Abraham, not Moses; see Gen 17:11), and the necessity of observing the Mosaic law. Nevertheless, the main concern is clear. These visitors from Judea insist that it is necessary that the Israelites living in non-Israelite regions who were totally assimilated to their neighbors should now embrace all Judean views and practices if they are to become Jesus group members. Paul (and Barnabas) obviously did not think so nor did they require it.

15:2: To resolve the controversy, the Antiochene community sends Paul, Barnabas, and some others to the apostles and presbyters in Jerusalem. The apostles are most likely Peter and John (see Gal 2:9). James, the brother of the Lord, was not an apostle, but likely was considered the leading elder in charge of the Jerusalem Jesus group.

15:3: On their way to Jerusalem, Paul and Barnabas share their success stories concerning Israelites living among non-Israelite majorities with fellow Israelite believers in Phoenicia (see Acts 11:19) and Samaria (Acts 1:8; 8:5). The news provides reason for all believers to rejoice.

15:4: Arriving in Jerusalem, the duo is welcomed by the community and its leaders, apostles and elders. To these they relate "all that God had done with them" (see Acts 14:27). God is the major actor in Luke's story.

15:5: Jesus group members from the Pharisaic party urged that the Israelites living among and assimilated to non-Israelite majorities to such a degree as to be indistinguishable from them should be circumcised and obliged to observe the law of Moses. This is how they interpret God's directives to Abraham (Gen 17:10-14) and to Moses (Deut 5:28-33). This is also how they interpret the implications of Jesus' command to Paul, to "bring my name before/among non-Israelites: both to kings and to the children of Israel" (Acts 9:15). This perception of Paul's way of dealing with Israelites living among non-Israelite majorities is repeated again in Acts 21:2, where James tells Paul of the great number of Judean Jesus group members in Jerusalem who "have been told about you that you teach all the Judeans who are among the non-Israelites to forsake Moses, telling them not to circumcise their children or observe the customs." This statement clearly describes Paul's audience: Judeans living among non-Israelites!

15:6: In accord with the requirements of their collectivistic culture, the apostles and elders call a meeting of the entire community (see v. 12) to resolve the disagreement (as in Acts 6:1-2). In such cultures, individuals always yield to the group consensus.

15:7: To imagine the "debate" it is important to keep in mind some key features of Mediterranean culture. Its agonistic character means the debate would be very lively. We might call it "hot." Moreover, the debate does not follow parliamentary rules of procedure but is rather a shouting match with unmediated interruptions.

Eventually, debaters tire out. At that point, Peter gives his opinion. His remarks can be divided into two sections: a report of his experience (Acts 15:7-9) and conclusions that he would draw from that experience (Acts 15:10-11).

15:7-9: Peter's experience in question is his encounter with Cornelius (Acts 10:1–11:18), a respectful stranger (the word used is *allophylos*, that is, member of another tribe) who was a centurion. Nothing is specified about his ethnic origin. There were Israelites in the Roman army. Peter's report (vv. 7-9) is yet a further interpretation of his own ASC experience (Acts 10:9-16) **Alternate States of Consciousness** in which he gained a divinely inspired insight into a new understanding of God's concern about purity. In the Lukan story line, Peter was the first one to alter this aspect of Judaism for a "God-fearer" who was similarly divinely inspired. Peter in turn taught him about God's place for Jesus in the forthcoming Israelite theocracy. Peter was the one "through whom the Gentiles would hear the message of the good news and become believers," referring to Cornelius and his household. What they believed was that the God of Israel raised Jesus from the dead with a view to a forthcoming Israelite theocracy. While no mention is made of any part in this theocracy for non-Israelites, they did receive the Holy Spirit, the Spirit of the God of Israel.

15:9: According to Peter, God still loves Israel but no longer discriminates between Israelites on the basis of observance or failure to observe traditional purity rules, but rather on the basis of faith in God's activity in raising Jesus and in God's promise of a forthcoming new and better Israelite theocracy.

15:10: "To put God to the test" is a grave dishonor. It involves tempting God, that is, checking on God's loyalty. Israelite experience demonstrated the impossibility of anyone fulfilling all the requirements of the Mosaic law (see Acts 13:38-39); hence, why impose it on God-fearers who are respectful toward Jesus groups in the Diaspora?

15:11: All Israelites will be saved "through the grace of the Lord Jesus," that is, through God's favor of acting in and through the Lord Jesus—hence the gift of faith, belief in what God accomplished for all Israelites by Jesus' life, death, and resurrection and loyalty to God.

15:12: With the debate conclusively brought to an end, the community now listens attentively to the report by Paul and Barnabas of all the "signs and wonders" that God accomplished among Israelites living in non-Israelite cities, as confirmation of their message about Jesus.

The Convocation: James's Proposals Acts 15:13-21

15:13 After they finished speaking, James replied, "My brothers, listen to me. 14 Simeon has related how God first looked favorably on the Gentiles, to take from among them a people for his name. 15 This agrees with the words of the prophets, as it is written,

16 'After this I will return,

and I will rebuild the dwelling of
     David, which has fallen;
from its ruins I will rebuild it,
     and I will set it up,
17 so that all other peoples may seek
     the Lord—
even all the Gentiles over whom

my name has been called.
Thus says the Lord, who has
been making these things
18 known from long ago.'
19 Therefore I have reached the decision
that we should not trouble those Gentiles
who are turning to God, 20 but we should

write to them to abstain only from things
polluted by idols and from fornication and
from whatever has been strangled and from
blood. 21 For in every city, for generations
past, Moses has had those who proclaim
him, for he has been read aloud every sabbath in the synagogues."

Textual Notes: Acts 15:13-21

15:13: This is not James the apostle (previously murdered, see Acts 12:2) but James "the brother of the Lord" (see Acts 12:17; Gal 1:19; 2:9, 12). He played an important role in the early Jerusalem Jesus group, as this report indicates. Eusebius (*Historia ecclesiastica* 3.32) tells of fifteen members of the house of Israel who served as supervisors of the Jerusalem Jesus group, beginning with James, a member of the actual family of Jesus; he was followed by another relative, Simeon. This sequence ended with the expulsion of Judeans from Jerusalem after the Bar Kokhba uprising (early second century C.E.).

The solution that James offers belongs to a different set of questions brought to his attention by delegates from Antioch. The problems addressed here are diet and marriage. The solution has two parts: first, the principle drawn from Scripture (Amos 9:11-12) upon which he based his decision (Acts 15:13b-18); and second, his solution to their practical questions supported by an appeal to Mosaic law (15:19-21).

15:14: This is only one of two times in the New Testament (see also 2 Pet 1:1) where Peter is called by his Israelite name, Simeon. Luke (through James) is defi-nitely referring to Peter, though historians suspect the person may have actually been Simeon who was called Niger (see Acts 13:2) who brought this different set of questions from Antioch to Jerusalem.

15:14: NRSV "looked favorably upon the Gentiles" is a doctrinally inspired misinterpretation of the Greek verb "be concerned with." James reports that through Peter, God for the first time in the Jesus group showed interest in taking from those among non-Israelites a "people to bear God's name" (see Jer 13:11 LXX; Zech 2:11 [LXX 2:15]). Whether those from among non-Israelites were practicing Judeans or assimilated Israelites is not determined. Perhaps, as previ-ously noted, this Cornelius, a Roman centurion, was like the nephew of Philo of Alexandria, Tiberius Julius Alexander, a Roman governor and certainly of Israelite lineage. In other words, these Israelites in name should now become true Israelites in fact, specifically by accepting the word of God and living out its consequences.

15:15-18: As one would expect in a message delivered to fellow Israelites, James quotes from the Scripture to support his argument. The actual citation reflects neither the Hebrew nor the Septuagint but is rather a Lukan adaptation of the Septuagint (Jer 12:15 and Amos 9:11-12). The procedure is hardly what one would expect of the historical James, but Luke is not reporting history as we understand it in the modern world. The Septuagint has made an interesting interpretation that lends itself readily to the traditional opinion that God cared at all about non-Israelites, here referred to as "humankind." The Hebrew "remnant of Edom" became "the remainder of humankind" in Greek because the Hebrew root *ʾdm* (Edom) could be interpreted as *ʾādām*, which in Greek becomes *anthrōpos*, or humanity. In the Amos passage, after rather total destruction of "David's tent," the God of Israel reconstitutes it so that what remains of humankind along with "all the *ethnē* (NRSV: Gentiles) over whom I call my name" may seek the Lord. In the passage from Amos "the *ethnē* (peoples) over whom I call my name" clearly refers to Israelites.

15:19: James offers his opinion and not a formal judgment. He basically supports Peter's position but offers yet another perspective. He is concerned not to add unnecessary burdens to fellow Israelites who have been assimilated to Hellenistic practices, and who have joined Jesus groups in the dispersion.

15:20: James lists four requirements that would ensure smooth relations between assimilated Israelites living among non-Israelite majorities and observant Israelites (Judeans) in Palestine or wherever they might be living. His four requirements reflect Leviticus 17–18, the so-called Holiness Code. Observance of these behavioral norms was expected of resident aliens in Israel (Lev 17:8). Thus, in comparison with Israelites in Palestine, those living in the dispersion were equated with resident aliens, that is, non-Israelites, living in Palestine. This indicates how very different these assimilated Israelites were judged to be from "Judeans" living in Palestine.

The first requirement is that they avoid foods sacrificed before images (NRSV "idols" is simply wrong; see Malina and Pilch 2006:92-93). Such activity would show disrespect to the God of Israel (see Lev 17:7-9). The second requirement is to avoid unchastity (Greek: *porneia*), that is, conduct forbidden by the Torah, hence unlawful conduct, not exclusively sexual (Lev 18:6-18). The third requirement is to avoid eating meat butchered without the appropriate ritual, namely, without the blood properly drained (Lev 17:15). The final requirement is not to eat food prepared from animal blood (Lev 17:10-11). After all, life is in the blood and belongs to God alone (Lev 17:14). By living according to these requirements, assimilated Israelites will avoid offending the sensitivities of observant Israelites among whom they live and with whom they interact in Jesus groups. Peace will reign in the community. Thus, while Peter agreed that assimilated Israelites joining Jesus groups did not have to be circumcised nor should they be compelled to observe the entire law of Moses, James suggests that assimilated Israelite believers at least observe what resident aliens in Palestine were expected to observe.

15:21: James concludes that even assimilated Israelites should be sufficiently aware of the minimum that was required of resident aliens, since it was traditionally discussed in the community centers. In other words, he does not endorse the demand of Pharisee believers.

The Letter Promulgating These Decisions Acts 15:22-29

15:22 Then the apostles and the elders, with the consent of the whole church, decided to choose men from among their members and to send them to Antioch with Paul and Barnabas. They sent Judas called Barsabbas, and Silas, leaders among the brothers, 23 with the following letter: "The brothers, both the apostles and the elders, to the believers of Gentile origin in Antioch and Syria and Cilicia, greetings. 24 Since we have heard that certain persons who have gone out from us, though with no instructions from us, have said things to disturb you and have unsettled your minds, 25 we have decided unanimously to choose representatives and send them to you, along with our beloved Barnabas and Paul, 26 who have risked their lives for the sake of our Lord Jesus Christ. 27 We have therefore sent Judas and Silas, who themselves will tell you the same things by word of mouth. 28 For it has seemed good to the Holy Spirit and to us to impose on you no further burden than these essentials: 29 that you abstain from what has been sacrificed to idols and from blood and from what is strangled and from fornication. If you keep yourselves from these, you will do well. Farewell."

Textual Notes: Acts 15:22-29

15:22: In accord with the collectivistic nature of Mediterranean culture, the group decision (apostles, elders, whole community) recorded in a written letter is delivered by another group (Paul, Barnabas, Judas, and Silas) to the communities in Antioch, Syria, and Cilicia. Though individuals are named, no one really stands out. Silas appears for the first time in Luke's narrative, and he becomes a regular companion of Paul on his journeys (called Silvanus in 1 Thess 1:1; 2 Cor 1:19). While he and Judas are here called "brothers," they are later identified as "prophets" (v. 32).

15:23: The form of this letter is standard in Greco-Roman letter writing: sender, addressees, greetings, message, formulaic conclusion. The addressees of this letter are described as "brothers *ex ethnōn*." NRSV translates "believers of Gentile origin." The phrase equally means, "brothers of non-Israelite regions or populations." We prefer the latter, of course. The addressees of the letter were assimilated Israelites living among majority non-Israelite populations. The letter is sent to these Jesus group members in Antioch (capital of Syria), Syria (a region), and Cilicia (a region), hence has to be carried there.

15:24: The gossip network informed the community at Jerusalem that some among them not authorized to do so were insisting that the assimilated Israelites in those regions submit to circumcision and obey the entire law of Moses, thus causing them great distress.

15:25-27: James and his associates "unanimously" agreed to send a personal delegation along with Barnabas and Paul to report the group decision. Luke ascribes distinctive honor to Paul and Barnabas. They have "risked [NRSV; or pledged or dedicated] their lives for the sake [NRSV; literally "name" or person] of our Lord Jesus Christ." Luke identifies the members of the delegation: Judas and Silas, who will orally tell what is written in the letter. This was common practice in antiquity, where less than one half of one percent of the population was literate. Moreover, the Mediterranean audience was interactive. It did not sit and listen in silence.

15:28-29: The community recognizes that its deliberations and conclusions are guided by the Holy Spirit, a distinctive feature of Jesus groups. Mention of the Holy Spirit likewise indicated divine direction and approval. The report is similar to what Luke had recorded earlier in v. 20. Scholars conjecture that Luke created his report of the deliberations on the basis of this letter, which was in his source. If assimilated Israelites avoid the four behaviors suggested, they will do well. The letter ends with the conventional closing of a Hellenistic letter: "be well."

How the Letter Was Received in Antioch Acts 15:30-35

15:30 So they were sent off and went down to Antioch. When they gathered the congregation together, they delivered the letter. 31 When its members read it, they rejoiced at the exhortation. 32 Judas and Silas, who were themselves prophets, said much to encourage and strengthen the believers. 33 After they had been there for some time, they were sent off in peace by the believers to those who had sent them. 35 But Paul and Barnabas remained in Antioch, and there, with many others, they taught and proclaimed the word of the Lord.

Textual Notes: Acts 15:30-35

15:31: Since only half of one percent of the ancient population may have been literate, that is, capable of reading and writing, it is more correct to understand that the letter was read to the gathered community. The news, of course, was good for this group of assimilated Israelites who had accepted Jesus as Messiah. To remain in the Jesus group, they were not obliged to accept the practices of strictly observant Israelites living in Judea and elsewhere. The directives given in the letter were considered "exhortations." In other words, the letter emanated not from some power or authority source but from a source that expected loyalty and solidarity.

15:32: Judas and Silas were those designated to relate the decision of the meeting in Jerusalem. Luke also mentioned "prophets" in Acts 11:27; 13:1; and 21:10. His view of Old Testament prophets is that they predicted future events, which would suit his practice of pointing to promise and fulfillment. In contrast, the Hebraic/Old Testament concept of prophet is one who speaks the will of God for the here and now. In general in the New Testament, as indicated here, prophets were inspired or gifted speakers who sometimes were capable of soothing unsettled or anxious groups.

15:33: If Judas and Silas return to Jerusalem, how could Paul select Silas to accompany him on his next journey? To resolve that discrepancy, less reliable manuscripts added v. 34: "But Silas decided to remain there, and only Judas left for Jerusalem." It is preferable to omit the verse and realize that Acts 15 is a conflated text.

15:35: Paul and Barnabas remain in Antioch, capital of the province of Syria, and continue to proclaim the word of the Lord, that is, the message about what God has done through Jesus Messiah and the significance of all this for these Israelite Jesus group members assimilated to Hellenism. Luke notes that they did this with many others. This notice implies the further expansion of Jesus movement groups.

Acts 15:36–21:26 Witnessing in the Aegean Region

In this section, there are five "public accusation type scenes" that follow a fixed literary pattern:

1. hostile detainment of visitors who are brought to a public tribunal;

2. explicit charges; and

3. a violent reaction from the crowd and authorities.

The five accusation scenes are leveled by a variety of personages: Greco-Roman fortune peddlers in Philippi (Acts 16:20-21); members of the house of Israel in Thessalonica (Acts 17:6-7) and in Corinth (Acts 18:13); Greco-Roman amulet-souvenir makers and peddlers in Ephesus (Acts 19:25-27); and Asian members of the house of Israel in Jerusalem (Acts 21:28). The accused, of course, are identified by the accusers as social deviants.

Conflict between Paul and Barnabas Acts 15:36-41

15:36 After some days Paul said to Barnabas, "Come, let us return and visit the believers in every city where we proclaimed the word of the Lord and see how they are doing." 37 Barnabas wanted to take with them John called Mark. 38 But Paul decided not to take with them one who had deserted them in Pamphylia and had not accompanied them in the work. 39 The disagreement became so sharp that they parted company; Barnabas took Mark with him and sailed away to Cyprus. 40 But Paul chose Silas and set out, the believers commending him to the grace of the Lord. 41 He went through Syria and Cilicia, strengthening the churches.

Textual Notes: Acts 15:36-41

This text segment reports how the harmonious—perhaps idyllic—collaboration of Paul and Barnabas collapses. Each selects another travel companion and sets out in a different direction. Barnabas and John Mark retrace their steps and cover old ground, while Paul and Silas strike out for new regions.

15:36: Paul suggests that he and Barnabas revisit the communities that accepted their proclamation of the word of God, that is, that the God of Israel raised Jesus from the dead, constituting him as Israel's Messiah to come in a context of a forthcoming Israelite theocracy. Paul acts as communicators of innovation should, since they must set up an information-exchange relationship to deal with problems and stabilize and prevent discontinuance. **Communication of Innovation.** In what preceded, Luke notes that there were Jesus groups in Salamis and Paphos on the island of Cyprus, Pisidian Antioch, Iconium, Lystra, Derbe, and Perga in Pamphylia (Acts 13:5-6, 14, 51; 14:1, 8, 20, 25).

15:37-38: A sharp disagreement erupts between Paul and Barnabas over Barnabas's cousin, John Mark (see Col 4:10). Barnabas wants to take him along on their journey as a co-worker. True to the nature of collectivistic societies and personalities, the early believers were tightly knit kin groups. Barnabas's aunt, Mary, was the mother of John Mark (Acts 12:12), who provided her house in Jerusalem for the Jesus group meeting there. Belief was a family affair, and women had a strong influence on the young males (2 Tim 3:14-15; 1:5). Still, Mediterranean allegiances tend to shift. As the proverb puts it: "I against my brother; I and my brother against our cousin(s); I, my brother and our cousins against the village; and so on." For some unknown reason, John Mark deserted his cousin and Paul at Pamphylia and returned to Jerusalem, quite likely to get home to his mother (Acts 13:13).

Paul was aggrieved by John Mark's departure. There is no indication of the nature of the disagreement between Paul and John Mark, but Paul strenuously resisted taking him along on this journey. There may have been a reconciliation later on, as suggested by Phlm 24 and Col 4:10.

15:39-41: At this point, however, Paul and Barnabas are so at odds that they decide to go their separate ways. Barnabas and John Mark head for Cyprus, where they have family, while Paul and Silas go forward with the blessing of the community at Antioch.

Paul Adds Timothy as a New Partner Acts 16:1-5

16:1 Paul went on also to Derbe and to Lystra, where there was a disciple named Timothy, the son of a Jewish woman who was a believer; but his father was a Greek. 2 He was well spoken of by the believers in Lystra and Iconium. 3 Paul wanted Timothy to accompany him; and he took him and had him circumcised because of the Jews who were in those places, for they all knew that his father was a Greek. 4 As they went from town to town, they delivered to them for observance the decisions that had been reached by the apostles and elders who were in Jerusalem. 5 So the churches were strengthened in the faith and increased in numbers daily.

Textual Notes: Acts 16:1-5

16:1-3: In Lystra, Paul meets Timothy for the first time. He reappears in Acts 17:14-15; 18:5; 19:22; 20:4. Timothy is already a "disciple" (*mathētēs*), that is, one who belongs to a Jesus group and embraces the values of the group. In Paul's letters he is also identified as an important co-worker and sometime collaborator in four of the Pauline letters (for example, 1 Thessalonians, 2 Corinthians, Philippians, and Philemon). He is the son of a Judean mother (anachronistically translated by NRSV as "Jewish"), that is, someone in the Diaspora who observed Judaic practices as in Jerusalem, and a Hellenized or thoroughly assimilated Israelite father (Greek is not his ethnic background; the word means rather "civilized," or one who participates fully in Greek culture and speaks the Greek language; see Acts 14:1). Thus, contrary even to traditional opinion, we hold that Timothy was indeed an Israelite living with his family among a majority non-Israelite population.

The question here particularly in the light of Acts 15 and Gal 2:3-4 as well as 1 Cor 7:18-19 is: Why did Paul circumcise Timothy? The traditional answer has been that it would remove a major problem for Paul as he continued to proclaim the word of God among Israelite groups usually consisting of some Judean traditionalists and assimilated Israelites, that is, Judeans and Greeks. This is what Luke states (v. 3). Assimilated Israelites, or course, were themselves not circumcised, nor did the Jerusalem leaders require it (Acts 15:10-12).

Note that Timothy rather quickly takes to the road with Paul after his circumcision—indicating that the full removal of the foreskin was not involved. As a matter of fact, that type of circumcision begins only after 150 c.e. The type of circumcision involved here would be nicking the foreskin so that some blood ran.

16:4: Paul and his companions Silas and Timothy journey on from town to town, while passing on to Israelite Jesus groups the decision reached in Jerusalem regarding circumcision and observance of the Mosaic law (Acts 15:7-11). Neither was required of assimilated Israelites, while traditionalist Judeans in the Jesus group would already be following those customs—but should now freely interact with assimilated Israelites in their group.

In Troas, Paul's ASC Commissions the Group for Macedonia Acts 16:6-10

16:6 They went through the region of Phrygia and Galatia, having been forbidden by the Holy Spirit to speak the word in Asia. 7 When they had come opposite Mysia, they attempted to go into Bithynia, but the Spirit of Jesus did not allow them; 8 so, passing by Mysia, they went down to Troas. 9 During the night Paul had a vision: there stood a man of Macedonia pleading with him and saying, "Come over to Macedonia and help us." 10 When he had seen the vision, we immediately tried to cross over to Macedonia, being convinced that God had called us to proclaim the good news to them.

Textual Notes: Acts 16:6-10

This passage describes how the traveling group got to Troas, passing through the regions of Phrygia, Galatia, by Mysia with the hope to getting to the region of Bithynia.

16:6: Paul and companions leave the area of southern Galatia and head northward toward Mysia (northwest Asia Minor) because the Holy Spirit forbade them to speak in Asia, very likely, at the provincial capital, Ephesus. Paul's journeys in Acts were inspired and initiated by the Spirit (13:2, 4, 9; 19:2, 6). References to the Spirit always involve human experiences in alternate states of consciousness. **Alternate States of Consciousness**. In this instance, Luke does not specify the exact experience, but it may have been while they were absorbed in prayer, or experiencing road trance while traveling, or daydreaming, or something similar.

16:7: By parallelism, Luke explains that the Holy Spirit is the Spirit of Jesus. Their attempt to travel east of Mysia to Bithynia is similarly thwarted by the Spirit.

16:8-9: Eventually they arrive at Troas, an important port of embarkation for trips across the Aegean Sea. There Paul has a night vision (cf. Acts 7:31; 9:10, 12; 10:3, 17, 19; 11:5; 12:9; 16:10; 18:9), perhaps a dream, in which he sees a human person rather than an angel or spirit. **Alternate States of Consciousness**. Paul identifies the person to be a Macedonian, that is, from a region called Macedonia, which is now northern Greece. How Paul knew this is not specified, but according to contemporary psychological anthropology, the visionary assigns meaning to the vision's content. This is how Paul interprets his vision. Paul being himself a collectivistic person would understand that this man also represents a collectivity. The man or collectivity invites Paul to come to Macedonia "and help us." It is not clear from this statement exactly what kind of help the man requests; the Greek word is too generic.

16:10: Paul and his companions interpret the dream to mean that God wants them to direct their efforts to a region different from the one they had intended. They are to leave Asia and go to Europe. There are two types of alternate states of consciousness experiences: individual and group. Paul had the dream, but the trio interpreted it together.

Significantly, this verse introduces the first of four "we" sections in Acts (16:10-17; 20:5-15; 21:1-18; 27:1—28:16), which many believe indicates Luke's personal and occasional participation in Paul's travels. However, the prologue to Luke-Acts (Luke 1:1-4) indicates that many narratives of what Jesus said and did already existed, and these narratives are third-generation products, while Paul himself belonged to the second Jesus group generation. For this reason it would seem that Luke the writer of this account belonged to the fourth Jesus group generation, or the third generation after Paul. **Generational Differences.** These "we" sections would then belong to some Lukan source, some person contemporary with and a companion of Paul. In context, the best candidates would be Silas (Silvanus) and Timothy—both of whom collaborated with Paul in composing letters, or Titus, a person quite significant in the Pauline letters, but not mentioned in Acts at all.

Witnessing in Philippi Acts 16:11-40

16:11 We set sail from Troas and took a straight course to Samothrace, the following day to Neapolis, 12 and from there to Philippi, which is a leading city of the district of Macedonia and a Roman colony. We remained in this city for some days. 13 On the sabbath day we went outside the gate by the river, where we supposed there was a place of prayer; and we sat down and spoke to the women who had gathered there. 14 A certain woman named Lydia, a worshiper of God, was listening to us; she was from the city of Thyatira and a dealer in purple cloth. The Lord opened her heart to listen eagerly to what was said by Paul. 15 When she and her household were baptized, she urged us, saying, "If you have judged me to be faithful to the Lord, come and stay at my home." And she prevailed upon us.

16 One day, as we were going to the place of prayer, we met a slave girl who had a spirit of divination and brought her owners a great deal of money by fortune-telling. 17 While she followed Paul and us, she would cry out, "These men are slaves of the Most High God, who proclaim to you a way of salvation." 18 She kept doing this for many days. But Paul, very much annoyed, turned and said to the spirit, "I order you in the name of Jesus Christ to come out of her." And it came out that very hour.

19 But when her owners saw that their hope of making money was gone, they seized Paul and Silas and dragged them into the marketplace before the authorities. 20 When they had brought them before the magistrates, they said, "These men are disturbing our city; they are Jews 21 and are advocating customs that are not law-

ful for us as Romans to adopt or observe." 22 The crowd joined in attacking them, and the magistrates had them stripped of their clothing and ordered them to be beaten with rods. 23 After they had given them a severe flogging, they threw them into prison and ordered the jailer to keep them securely. 24 Following these instructions, he put them in the innermost cell and fastened their feet in the stocks.

25 About midnight Paul and Silas were praying and singing hymns to God, and the prisoners were listening to them. 26 Suddenly there was an earthquake, so violent that the foundations of the prison were shaken; and immediately all the doors were opened and everyone's chains were unfastened. 27 When the jailer woke up and saw the prison doors wide open, he drew his sword and was about to kill himself, since he supposed that the prisoners had escaped. 28 But Paul shouted in a loud voice, "Do not harm yourself, for we are all here." 29 The jailer called for lights, and rushing in, he fell down trembling before Paul and Silas. 30 Then he brought them outside and said, "Sirs, what must I do to be saved?" 31 They answered, "Believe on the Lord Jesus, and you will be saved, you and your household."

32 They spoke the word of the Lord to him and to all who were in his house. 33 At the same hour of the night he took them and washed their wounds; then he and his entire family were baptized without delay. 34 He brought them up into the house and set food before them; and he and his entire household rejoiced that he had become a believer in God.

35 When morning came, the magistrates sent the police, saying, "Let those men go." 36 And the jailer reported the message to Paul, saying, "The magistrates sent word to let you go; therefore come out now and go in peace." 37 But Paul replied, "They have beaten us in public, uncondemned, men who are Roman citizens, and have thrown us into prison; and now are they going to discharge us in secret? Certainly not! Let them come and take us out themselves." 38 The police reported these words to the magistrates, and they were afraid when they heard that they were Roman citizens; 39 so they came and apologized to them. And they took them out and asked them to leave the city. 40 After leaving the prison they went to Lydia's home; and when they had seen and encouraged the brothers and sisters there, they departed.

Textual Notes: Acts 16:11-40

There are five different reports in this text segment: a continuation of the travel narrative and meeting Lydia (vv. 11-15); the exorcism of the slave girl, another of Paul's mighty deeds (vv. 16-18); the unhappy consequences of the exorcism for Paul and friends (vv. 19-24); rescue from prison by an earthquake (vv. 25-34); reaction by Philippian leaders to Paul's complaints about the treatment accorded to him and his companions (vv. 35-40).

Episode 1. 16:11-15: The trio now travel to the island called Samothrace, in the northeastern Aegean, then on to Neapolis, the port serving Philippi (located ten miles inland) where they eventually arrive, tarry for a while and meet Lydia. As noted, this is the first of five episodes in this text segment.

16:13: On the Sabbath, they go to the river. The closest river, Gangites, is too far away for a Sabbath journey. Hence, they more likely went to a creek close by, Crenides. Here they expected to find a place of prayer (not a synagogue, but a place where Israelites would gather as a group to pray). The ready availability of water for ritual ablutions makes the expectation plausible (see also Josephus, *Antiquities* 14.20.23). Indeed, Israelite women—the ones most likely to seek ablutions (see Lev 15:19-23)—are already gathered there.

Given the rigid separation of genders in ancient Mediterranean cultures, especially in public places, how is it that Paul and his companions were able to engage these women in conversation (see John 4:27)? The primary understanding and interpretation of space depend to a degree on the function it serves. In general, "public" space such as a river would be male. Yet some places can be used by males and females, but one gender generally has control over the space at any given time. If used for ablutions, the space could be under female control. If used by a teacher, women could gather there because that is where the (male) teacher sits and now controls the space.

16:14: The phrase "worshiper of God" (Greek: *sebomenos ton theon*, Acts 13:50; 16:14; 17:4, 17; 18:7; 19:27; cf 18:13; 19:27) is equivalent to the technical term "fearer of God" (Greek: *phoboumenos ton theon*, "God-fearer," Acts 10:2, 22, 25; 13:16, 26) which the Septuagint routinely uses to describe members of the house of Israel. The God in question, of course, is the God of Israel, indicating that the designation would include those assimilated Israelites who neglected circumcision and/or did not observe the Torah in its entirety. Lydia (and quite likely her household) are non-[fully]-observant Israelites.

Her place of origin, Thyatira, was in Asia Minor located near the Lycus River on the road from Pergamum to Sardis. The city was indeed noted for purple goods, a luxury item in the ancient world. Hence, one might hypothesize that Lydia owned a business that catered to elites. However, since animal urine was used in purple dyeing, Lydia and her workers might well have lived outside the city for obvious reasons.

16:15: Here we learn for the first time that part of the innovation proclaimed by Paul included the ritual of baptism. The fact that Lydia's entire household submits to baptism is typical of collectivistic societies (see Josh 24:14-15; also Acts 16:33). Everyone acts with a view toward harmony and promoting the common good. Individual choices and preferences simply do not factor into consideration. After the baptism, Lydia completes the informal dyadic contract again typical of Mediterranean societies. She offers them hospitality. **Hospitality.** She phrases her invitation in a way that will redound to her honor. "If you have judged me to be faithful to the Lord . . ." She is not the kind of woman described by the writer of 2 Tim 3:6-7, and Paul and his companions will affirm this if they accept her invitation. The word "prevail" accurately describes the Middle Eastern custom of insistently repeating an offer which the beneficiary is expected to refuse initially but to acquiesce only after the second or third offer (compare Gen 19:3; 1 Sam 28:23; 2 Kgs 2:17).

Episode 2. 16:16-18: The second episode associated with this place of prayer is Paul's role of holy man, revealed in his exorcising a slave girl from a "python spirit" correctly rendered by the NRSV "spirit of divination" (vv. 16-18). This is the only actual report of a disciple working an exorcism in the New Testament. It may be a Lukan creation intended to parallel the experience of Jesus (see Luke 4:33-34; 8:28-35). Through the girl in an alternate state of consciousness, the spirit world publicly testifies that these men serve the Most High God and offer "a way of salvation." That the girl shouts is an indication that she is in an ASC (see Pilch

2004:111). **Alternate States of Consciousness**. The reference to God as "Most High" is a typical Lukan way to refer to the God of Israel (Luke 1:32, 35, 76; 6:35; 8:28; Acts 7:48 and also very frequently in Judean writings such as 2 Esdras and Sirach; however, the name was also used in Hellenism). Paul and Silas are called slaves of the Most High God; slaves are people who are deprived of their freedom of decision and action with a view to the social utility of the enslaving agent, in this case, the God of Israel. Because Luke uncharacteristically does not use the definite article here with "way" as he does elsewhere (see Luke 9:57; 18:35; 19:36; 20:21; 24:32), it is plausible that Luke intentionally omitted the article here, allowing Paul to conclude that the girl was possessed by a deceptive spirit rather than one from the realm of the God of Israel. Hence the exorcism. What is clearly distressing to Luke/ Paul is that the girl's owners (plausibly a man and woman, a couple) were profiting financially from her soothsaying (v. 16).

Episode 3. 16:19-24: This third episode reports the consequences of Paul's good deed. Though her mediumship abilities brought profit to her masters, the ancient world ridiculed such profit-taking and considered the practice to be charlatanism (see Apuleius, *Metamorphoses* 8.26-30). Even so, Paul has infuriated her masters, who now seek revenge. They seize the men and bring them before the magistrates (*duoviri* of Philippi) charging that these Judeans are causing a disturbance by "advocating customs that are not lawful for us as Romans to adopt or observe" (v. 21). The charge is false on its face (as were those against Jesus; see Luke 23:1-16). On the other hand, since Paul and his companions interacted only with Israelites and told them of the word of the God of Israel meant solely for Israelites, it is quite possible that the possessed girl was herself an Israelite slave. After all, the mention of the "Most High God" indicates her knowledge of Israelite practices. Yet her masters do not seem to have been Israelites, or they could not have put themselves at risk with their charges. Further, Israel's political religion was permitted in the empire.

16:23: Paul recounts his mistreatment and flogging at Philippi in 1 Thess 1:1; Phil 1:30; 2 Cor 11:25. Of course, an obvious question arises: Why did Paul not invoke his Roman citizenship here as he does later in 22:25? After the humiliation of the flogging, they are locked in the innermost cell with their feet secured to a stake.

Episode 4. 16:25-34: This fourth episode reports the extraordinary rescue of the prisoners by means of an earthquake. In the first-century Mediterranean, earthquakes were said to be caused by celestial entities, often deities (see Acts 4:31). In accordance with this perception, Luke explains earthquakes as indications of divine intervention as throughout the Israelite tradition (see Acts 4:31; Exod 19:18; Judg 5:4; 1 Kgs 19:11; Matt 27:51, 54). God rescues his faithful agents. Impressed by the events as interpreted by Paul, the jailer and his family become believers in the God of Israel (v. 34).

16:25: While singing hymns to a "captive" audience at midnight sounds absurd to Western ears, this was honorable behavior in the ancient Mediterranean. According to the apocrypha, the patriarch Joseph fettered in Pharaoh's prison "sang praise . . . and rejoiced with cheerful voice, glorifying . . . God" (*Testament of Joseph* 8:5). The notice also fits Luke's motif emphasizing prayer.

Alexander of Macedonia. Roman portrait bust. Location: Museo di Villa Albani, Rome, Italy. Photo © Alinari / Art Resource, N.Y.

16:27-28: Immediately grasping the situation and its probable consequences for him (see Acts 12:19), the jailer prepares to take the honorable way out, when Paul stops him.

16:30: The jailer's question about "salvation" quite likely refers to rescue from anticipated aftershocks of the earthquake. In the Lukan narrative, the jailer's question echoes that posed by Israelites at the Pentecost event in Jerusalem (Acts 2:37). Luke gives the question a spin it may not have had on the jailer's lips.

16:31-33: Paul seizes the opportunity to instruct him and his household about the God of Israel and his activity in the life of Jesus. It is hardly likely that this would make sense to a devout non-Israelite in the Greco-Roman world. In a typical high-context document such as Acts, given Paul's gambit, we propose that the jailer was an assimilated Israelite who now realized the plan of the God of Israel revealed in the event of Jesus. This would cast the jailer's question in a new light: clearly the God of Israel has rescued you two by means of this earthquake. What must I now do to win such rescue ("salvation") from our God in times of duress? True to the nature of collectivistic culture, the jailer and his entire family were baptized (see Acts 16:15), following Paul's advice.

In these contexts where entire households were baptized, some have wondered whether children were included? It would seem that those baptized had to be capable of attentively listening to and understanding Paul's instruction. Scholars think this would exclude children. On the other hand, while individuals were baptized, in collectivistic societies children were part and parcel of their parents and the whole collectivistic ingroup—hence the baptism of a family's adults sufficed for the ingroup children as well.

16:34: Just like Lydia, so too the jailer reciprocates his good fortune by hosting his benefactors in his house. This is a normal response according to the terms of an implied dyadic contract embedded in circum-Mediterranean culture.

Episode 5. 16:35-40: This fifth and final episode in this chapter tells how the Philippian authorities respond to Paul's complaints. In Luke's story line, it seems that the magistrates' experience of the earthquake and their associating it with "those men" prompted them to send officers to command the jailer to let them go.

16:37: Paul's response to the magistrates' order that he and his companions be released from prison is to refuse until the magistrates come personally to release them. Paul informs them that he and Silas ("us" [v. 37]) are Roman citizens who have been totally dishonored by being publicly flogged without a trial to investigate the charges against them. Paul's claim to Roman citizenship (here and in Acts 22:28, but nowhere in his authentic letters) is either a Lukan presupposition (based on a datum that Paul was born in Tarsus), or a Pauline deception. It is honorable to lie to an outgroup person, but to be lied to is a challenge to honor.

> The reason for giving a word of honor is that moral commitment in telling the truth unambiguously in such honor cultures derives from the social commitment or loyalty to persons to whom such commitment is due. In first-century limited-good society, there was no such thing as universal, social commitment (e.g., the perception of all humans as equally persons, or even of all males in some brotherhood of all men). Rather, the right to the truth and the right to withhold the truth belong to the "person of honor" and to contest these rights is to place a person's honor in jeopardy, to challenge that person. Lying and deception are or can be honorable and legitimate. To lie in order to deceive an outsider, one who has no right to the truth, is honorable. In the Israelite tradition, Ben Zakaiists believed: "Men may vow to murderers, robbers, or tax-gatherers that what they have is heave-offering even though it is not heave-offering; or that they belong to the king's household even though they do not belong to the king's household" (Mishnah, *Nedarim* 3.4). (Malina 2003:41-42)

The point is, the magistrates had no right to the truth. On the other hand, how could the Philippian magistrates prove Paul was not a Roman citizen? Against the widely accepted opinion to the contrary, some would say Paul's Roman citizenship is a Lukan fiction (for example, Stegemann and Stegemann believe that Paul was a citizen neither of Rome nor of Tarsus [1999:302]; see Acts 22:3, 28). His own report of "countless beatings" (2 Cor 11:23-25) would seem to confirm he was no Roman citizen, since Roman law strictly forbade the flogging of a Roman citizen. Livy (59 B.C.E.–C.E. 17) reports:

> However, the Porcian law seems intended, solely, for the security of the persons of the citizens; as it visited with a severe penalty any one for beating with stripes or putting to death a Roman citizen. The Valerian law, after forbidding a person, who had appealed, to be beaten with rods and beheaded, added, in case of any one acting contrary thereto, that it shall yet be only deemed a wicked act. This, I suppose, was judged of sufficient strength to enforce obedience to the law in those days; so powerful was then men's sense of shame; at present one would scarcely make use of such a threat seriously. (Livy, *Historia* 10.9.4)

16:39: In any event, Paul shames the magistrates into publicly apologizing. At the same time in Luke's story line, the magistrates ask them to leave the city.

16:40: Paul and Silas head for Lydia's house (Acts 16:15), where they encourage those gathered and then proceed on their way. The identity of the "brothers" (NRSV "and sisters" is not in the Greek text) is puzzling to scholars. So far, we have learned only that Lydia joined the Jesus followers. However, since in this culture males are the significant personages, even though Paul goes to Lydia's house the cultural custom would be to mention the men only, as Luke and Luke's Paul literally do.

Witnessing in Thessalonica and Beroea Acts 17:1-15

The saga of Paul and Silas continues. After departing from Philippi, the duo make their way westward to Thessalonica. From that city, hostile Judeans force them to flee to Beroea, where the same scene repeats itself. Paul leaves his companions behind as he wends his way southward to Athens.

17:1 After Paul and Silas had passed through Amphipolis and Apollonia, they came to Thessalonica, where there was a synagogue of the Jews. 2 And Paul went in, as was his custom, and on three sabbath days argued with them from the scriptures, 3 explaining and proving that it was necessary for the Messiah to suffer and to rise from the dead, and saying, "This is the Messiah, Jesus whom I am proclaiming to you." 4 Some of them were persuaded and joined Paul and Silas, as did a great many of the devout Greeks and not a few of the leading women. 5 But the Jews became jealous, and with the help of some ruffians in the marketplaces they formed a mob and set the city in an uproar. While they were searching for Paul and Silas to bring them out to the assembly, they attacked Jason's house. 6 When they could not find them, they dragged Jason and some believers before the city authorities, shouting, "These people who have been turning the world upside down have come here also, 7 and Jason has entertained them as guests. They are all acting contrary to the decrees of the emperor, saying that there is another king named Jesus." 8 The people and the city officials were disturbed when they heard this, 9 and after they had taken bail from Jason and the others, they let them go. 10 That very night the believers sent Paul and Silas off to Beroea; and when they arrived, they went to the Jewish synagogue. 11 These Jews were more receptive than those in Thessalonica, for they welcomed the message very eagerly and examined the scriptures every day to see whether these things were so. 12 Many of them therefore believed, including not a few Greek women and men of high standing. 13 But when the Jews of Thessalonica learned that the word of God had been proclaimed by Paul in Beroea as well, they came there too, to stir up and incite the crowds. 14 Then the believers immediately sent Paul away to the coast, but Silas and Timothy remained behind. 15 Those who conducted Paul brought him as far as Athens; and after receiving instructions to have Silas and Timothy join him as soon as possible, they left him.

Textual Notes: Acts 17:1-15

17:1: The journey from Philippi to Thessalonica covered a distance of about ninety kilometers, or approximately fifty-four miles. In the ancient Mediterranean, a traveler on foot could average twenty-five kilometers a day, or fifteen miles, depending on the season and other conditions. Luke makes but brief mention of the journeys because he is writing about people and their interactions. Yet a reader should keep in mind the time and energy spent during travel to imagine the physical condition of the travelers when they arrived at their destinations.

Commentators note that while Paul passed by cities such as Amphipolis and Apollonia, he did not stop there, quite likely because there were no Judean community centers there. We take this as confirmation of our position that Paul was not interested in non-Israelites. The company found a Judean synagogue at Thessalonica and stopped there. Synagogue, as we note, is a gathering or assembly, as well as the place of gathering, hence a meeting place, a men's community center. Since Judeans might worship anyplace, these gathering centers might serve as a place of worship or a place of Torah study in the first century. The phrase "synagogue of the Jews" describes the participants. As previously noted, the word "Judean" was the general outgroup name for any Israelite, whether one fully devoted to the customs of Judea or one who followed Hellenistic customs and who was an assimilated Israelite who knew and kept Judean traditions in varying degrees. In the Roman Empire, the outgroup name for both devout Judeans and assimilated Israelite Greeks was "Judeans," as here in Thessalonica. Contrast this with the "synagogue of the Freedmen" in Jerusalem (Acts 6:9), consisting of Hellenistic Israelites from Cyrene, Alexandria, Cilicia, and Asia. Such Israelites would be less informed of the later alterations (traditions) emerging in Judea and Jerusalem, and more assimilated to the behaviors and values of non-Israelites around the Mediterranean. Perhaps because they were ostracized by local Jerusalemites, that is why they had their own meeting place in Jerusalem. In this latter synagogue there would likely be less discussion of traditions and perhaps just a better place for meeting socially and for Torah study based on Septuagint perspectives. The language in Hellenistic synagogues would very likely have been Greek.

17:2: In accord with his call to proclaim the word of God to Israelite minorities living among non-Israelite majorities, Paul regularly visited their meeting places, especially on the preferred gathering day, the Sabbath. Here he engaged them in discussions (preferable to "arguments" as in NRSV, though Middle Eastern discussions can sound like arguments to Westerners) for three Sabbaths. Such discussions could be day-long affairs that involved a vigorous, even heated exchange of opinions, here specifically about the significance of the resurrected Jesus of Nazareth and God's plan realized in him.

17:3: The Old Testament makes no reference to a suffering messiah; this notion is found exclusively in Luke (Luke 24:26, 46; Acts 26:23). The "necessity" of his suffering, according to Luke, is that it occurred "according to the definite plan and foreknowledge of God" (Acts 2:23). The notion of a messiah's being raised from the dead is also lacking in the Hebrew Scriptures. The "new idea" (innovation) that Paul announces to these Israelites is that the Messiah of Israelite expectation was Jesus of Nazareth, the Messiah still awaited by Israelites in 30 C.E. before the destruction of the temple in 70 C.E. Indeed, Jesus the Messiah lived and died before failed Messiah Simon bar Kokhba was "officially" identified as Israel's Messiah by Rabbi Aqiba in 135 C.E.

17:4: Paul succeeded in persuading some of the more observant Israelites, yet many more of the assimilated "civilized" Israelites (NRSV: "devout Greeks") as well as elite women. What are women doing in an exclusively male meeting place? First, they are elite, which means that other women in their households would tend to "women's work" (see Prov 31:10-31). Second, they would not only be free from "women's work" but, by reason of status, would have access to areas of male space generally not open to most women. Third, even if present, they would likely have been on the periphery, in a balcony or in an adjacent room. The significant males in these women's lives would have passed on the information given by Paul. These are Israelite women, prominently and frequently mentioned in Acts as attracted to the word of God with its resultant faith in Jesus as forthcoming Messiah (Acts 1:14; 5:14; 8:3, 12; 9:2; 12:12; 16:15, 40; 17:4, 12, 34; 18:2, 18, 26; 21:9).

17:5: The word translated "jealous" should be translated as "envious" (see also Acts 5:17; 7:9; 13:45). Envy basically consists of pain or distress caused by another's success accompanied by an intent to take that person down a notch, to cause damage. It is a negative and evil emotion. In contrast, jealousy is defense of one's family, property, or reputation. It is a positive and good emotion. In a limited-good society such as this, when one person gains, for example, honor or reputation, others lose. The gains of Paul and his companion, with some community members joining an emerging Jesus group, aggrieve some among the local Judeans. Given the patent loss to local fellow Israelites, some moral entrepreneurs among them foment a riot and attack the house of an otherwise unknown Jason, where Paul and Silas are lodging. They hire local "rabble" to assist them in their protest. They intended to haul the duo before an assembly of citizens who would deal with and adjudicate complaints against the twosome. **Establishment Violence.**

17:6-7: Not finding the duo, the crowd hauled Jason with other Israelite Jesus group members before the assembly. They included him in their complaints as harboring these troublemakers. Three charges are laid against Paul and Silas. First, they have been creating disturbances (see Acts 16:21). Literally, the charge is "turning the world upside down." Given the Roman obsession with order, this is much more serious than disturbing the peace. Typical Mediterranean agonistic personalities are ordinarily prone to conflict. Discussion can easily escalate into arguments, and, triggered by moral entrepreneurs motivated to defend the prevailing values of the group against innovation, disputes can erupt into violence, and result in bloodshed. **Establishment Violence.** Therefore, this is a very serious charge. Israelites appear to have been particularly prone to such behaviors (see *Acts of Isidore*, Papyrus Berolinensis 8877:22-24). The charge is plausible, since Paul's message about Jesus as Messiah was certainly and understandably sparking controversy wherever he went.

The second charge is that the men are acting "contrary to the decrees of the emperor," though none is specified. Third and perhaps most serious but patently false is that the men promote Jesus as king, presumably a Lord of cosmic proportions of greater status than even a divine Caesar. Paul and Silas are accused of steering loyalty from Caesar to Jesus. Outsiders could indeed perceive Messianists in this way (see Acts 8:12; 14:22; etc.).

17:8: As gossip spreads beyond the Israelite quarter, the charge throws the city and its leaders into turmoil. Even if confined to this minority group of assimilated Israelites, their internal conflict threatens civil order.

17:9: Jason and the others are required to post bail for themselves and for Paul and Silas lest they flee from the judicial process.

17:10: The local believers (literally, "brothers," an important kinship term describing how believers viewed themselves) do exactly that, dispatching Paul and Silas to Beroea under cover of night. Located eighty kilometers southwest of Thessalonica, Beroea was beyond the jurisdiction of the Thessalonian authorities. Upon arrival they went, as one might expect, to the local meeting place of fellow Israelites (synagogue).

17:11: The group here is described as "more noble" (NRSV: "more receptive"). Originally the word described origin but came to characterize attitude and behavior. This group did not allow gossip or prejudice to color their hearing. Thus, the message of the travelers about Jesus Messiah was received with enthusiasm. The group examined the Scripture "every day" (hence not a worship service but a study and investigation group) to determine whether the tradition confirmed the message. Indeed, the Greek word translated "examine" is usually used to describe legal examination of witnesses (see Acts 4:9; 12:19; 24:8; 28:18). This is quite appropriate, since Paul's witness is based on the witness of the Israelite traditions.

17:12: In contrast to the few Israelites at Thessalonica (Acts 17:4), many of these believed the message. So too did elite, assimilated Israelite women and men (not

Gentiles, who would hardly be interested in the Hebrew Scriptures or a Hebrew messiah). Luke demonstrates keen interest in receptive assimilated Israelite women (see Acts 1:14; 5:1; 8:3, 12; 9:2; 13:50; 16:1, 13, 14; 17:1, 2, 34; 18:2; 21:5; 22:4; 24:24).

17:13: When the "envious" Israelites in Thessalonica learn of Paul's activity in Beroea, they come to stir up the same trouble as before. **Establishment Violence.**

17:14: Since Paul is the source of irritation, the brothers (NRSV: "believers") send him to the coast to head toward Athens. In the Middle East, envy is an emotion that can motivate harm and even destruction to its object. Paul's escape is a matter of life and death.

17:15: Arriving in Athens, Paul instructs his entourage that Silas and Timothy should join him as soon as possible, although we are not told where Timothy might have been.

Witnessing in Athens 17:16-34

17:16 While Paul was waiting for them in Athens, he was deeply distressed to see that the city was full of idols. 17 So he argued in the synagogue with the Jews and the devout persons, and also in the marketplace every day with those who happened to be there. 18 Also some Epicurean and Stoic philosophers debated with him. Some said, "What does this babbler want to say?" Others said, "He seems to be a proclaimer of foreign divinities." (This was because he was telling the good news about Jesus and the resurrection.) 19 So they took him and brought him to the Areopagus and asked him, "May we know what this new teaching is that you are presenting? 20 It sounds rather strange to us, so we would like to know what it means." 21 Now all the Athenians and the foreigners living there would spend their time in nothing but telling or hearing something new.

22 Then Paul stood in front of the Areopagus and said, "Athenians, I see how extremely religious you are in every way. 23 For as I went through the city and looked carefully at the objects of your worship, I found among them an altar with the inscription, 'To an unknown god.' What therefore you worship as unknown, this I proclaim to you. 24 The God who made the world and everything in it, he who is Lord of heaven and earth, does not live in shrines made by human hands, 25 nor is he served by human hands, as though he needed anything, since he himself gives to all mortals life and breath and all things. 26 From one ancestor he made all nations to inhabit the whole earth, and he allotted the times of their existence and the boundaries of the places where they would live, 27 so that they would search for God and perhaps grope for him and find him—though indeed he is not far from each one of us. 28 For 'In him we live and move and have our being'; as even some of your own poets have said,

'For we too are his offspring.'

29 Since we are God's offspring, we ought not to think that the deity is like gold, or silver, or stone, an image formed by the art and imagination of mortals. 30 While God has overlooked the times of human ignorance, now he commands all people everywhere to repent, 31 because he has fixed a day on which he will have the world judged in righteousness by a man whom he has appointed, and of this he has given assurance to all by raising him from the dead."

32 When they heard of the resurrection of the dead, some scoffed; but others said, "We will hear you again about this." 33 At that point Paul left them. 34 But some of them joined him and became believers, including Dionysius the Areopagite and a woman named Damaris, and others with them.

Textual Notes: Acts 17:16-34

An inclusion that mentions Athens frames this episode (v. 15; and 18:1). Paul's speech is a Lukan composition telling what Paul would have said had he addressed localite Athenians. The speech has three parts: introduction (vv. 16-21a); proclamation (vv. 21b-31); conclusion (vv. 32-34). In this speech, Paul presents "common knowledge" about God (shared even by Israelites), which was rejected by Epicureans but welcomed by Stoics.

17:16: This sight of images of deities throughout Athens presumably annoys and distresses Paul. While commentators usually claim that such a sight offended Paul's monotheism, the truth is that Paul like his fellow Israelites were more plausibly henotheists (see 1 Cor 8:5-6; **Many Gods and Many Lords**). The Athenians had shrines to every god but the God of Israel (known in the Torah as Yhwh, read as "Adonai," or Lord). Paul was determined to address that issue.

17:17: Every day Paul had discussions in the Israelite meeting place (synagogue) with observant Judeans and devout but less observant Judeans. He also engaged passersby in the Agora (forum) in discussion. Ancient historians note that true to their agonistic culture, the Greeks vigorously pursued serious philosophical discussions in the marketplace. Paul was not an anomaly.

17:18: Epicureans (followers of Epicurus [341-270 B.C.E.]) denied divine providence and divine judgment, a life after death, and a postmortem retribution. Stoics (founded by Zeno [340-265 B.C.E.]) believed that knowledge would lead to and support virtue, that reason was the guiding principle of nature, and that humans should seek self-sufficiency in obedience to reason. Some Epicureans considered Paul a "babbler" (a disparaging Greek term), while some Stoics were interested in the foreign deities Paul was promoting. Some scholars believe that the Stoics understood "Jesus" (masculine noun) and *anastasis* (feminine noun, "resurrection") to be consorts, which was not at all the message of Paul. Other scholars doubt this, for Paul's phrase would have been something like "Jesus and the resurrection" (see Rom 10:9).

17:19: While there is a place, a hill, west-northwest of the Athenian acropolis known as the Areopagos, where speeches were delivered, vv. 22, 33, 34 suggest that Paul addressed a body of people, the council of the Areopagus. This was the supreme judicial council responsible for monitoring public instruction. They wanted a better understanding of his "new teaching."

17:20-21: Luke makes it clear that Paul is not on trial. He highlights rather the Athenian intellectual curiosity about novelty.

17:22-31: Paul's well-crafted speech can be outlined thus: vv. 22-23 introduction; vv. 24-25 the identity of the unknown god; vv. 26-27 the immanence of this creator god; vv. 28-29 the relationship of this god to human beings; vv. 30-31 conclusion—this god will judge through the risen Jesus.

17:22: Paul opens his speech with a customary comment intended to flatter the audience into paying serious attention (a gambit called *captatio benevolentiae*). In the ancient world, Athens had the reputation of being very devout, "the most pious of the Greeks" (Josephus, *Against Apion* 2.11 §130). The word might also mean superstition and may have been so intended when Luke placed the phrase on Paul's lips.

17:23: No such altar and inscription have been discovered in Greece. But there are inscriptions to "unknown gods." Luke may have changed the familiar plural to a singular for the henotheistic Paul to make his point about the God of Israel. But the God of Israel must surely have been already familiar to some Greeks. The Latin author Lucan speaks of "Judeans who pray before an unknown God . . ." (*Pharsalia* 2.668-69; c. 61-65 C.E.). Yet the fact that Israelites never used the actual Torah name of God undoubtedly indicated this was an unknown God. In line with Judean custom, instead of YHWH *elohim*, the Septuagint speaks of *kyrios ho theos* (the Lord God), a generic name and not a proper name for a god. Taking three key concepts widely known and commonly accepted (certainly by Stoics, but denied by Epicureans), Paul proceeds to demonstrate how the God of Israel is one who is honored but not yet fully understood by these Athenians. The concepts are: God

This altar with an inscribed dedication "To the Unknown Gods" was found in the Sanctuary of Demeter at Pergamum in northwest Asia Minor. The dedication is a unique parallel to the altar to the "Unknown God" in Athens, to which Paul refers in the Areopagus Speech (Acts 17:23). From Cities of Paul © 2004 The President and Fellows of Harvard College.

*The Areopagos is a rocky outcrop a short distance northwest of the Acropolis and above
the ancient Agora of Athens. See textual notes on Acts 17:19. From Cities of Paul © 2004
The President and Fellows of Harvard College.*

is creator (Acts 17:24), a benevolent creator who puts order into creation (17:26),
and one who will be a just judge (Acts 17:30). Such Stoic ideas would be warmly
welcomed by some in the audience.

17:24-25: God the creator does not need temples or sacrifices or anything made
by humans.

17:26-27: God the creator ordered all creation including humankind; God is
immanent, "not far from each one of us" (see Ps 145:18).

17:28-29: In Greek, the particle *for* that begins this sentence explains what has
just been previously said. How is God close to humans? The NRSV reports v. 28 as
a quotation and explains in a note that it is "sometimes attributed to Epimenides."
Contemporary scholarship prefers to recognize the sentence as a Lukan creation
reflecting a traditional and common pattern in the Greek language. Thus, the
quotation marks should be removed. The quotation from the Stoic poet Aratus
(*Phaenomena* 5) follows and asserts that humans are kin to God (see Psalm 139).
Luke, of course, traced Jesus' genealogy to Adam, "the son of God" (Luke 3:38). For
Luke, Israel's Torah indicates humans (Adam and his offspring) are kin to God.

17:30-31: Paul's speech concludes with an exhortation to repentance (see
also Acts 2:38; 3:19; 14:15) because this "unknown God" will render judgment,
and ignorance will no longer be an excuse (Acts 3:17; 13:27). The risen Jesus will
execute divine judgment.

17:32: The mixed response to Paul's message is, of course, by now familiar in
Acts. As Luke correctly notes, those who scoffed did so at hearing of a resurrected
being and not at Paul's theology, which was quite in harmony with Hellenistic

thought about the deity. Others whose interest was piqued hoped to hear more at another time, yet even they were not eager to set another date.

17:34: Some of these listeners became believers, and two are named: Dionysius and Damaris, both otherwise unknown. The meager response is plausible given Paul's message. Since he basically echoes Hellenistic theology, why would any non-Israelite want to change? While the Stoics were interested in the foreign deities they assumed he was introducing (see v. 18 above), most needed to hear more later. The question remains about those who joined Paul: were they non-Israelites? Or were they assimilated Israelites? We opt for the latter conclusion since so far in the story line, those were the only ones who joined the Jesus groups. The assimilated Israelites who joined Paul were likely so assimilated that they did not visit the meeting place (synagogue) very often or at all.

Witnessing in Corinth Acts 18:1-18

18:1 After this Paul left Athens and went to Corinth. 2 There he found a Jew named Aquila, a native of Pontus, who had recently come from Italy with his wife Priscilla, because Claudius had ordered all Jews to leave Rome. Paul went to see them, 3 and, because he was of the same trade, he stayed with them, and they worked together—by trade they were tentmakers. 4 Every sabbath he would argue in the synagogue and would try to convince Jews and Greeks.

5 When Silas and Timothy arrived from Macedonia, Paul was occupied with proclaiming the word, testifying to the Jews that the Messiah was Jesus. 6 When they opposed and reviled him, in protest he shook the dust from his clothes and said to them, "Your blood be on your own heads! I am innocent. From now on I will go to the Gentiles." 7 Then he left the synagogue and went to the house of a man named Titius Justus, a worshiper of God; his house was next door to the synagogue. 8 Crispus, the official of the synagogue, became a believer in the Lord, together with all his household; and many of the Corinthians who heard Paul became believers and were baptized. 9 One night the Lord said to Paul in a vision,

"Do not be afraid, but speak and do not be silent; 10 for I am with you, and no one will lay a hand on you to harm you, for there are many in this city who are my people." 11 He stayed there a year and six months, teaching the word of God among them.

12 But when Gallio was proconsul of Achaia, the Jews made a united attack on Paul and brought him before the tribunal. 13 They said, "This man is persuading people to worship God in ways that are contrary to the law." 14 Just as Paul was about to speak, Gallio said to the Jews, "If it were a matter of crime or serious villainy, I would be justified in accepting the complaint of you Jews; 15 but since it is a matter of questions about words and names and your own law, see to it yourselves; I do not wish to be a judge of these matters." 16 And he dismissed them from the tribunal. 17 Then all of them seized Sosthenes, the official of the synagogue, and beat him in front of the tribunal. But Gallio paid no attention to any of these things. 18 After staying there for a considerable time, Paul said farewell to the believers and sailed for Syria, accompanied by Priscilla and Aquila. At Cenchreae he had his hair cut, for he was under a vow.

Textual Notes: Acts 18:1-18

18:1: Corinth is about thirty-six miles from Athens and is located between two ports: Cenchreae and Lechaion. Such a location highlights its very diverse population.

18:2: Aquila and his wife, Priscilla (in Acts; in the epistles, she is named Prisca), are assimilated Israelites. He was a native of Pontus on the Black Sea, and if his marriage was arranged with a relative according to cultural custom, she very likely was an assimilated Israelite from the same region. As such, they moved to and lived in Rome and then came to Corinth perhaps around 49 C.E., because of Claudius's edict ("all the Judeans" is likely Lukan hyperbole). This forcible emigration confirms that Aquila was not a Roman citizen.

18:3: In the ancient Mediterranean world, artisans lived in their respective quarters. Hence, tentmakers lived in one place, and Paul, who plied this trade, would very naturally seek out lodging there. We agree with Stegemann and Stegemann (1999:300) that by Paul's own testimony (1 Thess 2:9; 1 Cor 4:12; 2 Cor 11:7) he worked hard, day and night, with fellow tradespersons for a daily wage in workshops.

18:4-5: On the Sabbath, he would join other Israelites in the community center or meeting place (NRSV: synagogue) and strive to convince both the observant (Judean) and assimilated (Greek) Israelites that Jesus was Israel's expected and awaited Messiah, as indicated by his being raised from the dead by the God of Israel. Eventually, Silas and Timothy arrived from Macedonia, presumably with aid (2 Cor 11:8-9). NRSV "argued" (v. 4) is probably too strong. It would be preferable to translate the term as "reasoned," that is, to think or reason carefully. This is confirmed in v. 5, where Paul is described as "totally absorbed in [proclaiming] the word" and witnessing that Israel's Messiah was Jesus (compare Acts 17:3).

18:6: When the people in the meeting place opposed and insulted him, Paul shook his cloak at them, a symbolic action (without words) of protest and total repudiation that signals breaking off a relationship. Luke told his audience of this ritual previously in Acts 13:51, after the advice of Jesus (in Luke 9:5; 10:11). Then he announced that they shall be held accountable for refusing to accept Jesus as Messiah: "Your blood be on your own heads" (see 2 Sam 1:16; Matt 27:25).

Who are these "Gentiles" (NRSV) to whom Paul is going? As we have argued in our commentary on Paul's undisputed letters (Malina and Pilch 2006: 5–7), Israelite ingroups use the Greek word translated "Gentiles" (*ethnē*) to refer to "people's other than us Israelites." But an ingroup member going among those "peoples other than us" is in reality going to fellow ingroup members residing among "the peoples other than us." Henceforth, Paul will continue to speak to fellow ingroup members but not primarily at the meeting place (synagogue). In fact, in the rest of Acts, Paul enters such a place only twice (Acts 18:19; 19:8), and in the latter case only after he has presumably met Israelite believers in Jesus Messiah elsewhere.

18:7: Confirmation of this is that Paul goes to the home of Titius Justus, an assimilated Israelite, who does not care to attend the meeting place. This is interesting, since his home is adjacent to the meeting place, obviously in the Israelite quarter of the city. Paul intentionally does not venture far from the meeting place.

18:8: Crispus, the president of the meeting place (NRSV: "official of the synagogue"), put his faith in God (probably the better referent for Lord; see Acts 16:34), the one who raised Jesus from the dead and made him cosmic Lord and forthcoming Messiah. True to the nature of collectivistic cultures, his entire household joined him. So too did many other assimilated Israelites living in Corinth with whom Titius was very likely associated. They submitted to the ritual of Jesus group affiliation, baptism.

Standing columns from the Temple of Apollo at Corinth. The temple was built probably in the mid-sixth century B.C.E. *From* Cities of Paul © 2004 *The President and Fellows of Harvard College.*

18:9-11: Luke notes how Paul's activity was punctuated by a vision, described in terms of a common literary pattern of "command and fulfillment." The command is outfitted with a reason for the encouragement not to be silent and a reason for the command to speak (noted by the use of "for").

Introduction:	One night the Lord said to Paul in a vision: Do not be afraid (v. 9a);
Command:	but speak and do not be silent (v. 9b);
Encouragement (to not be silent):	for I am with you, and no one will lay a hand on you to harm you (v. 10a);
Reason for the command (to speak):	for there are many in this city who are my people (v. 10b);
Fulfillment:	He stayed there a year and six months, teaching the word of God among them (v. 11).

18:9: As is very common in Mediterranean cultures (and in the Bible in general), Paul receives assurance about his decision in an ASC experience. **Alternate States of Consciousness**. NRSV translates "vision" but it could be a dream, one of more than thirty-five identified ASCs. The Greek word occurs in Acts 7:31; 9:10; 10:3, 17, 19; 11:5; 12:9; 16:9, 10, all but one (7:31) translated vision. Paul understands the message to come from the risen Jesus, who encourages him to speak boldly and not to be intimidated. In the literary form of ASCs, the advice "fear not" is intended to calm the visionary and is usually followed by self-identification of the being who is appearing. Paul knows who is speaking to him.

18:10: The motivation for speaking boldly is that Jesus promises to be with Paul. "Being with" is a phrase in the Old Testament that describes God aiding "his people" (Gen 21:22; 26:3; 31:3, 5; Exod 3:12, and the like). This is but one of a number of ASCs in the Lukan story line that give Paul assurance (Acts 18:9-10; 22:17-18; 23:11; 27:23-24). Jesus explains that no one will harm Paul, for many in the city will eventually join his group.

18:11: Thus assured, Paul fulfills the command and remains in Corinth eighteen months longer teaching "the word of God" about Jesus Messiah.

18:12: Gallio was proconsul for a short while, late spring to late autumn, 52 C.E. He was the older brother of the well-known philosopher Seneca. Once more, aggrieved and hostile Judeans take their conflict with Paul to the level of a dispute by hauling him before the tribunal. **Conflict Resolution.** It is preferable to think of the tribunal as a person rather than a place.

18:13: The charge against Paul as stated by localite Judeans was somewhat ambiguous. Which law was Paul violating: Roman or Israelite? No known Roman law would apply to Paul and his activity among fellow Judeans. If he is accused of violating Israelite law, that would be an internal problem. Perhaps the Israelite resident aliens (almost certainly not Corinthian citizens) were hoping that Gallio would think that Paul was promoting something "new" and distinct from Judaism, a way of worship and behavior (that is, a religion) that Rome could not legally accept. If that were the case, Gallio either misunderstood or deliberately misinterpreted the charge. He viewed it as an ingroup matter (see v. 15: "your own law").

18:14: Gallio sees through the ambiguity and speaks before Paul could begin to defend himself. He does not consider Paul's activity to be a crime or serious villainy; that is, Paul has not transgressed any Roman law.

18:15-16: He sees the problem as entirely internal to the Judean community. The dispute about words could point to differing Israelite views on "worshiping God" (v. 13). Assimilated and more observant Israelites held divergent views regarding circumcision and/or clean and unclean foods. "Names" could means "titles," for example, that Jesus is or is not the Messiah. These matters belong properly to the law of Moses and its interpretation, not Roman law. So Gallio dismisses the case.

18:17: In frustration and in dishonor, those denied a hearing by Gallio pounce on the leader of their meeting place, Sosthenes, and beat him in plain sight of Gallio, who paid no heed. They blame their dishonor on Sosthenes and take out satisfaction for their dishonor on that community leader.

18:18: The result was that Paul stayed even longer before bidding farewell to his fellow Jesus group members. In the company of Priscilla and Aquila, he set sail for Syria. Before his departure from the Corinthian port of Cenchreae, Paul cut his hair "because he was under a vow." So far in Luke's account, nothing is said of any vow (see Acts 21:23). Scholars debate the significance of this event.

Vows belong to the Hellenistic approach to the gods, which was a sort of nothing-ventured nothing-gained attitude, especially in situations of need. A vow is at bottom a deal with a deity. A vow is a promise to a deity to perform or refrain from performing some action provided the deity perform or refrain from performing some corresponding action. The behavior entailed in this approach was called a vow. Vows were a sort of *do ut des* contract, taken in the same spirit as such vows are taken today in the Mediterranean, witness the countless votive (= vow) offerings in countless churches in the region. Pachomius the monk, for example, when he was held in close custody against draft-dodging, promised the deity that if were freed from this obligation, he would serve God's will all the days of his life. Emperor Constantine did much the same after his alternate state of consciousness vision of a celestial Jesus group sign. Was Paul's behavior the fulfillment of a vow according to Israelite tradition (see Num 6:9, 19)? Or does it reflect the standard Greek cultural reaction to an ASC (dream) through which a person received divine guidance (see Juvenal, *Satirae* 12:81f.)? In either case, it further highlights Paul's devotedness to the God of Israel.

Witnessing in Ephesus Acts 18:19—19:41

Apollos Witnesses in Ephesus Acts 18:19-28

18:19 When they reached Ephesus, he left them there, but first he himself went into the synagogue and had a discussion with the Jews. 20 When they asked him to stay longer, he declined; 21 but on taking leave of them, he said, "I will return to you, if God wills." Then he set sail from Ephesus.

22 When he had landed at Caesarea, he went up to Jerusalem and greeted the church, and then went down to Antioch. 23 After spending some time there he departed and went from place to place through the region of Galatia and Phrygia, strengthening all the disciples.

24 Now there came to Ephesus a Jew named Apollos, a native of Alexandria. He was an eloquent man, well-versed in the scriptures. 25 He had been instructed in the Way of the Lord; and he spoke with burning enthusiasm and taught accurately the things concerning Jesus, though he knew only the baptism of John. 26 He began to speak boldly in the synagogue; but when Priscilla and Aquila heard him, they took him aside and explained the Way of God to him more accurately. 27 And when he wished to cross over to Achaia, the believers encouraged him and wrote to the disciples to welcome him. On his arrival he greatly helped those who through grace had become believers, 28 for he powerfully refuted the Jews in public, showing by the scriptures that the Messiah is Jesus.

Textual Notes: Acts 18:19-28

18:19: Paul continues his efforts among Israelite minorities living in non-Israelite regions. He goes to the meeting place (synagogue) in Ephesus to engage in discussion.

18:20: It is curious that Paul declines the invitation to stay longer. To suggest that this would interfere with Paul's plans is not a Mediterranean plausibility. These cultures are spontaneous and respond to a current cue even if it thwarts a different intention. Perhaps the invitation was given only once, or was not sufficiently insistent.

The Bema, the Court of Justice on the Forum of Corinth, where Paul was brought before Gallio (Acts 18:12-17). Acrocorinth in the background. Location: Corinth, Greece. Photo © Erich Lessing / Art Resource, N.Y.

18:21: The phrase "if God wills" is as frequent in the New Testament (1 Cor 4:19; 16:7; Heb 6:3; Jas 4:15) as it is common in the ancient (Plato, *Alcibiades* I.31 135d; Epictetus 1.1.17; Josephus, *Antiquities* 2.333; 7.373) and contemporary Middle Eastern world (Arabic: *In sha'a 'llah*). It is not a cliche, but rather an acknowledgment of the deity as the one who is ultimately in charge of and directs all human existence. Paul recognizes that God directs his travels. This curious trip from Ephesus to Caesarea and Jerusalem and on to Antioch serves no purpose in the story except to show Paul maintaining good relations with Jesus groups in communities which he himself did not found. Perhaps his fulfilling his vow in Jerusalem fits here (and not in Acts 21:23).

18:23: On the other hand, his departure from Antioch and his going "from place to place through the region of Galatia and Phrygia, strengthening all the disciples" is the typical and required behavior of a change agent to maintain an information exchange relationship and to stabilize and prevent discontinuance of the innovation he proclaimed there. **Change Agent.** After this detour, Luke turns to Apollos in Ephesus and picks up Paul in the same city later in Acts 19:1.

18:24-28: Mentions of the Scriptures in vv. 24 and 28 form an inclusion marking off a literary unit that deals with Apollos. Apollos was a traveling Israelite from Alexandria who arrived in Ephesus to proclaim Jesus as Israel's Messiah (see vv. 25 and 28). It seems he was familiar with the early story of Jesus only in relation to the proclamation and baptism of John. Again it is noteworthy that, like

Paul, Apollos too spreads his message among other Israelites in their meeting place (synagogue). "Way of the Lord" (v. 25) is likely in parallelism with "way of God" (v. 26); hence it describes what the God of Israel has done in Jesus and will do with the forthcoming Israelite theocracy. While Apollos had a basic grasp of the word of God, Priscilla and Aquila explain it to him more fully and accurately. It is also important to note that these fellow disciples of Paul are apparently also in the Israelite meeting place, the principal locus of all proclamation and teaching about Jesus.

To facilitate Apollos's desire to go to Achaia and make his proclamation to Israelite minorities there, the Ephesian believers give him a letter of recommendation (an important Jesus group practice [2 Cor 3:1; Rom 16:1; Col 4:10]). Such letters were essential in the ancient Mediterranean world, where once a person left the home village, life itself was always at risk. Hospitality (extended exclusively to strangers) was the cultural strategy for providing safe passage, but it depended on the availability of a person who could extend it. **Hospitality.** This letter would assure fictive kin (fellow believers) in other regions that this traveler (a stranger to them) was deserving of hospitality and did not have to be "tested" according to the cultural rules of extending hospitality.

18:28: Apollos has already been identified as an inspired speaker (v. 25, "fervent in spirit"). Now in Corinth he exhorts Messianists and publicly shames those Israelites who have not accepted Jesus as Messiah. This he does by demonstrating from Scripture that the Messiah they await is none other than Jesus.

Paul Incorporates the Baptist Faction into the Jesus Movement in Ephesus
Acts 19:1-7

19:1 While Apollos was in Corinth, Paul passed through the interior regions and came to Ephesus, where he found some disciples. 2 He said to them, "Did you receive the Holy Spirit when you became believers?" They replied, "No, we have not even heard that there is a Holy Spirit." 3 Then he said, "Into what then were you baptized?" They answered, "Into John's baptism." 4 Paul said, "John baptized with the baptism of repentance, telling the people to believe in the one who was to come after him, that is, in Jesus." 5 On hearing this, they were baptized in the name of the Lord Jesus. 6 When Paul had laid his hands on them, the Holy Spirit came upon them, and they spoke in tongues and prophesied—7 altogether there were about twelve of them.

Textual Notes: Acts 19:1-7

This section follows an A B C C' B' A' pattern. A (v. 1, some disciples) = A' (v. 7, twelve disciples). B (v. 2, Spirit not received) = B' (v. 6, Spirit came upon them). C (vv. 3-4, John pointed to Jesus) = C' (v. 5, John's disciples baptized in the name of Jesus).

19:1: The interior regions (literally, "upper regions") are the mountainous, inland part of Asia Minor, most likely the upper regions of Galatia and Phrygia (see Acts 18:23). Arriving at Ephesus, Paul meets some Jesus group disciples, that is, believers in Jesus as Israel's forthcoming Messiah.

19:2: For Jesus groups, receiving the Spirit signaled genuine ingroup belonging (Acts 2:38; 4:31; 6:3, 5; 7:55; 8:15-16, 19; 9:17; 10:44; 11:15-16; 13:9). These disciples claim not even to have heard about the Spirit, the experience of which was bound up with the proclamation of the gospel of God and subsequent baptism.

19:3-5: Since these disciples were baptized with only the baptism of repentance proclaimed and practiced by John, Paul baptizes them now with the baptism of Jesus, the forthcoming Messiah, with a view to experiencing the Holy Spirit.

19:6: Imposing his hands on them, Paul endows them with God's gift of the Holy Spirit (see Acts 6:6; 8:17) whose presence is confirmed by their spontaneous ecstatic speech ("tongues") and prophecies (compare Acts 10:44-46). In other words, these disciples enter into an alternate state of consciousness. **Alternate States of Consciousness**. This is the normal context for contact with the spirit world.

Paul Witnesses in Ephesus Acts 19:8-22

19:8 He entered the synagogue and for three months spoke out boldly, and argued persuasively about the kingdom of God. 9 When some stubbornly refused to believe and spoke evil of the Way before the congregation, he left them, taking the disciples with him, and argued daily in the lecture hall of Tyrannus. 10 This continued for two years, so that all the residents of Asia, both Jews and Greeks, heard the word of the Lord.

11 God did extraordinary miracles through Paul, 12 so that when the handkerchiefs or aprons that had touched his skin were brought to the sick, their diseases left them, and the evil spirits came out of them. 13 Then some itinerant Jewish exorcists tried to use the name of the Lord Jesus over those who had evil spirits, saying, "I adjure you by the Jesus whom Paul proclaims." 14 Seven sons of a Jewish high priest named Sceva were doing this. 15 But the evil spirit said to them in reply, "Jesus I know, and Paul I know; but who are you?" 16 Then the man with the evil spirit leaped on them, mastered them all, and so overpowered them that they fled out of the house naked and wounded. 17 When this became known to all residents of Ephesus, both Jews and Greeks, everyone was awestruck; and the name of the Lord Jesus was praised. 18 Also many of those who became believers confessed and disclosed their practices. 19 A number of those who practiced magic collected their books and burned them publicly; when the value of these books was calculated, it was found to come to fifty thousand silver coins. 20 So the word of the Lord grew mightily and prevailed.

21 Now after these things had been accomplished, Paul resolved in the Spirit to go through Macedonia and Achaia, and then to go on to Jerusalem. He said, "After I have gone there, I must also see Rome." 22 So he sent two of his helpers, Timothy and Erastus, to Macedonia, while he himself stayed for some time longer in Asia.

Textual Notes: Acts 19:8-22

This episode can be read in three distinct sections: vv. 8-12 summarize Paul's activity in Ephesus for a few months; vv. 13-16 recount his encounter with the sons of Sceva; and vv. 17-20 report the reaction of the Ephesians to this incident and to Paul's proclamation.

19:8: The heart of Paul's message to fellow Israelites is the forthcoming Israelite political religious theocracy (= kingdom of God; see Acts 1:3). The risen Jesus is coming soon as Israel's Messiah with power, and that will mark God's inauguration of that theocracy. The topic does not occur frequently as an explicit one in Paul's letters (1 Thess 2:12; 5:1ff.; Gal 5:21; 1 Cor 4:20; 6:9-10; 15:24, 50; Rom 14:17), perhaps because it was a focal topic in the original proclamation of the gospel of God. The letters are a follow up, not the first proclamation. The mentions of the kingdom in the letters is usually drawn from tradition. Kingdom of God is, however, central to Jesus' proclamation in the Synoptic tradition and occurs sporadically in Acts (8:12; 14:22; 19:8; 20:25; 28:23, 31).

19:9-10: The majority of the males in the community center (synagogue) reject Paul's message, but, worse than that, they publicly bad-mouth "the Way." This bad-mouthing is dishonoring as well as a threat to poison the minds not only of Jesus group members but also of others who might be interested in the Way. The gossip network in this culture can be very damaging. Instead of riposting, Paul withdraws with his disciples and believers and meets with them daily during the next two years (54-56 C.E.) in the lecture hall of Tyrannus. The locale is a meeting place for teachers and students; thus, Paul is instructing primarily disciples. News of his instruction spread among Israelite groups throughout the entire Roman province. "Jews and Greeks" as reported consistently in this commentary should be interpreted as two types of Israelites: Judeans who conserved and closely observed the customs of Judea, and Greeks who were Hellenized and assimilated in various degrees to the customs of Hellenism. Non-Israelites are not involved at all.

19:11: The Greek word translated by the anachronistic English term "miracles" (a post-Enlightenment word) literally is "powers, powerful deeds." Luke describes these deeds as "not ordinary." While NRSV "extraordinary" appears to be a reasonable translation, the literary Greek phrase occurs in Hellenistic literature to indicate something special or uncommon (for example, Artemidorus 2.13)—hence, in this case special, uncommon powerful deeds. Notice that God is the agent, not Paul. By means of these powerful deeds, God authenticates the work of his agents (see Rom 15:18-19).

19:12: The mention of the mighty deeds accomplished by God by means of "handkerchiefs or aprons [or belts]" touched to Paul, or the fringe of Jesus' garment (Luke 6:19 and 8:44), or Peter's shadow (Acts 5:15) introduces magic into the discussion. Scholars in many disciplines are not agreed on the definition of magic, although most would agree that magic is the attempt to control a celestial power by means of some ritual procedure. One accepted characteristic of the label "magic" is that it serves as a pejorative description of the worship activity of "others" which differs from "ours." For example, when "we" address God with repeated words of a litany, that is, prayer; when "they" do so, it is a magic incantation. Similarly, "our" (Israelite) mighty deeds are ascribed to Yahweh-God as agent. Mighty deeds performed by "others" are magic and not attributable to our God, Yahweh. The belief here is that the power to perform a mighty deed is bestowed by God upon some person, and that power is so strong that it can be transmitted by materials associated with the person such as handkerchiefs, belts, garment fringes, or other articles of clothing. The shadow is a different matter (see Acts 5:15). In antiquity, the shadow was considered to be a person's or animal's soul, life force, doppelgänger, or alter ego. It is possible to harm another person by working violence on his or her shadow. So Peter's shadow is his alter ego empowered by God to work mighty deeds.

Paul's mighty deeds had two effects. Sick people were restored to well-being, and the spirit-possessed were freed from malicious spirits. It is anachronistic to speak of diseases before the invention of the microscope—not to mention other technology by which organic malfunctions or infective agents invisible to the naked eye can be seen and identified. Since every significant effect in the ancient world was believed to require a personal cause, if no human agent could be identified, then the agent must have been other-than-human, that is, a spirit or demon. Spirits were part and parcel of ancient reality, that is, part of the "natural" order. They were not "supernatural."

19:13: Many in the ancient world (including Israelites) had power over spirits (recall Jesus' comment in Luke 11:19).

19:14: Previously we learned of the Israelite magician and prophet Bar Jesus (Elymas; Acts 13:8), blinded by the holy man Paul. Here seven brother priests, sons of a Judean high priest, attempt to perform an exorcism in the name of Jesus, although they were not Jesus group members. It was also common for exorcists in one tradition to use names known to be effective in another tradition. Origen (*Contra Celsum* 1.22) tells of non-Israelite exorcists who used the names of Solomon and of Jesus in their rituals (see among the magical papyri, *PGM* IV.3019-20: "I conjure you by the god of the Hebrews, Jesus . . .").

19:15-16: The attempt in this present instance, however, backfires on the exorcists. The possessed person overpowers them, causing them to flee naked and bruised. In other words, the shame of their failure is manifested in their naked flight! Other scholars suggest that nakedness indicates a broken relationship (Gen 3:7; 9:22-23; Luke 8:27). The reason that Luke gives for this failure is that the power exhibited by Paul is not a commodity (as in the story of Simon of Samaria; Acts 8:18) but rather the consequence of a personal relationship with the empowering one, in this instance, the risen Jesus. As a consequence, the would-be exorcists are ejected and isolated from the believing community. They have not been authentically authorized to attempt exorcisms in the name of Jesus.

19:17-20: The outcomes of this event are manifold. First, all the observant Israelites (NRSV: "Jews") and assimilated Israelites (NRSV: "Greeks") were awed when they heard of it, and their appreciation for the power of the name (= the person of the risen Jesus) grew immensely. This is a reference to honor, reputation. Second, many believers who were still hedging their bets by seeking to balance faith in Jesus with reliance on magic confessed and repented of this ambivalence. But, as scholars note, despite this external behavior many in antiquity continued to believe in magic. Third, some burned their magic books in public as an expression of their renunciation of their former way of life (but recall the previous comment and that most could not read such books anyway). Fourth, the word continued to spread with the power of the Lord. Still, magic continued to be a temptation among early Jesus groups. Justin Martyr as late as

165 writes: "we who formerly used magical arts, dedicate ourselves to the good and unbegotten God" (*1 Apology* 14).

19:21-22: These verses deal with travel plans, preparing Luke's audience for events to come. Paul resolved to remain in Ephesus for a while before heading toward Macedonia and Achaia, then to Jerusalem, and eventually on to Rome. (The word "spirit" here does not involve any spirit at all, and contrary to the NRSV should be lower case. One might translate it "mentally." Compare Acts 5:4 relative to "heart.") He sent advance men ahead of him to Macedonia: Timothy and Erastus. These verses, together with Acts 20:1-3, serve to bracket the report about the riot in Ephesus that follows. They form an inclusion.

In addition, Acts 19:21—21:17 has its matching scene in Luke 9:51—19:28. Paul and Jesus each make a journey to Jerusalem that is a passion journey under divine necessity and is characterized by their associates' lack of understanding. Specifically, Acts 19:21 reports Paul's resolve to go to Jerusalem echoing Jesus' determination to go to Jerusalem (Luke 9:51, 53).

Riotous Response to Paul's Witness in Ephesus Acts 19:23-41

19:23 About that time no little disturbance broke out concerning the Way. 24 A man named Demetrius, a silversmith who made silver shrines of Artemis, brought no little business to the artisans. 25 These he gathered together, with the workers of the same trade, and said, "Men, you know that we get our wealth from this business. 26 You also see and hear that not only in Ephesus but in almost the whole of Asia this Paul has persuaded and drawn away a considerable number of people by saying that gods made with hands are not gods. 27 And there is danger not only that this trade of ours may come into disrepute but also that the temple of the great goddess Artemis will be scorned, and she will be deprived of her majesty that brought all Asia and the world to worship her."

28 When they heard this, they were enraged and shouted, "Great is Artemis of the Ephesians!" 29 The city was filled with the confusion; and people rushed together to the theater, dragging with them Gaius and Aristarchus, Macedonians who were Paul's travel companions. 30 Paul wished to go into the crowd, but the disciples would not let him; 31 even some officials of the province of Asia, who were friendly to him, sent him a message urging him not to venture into the theater. 32 Meanwhile, some were shouting one thing, some another; for the assembly was in confusion, and most of them did not know why they had come together. 33 Some of the crowd gave instructions to Alexander, whom the Jews had pushed forward. And Alexander motioned for silence and tried to make a defense before the people. 34 But when they recognized that he was a Jew, for about two hours all of them shouted in unison, "Great is Artemis of the Ephesians!" 35 But when the town clerk had quieted the crowd, he said, "Citizens of Ephesus, who is there that does not know that the city of the Ephesians is the temple keeper of the great Artemis and of the statue that fell from heaven? 36 Since these things cannot be denied, you ought to be quiet and do nothing rash. 37 You have brought these men here who are neither temple robbers nor blasphemers of our goddess. 38 If therefore Demetrius and the artisans with him have a complaint against anyone, the courts are open, and there are proconsuls; let them bring charges there against one another. 39 If there is anything further you want to know, it must be settled in the regular assembly. 40 For we are in danger of being charged with rioting today, since there is no cause that we can give to justify this commotion." 41 When he had said this, he dismissed the assembly.

Textual Notes: Acts 19:23-41

This section has three parts: the cause of the riot (vv. 23-27); the riot itself (vv. 28-34); and the official response to the riot (vv. 35-41).

19:24-27: Modern scholars like to note that the cult of Artemis of Ephesus was syncretistic, since this goddess had little in common with Artemis of earlier Greek religion. She was fused with the older Phrygian Cybele or the Phoenician Astarte. All such historical niceties were of no concern to her first-century devotees. Her temple at Ephesus, the Artemision, was one of the seven wonders of the ancient world. Begun in the eighth century B.C.E., it was expanded about 550 B.C.E. but burned on the night Alexander the Great was born in 356 B.C.E. Its replacement was begun in 350 B.C.E.

Since in the ancient world religion as a social institution was embedded in kinship and politics, Paul's preaching that diminished the importance of Artemis and her temple was viewed as a political act, a challenge to political religion (like the political religious temple and its activities in Israel). Moreover, since economics, too, was not a freestanding social institution but was similarly embedded in kinship and politics, Demetrius and his fellow artisans' grievance against Paul concerned the damage to the political economy wrought by Paul's speeches (which in turn affected their domestic economic life). Demetrius's problem, of course, was with the effect of Paul's teaching among assimilated (= Hellenistic) Israelite worshipers who forsook Artemis to return to fidelity to the God of Israel and Israel's Messiah, Jesus. They ceased contributing to the temple of Artemis (Tertullian, *Apology* 42). Moreover, those who accepted Jesus as Messiah ceased purchasing silver amulets and sacrificial animals (Pliny, *Letters to Trajan* 10.96). If Paul is allowed to continue such teaching, pilgrimages will end and both the worship and businesses associated with the temple would slacken. The influence of Paul's proclamation extended widely in Asia. Artemis would suffer loss of honor (majesty, grandeur, reputation).

19:28-34: This section is bracketed by the phrase "Great is Artemis of the Ephesians!" Though it is clear why the artisans were enraged, there seems to be no reason for the citizenry who joined them other than that this is how riots in collectivistic cultures work. Even if the grievance is not known, it is imperative to support the fellow member(s) of a group who has/have the grievance. The same reasoning explains why Paul's travel companions would be dragged into the theater. They are considered as guilty as Paul, who upon hearing of their capture wanted to appear in the theater. Some scholars think Paul's spontaneous desire to go to the theater may have been to "evangelize" twenty-four thousand people in the theater. Given that he had no interest in non-Israelites, this is hardly likely. In such a culture, people act first and think later. Thus, it is more plausible that Paul wanted to rescue his fellow workers. True to Middle Eastern custom, others (disciples and friendly Asiarchs) intervened to prevent Paul's foolhardy, spontaneous, emotional, and potentially dangerous reaction to the fate of his travel companions. While free expression of emotions and spontaneity are normal circum-Mediterranean cultural

The "Beautiful Artemis" statue is one of three nearly complete statues of Artemis found in the Prytaneion in the agora in Ephesus and indicates the connection of the site with the worship of Artemis. From Cities of Paul © 2004 *The President and Fellows of Harvard College.*

reactions, these cultures also expect cooler heads in the group to intervene and keep the person from harming him or herself.

Alexander the Israelite, who likely wished to assure the crowd that Paul the troublemaker and his disciples should not be identified with himself and the Israelite minorities in their midst, was shouted down. Contrary to scholars who view this behavior as evidence of Ephesian anti-Semitism, it is preferable to interpret the crowd's behavior as a manifestation of the agonistic nature of Hellenistic culture. The crowd's grievance concerned blasphemy (discrediting Artemis and her temple) and the consequent loss of employment and income by the craftsmen. The crowd did not distinguish between Paul and his group and other Israelites. They were all considered assimilated Israelites, but suspiciously. Paul's teaching, however, now made it clear to the crowd that visiting Hellenistic Israelites were not really members of the larger ingroup (the majority population); hence they were all potential troublemakers.

19:35-41: After two hours of rioting and shouting, the crowd is silenced by the town clerk, who brings closure to the event. He begins by reminding the crowd that Artemis's reputation is solidly established and recognized. It cannot be denied. Second, Paul and his colleagues are not temple robbers (a serious crime), nor have they insulted the goddess by their teaching. The suspicion of blasphemy is baseless! Josephus confirms this judgment (*Against Apion* 2.237): "Our legislator has expressly forbidden us to deride or blaspheme the gods recognized by others, out of respect for the very word 'God.'" Third, anyone who has a serious grievance and can make a case of it should take it to the regular assembly or official court. The crowd in the theater is an illegal gathering. The final obvious statement ("we are in danger of being charged with rioting") is serious and not intended as a joke. Although the riot took place for at least two hours, obviously no one charged the city rioters. Rome would impose serious penalties for riots. The episode ends peaceably with Gaius and Aristarchus being set free.

Stabilizing Change in the Communities Acts 20:1–21:26

One of Paul's tasks as a change agent was to stabilize the changes he introduced and to prevent discontinuation of any part of it. **Change Agent.** Any reading of Paul's authentic letters reveals that the innovations he introduced to the communities produced at least two results: the people joining Jesus groups experienced the dissonance bound up with accepting the new and rejecting the old; and Paul himself faced challenges from change agents in competition with Paul (usually called "Judaizers"). The principal tool Paul used in order to firm up stability was to direct reinforcing messages to those who adopted the innovation. This kind of activity characterized Paul's travels described in this section of Acts.

Travel Summary Acts 20:1-6

20:1 After the uproar had ceased, Paul sent for the disciples; and after encouraging them and saying farewell, he left for Macedonia. 2 When he had gone through those regions and had given the believers much encouragement, he came to Greece, 3 where he stayed for three months. He was about to set sail for Syria when a plot was made against him by the Jews, and so he decided to return through Macedonia. 4 He was accompanied by Sopater son of Pyrrhus from Beroea, by Aristarchus and Secundus from Thessalonica, by Gaius from Derbe, and by Timothy, as well as by Tychicus and Trophimus from Asia. 5 They went ahead and were waiting for us in Troas; 6 but we sailed from Philippi after the days of Unleavened Bread, and in five days we joined them in Troas, where we stayed for seven days.

Textual Notes: Acts 20:1-6

20:1-2: Paul's encouragement should be understood in the sense of his intending to stabilize the change he introduced throughout the regions of Macedonia perhaps visiting Philippi, Thessalonica, Beroea, and settling finally in Corinth for three months (probably winter 57-58 C.E.).

20:2: This is the only time the word *Greece* (Greek: *Hellas*) appears in the entire New Testament. At the time of Luke, there was no national entity or country called "Greece" as there is today. The referent of Luke's "Greece" is probably the region frequently referred to as "Achaia."

20:3: The plot hatched by fellow Israelites against Paul was likely in response to the innovation that he proclaimed. We are not told how he learned of the plot, but that knowledge prompted Paul to cancel his trip by sea and to travel overland instead.

20:4: It is not important to identify precisely who Paul's travel companions were so much as to appreciate that as a collectivistic personality in a collectivistic culture Paul and his companions needed one another for far more than companionship. Scholars hypothesize that these men represented communities Paul founded and carried with themselves the collection they were delivering to Jerusalem. As such they formed a fictive kin group, a brotherhood. The number seven could be arbitrary or chosen to symbolize all the Israelite minority groups living outside of Palestine.

20:5: The second of four "we" sections begins here (Acts 16:10-17; 20:5-15; 21:1-18; 27:1—28:16). These sections seem to be part of a diary or travel notes kept by a some literate co-worker of Paul who occasionally journeyed with Paul (in the 50s). We hypothesized that the writer of those travel notes was Silvanus (Silas), Timothy, or Titus, persons of great significance in Pauline letters but mentioned little (Timothy) or not at all (Titus) in Acts. Yet all three were significant in Paul's authentic letters either as co-writers or close collaborators or both. Luke incorporated these recollections into Acts when he composed that work (in the third generation after Paul).

20:6: While the seven waited for Paul and colleagues in Troas, the latter stayed in Philippi to celebrate the feast of Passover with fellow Israelites. At this time it was a seven- or eight-day feast (Exod 12:17-20). They left from Neapolis and, after a five-day sail, arrived in Troas, where they spent seven days.

In Troas, Paul Works a Mighty Deed Acts 20:7-12

20:7 On the first day of the week, when we met to break bread, Paul was holding a discussion with them; since he intended to leave the next day, he continued speaking until midnight. 8 There were many lamps in the room upstairs where we were meeting. 9 A young man named Eutychus, who was sitting in the window, began to sink off into a deep sleep while Paul talked still longer. Overcome by sleep, he fell to the ground three floors below and was picked up dead. 10 But Paul went down, and bending over him took him in his arms, and said, "Do not be alarmed, for his life is in him." 11 Then Paul went upstairs, and after he had broken bread and eaten, he continued to converse with them until dawn; then he left. 12 Meanwhile they had taken the boy away alive and were not a little comforted.

Textual Notes: Acts 20:7-12

20:7: Paul and colleagues gather with the believers to "break bread," Luke's phrase for "celebrate the Eucharist" in Acts (for example, Acts 2:42), during which Paul spoke at great length (until midnight). The Greek word that the NRSV translates as "holding a discussion" is Luke's favored word for describing Paul's exchanges with fellow Israelites in the community centers (Acts 17:2, 17; 18:4, 19; 19:8, 9; 20:7, 9; 24:12, 25). While some think it suggests the Socratic method, more likely that word describes the rabbinic style of agonistic argumentation. This would entail raised voices (= shouting), differences of opinion, disputation, individuals speaking at the same time, each one trying to impose his point of view, and the like.

While this evening Eucharist calls to mind the Last Supper of Jesus with his disciples (Luke 22:14, after sundown), Luke may be using this report for apologetic purposes. In the ancient Mediterranean world, meetings at night were highly suspect. Most of the time, they were associated with political conspiracy (for example, Cicero, *In Catalinam* 1.1; 3.5-6; Pliny, *Letters to Trajan* 10.96) or with human sacrifice (usually infants whose blood was allegedly shared by participants) and sexual immorality. The latter charges were commonly made by Greeks and Romans against each other, or against Judeans, and Judeans against Jesus groups, even one Jesus group against another (see Jude 12-13)! In other words, it was a common accusation widely bandied about. Thus Luke's story defends the Jesus group gathering by indicating the abundance of lamps in the meeting (v. 8), and a young boy is restored to life rather than killed and eaten (vv. 10, 12)!

20:8: Paul's restoration of the boy to life echoes similar events featuring Israelite holy men (Elijah, 1 Kgs 17:2; Elisha, 2 Kgs 4:34; Jesus, Luke 7:11-17; 8:40-42, 49-56; and Peter, Acts 9:36-43). Paul thus stands in the line of holy men, including Jesus and Peter. Moreover, he performs this deed during a eucharistic worship gathering, thereby legitimating Jesus group worship at this suspicious hour.

In Miletus, Paul Bids Farewell to Ephesian Elites Meeting Him There
Acts 20:13-38

20:13 We went ahead to the ship and set sail for Assos, intending to take Paul on board there; for he had made this arrangement, intending to go by land himself. 14 When he met us in Assos, we took him on board and went to Mitylene. 15 We sailed from there, and on the following day we arrived opposite Chios. The next day we touched at Samos, and the day after that we came to Miletus. 16 For Paul had decided to sail past Ephesus, so that he might not have to spend time in Asia; he was eager to be in Jerusalem, if possible, on the day of Pentecost.

17 From Miletus he sent a message to Ephesus, asking the elders of the church to meet him. 18 When they came to him, he said to them:

"You yourselves know how I lived among you the entire time from the first day that I set foot in Asia, 19 serving the Lord with all humility and with tears, enduring the trials that came to me through the plots of the Jews. 20 I did not shrink from doing anything helpful, proclaiming the message to you and teaching you publicly and from house to house, 21 as I testified to both Jews and Greeks about repentance toward God and faith toward our Lord Jesus. 22 And now, as a captive to the Spirit, I am on my way to Jerusalem, not knowing what will happen to me there, 23 except that the Holy Spirit testifies to me in every city that imprisonment and persecutions are waiting for me. 24 But I do not count my life of any value to myself, if only I may finish my course and the ministry that I received from the Lord Jesus, to testify to the good news of God's grace.

25 And now I know that none of you, among whom I have gone about proclaiming the kingdom, will ever see my face again. 26 Therefore I declare to you this day that I am not responsible for the blood of any of you, 27 for I did not shrink from declaring to you the whole purpose of God. 28 Keep watch over yourselves and over all the flock, of which the Holy Spirit has made you overseers, to shepherd the church of God that he obtained with the blood of his own Son. 29 I know that after I have gone, savage wolves will come in among you, not sparing the flock. 30 Some even from your own group will come distorting the truth in order to entice the disciples to follow them. 31 Therefore be alert, remembering that for three years I did not cease night or day to warn everyone with tears. 32 And now I commend you to God and to the message of his grace, a message that is able to build you up and to give you the inheritance among all who are sanctified. 33 I coveted no one's silver or gold or clothing. 34 You know for yourselves that I worked with my own hands to support myself and my companions. 35 In all this I have given you an example that by such work we must support the weak, remembering the words of the Lord Jesus, for he himself said, 'It is more blessed to give than to receive.'"

36 When he had finished speaking, he knelt down with them all and prayed. 37 There was much weeping among them all; they embraced Paul and kissed him, 38 grieving especially because of what he had said, that they would not see him again. Then they brought him to the ship.

Textual Notes: Acts 20:13-38

This passage is significant in this story. Paul's command from God mediated through the resurrected Jesus to the prophet Ananias is that Paul is "to bring my name before/among Gentiles, both to kings and to the children of Israel" (Acts 9:15). His final words to Ephesian opinion leaders marks the end of his change agent activity among Judeans living among non-Israelites (see Acts 21:21). Now, led by the Spirit (Acts 20:22, "And now, as a captive to the Spirit"), he moves on to Jerusalem. The step will mark the first phase of his "bringing Jesus' name" before "kings," that is, political religious elites.

20:13-16: The passage opens with another travel summary in which the "we" section is concluded (v. 15). The point is that Paul is hastening toward Jerusalem hoping to arrive by Pentecost but necessarily making stops along the way. He arrives at Miletus, a port about thirty miles south of Ephesus, which overshadowed it.

20:17: Paul summons the opinion leaders of the Ephesian community. **Communication of Innovation.** Paul spent much time at Ephesus, the capital of the Roman province of Asia, and perhaps the Asian center of Jesus group activity. He asked the Ephesian leaders to meet him in Miletus, perhaps at the Israelite community center (synagogue) located close to the Harbor Stoa. There is a basilica type building (a nave flanked by two aisles) dating to the Roman period. The harbor on the Meander River has long been silted; the current city lies on a plain. Paul's decision not to go to Ephesus may have been based on his recollection of the violence he occasioned there not long ago.

Israelite communities recognized three types of elders: teaching elders (for example, Mark 7:5, 13); ruling elders (Luke 7:3, 5; Acts 22:5); and a ruling elder of a community center (synagogue; Luke 8:41, 49). Jesus group communities replicated this pattern: teaching elders (for example, 2 and 3 John); ruling elders (for example, Acts 20:17-35; Titus 1:5-9); and a ruling elder of the community (for example, 1 Tim 3:1-7). Paul summons the ruling elders of the Ephesian community to meet with him at Miletus. In the story of Acts, the Ephesian ingroup elites were the last of the Jesus groups founded by Paul to be addressed by Paul. This is Paul's final instruction.

20:18b-35: Luke composes a farewell speech for Paul. **Final Words.** Paul delivers this speech to the ruling elders of the Ephesian community assembled at Miletus. In the Bible, key figures spoke "final words" (or made a "farewell speech") before dying: Jacob (Gen 49:1-17), Moses (Deuteronomy 31–34, or Deuteronomy as a whole), Joshua (chapters 23–24), Samuel (1 Sam 12:1-25), David (1 Kgs 2:1-9). It is possible to consider these final words as similar to a "last will and testament" for their survivors, which included their children. Indeed, there is a collection of apocryphal literature known as the *Testament of the Twelve Patriarchs* (sons of Jacob).

In the modern Western world, where economics is the prevailing social institution, a last will and testament ordinarily assigns inheritance in terms of property and wealth. These cultures do not usually have special considerations for the firstborn son, as does Mediterranean culture (see Deut 21:15-17; compare Luke 12:13-15).

In the Mediterranean world, kinship is the focal social institution. At the death of the patriarch, the family is concerned about its impending loss. What will happen now? Will the family fall to pieces? Who will lead it? What dangers lie ahead? In the Mediterranean world, people at the brink of death are believed to know what is going to happen to persons who are near and dear. Because the dying person is closer to the realm of God than to the realm of human beings, that person is thought to become prescient. After all, human knowledge is limited, but God knows all things, even the forthcoming and the future.

With the final words, the last will and testament, a dying person strives to give advice on how to keep the family together, how to strengthen the loyalty of all its members. He or she gives good wishes and expresses concern for the ongoing well-being of the group. Though Luke does not state that Paul is not on the verge of death, we are told that Paul does not expect to see these people ever again. Thus this kind of speech is also fitting as a "departure speech."

The speech that Luke crafted for Paul is an insertion into a "we" section (Acts 20:5-15; 21:1-18). Though scholars debate the structure of Acts 20:18b-35, we accept the chiastic arrangement presented by Charles H. Talbert (1997:186-87).

> **A** Past record: "you yourselves know" (v. 18b)
> > **B** Present activity: "and now" (v. 22a)
> > > **C** Prophetic future: "I know" (v. 25a)
> > > "Therefore" (v. 26a)
> > > > **D** The charge: "keep watch" (v. 28)
> > > **C'** Prophetic future: "I know" (v. 29)
> > **B'** Present activity: "and now" (v. 32a)
> **A'** Past record: "you yourselves know" (v. 34a)

The main point in a chiastic arrangement is always found in the center. Paul's final words to the leaders are those of a change agent, affectionately urging his Ephesian clients to watch out for outsiders who might disturb the stability of their community. He alerts them to those who might trigger discontinuance of the gospel of God that he proclaimed. Hence they must monitor themselves and their flock and be on guard against "savage wolves" (outsiders) who will threaten them as well as against enemies within the community. This concept is also a commonplace in the ancient world. Jesus group members, too, believed that when their founding change agents died, godless error would creep in and corrupt the flock. Paul leaves them his personal example, also typical of ancient philosophers and sages. Luke leaves his audience with a stirring image of Paul, a model to be emulated.

20:21: To repeat once more, in this commentary, the phrase "Jews and Greeks" is preferably translated as "Judeans and Greeks," referring respectively to Israelites who sedulously observe Judean customs even outside Palestine, that is, observant Israelites or Judeans (= "Jews"); and assimilated Israelites or Greeks (= or Hellenists), that is, Israelites inculturated in the local Hellenism of the Roman Empire, who are Israelites largely in name (genealogy) only.

20:22: Paul's declaration of going to Jerusalem has its matching scene in Luke 13:22.

20:25: Once more at this important juncture, we are reminded that Paul's activity as change agent could be summarized in the phrase "to proclaim the kingdom," something that was of central concern to Jesus and of crucial ingroup concern to Israelites living outside Judea.

20:20-33: Paul makes a sort of negative confession, rather typical of honor-shame cultures:

> v. 20   *I did not shrink* from doing anything helpful
> v. 24   *But I do not count my life of any value to myself,*
> v. 26   Therefore I declare to you this day that *I am not responsible for the blood of any of you,*
> v. 27   *for I did not shrink from declaring to you the whole purpose of God.*
> v. 31   Therefore be alert, remembering that *for three years I did not cease* night or day to warn everyone with tears.
> v. 33   *I coveted no one's silver or gold or clothing*

Paul thus gives a personal example: he preached without fail (vv. 20, 27, 31); his final words alert them to imminent dangers; and he desired no one's wealth (v. 33). The elders ought to nourish the community (v. 28), be on the lookout for threatening dangers (vv. 29-31), and resist greed (vv. 33-35). These concerns were common to Messianist communities at the end of the first century. For example, the Pastorals, contemporary with Luke, evidence similar concerns: nourish the flock (1 Tim 3:2); be on the lookout for emerging error in the communities (all of the Pastorals); and avoid greed (1 Tim 3:3; Titus 1:7, 11). Perhaps this is a typical concern of the third Pauline generation as the old generation yields to the next one.

20:36-38: The elders are understandably grieved by the thought of never seeing Paul again, but they escort him to the ship. Kissing among males as greeting and mark of departure is still customary among Mediterraneans. Culturally, one kisses those persons with whom one can share food, both signs of ingroup affection.

In Caesarea, Paul Learns God's Will from Agabus the Prophet Acts 21:1-16

21:1 When we had parted from them and set sail, we came by a straight course to Cos, and the next day to Rhodes, and from there to Patara. 2 When we found a ship bound for Phoenicia, we went on board and set sail. 3 We came in sight of Cyprus; and leaving it on our left, we sailed to Syria and landed at Tyre, because the ship was to unload its cargo there. 4 We looked up the disciples and stayed there for seven days. Through the Spirit they told Paul not to go on to Jerusalem. 5 When our days there were ended, we left and proceeded on our journey; and all of them, with wives and children, escorted us outside the city. There we knelt down on the beach and prayed 6 and said farewell to one another. Then we went on board the ship, and they returned home.

7 When we had finished the voyage from Tyre, we arrived at Ptolemais; and we greeted the believers and stayed with them for one day. 8 The next day we left and came to Caesarea; and we went into the house of Philip the evangelist, one of the seven, and stayed with him. 9 He had four unmarried daughters who had the gift of prophecy. 10 While we were staying there for several days, a prophet named Agabus came down from Judea. 11 He came to us and took Paul's belt, bound his own feet and hands with it, and said, "Thus says the Holy Spirit, 'This is the way the Jews in Jerusalem will bind the man who owns this belt and will hand him over to the Gentiles.'" 12 When we heard this, we and the people there urged him not to go up to Jerusalem. 13 Then Paul answered, "What are you doing, weeping and breaking my heart? For I am ready not only to be bound but even to die in Jerusalem for the name of the Lord Jesus." 14 Since he would not be persuaded, we remained silent except to say, "The Lord's will be done."

15 After these days we got ready and started to go up to Jerusalem. 16 Some of the disciples from Caesarea also came along and brought us to the house of Mnason of Cyprus, an early disciple, with whom we were to stay.

Textual Notes: Acts 21:1-16

Luke continues to trace Paul's journey toward Jerusalem from Miletus to Cos, to Rhodes, to Patara, and then to Tyre, where they stayed for a week. From there Paul's group heads to Ptolemais and ultimately arrives at Caesarea. Of particular interest in this section is how believers evaluate and clarify the inspiration of the Spirit. Earlier, Paul felt inspired by the Spirit to journey to Jerusalem (Acts 19:21), and he resolved to do just that (Acts 20:22). Now at Tyre, fellow believers discern that the Spirit indicates that Paul should not travel to Jerusalem (Acts 21:4). A prophet, Agabus, arrives from Judea and by means of a symbolic action (v. 11) describes for Paul and the group the fate that awaits the apostle in Jerusalem. After discerning the differing interpretations of the Spirit's inspiration, Paul decides to continue his journey to Jerusalem, stopping at Caesarea (v. 8a).

21:1: The "we" section resumes (21:1-18).

21:4: Originally, the gospel tradition spoke of "those who followed" or "followers" of Jesus. This eventually gave way already in the gospels to the word disciples. Luke uses the term abundantly in Acts (beginning in 6:2). What is remarkable at

Tyre is that apart from Paul's proclamation, Israelite minorities living there some-how learned about Jesus designated Messiah by God raising him from the dead. They knew about Paul and his activity and expressed concern for his well-being. The attempt to dissuade Paul from journeying to Jerusalem (Acts 21:4) has its matching scene in Luke 13:33, where Jesus declares such a trip a divine necessity for him.

21:7: The NRSV translates the Greek word for "brothers" as "believers." "Brothers" is more appropriate (see RSV) since those who believed in Jesus formed a fictive kin group and described their mutual relationship with kinship terminology: "brothers" and "sisters" (Mark 3:31-35).

21:8: Arriving in Caesarea Maritima, Paul and his companions ("we") lodged with Philip the "evangelist" (Acts 8:40), one of the seven who served Greek-speaking Israelite widows (Acts 6:1-6, often mistakenly interpreted as "waiting on tables"). Philip was obviously an Israelite fully inculturated into Hellenistic culture, and as Luke indicates, he proclaimed the gospel. (The word *evangelist* is used in the New Testament only here and in Eph 4:11; 2 Tim 4:5.) His four daughters had the gift of prophesying, echoing the Israelite tradition of four prophetesses: Miriam (Exod 15:20); Deborah (Judg 4:4); Huldah (2 Kgs 22:14); and Noadiah (Neh 6:14). Compare also Ezek 13:17-23; Joel 2:28; Acts 2:17-18.

21:10-11: The prophet Agabus (Acts 11:28) comes from Judea and performs a symbolic prophetic action intended for Paul in the sight of the group. A symbolic prophetic action consists of the description of some symbolic action (usually commanded by God) performed by a prophet, followed by words that clarify the meaning of the action. Such an action invariably effects what it symbolizes because it is commanded by God. For example, in Ezekiel 5 God commands the prophet to cut off and divide some of the hair on his head and face; the described fate of this hair will be the fate of the Jerusalemites ("Thus says the Lord God: This is Jerusalem" [Ezek 5:5]; see also Isa 20:2; Ezek 4:1; Jer 13:1-14; 16:14; and so on). Here Agabus gets a divine command from the Holy Spirit and proceeds to bind his hand and feet with Paul's belt. The interpretation of the action, provided by the Spirit, is that Judeans of Jerusalem, Paul's fellow Israelites, will bind him and hand him over to the occupying Roman authorities (see Acts 28:17; compare Mark 10:33).

21:11-12: Agabus's message has its matching scene in Luke 17:11, where Jesus is described journeying through Samaria and Galilee on his way to Jerusalem.

21:12-16: Paul's traveling companions, along with the local community, urged him not to go to Jerusalem, but Paul insists on going. The group defers to Paul, who says: "The Lord's [God's] will be done" (compare Luke 22:42). Some of them accompany Paul on his journey to Jerusalem. He stops overnight at the house of a certain Mnason, a Cypriot, an early disciple. It is not clear whether he was evangelized by Paul (Acts 13:3-13) or by Barnabas the Cypriot (4:36).

21:13: Paul's admission that he is ready to die in Jerusalem has its matching scene in Luke 18:31, recording Jesus' determination to continue the journey to Jerusalem.

21:15: Making ready to go to Jerusalem has its matching scene in Luke 19:11, where Jesus was already near Jerusalem.

In Jerusalem, Paul Confers with Jesus Group Elites Acts 21:17-26

21:17 When we arrived in Jerusalem, the brothers welcomed us warmly. 18 The next day Paul went with us to visit James; and all the elders were present. 19 After greeting them, he related one by one the things that God had done among the Gentiles through his ministry. 20 When they heard it, they praised God. Then they said to him, "You see, brother, how many thousands of believers there are among the Jews, and they are all zealous for the law. 21 They have been told about you that you teach all the Jews living among the Gentiles to forsake Moses, and that you tell them not to circumcise their children or observe the customs. 22 What then is to be done? They will certainly hear that you have come. 23 So do what we tell you. We have four men who are under a vow. 24 Join these men, go through the rite of purification with them, and pay for the shaving of their heads. Thus all will know that there is nothing in what they have been told about you, but that you yourself observe and guard the law. 25 But as for the Gentiles who have become believers, we have sent a letter with our judgment that they should abstain from what has been sacrificed to idols and from blood and from what is strangled and from fornication." 26 Then Paul took the men, and the next day, having purified himself, he entered the temple with them, making public the completion of the days of purification when the sacrifice would be made for each of them.

Textual Notes: Acts 21:17-26

This meeting with the elders in Jerusalem in Acts 21 mirrors a previous meeting in Jerusalem reported in Acts 15:1—16:5. Paul goes to Jerusalem; he meets with the elders and James. Paul relates what God has done through him among Israelites living in non-Israelite cities. Many of these Israelites were assimilated to Hellenism, hence "Greek." The Jerusalem meeting in Acts 15:1—16:5 (called the council of Jerusalem) resulted in a decree that stated how much of the Torah these Israelite "Greeks" should observe as Jesus group members. Paul accommodated himself for the sake of unity in the community. Now we have another meeting in Jerusalem.

21:17: The arrival of Paul in Jerusalem has its matching scene in Luke 19:28, 45, when Jesus goes up to Jerusalem and enters the temple. The warm greeting received by Paul is what one would expect among fictive kin ("brothers").

21:17-20a: The scene of Paul receiving a good reception and God being glorified or honored for what Paul has accomplished among assimilated Israelites has its matching scene in Luke 19:37, where Jesus received a good reception and people praise God for the works they have witnessed.

21:18: James, the brother of the Lord (Acts 15:13; Matt 13:55; Gal 1:19), thus real kin to Jesus, is clearly the head of the believing community in Jerusalem. Tradition indicates that after the destruction of Jerusalem during the Bar Kokhba uprising (c. 135 C.E.), those of the family of Jesus in Jerusalem moved to Galilee and governed the believing community in the region for three centuries (Bagatti 1971). "All" the elders is probably Lukan hyperbole. This verse concludes the "we" section(s).

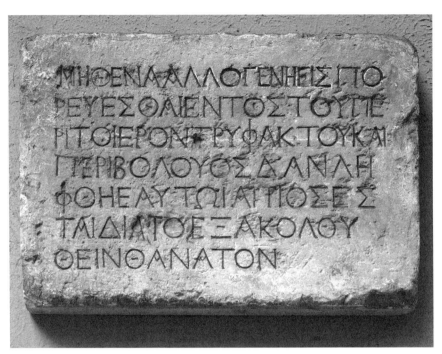

Interdiction prohibiting non-Jews from entering the Inner Sanctum of the temple in Jerusalem. Greek inscription from the outer wall of the temple. Paul was falsely accused of introducing a former pagan into the precinct. Plaster cast; third century B.C.E.–*first century* C.E. *Location: Museo della Civilta Romana, Rome, Italy. Photo © Erich Lessing / Art Resource, N.Y.*

21:19-20: The elders respond to Paul's report of his success among Israelites resident in non-Israelite cities by giving appropriate praise [honor] to God. At the same time, the elders remind Paul that even greater numbers (literally, "myriads," that is several ten-thousands, another Lukan hyperbole) of "observant" Israelites ("Judeans zealous for the law") have accepted Jesus as Messiah but are troubled by rumors concerning the behavior deriving from Paul's proclamation of the word of God.

21:21: The gossip network spreads rumors—true and false, for better or worse—about Paul's teachings (see Rohrbaugh 2001). The rumor is that Paul exhorted Judeans living among non-Israelites to forsake Moses, to disregard circumcising their sons, and to reject the customs characteristic of the Judean way of life. Of course, there is no evidence for any of this at all in Acts. It is gossip very likely passed on by some anti–Jesus group Judeans in the Diaspora who opposed Paul and those Judeans who accepted his word of God. Assimilated Israelites living among non-Israelite majorities ("Greeks") likely ignored circumcision or did not even hear about a practice introduced by the Maccabees in Judea (after c. 150 B.C.E.).

21:22-24: James and the elders advise Paul to follow a plan that they have devised to discredit the Judean gossip about him. Paul is to publicly purify himself from the pollution incurred by passing through non-Israelite lands (*Mishnah Ohalot* 2:3) and pay the considerable expenses associated with the Nazirite vow undertaken by four needy males (see Num 6:14-15; on vows, see the note on Acts 18:18). Paul willingly undertook this accommodation and entered the temple with the men the next day. This public testimony to his Torah observance thus gave the lie to the gossip circulating about Paul.

21:25: The mention of "non-Israelites who have become believers" may be the way Jesus group leaders located at Israel's sacred center of Jerusalem regarded Israelites who assimilated to non-Israelite practices. For all practical purposes, they were "non-Israelites," not unlike Samaritans. We find a similar assessment in the most Judean of the Gospels, Matthew, for whom Jesus pronounces as "non-Israelites" (Gentiles) those in the Jesus group who do not share group attitudes and behaviors (see Matt 18:17; see also 5:47; 6:7, 32). According to the decree of Acts 15, they were like resident aliens in Judea.

21:26: So Paul complies with the advice of the Jerusalem Jesus group leaders and goes through with the temple sacrifice. Paul's friendly attitude toward the temple has its matching scene in Luke 19:45-48, which reports Jesus' entry into the temple and his friendly attitude toward it.

Acts 21:27–28:31 Paul Witnesses from Jerusalem to Rome

In this final section of the Acts of the Apostles, Paul moves from Jerusalem to Caesarea to Rome. The section marks the fulfillment of two noteworthy statements in Luke-Acts. First of all, there is the statement in Jesus' final words concerning his disciples: "But before all this occurs, they will arrest you and persecute you; they will hand you over to synagogues and prisons, and you will be brought before kings and governors because of my name. This will give you an opportunity to testify" (Luke 21:12-13). Paul will now find himself "brought before kings and governors because of Jesus' name," and thus will get significant opportunity to bear witness to the gospel of God. Second, there is the resurrected Jesus' own prognosis of Paul's activity: "I have chosen [Paul] to bring my name before non-Israelites: both kings and before the people of Israel" (Acts 9:15; NRSV is slightly different). Paul has completed his task before the people of Israel resident among non-Israelites. It remains for him now to do so among "kings," occasioned by his being arrested by Judeans in Jerusalem's temple.

Modifying Talbert (1997:226), we structure Acts 21–28 as a well-integrated unit in this way:

A Paul's Witness before Fellow Judeans in Jerusalem (Acts 21:27 — 23:10)
  Paul's Witness before the Jerusalem Crowd (Acts 21:27–22:29)
  Paul's Witness before the Jerusalem Council (Elites) (Acts 22:30 — 23:10)

B Rulers Pronounce Paul Innocent (Acts 23:12—26:32)
    Paul's Witness before Tribune Claudius Lysias (Acts 23:11-35)
    Paul's Witness before Governor Felix (Acts 24:1-27)
    Paul's Witness before Governor Festus (Acts 25:1-27)
    Paul's Witness before King Agrippa (Acts 26:1-32)
B' God Pronounces Paul Innocent (Acts 27:1—28:1-16)
    Ordeal by Shipwreck on the Way to Rome (Acts 27:1—28:15)
A' Paul' Proclamation and Witness to Fellow Judeans in Rome (28:16-31)
    Paul's Proclamation and Witness in Rome before Judeans (Acts 28:16-31)

Acts 21:27—23:10 Section A: Paul Witnesses in Jerusalem to Fellow Israelites

Paul Witnesses before the Jerusalem Crowd Acts 21:27—22:29

21:27 When the seven days were almost completed, the Jews from Asia, who had seen him in the temple, stirred up the whole crowd. They seized him, 28 shouting, "Fellow Israelites, help! This is the man who is teaching everyone everywhere against our people, our law, and this place; more than that, he has actually brought Greeks into the temple and has defiled this holy place." 29 For they had previously seen Trophimus the Ephesian with him in the city, and they supposed that Paul had brought him into the temple. 30 Then all the city was aroused, and the people rushed together. They seized Paul and dragged him out of the temple, and immediately the doors were shut. 31 While they were trying to kill him, word came to the tribune of the cohort that all Jerusalem was in an uproar. 32 Immediately he took soldiers and centurions and ran down to them. When they saw the tribune and the soldiers, they stopped beating Paul. 33 Then the tribune came, arrested him, and ordered him to be bound with two chains; he inquired who he was and what he had done. 34 Some in the crowd shouted one thing, some another; and as he could not learn the facts because of the uproar, he ordered him to be brought into the barracks. 35 When Paul came to the steps, the violence of the mob was so great that he had to be carried by the soldiers. 36 The crowd that followed kept shouting, "Away with him!"

37 Just as Paul was about to be brought into the barracks, he said to the tribune, "May I say something to you?" The tribune replied, "Do you know Greek? 38 Then you are not the Egyptian who recently stirred up a revolt and led the four thousand assassins out into the wilderness?" 39 Paul replied, "I am a Jew, from Tarsus in Cilicia, a citizen of an important city; I beg you, let me speak to the people." 40 When he had given him permission, Paul stood on the steps and motioned to the people for silence; and when there was a great hush, he addressed them in the Hebrew language, saying: 22:1 "Brothers and fathers, listen to the defense that I now make before you."

2 When they heard him addressing them in Hebrew, they became even more quiet. Then he said:

3 "I am a Jew, born in Tarsus in Cilicia, but brought up in this city at the feet of Gamaliel, educated strictly according to our ancestral law, being zealous for God, just as all of you are today. 4 I persecuted this Way up to the point of death by binding both men and women and putting them in prison, 5 as the high priest and the whole council of elders can testify about me. From them I also received letters to the brothers in Damascus, and I went there in order to bind those who were there and to bring them back to Jerusalem for punishment.

6 While I was on my way and approaching Damascus, about noon a great light

from heaven suddenly shone about me. 7 I fell to the ground and heard a voice saying to me, 'Saul, Saul, why are you persecuting me?' 8 I answered, 'Who are you, Lord?' Then he said to me, 'I am Jesus of Nazareth whom you are persecuting.' 9 Now those who were with me saw the light but did not hear the voice of the one who was speaking to me. 10 I asked, 'What am I to do, Lord?' The Lord said to me, 'Get up and go to Damascus; there you will be told everything that has been assigned to you to do.' 11 Since I could not see because of the brightness of that light, those who were with me took my hand and led me to Damascus.

12 "A certain Ananias, who was a devout man according to the law and well spoken of by all the Jews living there, 13 came to me; and standing beside me, he said, 'Brother Saul, regain your sight!' In that very hour I regained my sight and saw him. 14 Then he said, 'The God of our ancestors has chosen you to know his will, to see the Righteous One and to hear his own voice; 15 for you will be his witness to all the world of what you have seen and heard. 16 And now why do you delay? Get up, be baptized, and have your sins washed away, calling on his name.'

17 "After I had returned to Jerusalem and while I was praying in the temple, I fell into a trance 18 and saw Jesus saying to me, 'Hurry and get out of Jerusalem quickly, because they will not accept your testimony about me.' 19 And I said, 'Lord, they themselves know that in every synagogue I imprisoned and beat those who believed in you. 20 And while the blood of your witness Stephen was shed, I myself was standing by, approving and keeping the coats of those who killed him.' 21 Then he said to me, 'Go, for I will send you far away to the Gentiles.'"

22 Up to this point they listened to him, but then they shouted, "Away with such a fellow from the earth! For he should not be allowed to live." 23 And while they were shouting, throwing off their cloaks, and tossing dust into the air, 24 the tribune directed that he was to be brought into the barracks, and ordered him to be examined by flogging, to find out the reason for this outcry against him. 25 But when they had tied him up with thongs, Paul said to the centurion who was standing by, "Is it legal for you to flog a Roman citizen who is uncondemned?" 26 When the centurion heard that, he went to the tribune and said to him, "What are you about to do? This man is a Roman citizen." 27 The tribune came and asked Paul, "Tell me, are you a Roman citizen?" And he said, "Yes." 28 The tribune answered, "It cost me a large sum of money to get my citizenship." Paul said, "But I was born a citizen." 29 Immediately those who were about to examine him drew back from him; and the tribune also was afraid, for he realized that Paul was a Roman citizen and that he had bound him.

Textual Notes: Acts 21:27–22:29

21:27: When Diaspora Israelites in Jerusalem for the Feast of Weeks saw Paul in the temple, they agitated the crowds against him and seized him with a view to removing him from the temple and killing him. **Establishment Violence.** Given the prevalent tendency for Diaspora Israelites to assimilate, devout Diaspora Israelites who took pains to make a pilgrimage to Jerusalem were very observant and would tolerate no deviance such as they accused Paul of.

21:28-29: Despite Paul's public observance of Israelite customs with the four men, the Diaspora Israelites repeat the unfounded and undocumented gossip that he teaches against Israelites, the Torah, and the temple. To this they add the charge that Paul brought non-Israelites into the temple, thereby defiling it. The charge is, of course, ridiculous. All they actually witnessed was Paul walking with his traveling companion, Trophimus the Ephesian (Acts 20:4), in the city. Why would Paul or anyone bring a non-Israelite into the temple when the threat of death was clearly posted? Moreover, of what interest would the temple and its activities be to a non-Israelite? Trophimus was most plausibly an assimilated Israelite living in Ephesus, where he met Paul and then accompanied him to Jerusalem to deliver the collection for the poor.

21:30-31: Reaction to the gossip spreads rapidly. These Israelites seize Paul and intend to kill him quite in accord with Israelite custom relative to fellow Israelites who blatantly ignore Torah (for example, Philo, *Special Laws* 1.315-18).
Establishment Violence.

21:30: The mob that seizes Paul has its matching scene in Luke 22:54, where a mob seizes Jesus.

21:32-36: The commander and his Roman cohort garrisoned in the Antonia Fortress next to the Jerusalem temple rushed to quell the disturbance and, presuming Paul to be guilty of something, arrested and bound him with double chains (that is, to a soldier at each side). Unable to learn anything from Paul because of the dangerously unruly crowd, the commander has Paul carried into the fortress.

21:36: The cry of the Judeans "Away with him [Paul]!" finds its matching scene in Luke 23:18, where the Judeans say the same about Jesus: "Away with him!"

21:37-40: Paul surprises the commander by speaking to him in Greek. The commander assumed he had captured a Judean Egyptian who instigated a riot with a band of four thousand in the wilderness but who escaped though many of his associates were killed (see Acts 5:36). Paul identifies himself as Judean Tarsian, a native of Tarsus in Cilicia, and not an Egyptian. Paul requests and receives permission to address the crowd in Aramaic.

22:1-21: Once more, we follow Talbert's analysis (1997:197) of this first of five "defense" (better: witness) speeches (22:1) by Paul as chiastically arranged:

A Paul came from regions where Israelites were a minority (Tarsus) to Jerusalem, where they are a majority (v. 3)
  B Paul persecuted the Way (vv. 4-5a)
    C Paul journeyed from Jerusalem to Damascus (v. 5b)
      D Paul has an ASC experience on the road to Damascus (vv. 6-11)
        E Ananias restores Paul's sight (vv. 12-13)
          F Ananias tells Paul his mission (vv. 14-15)
        E' Ananias urges Paul be baptized (v. 16)
      D' Paul has an ASC experience in Jerusalem (vv. 17-18a)
    C' Paul is commanded to leave Jerusalem (v. 18b)
  B' Paul reminisces about his days as a persecutor (vv. 19-20)
A' Paul is sent from Jerusalem to lands where Israelites are a minority population (v. 21)

The speech is framed by two exchanges with the commander (Acts 21:37-40 and 22:22-29), which form an inclusion. The central point of the speech (F, vv. 14-15) is that Paul is to be a witness (note the word field for "witness": Acts 22:5, 15, 18, 20) of what he has seen and heard in his ASC experience.

22:2: Paul surprises this crowd, for he addresses it in Aramaic rather than the Greek that was common among Israelites living in the Diaspora.

22:3: As previously noted (Acts 16:37), the historical Paul was quite likely a citizen neither of Tarsus nor of Rome as he claims in Acts (16:37; see Stegemann and Stegemann 1999:302). Birth did not automatically confer citizenship in antiquity; it did confer belonging to some group bound by common ancestry, hence genealogical belonging. This claim to Tarsus citizenship placed on Paul's lips is part of Luke's strategy for elevating Paul's social status to a level that the artisan (and his family of origin) did not have in real life. Paul's letters do not support this claim.

22:5: The high priest at the time of Paul's defense speech (58 C.E.) would have been Ananias, son of Nedebaeus (see Acts 23:2), but the one who commissioned Paul to go to Damascus in 36 C.E. would have been Joseph Caiaphas, son-in-law of Annas.

22:6-11: This passage reports Paul's core experience on the road to Damascus. This is the *narratio* part of the defense speech. The three reports in Acts are essentially consistent in describing Paul's core experience (Acts 9:4-5; 22:7-8; 26:14-15), and two conclude with a commissioning as change agent (Acts 22:14; 26:16). This is an ASC experience quite common in the ancient circum-Mediterranean world (see Pilch 2004:68-78). **Alternate States of Consciousness.** The experience is better identified as Paul's call to be a prophet of the God of Israel, a change agent to communicate the innovation of what the God of Israel has done through the death and resurrection of Jesus. Paul did not "convert," since there was nothing to convert to. Paul remained an observant and obedient Israelite and did not "convert" to any new or different group. He continued in his obedience to the God of Israel by accepting Jesus crucified and raised by God as Israel's Messiah and proclaimed Jesus' imminent return to establish theocracy in Israel, God's rule on the land of Israel (often inaccurately called "earth").

22:12-16: In this account, Ananias interprets the ASC for Paul. Interpretation is important, for without it, an ASC experience remains vacuous. The visionary and/ or associates interpret and reinterpret the experience as they remember and retell it. This helps explain the differences in Luke's three reports of this event in Acts. Ananias announces that the God of Israel has elected Paul to be a witness. Ananias is described as "a devout observer of the law," which indicates that he is an Israelite holy man (*ḥāsîd*). In all cultures, such a person has direct contact with the deity and mediates information and favor from the realm of God to this one.

First, the holy man Ananias restores Paul's sight. One of the most important gifts a holy man brings from the world of God to this world is healing. Second, Ananias identifies God as the agent of the ASC and tells Paul of God's intentions. Paul will eventually learn God's will since this experience is Paul's vocation to be a holy man. "I know better than any man that the gods reveal their intentions to holy and wise men" (Philostratus, *Vita Apollonii* 8.7.10). Ananias further identifies the person whom Paul saw in the ASC as "the Righteous One," that is, the risen Jesus. Finally, Paul will gain information from the risen

Jesus. "Righteous One" is a Greek term that described Noah in the Septuagint (Gen 6:9; Sir 44:17) and was applied by Peter to Jesus (Acts 6:14). However, Paul's Israelite audience would recognize the word as describing a descendant of David (Jer 23:5-6; 33:15).

Paul's charge is to be a witness about what he has learned in his ASC experience to "all human beings" (RSV: "to all men"). The NRSV neglects the context (Acts 21:21) and mistranslates the phrase as "to all the world." Would "all the world" be interested in the God of Israel, Jesus of Nazareth, and descendants of David? As Acts 21:21 makes clear, Paul deals with Israelites living among non-Israelite majorities, so an even better rendition would be "to all fellow Israelites."

Finally, Ananias directs Paul to be baptized (see Acts 9:18, which highlights Paul's baptism).

22:17-21: The Lucan Paul then recounts yet another ASC experience, which he had while praying in the Jerusalem temple after returning from Damascus. The significance of this event is that even after gaining a new understanding of Jesus, thanks to the God of Israel, Paul continued to pray in Israel's temple! It is foolish to say that he rejected or demeaned that institution (Acts 21:28-29). In this ASC experience, the risen Jesus himself (not simply Jerusalemites; Acts 9:29-30) sends Paul "far away" to proclaim the word of God among Israelite minorities living in places dominated by non-Israelite populations (Acts 21:21).

22:22-29: Paul's mention of his work among majority non-Israelite populations inflames his observant Israelite audience against him once more. Jerusalemites did not look kindly upon assimilated nonobservant Israelites living outside Judea.

22:27-28: Luke's Paul claims: "I was born a citizen." This is a problem and is debated by scholars. As noted above (Acts 16:37), we follow Stegemann and Stegemann (1999), who deny this fact on the basis of Paul's letters, which do not support the claim. Not only does Paul never mention his Roman citizenship, but his flogging (2 Cor 11:24-25; five times in a synagogue; three times by Roman authorities) could never have been meted out to a Roman citizen. "To bind a Roman citizen in a crime, to flog him is an abomination, to slay him is almost an act of murder; to crucify him is—what? There is no fitting word that can possibly describe so horrible a deed" (Cicero, *In Verrem* 2.5.66 §170). Moreover, if Paul's father had indeed gained Roman citizenship (which Paul would inherit by birth from a free or freed father), it would have moved him into elite circles of Tarsus. In this position, he would have been obliged to participate in local, non-Israelite cultic events, which would prove troublesome to assimilated Torah-observant Israelites, not to mention Pharisees. Paul could never claim to be blameless as to the law as he does (Phil 3:6).

On the other hand, as we observed in the textual note on Acts 16:37, Paul may be practicing deception by lying to outgroup people. That is an honorable line of behavior and serves to challenge the outgroup. Yet it is possible that the writer believed Paul was a Roman citizen because of the tradition that he was beheaded (a tradition that Luke does not mention).

Paul Witnesses before the Jerusalem Council (Elites) Acts 22:30—23:10

22:30 Since he wanted to find out what Paul was being accused of by the Jews, the next day he released him and ordered the chief priests and the entire council to meet. He brought Paul down and had him stand before them. 23:1 While Paul was looking intently at the council he said, "Brothers, up to this day I have lived my life with a clear conscience before God." 2 Then the high priest Ananias ordered those standing near him to strike him on the mouth. 3 At this Paul said to him, "God will strike you, you whitewashed wall! Are you sitting there to judge me according to the law, and yet in violation of the law you order me to be struck?" 4 Those standing nearby said, "Do you dare to insult God's high priest?" 5 And Paul said, "I did not realize, brothers, that he was high priest; for it is written, 'You shall not speak evil of a leader of your people.'"

6 When Paul noticed that some were Sadducees and others were Pharisees, he called out in the council, "Brothers, I am a Pharisee, a son of Pharisees. I am on trial concerning the hope of the resurrection of the dead." 7 When he said this, a dissension began between the Pharisees and the Sadducees, and the assembly was divided. 8 (The Sadducees say that there is no resurrection, or angel, or spirit; but the Pharisees acknowledge all three.) 9 Then a great clamor arose, and certain scribes of the Pharisees' group stood up and contended, "We find nothing wrong with this man. What if a spirit or an angel has spoken to him?" 10 When the dissension became violent, the tribune, fearing that they would tear Paul to pieces, ordered the soldiers to go down, take him by force, and bring him into the barracks.

Textual Notes: Acts 22:30—23:10

22:30: This verse serves as an introduction to the following scene. In the Lukan story line, Paul's claim of Roman citizenship not only spares him torture but allows the tribune to gather the chief priests and entire council in order to question Paul concerning the accusations made by fellow Israelites against him.

Chapters 23–26 present four trials or occasions for witness by Paul as he gives testimony before the Sanhedrin, Felix, Festus, and Herod Agrippa. These have their matching scenes in Luke 22:26; 23:1; 23:8; 23:13, where Jesus is on trial before the Sanhedrin, Pilate, Herod, and Pilate again.

23:1: The Greek word translated "look intently" occurs just fourteen times in the New Testament, ten times in Acts (1:10; 3:4, 12; 6:15; 7:55; 10:4; 11:6; 13:9; 14:9; 23:1). It can also be translated "gaze" or "stare (at)." In most occurrences it signals an alternate state of consciousness experience (ASC). **Alternate States of Consciousness.** Given the challenge Paul faced, it is quite likely that he—like performing musicians and orators, among others—slipped into an ASC in order to enhance the effect of his words. Or alternatively, he might hope through intense eye contact with this group to "entrance," captivate, or charm his listeners and win them over to his views. The question of the Pharisees that follows Paul's declaration of belief in the resurrection ("What if a spirit or an angel has spoken to him?" [v. 9]) indicates that Paul occasionally—and perhaps even on this occasion—slipped into ASCs. It also confirms the promise Jesus made to his disciples: "Make up your minds not to prepare your defense in advance; for I will give you words and a wisdom that none of your opponents will be able to withstand or contradict" (Luke 21:14-15). Quite plausibly such inspiration comes in an ASC.

23:2: The reason for the high priest's order to strike Paul on the mouth is not clear. At the very least, it is a shaming strategy. Or it may be that the high priest chooses to believe the gossip about Paul as rejecting tradition rather than Paul's own declaration of a "clear conscience." It is also plausible that the high priest wanted to break Paul's trance and abort its powerful potential.

23:2: The slapping of Paul at the high priest's command has its matching scene in Luke 22:63-64, where Jesus is slapped by the priest's assistants.

23:3: "God will strike you" is a curse formula echoing Deut 28:22 and invoking God to redress Ananias's unjust order. In ancient Israel, the accused was presumed innocent until proven guilty (Lev 19:15).

23:5: Paul apologizes, perhaps with tongue in cheek, for not recognizing and respecting Ananias as high priest. Once again he proves his fidelity to the Torah by quoting Exod 22:27—"You shall not revile God, or curse a leader of your people"—in acknowledging his inculpable guilt.

23:6-10: Recognizing that the group was mixed (Pharisees and Sadducees), Paul aligns himself with the Pharisees and quite correctly acknowledges the source of his difficulties: his belief in the resurrection of the dead (and implicitly Jesus being raised by God from the dead). In the ensuing discussion, the Pharisees exonerate Paul. And their declaration acknowledges that Paul and other Israelite believers in Jesus raised by the God of Israel from the dead are equally another legitimate political religious party in Israel. Fearing that the Sadducee disagreement may turn violent, the tribune takes Paul into the Antonia Fortress.

23:6-9: The report that Sadducees do not believe in the resurrection but that the scribes support him has its matching scene in Luke 20:27-39, where Jesus has a similar experience with Sadducees and scribes.

Moreover, in Acts 23:9; 25:25; and 26:31, three men—Lysian, Festus, and Agrippa—declare Paul innocent. These instances have matching scenes in Luke 23:4, 14, 22, where Pilate declares Jesus innocent three times.

Acts 23:11—26:32 Section B: Rulers Pronounce Paul Innocent

Paul Witnesses before Tribune Claudius Lysias Acts 23:11-35

23:11 That night the Lord stood near him and said, "Keep up your courage! For just as you have testified for me in Jerusalem, so you must bear witness also in Rome."

12 In the morning the Jews joined in a conspiracy and bound themselves by an oath neither to eat nor drink until they had killed Paul. 13 There were more than forty who joined in this conspiracy. 14 They went to the chief priests and elders and said, "We have strictly bound ourselves by an oath to taste no food until we have killed Paul. 15 Now then, you and the council must notify the tribune to bring him down to you, on the pretext that you want to make a more thorough examination of his case. And we are ready to do away with him before he arrives."

16 Now the son of Paul's sister heard about the ambush; so he went and gained entrance to the barracks and told Paul.

17 Paul called one of the centurions and said, "Take this young man to the tribune, for he has something to report to him." 18 So he took him, brought him to the tribune, and said, "The prisoner Paul called me and asked me to bring this young man to you; he has something to tell you." 19 The tribune took him by the hand, drew him aside privately, and asked, "What is it that you have to report to me?" 20 He answered, "The Jews have agreed to ask you to bring Paul down to the council tomorrow, as though they were going to inquire more thoroughly into his case. 21 But do not be persuaded by them, for more than forty of their men are lying in ambush for him. They have bound themselves by an oath neither to eat nor drink until they kill him. They are ready now and are waiting for your consent." 22 So the tribune dismissed the young man, ordering him, "Tell no one that you have informed me of this."

23 Then he summoned two of the centurions and said, "Get ready to leave by nine o'clock tonight for Caesarea with two hundred soldiers, seventy horsemen, and two hundred spearmen. 24 Also provide mounts for Paul to ride, and take him safely to Felix the governor." 25 He wrote a letter to this effect:

26 "Claudius Lysias to his Excellency the governor Felix, greetings. 27 This man was seized by the Jews and was about to be killed by them, but when I had learned that he was a Roman citizen, I came with the guard and rescued him. 28 Since I wanted to know the charge for which they accused him, I had him brought to their council. 29 I found that he was accused concerning questions of their law, but was charged with nothing deserving death or imprisonment. 30 When I was informed that there would be a plot against the man, I sent him to you at once, ordering his accusers also to state before you what they have against him."

31 So the soldiers, according to their instructions, took Paul and brought him during the night to Antipatris. 32 The next day they let the horsemen go on with him, while they returned to the barracks. 33 When they came to Caesarea and delivered the letter to the governor, they presented Paul also before him. 34 On reading the letter, he asked what province he belonged to, and when he learned that he was from Cilicia, 35 he said, "I will give you a hearing when your accusers arrive." Then he ordered that he be kept under guard in Herod's headquarters.

Textual Notes: Acts 23:11-35

23:11: In a night vision, Paul receives encouragement directly from Jesus (see also Acts 18:9-10; 22:17-18; 26:31-32), who tells him his journey is not yet ended. He must also witness in Rome. **Alternate States of Consciousness.** Like all holy men (and women), so too for Paul, many ASC experiences followed upon the initial call from or contact with the spirit world in an ASC (Acts 9; Gal 1:11-12, 15-16). He reminded Corinthian believers of this fact (2 Cor 12:1).

23:12-35: This section reports the plot against Paul's life (Acts 23:12-15), the discovery of the plot (Acts 23:16-22), and the thwarting of the plot (Acts 23:23-25). Paul's innocence is also recognized (Acts 23:29).

23:12-15: Plots were and are quite common in the circum-Mediterranean world (for example, Daniel 3; 6) and especially in pre-70 Jerusalem. These men put themselves under a curse (NRSV: "oath") if they failed to kill Paul because of his alleged deviant teaching and behavior. An oath is a promise made to God with a view to some divine benefaction. What triggers the oath here is belief that Paul is dishonoring God. The oath takers seek to defend God's honor. For similar "self-curses" as part of an oath see Ruth 1:16-17; Matt 26:74. They present their plot to the religious leaders.

23:16-22: Paul's nephew reports the plot to Paul and eventually to the tribune. In the circum-Mediterranean world, the closest emotional bond is between mother and son, but a very close second, nearly equal to this, is brother and sister. In the light of this cultural fact, it is quite surprising that Paul never mentions a sister in his letters. On the other hand, the fact that his married sister resides in Jerusalem suggests other interesting connections. Since the ideal marriage partner in the Mediterranean world is a patrilateral parallel cousin, Paul's sister was married to their father's brother's (= uncle's) son. The wife always leaves her family home to live with the groom in his father's compound. In this case, the brother of Paul's father lived in Jerusalem. Paul's father likely lived there too. Paul and his family may well have moved to Jerusalem from Tarsus when Paul was quite young. Thus Acts 23:16 (along with Acts 22:3) indicates that Paul was educated in Jerusalem rather than Tarsus.

We have no idea how Paul's nephew learned of the plot, nor do we know whether Paul's sister and/or her family shared Paul's understanding of Jesus and were Jesus followers. The fact of the nephew's concern for Paul's life basically testifies to the strength of Middle Eastern kinship bonds "no matter what" or "in spite of everything and anything." In the Middle East, blood is indeed thicker than water and stronger than conflicting ingroup beliefs. Had Paul denounced the God of Israel, he would most probably be disowned by the family.

23:23-35: The tribune arranges for a military escort to ensure Paul's safe passage to Caesarea Maritima, where he is to explain his case to Felix the governor. This Felix was a Roman freedman who was procurator of Judea, Samaria, Galilee, and Perea. Of him, Tacitus wrote: "Since kings had died or been reduced in control, Claudius [the emperor] entrusted the province of Judea to Roman knights or freedmen, one of whom was Anconeus Felix, who with all cruelty and lust wielded the power of a king, with the mentality of a slave" (*Historiae* 5.9). This Felix was in part responsible for the revolt against Rome in 66 C.E.

The letter was required for the transfer of a prisoner to a higher authority. Its significance is that the tribune characterizes Paul's difficulties as a problem of concern to Judeans. He was not guilty of any anti-Roman criminal acts (v. 29). Felix keeps Paul in custody awaiting the arrival of his accusers from Jerusalem so that he could hold a hearing.

In Caesarea Acts 24:1—26:32

Paul's Witness before Felix the Governor Acts 24:1-27

24:1 Five days later the high priest Ananias came down with some elders and an attorney, a certain Tertullus, and they reported their case against Paul to the governor. 2 When Paul had been summoned, Tertullus began to accuse him, saying:

"Your Excellency, because of you we have long enjoyed peace, and reforms have been made for this people because of your foresight. 3 We welcome this in every way and everywhere with utmost gratitude. 4 But, to detain you no further, I beg you to hear us briefly with your customary graciousness. 5 We have, in fact, found this man a pestilent fellow, an agitator among all the Jews throughout the world, and a ringleader of the sect of the Nazarene. 6 He even tried to profane the temple, and so we seized him. 8 By examining him yourself you will be able to learn from him concerning everything of which we accuse him."

9 The Jews also joined in the charge by asserting that all this was true.

10 When the governor motioned to him to speak, Paul replied:

"I cheerfully make my defense, knowing that for many years you have been a judge over this nation. 11 As you can find out, it is not more than twelve days since I went up to worship in Jerusalem. 12 They did not find me disputing with anyone in the temple or stirring up a crowd either in the synagogues or throughout the city. 13 Neither can they prove to you the charge that they now bring against me. 14 But this I admit to you, that according to the Way, which they call a sect, I worship the God of our ancestors, believing everything laid down according to the law or written in the prophets. 15 I have a hope in God—a hope that they themselves also accept—that there will be a resurrection of both the righteous and the unrighteous. 16 Therefore I do my best always to have a clear conscience toward God and all people. 17 Now after some years I came to bring alms to my nation and to offer sacrifices. 18 While I was doing this, they found me in the temple, completing the rite of purification, without any crowd or disturbance.

19 But there were some Jews from Asia—they ought to be here before you to make an accusation, if they have anything against me. 20 Or let these men here tell what crime they had found when I stood before the council, 21 unless it was this one sentence that I called out while standing before them, 'It is about the resurrection of the dead that I am on trial before you today.'"

22 But Felix, who was rather well informed about the Way, adjourned the hearing with the comment, "When Lysias the tribune comes down, I will decide your case." 23 Then he ordered the centurion to keep him in custody, but to let him have some liberty and not to prevent any of his friends from taking care of his needs.

24 Some days later when Felix came with his wife Drusilla, who was Jewish, he sent for Paul and heard him speak concerning faith in Christ Jesus. 25 And as he discussed justice, self-control, and the coming judgment, Felix became frightened and said, "Go away for the present; when I have an opportunity, I will send for you." 26 At the same time he hoped that money would be given him by Paul, and for that reason he used to send for him very often and converse with him.

27 After two years had passed, Felix was succeeded by Porcius Festus; and since he wanted to grant the Jews a favor, Felix left Paul in prison.

Textual Notes: Acts 24:1-27

Paul's witness before Felix is presented in three sections: (1) Felix hears the charges against Paul (vv. 1-9); (2) Felix hears Paul's defense/witness (vv. 10-21); (3) Felix disposes of Paul's case (vv. 22-27).

24:1-9: Legal proceedings in the ancient world, just as in the modern world, did not guarantee justice. Just as U.S. legal proceedings are concerned with winning, in parallel fashion ancient Mediterranean legal proceedings were concerned with dishonoring one's opponents. The best situation was to avoid legal proceedings. In fact, a person who was unable to head off a legal proceeding was considered a loser (cf. Prov 25:7c-10; Matt 5:25), all the more if he could not afford to bribe the judge (Matt 5:26; Acts 24:26). Luke continues his idealized presentation of Paul.

24:5: Tertullus, the "attorney" for Jerusalem's political religious leaders, levels four charges against Paul. First, he is a "pestilent fellow" (NRSV) or, more accurately, a "public enemy," that is, one who threatens the common good. The literal meaning of the Greek word ("pestilence, disease") would also connote contagion. Second, he is an "agitator," charges previously made in Acts 16:20 and Acts 17:6. Third, he is a ringleader of the "faction of the Nazoreans." The NRSV "sect" is anachronistic and ought to be translated as "faction," or "coalition" **Coalitions/Factions.** A person-centered faction is a kind of coalition formed around a central person (in this case, Jesus of Nazareth during his lifetime; see Malina 1996:143-75). After the death and resurrection of Jesus, his faction continued to exist but evolved into a new form. Where factions exist in a relatively stable environment wherein conflict with other factions persists, they become increasingly structured and become collectivistic coalitions or parties. The collectivistic quality of the group indicates group-centeredness as the key virtue for the faction (see Matt 23:8-12; 1 Cor 1:13ff.). Thus as Acts documents, the faction centered on Jesus of Nazareth that was in on-going conflict with many Judeans in general and other Judean factions in particular developed into a group-centered coalition or party (see Acts 4:32-37; contrast Acts 5:1-11). Finally, Paul is charged with desecrating the temple (Acts 21:28-30). This last is perhaps the most serious of the four charges, since Rome perceived itself as a protector of the temple as a holy site (Josephus, *Jewish War* 6.2.4 §128).

24:10-21: In this second section, Paul defends himself against the charges and continues to bear witness. Regarding disturbing the peace (v. 5), his purpose for going to Jerusalem was worship (v. 11). He was neither disputing nor agitating (vv. 12-13). As for the charge of being a ringleader of the Nazoreans, Paul rejects their identification of it as a "sect" but insists that he and the Nazoreans, a group-centered coalition, are in continuity with the ancestors of the house of Israel. They worship the God of Abraham, Isaac, and Jacob; hold fast to the law and the prophets; and, like the Pharisee group-centered coalition, they too believe in a resurrection.

The ancient harbor of Caesarea, built by Herod the Great in 22–10 B.C.E. Caesarea was the Roman administrative center of Judea and a place where Paul was judged. Location: Israel. Photo © Erich Lessing / Art Resource, N.Y.

As for desecrating the temple (v. 6), Paul was completing a purification rite and brought alms for the needy (vv. 17-18). The fact that those who originally made these false accusations are not present at this hearing suggests they abandoned their case. The real issue for Paul is that his accusers fault him for a belief he shares with the Pharisees, namely, the resurrection of the dead (vv. 20-21).

24:22-27: Felix adjourns the trial but keeps Paul in custody for two years (v. 27). Some days later, Paul has yet another opportunity to bear witness when Felix and his Judean wife, Drusilla, summon Paul to speak precisely about faith in the Messiah Jesus. Drusilla had been married to Azizus, king of Emesa (Syria), when Felix was smitten by her and took her to wife. She was quite plausibly the reason why Felix was "well informed about the Way" (v. 22). Paul presented his reflections on faith in (which means loyalty to) Messiah Jesus through the prism of "justice, self-control, and the coming judgment."

In the ancient, Greco-Roman world, a just or upright person was someone who knew and played by the specific cultural rules of the game in his cultural context (see Neyrey 1998:108-13). The virtue of justice pertained to three areas: gods, parents, and fatherland. This implied a shared "local code" concerning such things as patron–client relationship, piety, hospitality, and marriage ties among other things. Self-control (especially with reference to matters of sex) was treated extensively by Aristotle (*Nicomachean Ethics* 7, 1145a–1154b) and listed by Paul as one fruit of the Spirit (Gal 5:23). Finally, the coming judgment (see Rom 2:2-3), when virtue would be rewarded and wickedness punished, was integral to the Israelite tradition. No wonder that this trio of topics, natural lifestyle consequences of loyalty to (faith in) Messiah Jesus, would certainly strike fear in the hearts of Felix and Drusilla (v. 25). On the other hand, perhaps Luke has exaggerated what may have been nothing more than momentary embarrassment. The fear was obviously not sufficiently powerful to deter Felix from expecting a bribe. Though Roman law explicitly forbade this practice, it did exist (see Josephus, *Jewish War* 2.14.1 §273, concerning Albinus, the governor of Judea).

Paul Witnesses before Festus Acts 25:1-27

25:1 Three days after Festus had arrived in the province, he went up from Caesarea to Jerusalem 2 where the chief priests and the leaders of the Jews gave him a report against Paul. They appealed to him 3 and requested, as a favor to them against Paul, to have him transferred to Jerusalem. They were, in fact, planning an ambush to kill him along the way. 4 Festus replied that Paul was being kept at Caesarea, and that he himself intended to go there shortly. 5 "So," he said, "let those of you who have the authority come down with me, and if there is anything wrong about the man, let them accuse him."

6 After he had stayed among them not more than eight or ten days, he went down to Caesarea; the next day he took his seat on the tribunal and ordered Paul to be brought. 7 When he arrived, the Jews who had gone down from Jerusalem surrounded him, bringing many serious charges against him, which they could not prove. 8 Paul said in his defense, "I have in no way committed an offense against the law of the Jews, or against the temple, or against the emperor." 9 But Festus, wishing to do the Jews a favor, asked Paul, "Do you wish to go up to Jerusalem and be tried there before me on these charges?" 10 Paul said, "I am appealing to the emperor's tribunal; this

is where I should be tried. I have done no wrong to the Jews, as you very well know. 11 Now if I am in the wrong and have committed something for which I deserve to die, I am not trying to escape death; but if there is nothing to their charges against me, no one can turn me over to them. I appeal to the emperor." 12 Then Festus, after he had conferred with his council, replied, "You have appealed to the emperor; to the emperor you will go."

13 After several days had passed, King Agrippa and Bernice arrived at Caesarea to welcome Festus. 14 Since they were staying there several days, Festus laid Paul's case before the king, saying, "There is a man here who was left in prison by Felix. 15 When I was in Jerusalem, the chief priests and the elders of the Jews informed me about him and asked for a sentence against him. 16 I told them that it was not the custom of the Romans to hand over anyone before the accused had met the accusers face to face and had been given an opportunity to make a defense against the charge. 17 So when they met here, I lost no time, but on the next day took my seat on the tribunal and ordered the man to be brought. 18 When the accusers stood up, they did not charge him with any of the crimes that I was expecting. 19 Instead they had certain points of disagreement with him about their own religion and about a certain Jesus,

who had died, but whom Paul asserted to be alive. 20 Since I was at a loss how to investigate these questions, I asked whether he wished to go to Jerusalem and be tried there on these charges. 21 But when Paul had appealed to be kept in custody for the decision of his Imperial Majesty, I ordered him to be held until I could send him to the emperor." 22 Agrippa said to Festus, "I would like to hear the man myself." "Tomorrow," he said, "you will hear him."

23 So on the next day Agrippa and Bernice came with great pomp, and they entered the audience hall with the military tribunes and the prominent men of the city. Then Festus gave the order and Paul was brought in. 24 And Festus said, "King Agrippa and all here present with us, you see this man about whom the whole Jewish community petitioned me, both in Jerusalem and here, shouting that he ought not to live any longer. 25 But I found that he had done nothing deserving death; and when he appealed to his Imperial Majesty, I decided to send him. 26 But I have nothing definite to write to our sovereign about him. Therefore I have brought him before all of you, and especially before you, King Agrippa, so that, after we have examined him, I may have something to write—27 for it seems to me unreasonable to send a prisoner without indicating the charges against him."

Textual Notes: Acts 25:1-27

25:1-12: Festus hears the charges against Paul (vv. 1-7), listens to Paul's defense and appeal to Caesar (vv. 8-11), and agrees to send him to Caesar (v. 12).

25:8: Paul denies having done anything illegal. He has not transgressed Mosaic law, nor has he desecrated the temple, nor has he violated Roman law.

25:11: Paul's appeal to Caesar is not a light request since he would have to pay travel costs and lodging in Rome, as well as the cost of litigating his case.

25:13-27: Agrippa II and Bernice are brother and sister. After she was widowed, Bernice lived at her brother's court. Gossip claimed she had a liaison with her brother (Josephus, *Jewish War* 2.11.5 §217). Neither of them was liked by fellow Judeans. Festus seeks Agrippa's opinion on Paul's case, since he has no idea what to write in the letter that must accompany Paul to Rome to inform the tribunal there of the particulars. Festus acknowledged that Paul was innocent of criminal charges (vv. 18-19, 25). Agrippa requests to hear Paul in person (v. 22).

25:13—26:32: Herod hears Paul with the permission of Festus. This has its matching scene in Luke 23:6-12, where Pilate sends Jesus to Herod for questioning.

25:19: NRSV "religion" is anachronistic since in antiquity "religion" was embedded in kinship and politics and was not a freestanding social institution as it is in the contemporary Western world. RSV "superstition" is possible but implausible here, given Rome's general tolerance regarding relations with the realm of the deity (Josephus, *Antiquities* 14 §228). The Greek word basically means reverence for deities, devotion to the gods; hence a more appropriate translation would be "disputes about their [Judean] *beliefs* [about their god]." The following statement specifies one dispute concerning Jesus who died, but whom Paul claimed was alive. This is a Roman view of the matter and not Paul's understanding. The majority of Paul's opposing fellow Judeans denied Paul's claim that Jesus was raised by God.

Paul Witnesses before King Agrippa Acts 26:1-32

26:1 Agrippa said to Paul, "You have permission to speak for yourself." Then Paul stretched out his hand and began to defend himself: 2 "I consider myself fortunate that it is before you, King Agrippa, I am to make my defense today against all the accusations of the Jews, 3 because you are especially familiar with all the customs and controversies of the Jews; therefore I beg of you to listen to me patiently.

4 All the Jews know my way of life from my youth, a life spent from the beginning among my own people and in Jerusalem. 5 They have known for a long time, if they are willing to testify, that I have belonged to the strictest sect of our religion and lived as a Pharisee. 6 And now I stand here on trial on account of my hope in the promise made by God to our ancestors, 7 a promise that our twelve tribes hope to attain, as they earnestly worship day and night. It is for this hope, your Excellency, that I am accused by Jews! 8 Why is it thought incredible by any of you that God raises the dead?

9 Indeed, I myself was convinced that I ought to do many things against the name of Jesus of Nazareth. 10 And that is what I did in Jerusalem; with authority received from the chief priests, I not only locked up many of the saints in prison, but I also cast my vote against them when they were being condemned to death. 11 By punishing them often in all the synagogues I tried to force them to blaspheme; and since I was so furiously enraged at them, I pursued them even to foreign cities.

12 With this in mind, I was traveling to Damascus with the authority and commission of the chief priests, 13 when at midday along the road, your Excellency, I saw a light from heaven, brighter than the sun, shining around me and my companions. 14 When we had all fallen to the ground, I heard a voice saying to me in the Hebrew language, 'Saul, Saul, why are you persecuting me? It hurts you to kick against the goads.' 15 I asked, 'Who are you, Lord?' The Lord answered, 'I am Jesus whom you are persecuting. 16 But get up and stand on your feet; for I have appeared to you for this purpose, to appoint you to serve and testify to the things in which you have seen me and to those in which I will appear to you. 17 I will rescue you from your people and from the Gentiles—to whom I am sending you 18 to open their eyes so that they may turn from darkness to light and from the power of Satan to God, so that they may receive forgiveness of sins and a place among those who are sanctified by faith in me.'

19 After that, King Agrippa, I was not disobedient to the heavenly vision, 20 but declared first to those in Damascus, then in Jerusalem and throughout the countryside of Judea, and also to the Gentiles, that they should repent and turn to God and do deeds consistent with repentance. 21 For this reason the Jews seized me in the temple and tried to kill me. 22 To this day I have had help from God, and so I stand here, testifying to both small and great, saying nothing but what the prophets and Moses said would take place: 23 that the Messiah must suffer, and that, by being the first to rise from the dead, he would proclaim light both to our people and to the Gentiles."

24 While he was making this defense, Festus exclaimed, "You are out of your mind, Paul! Too much learning is driving you insane!" 25 But Paul said, "I am not out of my mind, most excellent Festus, but I am speaking the sober truth. 26 Indeed the king knows about these things, and to him I speak freely; for I am certain that none of these things has escaped his notice, for this was not done in a corner. 27 King Agrippa, do you believe the prophets? I know that you believe." 28 Agrippa said to Paul, "Are you so quickly persuading me to become a Christian?" 29 Paul replied, "Whether quickly or not, I pray to God that not only you but also all who are listening to me today might become such as I am—except for these chains."

30 Then the king got up, and with him the governor and Bernice and those who had been seated with them; 31 and as they were leaving, they said to one another, "This man is doing nothing to deserve death or imprisonment." 32 Agrippa said to Festus, "This man could have been set free if he had not appealed to the emperor."

Textual Notes: Acts 26:1-32

This fifth and last "self-defense" speech made by Paul in Acts ends up being a testimony (vv. 23, 28) as he continues to bear witness to Jesus. This is in accord with the information Ananias received from the risen Jesus concerning Paul's newly assigned task (Acts 9:15). We follow the structure proposed by Talbert (1997:211-12):

Captatio benevolentiae (vv. 2-3), flattering the listener
  A Autobiography: Paul's life as a faithful Judean (vv. 4-5, marked by the Greek particle *men oun*)
    B The issue: resurrection (vv. 6-8, marked by the verb "stand")
      A' Autobiography: Paul's life as a faithful Judean, his call or recruitment by God, and his preaching (vv. 9-21, marked again by the Greek particle *men oun*)
        B' The issue: resurrection (vv. 22-23, marked again by the verb "stand")

26:2-3: Paul is pleading his case before a "half Judean" by genealogy. But by his Hellenistic Judean inculturation, Agrippa would be quite familiar with the "customs and controversies" of Judeans. True to the agonistic nature of circum-Mediterranean cultures, Judeans were continually involved in never-ending discussions and disputes as is reflected in much later rabbinic literature.

26:4-5: The Lukan Paul describes himself just as he does in his authentic writings (for example, Phil 3:4b-6): a Pharisee. He has lived in Jerusalem since youth; hence he and his lifestyle are well known to fellow Judeans of that place.

26:6-8: Once again Paul emphasizes that the problem fellow Judeans in Jerusalem have with him is theological, not political. Paul's "hope" is for the resurrection of the dead (v. 8; see also Acts 24:15; 26:8). That hope is rooted in a divine promise (perhaps Dan 12:2-3; or even Isa 26:19; Hos 6:2; Ezek 37:1-14) to all Judeans ("our ancestors [literally "fathers"] and "our twelve tribes"). This belief, rooted in Persia, is shared by Pharisees and Essenes.

26:9: "Name" in Luke as in the Bible in general stands for the real person. Hence, "the name of Jesus" means quite simply "Jesus." In collectivistic society, however, those who believed in Jesus crucified and raised were considered to be one with him. So Paul interprets his persecution of believers as opposing the person of Jesus as preached by these believers.

26:10: For the first and only time, Paul claims this activity took place in Jerusalem (see Acts 8:3).

26:11: Luke's Paul reveals a new detail about his persecution strategy. He claims to have resorted to violence in the community centers (synagogues). "Punish" could refer to flogging such as Paul himself experienced (2 Cor 11:24). The ancient Mediterranean world was filled with violence, and such behavior in Judean community centers would not be unusual. **Establishment Violence.**

The only "foreign city" in which Paul attempted to carry out his persecution was Damascus, but he was literally stopped in his tracks before he could even begin his task there.

26:12-18: Luke's third retelling of Paul's ASC experience on the road to Damascus exhibits some differences with the other accounts. As previously noted (see Acts 9 and 22 above), there are two possible explanations. One is that Luke is interpreting (and embellishing) the basic information he received from Paul. A second explanation is that such differences are normal in recalling ASC experiences. Paul, who reported his experience quite tersely in Gal 1:12, 15-16, would normally have reinterpreted it as he repeated it to others throughout his career. Even Luke's sources may have recorded it from Paul more than once. Quite likely both explanations are valid here.

26:13: The intensity of the light grows with each report (Acts 9:3; 22:6). Light has two meanings. Neurologically, it signals that a person is entering an ecstatic trance. The level of awareness is shifting. Noting increased intensity of light in each account indicates that the trance was deep. Second, light is associated with God in the Israelite tradition (Exod 24:5; Deut 5:24; see Jas 1:17). That is the meaning given to an experience of light. Hence, Paul instantly recognized that God was initiating personal contact with him.

26:14: Whether all fell to the ground or only Paul (Acts 9:4, 7; 22:7) is insignificant for the ASC experience. Nothing in those passages precludes his companions from falling to the ground also. On the other hand, if Paul alone heard the voice (as here and in Acts 9:4, 7; 22:7, 9), his fellow travelers either did not share the ASC experience, or it was vacuous for them without the soundtrack which they were unable to provide. Yet according to Acts 9:7, his fellow travelers did hear the voice too. This might indicate that Paul's fellow travelers did not share his new understanding of Jesus Messiah. They may have heard the voice but failed to understand its message, not uncommon in ASC experiences (see John 12:27-29). They might have remained staunch persecutors of these deviant Israelites.

Some scholars find a contradiction in Paul's hearing a voice speaking Aramaic but quoting a Greek proverb. In Greek literature, the proverb he quotes expressed the futility of resisting divine influence in future activities, a notion appropriate to Paul's situation. This notion may have been familiar in Hellenistic culture (see *Pss. Sol.* 16:4 [125 B.C.E. to early first century C.E.]; Philo, *Decalogue*, 87). Paul, of course, knew both Aramaic and Greek. Since the visionary provides the soundtrack for the ASC experience, it is no surprise that he hears Jesus speaking Aramaic and Greek. ASC research by members of Cuyamungue: The Felicitas D. Goodman Institute confirms the multilingual soundtracks of trance experiences.

26:16-18: "Stand on your feet" does not appear in Acts 9:6 and 22:10. It is plausibly an allusion to Ezek 2:1-3 in the Septuagint, with which Paul and Luke were quite familiar. The allusion—the first of a few allusions in this report—highlights Paul as a prophet (v. 17 = Jer 1:7-8; v. 18 = Isa 35:5; 42:7, 16). In Acts 9, he is presented as a chosen instrument (Acts 9:15), while in Acts 22 he is presented as a witness (Acts 22:15, 18, 20). This triple report is very likely Luke's effort to clarify how Paul perceived himself (see Gal 1:15) and how he was perceived by others. The latter perception is very important to dyadic personalities such as Paul. They depend very strongly on the opinions of others ("Who do people say that I am?" [Mark 8:27] is not a quiz but rather a genuine concern of a collectivistic person about the opinion of others).

Paul's charge from the risen Jesus is similar to that given by God to the prophets: he is to open the eyes of his people (Israel), even those living as minorities among non-Israelite populations ("Gentiles"). He is to lead them to faith in Israel's Messiah, Jesus of Nazareth, raised by the God of Israel with a view to a forthcoming and new political religious kingdom.

26:19-21: As any Roman would understand, Paul obeyed the vision. Livy (2.36) tells of a man who had a vision of Jupiter sending him with a message to the Senate. The man ignored the vision even though he had it two more times. Then his son died and he became palsied. After delivering the divine message to the Senate from his litter, he rose and walked out unaided.

Paul, in turn, insists on his obedience to God. He describes his activity in a way reminiscent of the holy man, John the Baptist: Paul proclaimed repentance to fellow Israelites in Damascus, then Jerusalem, throughout Judea and also among Israelites living in non-Israelite cities. This repentance entails turning to the God of Israel and producing works of repentance. Fellow Israelites seized him in the temple and sought to kill him because, in Paul's view, he was obedient to the divine commission.

26:22-23: Luke's Paul focuses again on the true issue: the resurrection of Jesus. Though the Old Testament nowhere speaks of a suffering Messiah (yet Qumran seems to in the Dead Sea scrolls: 4Q285), Luke makes that notion central to his interpretation of tradition (Luke 24:26, 46; Acts 17:3; 26:23), which he claims coheres with what is contained in the Law and the Prophets. Paul proclaims that Jesus is the first to be raised from the dead (compare 1 Cor 15:20).

26:24-32: The reaction to Paul's witness is varied. Festus thinks he is mad; Agrippa sneers at the implication that Paul is trying to win him over. In the end, Agrippa admits and Festus agrees that Paul is innocent of any crime.

26:32: Agrippa's declaration: "This man could have been set free . . ." has its matching scene in Luke 23:16, 22, where Pilate says he will release Jesus. The same Greek word appears in both places.

26:24-25: It was common in antiquity to charge philosophers with being mad. Dio Chrysostom was so charged but denied the accusation and insisted that he spoke the truth (*De Invidia* [*Or 77/78*] 41-42). Paul does the same. Festus attributes Paul's alleged madness to his learning. The charge (madness due to learning) is a Lukan strategy for emphasizing the elevated social status of Paul and other believers.

26:26-28: Paul addresses Agrippa directly and makes two points: (1) The events Paul discusses did not occur "in a dark corner," that is, in secret. Romans were highly suspicious and fearful of secret societies, secret rites, secret teachings (Pliny, *Letters to Trajan* 10.96). Jesus groups are not a secret society. (2) Paul challenges Agrippa on the basis of his familiarity with Israelite traditions and the Prophets to accept Paul's conclusions about Jesus. Agrippa parries the thrust by rejecting the possibility of an instantaneous change of heart, which was derided by the ancients (Plutarch, *Moralia* 75C-E).

The title "Messianist" (Greek: *Christianoi*) occurs only three times in the New Testament (Acts 11:26; 26:28; 1 Pet 4:16). It was used by outsiders and always in a denigrating sense. Jesus group members never identified themselves as Messianists, but rather preferred "followers of the Way" (see Acts 9.2).

Acts 27:1–28:14 Section B' On the Way to Rome: God Pronounces Paul Innocent

27:1 When it was decided that we were to sail for Italy, they transferred Paul and some other prisoners to a centurion of the Augustan Cohort, named Julius. 2 Embarking on a ship of Adramyttium that was about to set sail to the ports along the coast of Asia, we put to sea, accompanied by Aristarchus, a Macedonian from Thessalonica. 3 The next day we put in at Sidon; and Julius treated Paul kindly, and allowed him to go to his friends to be cared for. 4 Putting out to sea from there, we sailed under the lee of Cyprus, because the winds were against us. 5 After we had sailed across the sea that is off Cilicia and Pamphylia, we came to Myra in Lycia. 6 There the centurion found an Alexandrian ship bound for Italy and put us on board. 7 We sailed slowly for a number of days and arrived with difficulty off Cnidus, and as the wind was against us, we sailed under the lee of Crete off Salmone. 8 Sailing past it with difficulty, we came to a place called Fair Havens, near the city of Lasea. 9 Since much time had been lost and sailing was now dangerous, because even the Fast had already gone by, Paul advised them, 10 saying, "Sirs, I can

see that the voyage will be with danger and much heavy loss, not only of the cargo and the ship, but also of our lives." 11 But the centurion paid more attention to the pilot and to the owner of the ship than to what Paul said. 12 Since the harbor was not suitable for spending the winter, the majority was in favor of putting to sea from there, on the chance that somehow they could reach Phoenix, where they could spend the winter. It was a harbor of Crete, facing southwest and northwest.

13 When a moderate south wind began to blow, they thought they could achieve their purpose; so they weighed anchor and began to sail past Crete, close to the shore. 14 But soon a violent wind, called the northeaster, rushed down from Crete. 15 Since the ship was caught and could not be turned head-on into the wind, we gave way to it and were driven. 16 By running under the lee of a small island called Cauda we were scarcely able to get the ship's boat under control. 17 After hoisting it up they took measures to undergird the ship; then, fearing that they would run on the Syrtis, they lowered the sea anchor and so were

driven. 18 We were being pounded by the storm so violently that on the next day they began to throw the cargo overboard, 19 and on the third day with their own hands they threw the ship's tackle overboard. 20 When neither sun nor stars appeared for many days, and no small tempest raged, all hope of our being saved was at last abandoned.

21 Since they had been without food for a long time, Paul then stood up among them and said, "Men, you should have listened to me and not have set sail from Crete and thereby avoided this damage and loss. 22 I urge you now to keep up your courage, for there will be no loss of life among you, but only of the ship. 23 For last night there stood by me an angel of the God to whom I belong and whom I worship, 24 and he said, 'Do not be afraid, Paul; you must stand before the emperor; and indeed, God has granted safety to all those who are sailing with you.' 25 So keep up your courage, men, for I have faith in God that it will be exactly as I have been told. 26 But we will have to run aground on some island."

27 When the fourteenth night had come, as we were drifting across the sea of Adria, about midnight the sailors suspected that they were nearing land. 28 So they took soundings and found twenty fathoms; a little farther on they took soundings again and found fifteen fathoms. 29 Fearing that we might run on the rocks, they let down four anchors from the stern and prayed for day to come. 30 But when the sailors tried to escape from the ship and had lowered the boat into the sea, on the pretext of putting out anchors from the bow, 31 Paul said to the centurion and the soldiers, "Unless these men stay in the ship, you cannot be saved." 32 Then the soldiers cut away the ropes of the boat and set it adrift.

33 Just before daybreak, Paul urged all of them to take some food, saying, "Today is the fourteenth day that you have been in suspense and remaining without food, having eaten nothing. 34 Therefore I urge you to take some food, for it will help you survive; for none of you will lose a hair from your heads." 35 After he had said this, he took bread; and giving thanks to God in the presence of all, he broke it and began to eat. 36 Then all of them were encouraged and took food for themselves. 37 (We were in all two hundred seventy-six persons in the ship.) 38 After they had satisfied their hunger, they lightened the ship by throwing the wheat into the sea.

39 In the morning they did not recognize the land, but they noticed a bay with a beach, on which they planned to run the ship ashore, if they could. 40 So they cast off the anchors and left them in the sea. At the same time they loosened the ropes that tied the steering-oars; then hoisting the foresail to the wind, they made for the beach. 41 But striking a reef, they ran the ship aground; the bow stuck and remained immovable, but the stern was being broken up by the force of the waves. 42 The soldiers' plan was to kill the prisoners, so that none might swim away and escape; 43 but the centurion, wishing to save Paul, kept them from carrying out their plan. He ordered those who could swim to jump overboard first and make for the land, 44 and the rest to follow, some on planks and others on pieces of the ship. And so it was that all were brought safely to land.

28:1 After we had reached safety, we then learned that the island was called Malta. 2 The natives showed us unusual kindness. Since it had begun to rain and was cold, they kindled a fire and welcomed all of us around it. 3 Paul had gathered a bundle of brushwood and was putting it on the fire, when a viper, driven out by the heat, fastened itself on his hand. 4 When the natives saw the creature hanging from his hand, they said to one another, "This man must be a murderer; though he has escaped from the sea, justice has not allowed him to live." 5 He, however, shook off the creature into the fire and suffered no harm. 6 They were expecting him to swell up or drop dead, but after they had waited a long time and saw that nothing unusual had happened to him, they changed their minds and began to say that he was a god.

7 Now in the neighborhood of that place were lands belonging to the leading man of the island, named Publius, who received us and entertained us hospitably for three days. 8 It so happened that the father of Publius lay sick in bed with fever and dysentery. Paul visited him and cured him by praying and

putting his hands on him. 9 After this happened, the rest of the people on the island who had diseases also came and were cured. 10 They bestowed many honors on us, and when we were about to sail, they put on board all the provisions we needed.

11 Three months later we set sail on a ship that had wintered at the island, an Alexandrian ship with the Twin Brothers as its figurehead. 12 We put in at Syracuse and stayed there for three days; 13 then we weighed anchor and came to Rhegium. After one day there a south wind sprang up, and on the second day we came to Puteoli. 14 There we found believers and were invited to stay with them for seven days. And so we came to Rome.

Textual Notes: Acts 27:1–28:14

This last of the "we" sections (Acts 27:1—28:16) is constructed around a sea-voyage narrative, a very popular literary form in antiquity. Examples can be found in Greek (Homer, *Odyssey* 4.449-511; 5:291-453), Roman (Virgil, *Aeneid* 1.122-252; 3:253-75), and Israelite literature (Jonah 1:3-17; *Testament of Naphthali* 6:1-10; Josephus, *Life* 13–16). Rhetorical training in the Roman period required extensive practice in composing such accounts. They all shared common elements such as a warning not to sail, sailing in a bad season, the ship's breaking up, survivors swimming to shore where helpful, simple folk meet them on the shore, and so on. The stories were so predictable that satirists lampooned them (Juvenal, *Satirae* 12.17-82).

A common feature of these stories is that they are very high context, both as to geographical locations and as to the fine points of sailing in the Mediterranean. Perhaps it was common knowledge that one did not sail (or even travel by land) during the rainy season from mid-October to mid-March. By Israelite reckoning that would be from the Day of Atonement (the fast of Acts 27:9) to when the rains stop before Passover. Sailing at any time was precarious. The seas were in the control of Poseidon (for Hellenists), or Neptune (for Romans), [or Tehom/Tiamat (for Semites)]. It was common to offer sacrifice to Poseidon/Neptune before a sea journey. Shipwrecks might be ascribed to any of those deities, who in the Greco-Roman period were considered the same personage. Yet for Israelites like Paul, it is the God of Israel who is in charge of the sea, earth, and sky that he created.

Of course, the focus of this story is Paul, innocent yet on his way to Rome for a hearing before the emperors. The sea voyage during the Mediterranean storm season would have one wonder whether Paul will in fact make it to Rome. While Paul acts as Israelite holy man in charge, the storm and shipwreck are a sort of ordeal by cosmic forces testing Paul's ultimate guilt or innocence. As is well known, an ordeal is "a practice of trial in which an accused person is subjected to a test, usually involving physical pain or danger, overcoming of which is taken as divine proof of innocence" (Oxford English Dictionary, *ad verbum*). Paul's survival is clear divine proof of his innocence.

Luke's sea-voyage account can be divided thus:

Introduction (Acts 27:1-8): Leaving Caesarea
Itinerary presented in three acts or scenes (Acts 27:9-12; 27:13-44; 28:1-10)

27:9-12: Centurion's dangerous decision at Fair Havens
27:13-44: Storm and shipwreck
28:1-10: Safety at Malta
Conclusion (Acts 28:11-14): On to Rome

Into this sea-voyage account, the writer inserted a number of comments about Paul, revealing his role as Israelite holy man. **Holy Man.** In the first scene, on land before embarking, Paul warns of danger and is disregarded; the danger is eventually realized (Acts 27:9-11). In the central scene, at sea, Paul declares that the God of Israel will save all (Acts 27:21-26); he then intervenes to thwart the mutiny of the sailors (Acts 27:31); and finally Paul urges everyone to eat (Acts 27:33-36); at the conclusion, the centurion rescues Paul (Acts 27:43). In the final scene on Malta, Paul is saved from a viper (Acts 28:2b-6) and heals his host's father as well as all who were sick on the island (Acts 28:8-9).

Introduction (Acts 27:1-8): Leaving Caesarea

27:1-8: The centurion, Julius, treats Paul according to Festus's recommendation (Acts 24:23; see here 27:3). Particularly noteworthy is the mention of Aristarchus (v. 2b), a member of the "we" in addition to the author of the "we" section (either Timothy or Silvanus or Titus). He illustrates true Middle Eastern loyalty (usually translated "faith" but actually meaning "I'm sticking with you no matter what") to his friend Paul (see Acts 19:29; 20:4; Col 4:10; Phlm 24). At Myra (v. 6), the centurion transfers Paul and company to a grain ship heading from Alexandria (Rome's breadbasket at that time) to Rome. Financial guarantees by Rome ensured that these ships would travel even in bad sailing season.

27:3: This verse reports that a centurion has a favorable relationship with Paul. This has its matching scene in Luke 23:47, where a centurion has a favorable opinion of Jesus.

Itinerary Presented in Three Acts or Scenes (Acts 27:9-12; 27:13-44; 28:1-10):

27:9-12: Centurion's dangerous decision at Fair Havens
27:13-44: Storm and shipwreck
28:1-10: Safety at Malta

Scene One (Acts 27:9-12): Centurion's dangerous decision at Fair Havens
27:9-12: Fully aware of this risky time for sea travel on the Mediterranean (v. 9), Paul predicts disaster (v. 10, loss of cargo and human life). As a holy man in contact with the divine realm, presented in the preceding chapter as a prophet, Paul communicates his understanding of the divine will. Human beings who ignore the rhythms that God has programmed into nature disobey the will of God. They will pay serious consequences. Greed of the pilot and ship owner (v. 11), however, overrides Paul's prudent and inspired advice, and an unsuitable harbor prompts the

group to risk sailing further in search of a safer harbor. "Fast" (v. 9) refers to the Day of Atonement, a Judean feast whose calendrical position (September/October) also identifies a time after which sailing on the Mediterranean grew dangerous. Paul's experience of shipwrecks (three times!—2 Cor 11:25) qualified him as someone to heed.

Scene Two (Acts 27:13-44): Storm and shipwreck

27:13-44: This section describes the storm and shipwreck continuing in the stereotypical literary form of a sea voyage.

27:13-20: A gentle south wind begins to take them on their chosen course to a safer harbor (v. 13). The storm, however, breaks (v. 14) and grows in intensity. They jettison cargo and tackle (v. 19) but soon abandon hope of surviving (v. 20) because conditions made it impossible to navigate by sun or stars.

27:21-26: Luke creates a speech for Paul and inserts it at this point. Paul is motivated by the fact that the passengers have not eaten in quite a while (due to fear, seasickness, anxiety, or all of the above and more; v. 21). He begins his speech with something of an "I told you so." The danger they now experience has resulted from refusing to heed his earlier warning. Seneca (*Ad Lucilium* 14.8) notes that wise pilots pay attention to those on board who are familiar with the sea. As he continues (v. 21), Paul says that, contrary to what he earlier predicted, there will be no loss of human life (see v. 11). He learned this in an ASC experience during which a messenger from the divine realm assured him that the passengers would be safe and that Paul would eventually reach Rome (vv. 23-24). Whether his first prediction was the result of an ASC experience or not, research in ecstatic trance experiences indicates that visionaries routinely revise the content, including the message of the experience. ASC experiences are not as clear as digital photographs or stereophonic sounds. They lack clarity that gains sharper focus as the experience is repeated or as the visionary continues to reflect upon the experience. Luke's Paul is explicit that this information comes from "the God to whom I belong and whom I worship," that is, the God of Israel. Paul concludes his exhortation by assuring everyone that events will turn out exactly as he has been told, though shipwreck is not a result of divine judgment but rather the consequence of sailing at a dangerous time of year. This is God's will or plan but not divine judgment (in v. 26 the Greek word translated "*have to* [run aground]" is Luke's way of indicating that events of history take place according to God's plan [Acts 1:16, 21; 3:21; 4:12; 9:16; 17:3; 23:11; 27:24, 26]).

27:27-44: As they drift on the sea, the sailors think they are nearing shore and, fearful of the danger of shipwreck, attempt to mutiny (v. 30). This, too, is a stock element in sea-voyage journeys. Paul—either because he has knowledge from the divine realm or because he has experience with behavior on shipwrecks—warns the centurion, and the mutiny is thwarted (v. 32). Then Paul encourages them to eat for their own well-being. They have not eaten in two weeks! Though Luke may have overlaid eucharistic overtones on this report (vv. 33-38), scholars interpret it as nothing more than a meal eaten according to customary Israelite tradition (blessing, breaking bread). Paul is apparently the only follower of the Way on board.

27:35: The meal Paul shares with colleagues has its matching scene in Luke 22:19a depicting Jesus at the Last Supper. The Greek words are nearly identical.

At daybreak, the sailors attempt to beach the craft, and the soldiers plan to kill the prisoners. If any should escape, the soldiers would pay with their own lives. The centurion, however, intervenes and saves Paul and the others. This, again, is according to the divine will. The passengers head to shore, some by swimming and others on planks or other pieces of the ship.

Scene Three (Acts 28:1-10): Safety at Malta

28:1-6: The shipwrecked survivors are greeted on the shore of Malta by local inhabitants. NRSV "natives" is partly correct, in that these people live there; however, the Greek word (*barbaroi*) essentially makes a linguistic reference and identifies those who do not speak Greek. Scholars believe that these "ordinary folk" who met the survivors probably spoke Punic, related to Phoenician. It is possible that these inhabitants and the survivors could communicate only non-verbally, aside from Paul who knew Aramaic, a language related to Punic.

28:3: The locals light a fire for the survivors, and while adding twigs to this fire Paul is bitten by a viper, which "fastened itself on his hand." There are no poisonous snakes on Malta now, and some scholars argue that there were none in antiquity either. If this was a poisonous snake, scholars propose that the island is Cephallenia, which has poisonous snakes and heavier rainfall than Malta. On the other hand, Luke may have embellished the event to further highlight Paul as a holy man. Recall Jesus' bestowal of power on his disciples to "tread upon serpents and scorpions . . . and nothing will hurt you" (Luke 10:19; compare Mark 16:18).

Documented research on behavioral signs of ASCs include handling poisonous snakes without suffering ill effects (Pilch 2004:53). Paul the holy man may well have entered an ASC by staring at the fire or by reflecting intensively on the experience all have just lived through. This could explain why the snakebite did not harm him if indeed the snake was poisonous.

In the ancient Mediterranean world, a serpent frequently served as a vehicle for divine justice (see *Greek Anthology* 7.29 for a similar event following a shipwreck). The later Israelite tradition tells the experience of the holy man Ḥanina ben Dosa (before 70 C.E.), who was bitten by a snake while praying. He continued praying unharmed, but the snake died at the entrance to its lair. Ḥanina's comment was: "It is not the snake that kills, but sin" (Babylonian Talmud, *Berakhot* 33a).

28:4-6: "Justice" (NRSV) is the name of a Greek goddess, Dike, who inflicts punishments on evildoers (Sophocles, *Antigone* 538). The locals concluded that Paul must be guilty of a crime (murder). Having escaped "Justice" at sea, he will now die from the viper's bite. When Paul remains unharmed, they conclude that he must be a god.

28:7: "Leading man" (or chief man) (NRSV) literally means first, most important, and pertains to prominence. As such, Publius was likely a Roman landowner or local official, hence in a good position to treat the survivors (see Acts 27:36) generously for three days.

28:8: The dysentery accompanied by a fever is a plausible response to a food-borne bacterial enterotoxin. This is a microorganism that causes gastrointestinal problems that are self-limiting; that is, they don't last beyond twenty-four to forty-eight hours (Pilch 2004:153). In 1887, a microorganism that infected the milk of Maltese goats was identified as a cause of "Malta fever." However, it produces dysenteric symptoms in only 7 percent of cases and is not therefore a plausible explanation for the problems (fever and dysentery) suffered by Publius's father.

Paul remedies the problem through prayer and laying on of hands. Prayer proves that Paul is not a god, as the locals concluded. Rather, the fact that Paul's prayers were heard (by the God of Israel, of course) confirms that he is a holy man (cf. John 9:31; Jas 5:16b-18) whose principal function in cross-cultural literature is healing. Laying on of hands relative to healing is not mentioned in the OT or in rabbinic literature. It is mentioned in one of the Dead Sea scrolls, the *Genesis Apocryphon* (1QapGen 20:21-22, 28-29), which tells of Abraham praying and laying hands on the pharaoh to remove the afflictions affecting him and his household for having taken Abraham's wife, Sarai, though he was completely unaware of their relationship (Gen 12:17-20). This suggests that laying on of hands and prayer were already associated as a healing strategy in the first century C.E. **Three Zones of Personality.**

28:9: "Diseases" (NRSV) is an anachronistic and ethnocentric rendition of the Greek word, which literally means "lack of strength." It is therefore best described as debilitating sicknesses (Pilch 2000:24-25). Likewise, Paul did not "cure" (NRSV) these conditions (see W. Bauer et al., *A Greek-English Lexicon of the New Testament and Other Early Christian Literature* [3rd ed.; Chicago: University of Chicago Press, 1999] s.v. *therapeuō*) but rather "healed" (RSV) them or "restored" them to wholeness or well-being (Pilch 2000:24-25).

28:10: "Bestowed many honors (literally, "honored us with many honors") (NRSV) could also be rendered "paid us with many fees." Since Paul would not leave for another three months, some have hypothesized that he set up a medical practice operating on "fee for service." This hypothesis is baseless. "Honors" is preferable to "fees" (see Sir 38:1), since the locals provision Paul and his company when they are about to embark. This fits not only with the core cultural values of honor and shame (v. 10a) but also with the interactions typical of dyadic contracts (v. 10bc).

Conclusion (Acts 28:11-14): On to Rome

28:11-13: These verses bring Paul's itinerary finally to Rome (actually, Puteoli on the Gulf of Naples) with stops along the way at Syracuse and Rhegium.

28:14: It seems that Jesus groups at Puteoli invited Paul and his company to stay for a week. Josephus knew of Judeans at Puetoli (*Jewish War* 2.7.1 §104), and some had embraced Jesus as Israel's Messiah before Paul's arrival.

Acts 28:16-31 Section A': Paul Witnesses in Rome to Fellow Israelites

28:16 When we came into Rome, Paul was allowed to live by himself, with the soldier who was guarding him.

17 Three days later he called together the local leaders of the Jews. When they had assembled, he said to them, "Brothers, though I had done nothing against our people or the customs of our ancestors, yet I was arrested in Jerusalem and handed over to the Romans. 18 When they had examined me, the Romans wanted to release me, because there was no reason for the death penalty in my case. 19 But when the Jews objected, I was compelled to appeal to the emperor—even though I had no charge to bring against my nation. 20 For this reason therefore I have asked to see you and speak with you, since it is for the sake of the hope of Israel that I am bound with this chain." 21 They replied, "We have received no letters from Judea about you, and none of the brothers coming here has reported or spoken anything evil about you. 22 But we would like to hear from you what you think, for with regard to this sect we know that everywhere it is spoken against."

23 After they had set a day to meet with him, they came to him at his lodgings in great numbers. From morning until evening he explained the matter to them, testifying to the kingdom of God and trying to convince them about Jesus both from the law of Moses and from the prophets. 24 Some were convinced by what he had said, while others refused to believe. 25 So they disagreed with each other; and as they were leaving, Paul made one further statement: "The Holy Spirit was right in saying to your ancestors through the prophet Isaiah, 26 'Go to this people and say, You will indeed listen, but never understand, and you will indeed look, but never perceive. 27 For this people's heart has grown dull, and their ears are hard of hearing, and they have shut their eyes; so that they might not look with their eyes, and listen with their ears, and understand with their heart and turn—and I would heal them.' 28 Let it be known to you then that this salvation of God has been sent to the Gentiles; they will listen." [29]

30 He lived there two whole years at his own expense and welcomed all who came to him, 31 proclaiming the kingdom of God and teaching about the Lord Jesus Christ with all boldness and without hindrance.

Textual Notes: Acts 28:15-31

28:15: Whereas in the previous verse Luke notes, "and so we came to Rome," Paul and his entourage still have a ways to travel to actually enter Rome. Since it is a five-day walk from Puteoli to Rome (200 km), and Paul stayed in Puteoli for a week, news of his arrival reached Rome by the gossip network. Some set out immediately to meet him along his way and got as far as the Appian Forum (65 km from Rome). Others went a bit shorter distance to Three Taverns (about 50 km from Rome). Both places were along the Appian Way. How might these Jesus group members have recognized Paul, a person they never met? Surely the military entourage was indicative of the presence of a prisoner. But which prisoner? Perhaps rumor of his appearance as recorded in the second-century document *The Acts of Paul and Thecla* had already been circulating: "a man small of stature, with a bald head and crooked legs, in a good state of body, with eyebrows meeting and nose somewhat hooked, full of friendliness; for now he appeared like a man, and now he had the face of an angel" (*Acts of Paul* 3:2; see Malina and Neyrey 1996:128). Admittedly this stereotypical description might not at all have matched the reality; however, one cannot minimize the important role of the gossip network. Word spread rapidly, and those greeting

Paul would form a wider entourage for his entry into the city. The passages have the following structure:

> Introduction Acts 28:16: vv. 16 and 30-31 form an inclusion (v. 16: Paul lives by himself albeit with a guard; v. 30: Paul receives visitors in his own rented lodging) that binds these verses together as a literary unit having two scenes:
> 28:17-22: Paul states that his innocence among Judeans is affirmed
> 28:23-28: Paul testifies to the kingdom and proclaims Jesus among Judeans
> Conclusion: Acts 28:30-31.

Introduction: Acts 28:16

Scene One (28:17-22): Paul states that his innocence among Judeans is affirmed
28:17-22: Since he is under house arrest and cannot visit Judean community centers (synagogues), Paul invites prominent leaders to visit him and hear him (v. 17), following his practice in cities with Israelite minorities. These are not Jesus group members. In fact they express interest in learning Paul's assessment of the Jesus group, the group within Judaism that is widely spoken against, resisted, and rejected (v. 22). They claim not to have received any information from Judea about Paul. Neither have any travelers from there reported "any evil" about him (v. 21). Given James's statement (Acts 21:21) that gossip about Paul's deviant preaching has spread all over the circum-Mediterranean world, it seems James was exaggerating. The ignorance of Roman Israelites about Paul is highly likely to have been the case. There is no indication of an effective information network running from Jerusalem to Rome and back in antiquity. For this reason alone, many Israelite communities around the Mediterranean developed their own form of Judean traditions.

This (vv. 21-22) is their response to Paul's declaration of innocence (vv. 17-20). He explains how political religious authorities in Jerusalem had the Romans arrest him, but Roman authorities found him innocent of any crime. To escape the plots of fellow Judeans, Paul appealed to Caesar, which explains why he is in Rome at the present moment. What he wanted to discuss with these leaders is the hope of Israel, which they share. This hope, according the Paul's Pharisaic beliefs, is in "the resurrection of the dead" (see Acts 23:6).

Scene Two (28:23-28): Paul witnesses to the kingdom and proclaims Jesus among Judeans
28:23-28: These leaders and many other Judeans return to Paul's lodging at a mutually agreeable time. Paul "witnesses" (NRSV: "testifying") to them for an entire day concerning the forthcoming Israelite political religious theocracy to be definitively established by Israel's Messiah Jesus, raised from the dead by the God of Israel, as the Law and the Prophets confirm. Paul's message is that Jesus group members stand in continuity with Judaism and its sources. As in the Gospels,

reaction is mixed: some were convinced, while others refused to believe. The visitors left disagreeing with each other.

Paul's final indicting words (vv. 26-27) quote Isa 6:9-10 and form an inclusion with the opening of Luke's story in Galilee (Luke 4:18-19), where in Nazareth Jesus reads from Isa 61:1-2. This inclusion further signals Luke's intention that his two volumes form a single work and should be read and understood as such. The quotation from Isaiah in the Gospel can be structured thus:

> **A** Bring good news to the poor
> >**B** Release to the captives/debtors
> > >**C** SIGHT TO THE BLIND
> >**B'** Release to the oppressed
> **A'** announce a year of favor from the Lord.

The chiastic or concentric arrangement of these verses focuses on blindness, which is a significant concern in Luke's works (see Luke 4:18; 6:39; 7:21-22; 11:34-36; 18:35-43; Acts 9:18//22:13; 13:11). In addition to these references to physical blindness, there are many references to sociocultural blindness or lack of understanding. In the Gospel, there is a parable about judging (Luke 6:39-42); a parable of the sower (Luke 8:9-16); a parable of the lamp (Luke 8:16-18); a makarism (more appropriate word for "beatitude") on seeing (Luke 10:21-24); the sign of Jonah (Luke 11:29-32); a parable on the lamp (Luke 11:33-36); signs on the earth and in the sky (Luke 12:54-56); yearning to "see" the Son of Man's day (Luke 17:22.30); Herod's hope to see a sign (Luke 23:8); crowds seeing and beating their breasts at Jesus' death (Luke 23:48); Jesus' final words: you are witnesses (Luke 24:48).

The Acts theme is "you will be my witnesses" (Acts 1:8) and dwells on the inability to see in reports about Peter (Acts 10:39, 41), Stephen (Acts 7; 22:20), Philip (Acts 8:5-8), and Paul. In Acts, even though the physical blindness of some was remedied—Paul (Acts 9:18//22:13) and Elymas (Acts 13:11)—others such as Paul's Judean visitors (Acts 28:25) chose to remain blind by their refusal to understand what they heard. Paul's "parting shot" to his Judean visitors, a quotation from Isa 6:9-10, can be structured in this way:

Go to this people, and say:

> **A** You shall indeed hear but never understand
> >**B** and you shall indeed see but never perceive
> >**B** for this people's heart has grown dull
> **A** and their ears are heavy of hearing
> >**B** and their eyes they have closed
> >**B** lest they should perceive with their eyes
> **A** and hear with their ears
> >**B** and understand with their heart
> >**B** and turn to me to heal them.

Of the three zones of the body (A = mouth-ears; B = heart-eyes; C = hands-feet) identified in the traditional Mediterranean view as well as throughout the Bible (see Pilch 2000:106-11), this Isaian passage focuses on mouth-ears, or self-expressive speech (A), and heart-eyes, or emotion-fused thought (B). Zone C, the symbolic bodily zone represented by "hands-feet," the zone of purposeful action, is entirely lacking. **Three Zones of Personality.** In Acts there are many speeches (Zone A), and many listeners understand (Zone B) and act upon what they hear (Zone C, for example, being baptized: Lydia in Acts 16:14-15; the jailer in Acts 16:33; and the like). However, some of Paul's visitors at this moment, like his Judean opponents throughout Acts, refuse to act on what they hear (Zone C: believe, repent, be baptized).

28:28: Scholars suggest Isa 40:5 and Ps 67:3 as possible influences on Paul's statement that "this salvation of God has been sent to the Gentiles." They interpret it to mean that Paul has proclaimed the Israelite kingdom of God and the Israelite Messiah to non-Israelites, and these have accepted his very Israelite message. Aside from the problems of making sense of such behavior, a closer look at those passages (Isaiah and the Psalm) and others like them suggests rather that non-Israelites form an appreciative audience or cheering section when they see what Yahweh God does for those of divine election. They applaud such a God.

Others have suggested Ezekiel 3 as background for Paul's statement: "they [presumably Gentiles] will listen to it." Ezekiel's charge from God, however, was to continue to preach to obstinate fellow Israelites. God's statement that non-Israelites would listen and respond is intended as a contrary-to-fact contrast with Ezekiel's assigned audience. As a consequence, we repeat our conviction that Paul's statement indicates his determination to continue to speak to assimilated Israelites living as minorities among majority non-Israelite populations. Some have already listened obediently, and some will likely listen congenially in the future. Who else would be able to appreciate or even be interested in Paul's arguments rooted in Israelite traditions and Pharisaic beliefs?

28:29: This verse is not attested in the best Greek manuscripts; hence, it appears in a note in most translations (as in the NRSV; it is included in the KJV text).

Conclusion 28:30-31

28:30-31: For two more years Paul proclaimed the forthcoming political religious theocracy ("kingdom of God") and taught about Lord Jesus Messiah. As with the Eleven (Twelve) from the outset of the story, Paul proclaims "with boldness," that is, without respect for the social status of his hearers. Luke adds that he does so unhindered, unlike his experiences with Judeans in various cities of the Mediterranean and in Jerusalem. Note that "kingdom of God" (v. 31) forms an inclusion with Acts 1:3.

Acts 28, which forms the conclusion of Acts, reports that Paul's work ends on the positive note of the fulfillment of Scripture. It has its matching scene in Luke 24, where Jesus' work concludes on the positive note of the fulfillment of Israel's Scriptures.

Appendix: Recurring Scenes in Luke and Acts

The prologue to Acts notes that this document is the second of a two-volume work. Luke and Acts form a diptych, that is, a work made up of two sets of more or less matching scenes. Charles H. Talbert (1974) and G. W. Trompf (1979) have adequately demonstrated this feature. There have been many explanations for this procedure. Perhaps Trompf states it best:

> Luke was fundamentally interested in more directly historical connections as an historian of the Hellenistic period. He wrote as though established historical events, which were for him divinely guided, had their own inner relatedness, connections between events amounting to the virtual reenactment of special happenings or the repetition of an earlier state of history in a later one, or even the recurrent operation of certain laws or principles. By the time Luke-Acts was written many connections between Jesus and the Old Testament and between the work of the Church and Jesus' ministry had already been forged. Luke appears to have interpreted this inheritance under the influence of his historiographical assumptions. As with Polybius, these assumptions were bound to affect the reliability of his account. But the main point is that he emerges as an historian comparable to Polybius (who, after all, managed to infuse a theological significance into his work), rather than as someone concerned to make a series of evangelistic and theological assertions in the form of a narrative. (Trompf 1979:129)

1. Acts 1:1-5. The first matching scene is the dedication of each book (Luke and Acts) to Theophilus (Luke 1:1-14 and Acts 1:1-5).

2. Acts 1:14, 24. The matching scene (see Textual Notes 1:1-2) for Acts 1:14, 24 (the disciples praying) is Luke 3:21 (Jesus praying at his baptism).

3. Acts 2:1-13. This scene (the Spirit "falls" on the disciples) has its match in the scene of Jesus' baptism and the descent of the Spirit upon him in physical form (Luke 3:22).

4. Acts 2:14-40. This scene, with a sermon giving a theme for what follows—fulfillment of prophecy and rejection of Jesus—has its matching scene in the Gospel with the same content (Luke 4:16-30).

5. Acts 2:14—12:17. The whole passage is a text-segment that sounds the theme of fulfillment, illustrated by examples of prophesying and wonders. Persecutions illustrate the note of unbelief. Its matching scene is

Luke 4:31—8:46, which sounds the same themes: fulfillment (Luke 4:16-30) illustrated by examples of preaching and healing. Conflicts illustrate the note of rejection.

6. Acts 3:1-10. This text-segment, which relates the healing of a lame man in the name of Jesus, has its matching scene in the Gospel's account of a similar healing (Luke 5:17-26).

7. Acts 4:1—8:3. The scene reports conflicts with religious leaders and has its matching scene in Luke 5:29—6:11, where Jesus experiences the same.

8. Acts 7:60. Stephen's attitude of forgiveness or waiving the need for satisfaction matches that of Jesus (Luke 23:34).

9. Acts 9:36-43. This passage concerning widows and a resurrection has its matching scene in Luke 7:11-17 (a widow and the raising of her son).

10. Acts 10:1-8. The report about Cornelius, a Roman centurion, has its matching scene in Luke 7:1-10, where a centurion, well regarded by Israelites, sends men to Jesus to ask him to come to his house.

11. Acts 11:1-18. The scenario here, in which the Pharisee party criticizes Peter for associating with non-Israelites, has its matching scenario in Luke 7:36-50, where Pharisees criticized Jesus for being touched by the wrong kind of woman.

12. Acts 12:1-4. This scene very much matches what happened in the case of Jesus (Luke 21:1-7; 23:7-15). In this case Jesus' disciple and one of the Twelve, James son of Zebedee, is killed by Herod during the feast of Unleavened Bread. Immediately, after that, because it pleased the Judeans, Herod seized Peter, to bring him out to the people right after the Passover.

13. Acts 13–20. The scene painted by Luke in Acts 13–20, wherein he traces the journeys of Paul, has its matching scene in Luke 12:1-12, which describes the mission of the seventy.

14. Acts 19:21—21:17. This passage has its matching scene in Luke 9:51—19:28. Paul and Jesus each make a journey to Jerusalem that is a passion journey under divine necessity and characterized by their associates' lack of understanding.

15. Acts 19:21. This passage reports Paul's resolve to go to Jerusalem, echoing Jesus' determination to go to Jerusalem (Luke 9:51, 53).

16. Acts 20:22. Paul's declaration of going to Jerusalem has its matching scene in Luke 13:22.

17. Acts 21:4. The attempt to dissuade Paul from journeying to Jerusalem has its matching scene in Luke 13:33, where Jesus declares such a trip a divine necessity for him.

18. Acts 21:11-12. Agabus's message has its matching scene in Luke 17:11, where Jesus is described as journeying through Samaria and Galilee on his way to Jerusalem.

19. Acts 21:13. Paul's admission that he is ready to die in Jerusalem has its matching scene in Luke 18:31, recording Jesus' determination to continue the journey to Jerusalem.

20. Acts 21:15. Making ready to go to Jerusalem has its matching scene in Luke 19:11, where Jesus was already near Jerusalem.

21. Acts 21:17. The arrival of Paul in Jerusalem has its matching scene in Luke 19:28, 45, when Jesus goes up to Jerusalem and enters the temple.

22. Acts 21:17. The scene of Paul receiving a good reception and God being glorified or honored for what Paul has accomplished among assimilated Israelites has its matching scene in Luke 19:37, where Jesus receives a good reception and people praise God for the works they have witnessed.

23. Acts 21:26. Paul's friendly attitude toward the temple has its matching scene in Luke 19:45-48, which reports Jesus entry into the temple and his friendly attitude toward it.

24. Acts 21:30. The mob that seizes Paul has its matching scene in Luke 22:54, where a mob seizes Jesus.

25. Acts 23–26. These chapters present four trials or occasions for witness by Paul as he gives testimony before the Sanhedrin, Felix, Festus, and Herod Agrippa. These have their matching scenes in Luke 22:26; 23:1; 23:8; and 23:13, where Jesus is on trial before the Sanhedrin, Pilate, Herod, and Pilate again.

26. Acts 23:2. The slapping of Paul at the high priest's command has its matching scene in Luke 22:63-64, where Jesus is slapped by the priest's assistants.

27. Acts 23:6-9. The report that Sadducees do not believe in the resurrection but that the scribes support Jesus has its matching scene in Luke 20:27-39, where Jesus has a similar experience with Sadducees and scribes.

28. Acts 23:9; 25:25; and 26:31. Three men—Lysian, Festus, and Agrippa—declare Paul innocent. These instances have matching scenes in Luke 23:4, 14, 22 where Pilate declares Jesus innocent three times.

29. Acts 25:13—26:32. Herod hears Paul with the permission of Festus. This has its matching scene in Luke 23:6-12, where Pilate sends Jesus to Herod for questioning.

30. Acts 26:32. Agrippa's declaration: "This man could have been set free . . ." has its matching scene in Luke 23:16, 22, where Pilate says he will release Jesus. The same Greek word appears in both places.

31. Acts 27:3, 43. These verses report that a centurion has a favorable relationship with Paul. This has its matching scene in Luke 23:47, where a centurion has a favorable opinion of Jesus.

Reading Scenarios for the
Acts of the Apostles

Alternate States of Consciousness (ASC)

Anthropologists studying cross-cultural psychology define altered (preferably, alternate) states of consciousness as conditions in which sensations, perceptions, cognition, and emotions are altered. Such states are characterized by changes in sensing, perceiving, thinking, and feeling. When a person is in such a state, the experience modifies the relation of the individual to the self, the body, one's sense of identity, and the environment of time, space, or other people. One scholar has identified more than thirty such states of consciousness, including dreams, daydreams, nightmares, incubation dreams, directed imagings, hallucinations, *dédoublements de conscience*, illusions, visions, depersonalization, derealization, bodiliness, the stare, fugue states, sexual ecstasy, mystical ecstasy, prayerfulness, inspiration, furor, aesthetic contemplation, *Ergriffenheit* (being seized), being charmed, transported (in the French sense of *transporter*), entranced hypnotic trance, possession trance, television trance, distraction, soul loss, soul flight, shamanistic trance, nirvana-like experiences, *susto* (sudden, overwhelming fear), near-death experiences, and a host of drug-induced experiences of varying intensity and phenomenology, not to mention "normal" consciousness. In trance or in any other alternate state of consciousness, a person encounters, indeed enters, another level or aspect of reality registered physiologically in the brain in the same way "normal" experiences are. Culturally "normal" or consensual reality is that aspect or dimension of reality of which a person is most commonly aware most of the time.

Alternate reality describes that dimension of reality in which nonhuman personages such as spirits and/or the deity reside, and which human beings from culturally "normal" reality can sometimes visit in ecstatic trance by taking a journey (variously called "sky journey" or "soul loss" and the like), and to which people go when they die. The experience of alternate reality is nonrational but not irrational, as claimed by those who do not believe any of these things. From the perspective of these latter persons, such experiences would be appropriately described as experiences of nonconsensual reality.

185

In the book of Acts, there is an endless series of episodes depicting alternate state of consciousness experiences: 1:1-11 (ascension of the risen Jesus); 2:1-4 (descent of spirit); 2:5-13 (glossolalia); 6:1—8:3 (Stephen [7:55-56]); 8:4-40 (Philip); 9:1-9 (Paul); 9:10-19 (Ananias); 9:43—10:8 (Cornelius); 10:9-16 (Peter); 10:17-23 (interpretation of Peter's vision); 10:23-48 (soldier's house in Caesarea: Cornelius repeats; Peter explains; glossolalia; trance experience); 11:1-18 (Peter explains in Jerusalem); 12:5-19 (Peter escapes arrest); 12:12-17 (maid's reaction); 13:1-3 (commission in Antioch), 4-12 (Paul and the curse); 14:1-20 (healing); 16:6-10 (ASC experience of Spirit); 18:1-17 (Paul encouraged by the Lord); 18:18—19:4 (glossolalia in Corinth); 20:23 (experience of the Spirit); 22:6-21 (Paul's vision); 23:10-11 (Lord speaks to Paul); 26:9-18 (Paul's vision, again); 27:23-26 (angel tells Paul his destiny) (see Pilch 2004). The whole book of Revelation depends on the alternate state of consciousness experiences of the prophet John (see Malina and Pilch 2000).

During the centuries before and after Luke, countless persons reported a range of visions and appearances involving celestial entities. Their experiences have to be interpreted within the framework of *their* own culture's consensus reality rather than ours. There is no reason not to take seriously what these persons say of their experiences. Paul ascribes his call by the God of Israel to undertake his change-agency task to an alternate state of consciousness experience initiated by God (Gal 1:1, 12). His descriptions of Jesus group experiences, which he ascribes to God's Spirit, are all instances of such alternate states events, as indicated repeatedly in our commentary. Paul himself notes his personal sky journey in which he experienced the ineffable, in "Paradise" (2 Cor 12:1-7). Paradise in Israelite lore, of course, was the name of the garden of pleasure created by God for the first human beings (Genesis 2). By Paul's day, however, this place of blessedness was transposed into the sky (see Luke 23:43), often referred to as the third or highest level of the sky, where the righteous dead dwell awaiting the resurrection of the dead. Paul himself frequently receives directives from the realm of God (Rom 16:26; Gal 2:2; 2 Cor 12:8). Of course, Paul ascribes the visions of the resurrected Jesus to such alternate state experiences (1 Cor 15:5-8).

Aside from dreams and angelic appearances, the Synoptics report five main incidents of such visions and/or appearances in the career of Jesus: two by Jesus: at his baptism (Mark 1:9-11//Matt 3:13-17//Luke 3:21-22), and at his being tested as holy man (Mark 1:12-13//Matt 4:1-11//Luke 4:1-13); and three by various disciples: their vision of Jesus walking on the sea of Galilee (Mark 6:45-52//Matt 14:22-33//John 6:16-21); their vision of Jesus transformed (Mark 9:2-10//Matt 17:1-9//Luke 9:28-36), and finally the various resurrection appearances, including the final appearance of Jesus, in God's name, commissioning the apostles to proclaim the gospel of God.

Mainstream U.S. culture frowns on and even denies the human capacity for visions, trances, and experiences of alternate realities. We are very curious about nonrational dimensions of human existence but tend to label all such occurrences as irrational. John Pilch cites the work of Erika Bourguignon, who compiled a sample of 488 societies in all parts of the world, at various levels of technological complexity, and found that 90 percent of these societies evidence "alternate states of consciousness." Her conclusion: "Societies which do not utilize these states clearly are historical exceptions which need to be explained, rather than the vast majority of societies that do use these states" (cited by Pilch 1993:233). Thus, it would be quite anachronistic and ethnocentric to take our post-Enlightenment, post–Industrial Revolution, technologically obsessed society as normative for judging anyone other than ourselves. For most of the world, even today, a report of alternate states of awareness would be considered quite normal.

Cross-cultural comparison suggests that the Gospel authors describe experiences of alternate states of awareness. This may be difficult for us to believe because we have been inculturated to be selectively inattentive to such states of awareness except in dreams or under the influence of controlled substances. Pilch (1993:233) notes:

> The physician-anthropologist Arthur Kleinman offers an explanation for the West's deficiency in this matter. "Only the modern, secular West seems to have blocked individual's access to these otherwise pan-human dimensions of the self." What is the Western problem? The advent of modern science in about the seventeenth century disrupted the bio-psycho-spiritual unity of human consciousness that had existed until then. According to Kleinman, we have developed an "acquired consciousness," whereby we dissociate self and look at self "objectively." Western culture socializes individuals to develop a metaself, a critical observer who monitors and comments on experience. The metaself does not allow the total absorption in lived experience which is the very essence of highly focused ASCs (= alternate states of consciousness). The metaself stands in the way of unreflected, unmediated experience which now becomes distanced.

If we recognize that "objectivity" is simply socially tutored subjectivity, we might be more empathetic with persons of other cultures who report perceptions that we find incredible just because they are socially dysfunctional for us. (For more on the subject, see Pilch 2002a, 2002b, 2004.)

Ancestor Reverence

Ancestor reverence, also known as ancestrism or ancestor worship, refers to ritualized activities that honor those to whom we effectively owe our existence and continued well-being. In Mediterranean antiquity, the virtue of religion (Greek: *eusebeia*) dealt with the virtue of respecting and honoring those who have given and/or maintain our existence in society: God, king, parents. But in a special way it likewise includes those persons who have preceded us in our family and/or fictive family, that is ancestors. Some call this "memorialism."

What shaped ancestrism most was the prevailing family dyad (twosome) on which people focus, which they find "natural." A family dyad consists of two individuals, each standing in some role relative to the other, such as father and son, husband and wife, mother and son, mother and daughter (and father and daughter). The Mediterranean focus was on the prevailing patriarchalism emphasizing father and son.

Ancestrism is an essential expression of the inherent rules of behavior of the kinship system in the first place and of the specific society in general. Strong, positive ancestral concerns are likely to be found in a society where the father–son relationship is dominant. Father–son dyad focus exhibits the following traits: maintenance of ties with the past (continuity); close links between generations (inclusiveness); high value accorded to and respect for the aged; the normality of intervention by elders in the affairs of younger family members; authoritarian orientation; duties and obligations for family members viewed as superior and subordinate relations; strong and positive ancestor reverence.

Thus, in Israel, along with reverence for parents, one was expected to reverence (worship) the ancestral deity(ies) (God of Abraham, Isaac, and Jacob) and to observe the tradition of the elders, that is ancestral tradition (Matt 15:2, 3, 6; Mark 7:3, 4, 5, 8, 9, 13; 1 Cor 11:2; Gal 1:14; Col 2:8; 2 Thess 2:1; 3:6). The chief ancestor, Abraham, is mentioned in this role some seventy-three times in the New Testament; he variously receives the dead, rejoices with his offspring, is the source of merit for all his offspring, is the recipient of God's promises for his offspring, and so on.

This dominant father–son dyad correlates with spirit beliefs emphasizing rewarding and punishing ancestral spirits and deity(ies) as well as benevolent and just ancestral spirits and deity(ies). The frequent interactions of New Testament personages and angels sent from God point to this feature.

There are two aspects of ancestor reverence in the New Testament. First, there is the usual reverence for ancestors Abraham, Isaac, and Jacob, and their deity (the God of Abraham, Isaac, and Jacob), known as the God of our fathers (NRSV: ancestors). Acts makes mention of David as ancestor, and if we focus exclusively on Acts, we find reference to ancestors in 3:13, 25; 4:25; 5:30; 7:2, 4, 8, 9, 11, 12, 15, 19, 32, 38, 39, 44, 45, 51, 52; 13:17, 32, 36; 15:10; 22:14; 26:6; 28:25. The basis of Stephen's speech in Acts 7 is overwhelmingly rooted in rhetoric about Israel's ancestors.

Along with this reverence and remembrance of ancestors of old, there is a new perspective that considers the resurrected Jesus as an ancestor worthy of ancestor reverence and worship. He is the ancestor of the fictive kin group of all "in Christ," a group that shares a social identity, as do descendants of a common ancestor. To begin with, there is Jesus' request for remembrance at his final meal with his disciples (note his request in "remembrance of me" in Luke 22:19; 1 Cor 11:24; Justin, *1 Apology* 66.3). Further, Jesus claims, "For where two or three are gathered in my name, there am I in the midst of them" (Matt 18:20), thus assuring his continued ancestral presence, even for all days, "I am with you all days" (Matt 28:20). Actions done "in the name of the Lord" are done in the name of an ancestor who lives on (Acts 2:38; 3:6; 4:18; 5:40; 8:16; 9:27, 29; 10:48; 16:18; 19:5; 26:9; 1 Cor 1:13; 5:4; 6:11; Eph 5:20; Col 3:17; 2 Thess 3:6; Jas 5:10, 14; 1 John 3:23; 5:13).

*Abraham. Fresco, c. 239 C.E. from the
Synagogue in Dura Europos, Syria. Photo © Art
Resource, N.Y.*

Just as descendants of Abraham found themselves "in Israel," so now descendants of Jesus find themselves "in Christ." Jesus groups "in Christ" formed fictive kinship groups, just as previously those "in Israel" formed fictive extended kinship groups. The roles, statuses, goals, and values of the kinship system were contextualized to fit the roles, statuses, goals, and values of brothers and sisters "in Christ." The father–son patterns of being subject prevailed, although group members were to subject themselves to each other "in Christ." As befits people who reverence their ancestors, "in Christ" people remembered Jesus.

In sum, as one might expect of a group devoted to ancestor reverence, those "in Christ" formed an ingroup. And ingroup is a collection of individuals who perceive themselves to be members of the same social category, share some emotional involvement in this common definition of themselves, and achieve some degree of social consensus about the evaluation of their group and of their membership in it. Those not "in Christ" formed outgroups. A social outgroup is a collection of individuals who are perceived to be members of a different social category, to share some emotional involvement in some common definition of themselves, and to have in common a number of traits negatively evaluated by the other group but typical of this outgroup and of its membership.

Readers of Luke-Acts were ingroup members recognizing their roots in their founding ancestor—Jesus of Nazareth, Israel's Messiah and cosmic Lord, raised from the dead by the God of Israel (now the God of Jesus Christ), with a view to a forthcoming theocracy.

Baptism

Baptism is a prophetic symbolic action originally associated with the prophet John the Baptist. The Greek word *baptisma* is usually not translated, but simply written in the Latin alphabet. The Greek means dipping in some liquid. In antiquity people used water for purification rituals, which they undertook by themselves, on their own behalf. Such rituals restored people to some proper state after having stepped out of that state. John's baptism, however, was not a purification ritual, if only because it required dipping in water by a person other than oneself. John administered baptism as a symbolic act of the forgiveness of sin among Israelites in preparation for the forthcoming Israelite theocracy (see Acts 11:16; 13:24; 19:3-4). Sin was an act of dishonoring or shaming God that, in turn, required divine satisfaction lest God be shamed in the sight of people who knew about the sin. John's baptism, as a prophetic symbolic action, effectively removed the expected divine satisfaction. Jesus groups took up this practice but expanded its significance. Along with the meaning attributed to baptism by John, baptism was now "in Christ," symbolizing new birth into a Jesus group (Acts 2:38; 19:5).

In either case, baptism was an administered ritual dipping by means of which people were brought across social lines into a changed social status. Some recognized status transformation rituals in our society include marriage or taking office. Along with forgiveness of sin, baptism was a status transformation ritual symbolizing new birth "in Christ" through which Israelites were brought across the social line separating outsiders from insiders and transformed from the status of a nonmember to being a member of a Jesus group. Israelite Jesus group members looked upon themselves as forming a group of people in Christ, much like old Israel was a group of people in Israel (which is the name of the patriarch Jacob [Gen 32:28]). With the new birth came a new life marked by the presence of the spirit (Acts 1:5), usually manifested in alternate states of consciousness experiences. The highlight of Paul's call to be a holy man and prophet in Israel was his baptism in Christ (9:18).

Change Agent

The persons featured in the narrative of Acts are persons who communicate information about an innovation wrought by the God of Israel to the designated receiving group, the people of Israel, on behalf of an agency behind the change, specifically the God of Israel. Such persons (communicators) are called change agents. Such change agents attempt to influence an innovation decision in a direction deemed desirable by the change agency. Thus the change agent functions as a communication link between two or more social entities, the change agency responsible for the innovation and those to and for whom the innovation is directed. Change agents are usually professionals in that the task of diffusing the innovation in question constitutes a master status and is a full-time occupation.

In the Gospel documents, apostles were persons sent with a commission by some commissioning agency. The commission is to proclaim the forthcoming kingdom of God (= theocracy), based on Jesus' being commissioned by the God of Israel to make such a proclamation. In Acts, the characteristic feature of the change agent role of apostle is that it entails being commissioned by the God of Israel through the mediation of the resurrected Jesus. In the letters of Paul, the earliest documents of the New Testament, Paul insists on having been commissioned by the God of Israel in his revelation experience of the resurrected Jesus (an ASC; Gal 1:1, 10-12). In third- and fourth-generation Jesus group documents, we find mention of such authorization given to the Twelve through the resurrected Jesus (ASC experiences; Matt 28:18-20; Acts 1:8).

There are seven tasks that a change agent must undertake. The book of Acts describes several of these tasks in its high-context presentation, although all of them will have been present. The first and last tasks take place in that sequence; the other five take place variously and may be repeated. A change agent (1) develops need for change; (2) establishes an information exchange relation; (3) diagnoses problems; (4) creates intent to change; (5) translates intent into action; (6) stabilizes and prevents discontinuance; and (7) terminates relationship with the clients.

1. *Develops need for change.* A change agent is often initially required to bring awareness or knowledge to persons in some social grouping by pointing out alternatives to existing problems, by dramatizing these problems, and by convincing would-be clients that they are capable of confronting these problems. In collectivistic settings, a change agent attempts to influence opinion leaders by emphasizing a broader, forthcoming horizon (hence emphasis on the coming Israelite theocracy and the age to come), a higher contentment motivation (hence theme of reversal and righteousness through faith), a lower fatalism (hence theme of need for change and responsibility), and higher aspirations (in terms of the newly introduced symbol system focused on the presence of the Spirit of the resurrected Jesus). The change agent not only assesses the would-be clients' needs at this stage but also helps to create these needs in a consultive and persuasive manner.

2. *Establishes an information exchange relationship.* In collectivistic societies, would-be clients must accept the change agent before they will accept the innovations the agent promotes (hence the effectiveness of Paul's insistence that he is "all things to all men," or the significance of Peter's willingness to eat with Cornelius [Acts 10] in collectivistic Hellenistic society). While initial contact with prospective clients must leave an impression of credibility, trustworthiness, and empathy with their needs and problems, the change agent must maintain an information exchange relationship with those clients to maintain and develop social identity based on the proclaimed innovation. In Acts, Paul's return visits to various Jesus groups marks this feature (Acts 15:36). Interestingly, Luke makes no mention of Paul's letters, a prime example of an information exchange relationship.

3. *Diagnoses the problems.* The change agent is responsible for analyzing his clients' problems to point up why existing alternatives do not meet their needs. In arriving at his diagnostic conclusions, the change agent must view the situation empathetically, from his clients' perspective and not his own. (Such empathy is the ability of an individual to project oneself into the role of another; sympathy is

The restored inscription on white marble stone reads "Synagogue of the Hebrews." Many have suggested that the stone may have come from the synagogue in which Paul taught (see Acts 18:4); however, a post-Pauline date is more likely. From Cities of Paul © 2004 The President and Fellows of Harvard College.

the ability of an individual to project another into one's own role.) Change agent empathy is positively related with success in implementing an innovation (provided the change agent is not so empathetic that he completely takes the role of his clients and does not wish to change them in the direction desired by the change agency. Such over-empathy would have Peter (Acts 15:10) and later Paul (Acts 21:21) acquiesce in the acceptance of Israelite Torah obligations insisted upon by Judaizers and practiced by "the weak."

4. *Creates intent to change in the client.* Here the change agent's role is to motivate intent to change. Just like the innovation that the change agent makes known, so too the motives should be client-centered in order to be effective. Hence the repeated insistence on what God has done "for us" (Acts 13:33), or that Jesus died "for us," and descriptions of what the forthcoming theocracy holds "for us." Of course, change agent–centered motivation (for example, Paul in the apocryphal *Acts of Paul and Thecla*) and change agency–centered motivation (for the sake of the survival of "the church," or the Jesus group) are equally possible, but in the long run ineffective.

5. *Translates intent into action.* The change agent is after action or behavioral change, not simply intellectual agreement. In essence, the agent works to promote compliance with the program he advocates, but compliance rooted in attitudinal change as well. Paul's exhortation in terms of virtues that would develop Jesus group character are instances of emphasis on activity. As a good change agent, Paul presents both "how-to" knowledge (the theme of imitating Paul: 1 Thess 1:6; 2:14; 1 Cor 4:16; 11:1; Phil 3:17) and "why" knowledge (principles). Here a sort of learning by doing (orthopraxy) precedes orthodoxy. Emphasis on orthodoxy alone prior to the actual innovation decision to adopt the change leads to "temporizing"—hence to no change at all (this is faith without Jesus group works). On the other hand, emphasis on orthodoxy after orthopraxy, after actual adoption, serves a confirmation function and leads to self-reliance and self-renewal in client behavior (this is Jesus group works coupled with faith).

6. *Stabilizes change and prevents discontinuances.* Here the change agents seek to stabilize the new behavior, especially by directing reinforcing messages to those

who have adopted the change. At this stage, "why" knowledge (orthodoxy or faith) and exhortation deriving from "why" knowledge serve to allay the dissonance that is bound up with adoption of the new and rejection of the old. Much of what Paul writes to his churches is of this sort, helping to "freeze" new behavior in the face of dissonance as well as in the face of other change agents.

7. *Terminates the relationship.* Paul's goal is to establish local Jesus groups with members who behave according to their new social identity as they await the coming of the Lord Jesus and the Israelite theocracy. This is fully in line with the goal of all change agents. The end goal for any change agent is development of self-renewing behavior on the part of his or her clients. Change agents should seek to put themselves out of business by developing their clients' ability to be their own change agents. In other words, the change agent must seek to shift the clients from a position of reliance on the change agent to reliance on themselves. This, indeed, is the situation of Jesus, whose clients, the Twelve, end up with their own leader, Peter (Acts 1–2), as well as the situation of the Jerusalem Jesus group with James, the brother of the Lord, in charge (Acts 15), and of the Pauline group at Ephesus, whose leadership comes to hear Paul for the last time (Acts 20:18-36).

Coalitions/Factions

A coalition is a type of impermanent group gathered for specific purposes over a limited time period. In social-scientific terminology, it is a fluid, impermanent, multidimensional network of relations focused on limited goals. Coalitions characterized both elites (for example, Herodians with Romans, Herodians with Pharisees) and non-elites in the first-century Mediterranean world. In contrast to coalitions stood "corporate groups" such as political religious parties (Pharisees, Sadducees, and, in Acts, Jesus groups) or closed statuses among elites. Corporate groups were based on enduring principles: for example, birth and marriage (Sadducee party and its priestly basis); birth and political allegiance (Herodians); or tested fictive kinship rooted in commitment to a common ideology (the purity fellowship of the Pharisees; community members of Qumran's Essenes). Corporate groups were rather formal—tightly knit with social rules. Coalitions were informal, elective, and loosely knit. Identifying with a coalition did not override membership or commitments to more fundamental groups such as the family. But membership in a corporate group, such as the Pharisaic movement groups, involved one's family as well.

In the Luke-Acts story, Jesus begins by forming a faction. A faction is a type of coalition formed around a central person who recruits followers for a certain purpose, for a given time. Group members have loyalty to the faction founder, not to one another. Factions share the common goal of the person recruiting the faction. Membership is based on a relationship with that central personage. This relationship results in a core group of those with distinct and rather permanent, ongoing relationships for the duration of the faction. Peripheral members sometimes divide their loyalty with other factions and their leaders and thus can threaten a faction's effectiveness. Rivalry with other groups is basic; hence, hostile competition for honor, truth (an ideological justification), and resources is always present.

The recruitment of core disciples (Matt 4:18-22; Mark 1:16-20; Luke 5:1-11) clearly identifies the Jesus movement group as such a faction and may also explain the rivalry with groups surrounding John the Baptist (John 3:22-23). Matthew and Luke try to put this rivalry to rest by indicating how Jesus' message was identical with that of John (Matt 3:2; 4:17; 9:14; 11:2-13; 14:1-2; 21:25; Luke 3:15ff.; 5:33; 7:19ff.; 9:7ff.; 11:1; 16:16; 20:4ff.). Mark, however, suggests that the Jesus group was an offshoot of John's group. He presents John as baptizing and preaching reconciliation with God (Mark 1:4), while Jesus proclaims God's forthcoming patronage to all Israel in the theocracy about to emerge (Mark 1:14-15; see also 2:18; 6:30-31; 11:27-33). Much of the Gospels' portrayal of Jesus as the honored Son of God, and especially their depiction of Jesus' success in the game of challenge-riposte, can be understood as justification of Jesus' leadership of the faction that he recruited. Note that it was the first follower recruited, Simon Peter, who proves to be the moral entrepreneur promoting Jesus' central place of honor (Matt 16:16; Mark 8:29). **Moral Entrepreneur.**

In Acts 1–2, Luke describes the re-forming of the faction clustered about Jesus and his program. Central to this process was the presence of the resurrected Jesus and the leadership of Peter. In their new social shape, the small group of Jesus followers in Jerusalem develop into a corporate group, a true political religious party as previously described.

Communication of Innovation

The story told in Acts is the story of the successful proclamation of the word of the God of Israel relative to Jesus of Nazareth, Israel's forthcoming Messiah and resurrected Lord. This word of the God of Israel is an innovation, information perceived as new by an individual. Innovations such as this word may have two components: an idea component (here what the proclaimed word communicates) and an object component (here the new behavior, group formations, collaborative actions).

Proclamation of the word of God among Israelites resulted in an innovation decision. Such a decision was the mental process of passing from first knowledge of the innovation to a decision to adopt or reject, followed by the confirmation of the decision among those who adopt it. The repeated notice of the swelling numbers of Israelites who decide to adopt the innovation points to people who have made a positive innovation decision. On the other hand, no notice is given of how many made the decision to reject. One such rejecter was Paul the Pharisee, who after his initial encounters with Jesus group members (notably Stephen in Acts 7:58) decided to persevere in traditional Israelite belief, as his persecutory behavior indicates.

Rogers with Shoemaker argues for four main steps to the innovation-decision process: knowledge, persuasion, decision, and confirmation.

1. *Knowledge* occurs when the individual is exposed to the innovation's existence and gains some understanding of how it functions. This step, of course, is what proclaiming the word of God is all about.

2. *Persuasion* occurs when the individual forms a favorable or unfavorable attitude toward the innovation. There is no external behavior that might evidence

persuasion. Hence, it is presumed to have existed when verified in an individual's subsequent behavior.

3. *Decision* occurs when the individual engages in activities that lead to a choice to adopt or reject the innovation. Behavior such as joining a Jesus group, being baptized, offering hospitality to Jesus change agents, and the like point to the fact that an individual has chosen to adopt the innovation. In Acts, the reception of the Holy Spirit made known in various actions likewise points to an individual's positive decision. Rejection is obvious in the behavior of those aggrieved by seeing their fellows adopt the innovation.

4. *Confirmation* occurs when the individual seeks reinforcement for the innovation decision s/he has made, but s/he may reverse the previous decision if exposed to conflicting messages about the innovation. Ingroup activities of Jesus groups point to individuals being reinforced in their innovation decisions. The Acts narrative has much information about steps (1) and (4), but for the most part, the story told in Acts is the story of change agents attempting to affect the innovation decisions of others. This leads to the next point, the types of innovation decisions.

Acts describes two types of decisions to adopt the innovation wrought by the God of Israel. The first is the "optional decision" made by an individual regardless of the decision of other members of society. In this case, the first part of Acts deals with Israelite society in Judea, Samaria, and surrounding regions. The second part of Acts deals with Israelite minorities in majority non-Israelite cities. In both cases, the individual's decision is undoubtedly influenced by the norms of the prevailing social system and the need to conform to group pressures. In the Israelite heartland, Jesus groups might emerge as competing Israelite political religious parties. But around the Mediterranean in the rather small Israelite populations in individual Greco-Roman cities, Israelites joining Jesus groups would appear as unfaithful to the small Israelite community, resulting in leaving community members aggrieved and ready to engage in conflict.

The second type of decision in Acts is the "collective decision," in which embedded individuals such as wife, children, slaves, and perhaps other family members agree to the decision made by the head of the family group, for example, Cornelius (Acts 10:44-48), Lydia (Acts 16:14-15), and the unnamed jailor (Acts 16:32-33). All group dependents must conform to the central person's decision once it is made.

Why would any first-century Israelite adopt the innovation proclaimed by Jesus group change agents? Obviously, the innovation was seen to be a solution to the problem Israelites faced in the first century. Redemption by the God of Israel meant the restoration of Israel's collective honor. It meant non-Israelites would look with awe at what the Israelite God had done to and for his people (as frequently noted in the writing prophets). The innovation had to fit into Israel's traditional ancestral kinship religion, as the countless citations of Israel's sacred writings indicated.

Ancestor Reverence.

Use of Israel's Sacred Scriptures further underscores the conviction of early Jesus group members that the "founder" of what was inaugurated by Jesus as well as by the postresurrection Jesus groups was none other than the God of Israel.

The innovation that Jesus proclaimed was a forthcoming Israelite theocracy, or the kingdom of heaven/God. The innovation that the Twelve and later Paul and his associates proclaimed was that the God of Israel raised Jesus from the dead, thus revealing Jesus to be Israel's Messiah (Christ) and cosmic Lord, with a view to the forthcoming Israelite theocracy. According to these New Testament witnesses, then, the founder or change agency of Jesus groups and their ideology is God, the God of Israel. God's directly authorized change agents, such as John the Baptist, Jesus, the Twelve, or Paul all functioned for the same change agency, the God of Israel. To shift the thrust from the agency (God) to the agent (for example, Jesus or Paul) is to miss the thrust of early Jesus group activity that emerged eventually as "Christianity." **Change Agent.**

Conflict Resolution

Conflict, whether interpersonal or social, refers to the antagonistic state or action of persons or groups and their divergent interests, values, and ideas. In the Acts narrative, it is the opposition of persons and/or groups that gives rise to the dramatic action in the story. At bottom, conflicts begin with some aggrieved person in some group. When an aggrieved person or group faces down the person or group believed to cause the grievance, the outcome is conflict. And when third parties are interjected into the conflict for whatever reason, the result is a dispute. Thus:

1. *Grievance* or *preconflict* refers to the real or imagined circumstances or conditions that one person or group perceives to be unjust and to be the grounds for resentment or complaint. Since only one party is aware of misconduct, this phase is monadic. Any unfolding of a dispute process depends on steps taken by the offended party. In the Acts story, the aggrieved party is often the group from which some members accept the word of the Lord and adhere to a developing Jesus group. At other times, it is Judeans in Jerusalem who stand against Jesus groups, and the offended party here is Paul. Of course, the implied question is, Why should Paul be aggrieved?

2. *Conflict* emerges if the offended party opts for confrontation and communicates disapproval, resentment, or a feeling of injustice toward the offending party. The offending party will seek redress. Both parties are now aware of antagonism— hence a dyadic phase. The further development of the process depends on steps taken by the offending party or by the offended party (see below).

3. *Dispute* is marked by an escalation of the conflict by its being made public. A third party (the public: a person or group) is now actively involved—hence a triadic phase. Peter and John being haled before the high priest by people whom they have aggrieved is an instance of a dispute. In addition, the several instances when Paul is brought before officials are cases of disputes.

All societies have developed procedures that are called into operation when interpersonal or intergroup antagonism arises. These are called conflict/dispute management procedures. The same basic procedural modes (although they might have other names) are used worldwide in attempts to deal with grievances, conflicts, or disputes: lumping it, avoidance, coercion (conquest), negotiation, mediation, arbitration, adjudication (Nader and Todd 1978:8-11).

Briefly, each can be defined as follows:

a. *Lumping it* is the failure of an aggrieved party to press his claim or complaint, ignoring the problem that gave rise to the disagreement and continuing the relationship with the offending party. Thus, lumping it means ignoring the issue in dispute and continuing the relationship. Reasons for lumping it are lack of information or access to persons who can help, perception of low gain/high cost (including psychic and social costs and gains). This form of dealing with conflict does not involve any third party. Its expected outcome is continued relations, and it is based on the unilateral decision of the one lumping it. In Mediterranean society, while women, children, and slaves were expected to behave in this fashion, lumping it was certainly no option for an honorable male. Paul's escape in a basket over the wall of Damascus is an example of lumping it (Acts 9:25; 11:19).

b. *Avoidance* means withdrawing from a situation or curtailing or terminating a relationship by leaving, finding new interacting partners, and so on. This way of dealing with conflict might also be called *exiting*. It also involves no third party, and its outcome is the reduction or termination of social interaction on the basis of unilateral decision. Paul's leaving Athens after rather unsuccessful interaction with philosophers is an instance of avoidance (Acts 18:1).

c. *Coercion* means the threat or actual use of force to resolve a dispute. Conquest is synonymous with such coercion. There is no third party involved in such conflict management. The expected outcome is violent settlement and often aggravation of conflict based on the unilateral decision of the one exerting force. Instances of such coercion include the apprehension of Peter and John (Acts 4:3; 5:18), Peter alone (Acts 12:5-6), Paul and Silas (Acts 16:19), or Paul alone (Acts 21:33).

d. *Negotiation* is a dyadic arrangement of mutual influence. The two principal parties are the decision makers, and the settlement is one to which both parties agree by mutual persuasion. "They seek not to reach a solution in terms of rules, but to create the rules by which they can organize their relationship with one another" (Gulliver 1973:2-3). Thus, although there is no third party involved, the outcome of negotiation is new rules of social interaction mutually consented to. It is thus a dyadic arrangement.

e. *Mediation* refers to the intervention by a third party, agreed to by both principals, to aid the principals in reaching agreement. Here a third party is present. The outcome of the procedure is new rules of social interaction mutually consented to. Thus, the arrangement is triadic. Although it would seem that all honor–shame interactions based on challenge and riposte are rooted in a form of mediation, adjudication (see below) seems more appropriate, since there are winners and losers. In mediation, both parties "win." Peter mediates in Acts 15:6-11.

f. *Arbitration* refers to the intervention by a third party, agreed to by both principals, whose judgment they must agree to accept beforehand. This third party may be human or divine. Thus, when both parties agree to perform an ordeal or a divination, or even a duel, and accept the outcome as a decision, the third party in the arbitration is a nonhuman agent. Here, too, some third party is present. The outcome is a decision based on present rules or rules newly formulated by the arbitrator and perceived as binding. This, then, is another triadic arrangement. James's judgment in Acts 15:13-19, ending with the words, "Therefore I have reached the decision . . . ," is a case of arbitration. Further, from the perspective of cultures accustomed to ordeals and duels, Paul's journey by sea into the perils of a storm is a form of ordeal, arbitrated by God (Acts 27:3-44; for a Torah-sanctioned trial by ordeal, see Num 5:16-28). Similarly, arbitration with God as arbiter is also to be found in the drawing of lots (Acts 1:26).

g. *Adjudication* refers to the intervention of a third party who has the authority to intervene in a dispute whether the principals wish it or not, and the authority to render a decision with the means at his/her disposal, and to enforce compliance with that decision. Here a third party is present and the outcome is an enforced decision based on past/present rules. Of course, this is a triadic arrangement. The trials of Paul before the governor, Felix (Acts 24), then before governor Festus (Acts 25:1-12), and finally before King Agrippa (Acts 25:13—26:32) are instances of adjudication.

What determines which of these seven procedures will be used in a given society and a given case to manage conflict? Variables include: (1) the social position of the disputant in relation to the opponent (social rank; political, economic situation; lineage); (2) the social position of both disputants vis-à-vis the helping agent, when one is involved; and (3) the goal or aim of those involved: to restore goods, honor; to get satisfaction; to retaliate; to prevent escalation; to disrupt status differences, that is, to challenge; to restate village power and status relationships.

Establishment Violence

Violence is about coercing others in a way that social norms do not endorse. The story told in the book of Acts is full of instances of persons, visible and invisible, doing or planning violence toward others in the name of the status quo. These persons ostensibly intend to maintain established values. Consider the persons responsible for the *arrest* of Peter and John (Acts 4:3), *violence* by unseen agents to Ananias and Sapphira (Acts 5:5, 10), the *arrest* of the apostles out of jealousy (Acts 5:18), the council's desire *to kill* them (Acts 6:33), the vigilante treatment of Stephen by a provoked crowd (Acts 7:54-60). Then Luke tells of Saul's joining in the vigilante violence against Stephen (Acts 7:58b), becoming a full-blown and devoted vigilante (Acts 8:3) doing violence against Jesus group members in the name of the status quo.

It was on one of his vigilante escapades supported by the Jerusalemite high priest that Saul had his ASC experience with the resurrected Jesus (Acts 9:1-2). Judeans of Damascus soon plot to kill Paul (Acts 9:22-23). In Thessalonica, a group of envious Judeans hire a group of street toughs to grab up Paul and Silas to arraign them before city authorities, but unsuccessfully. Instead they attack the house of Jason, the host of Paul and Silas, and eventually take Jason and some Jesus group neighbors to the city authorities (Acts 17:2-10). These Judeans follow Paul and Silas

The Politarch Inscription from ancient Thessalonica dates from the early first century B.C.E. *to the mid-second century* C.E. *It lists the names of some of the city's principal officials: politarchs, treasurer, and gymnasiarchs. From* Cities of Paul © 2004 *The President and Fellows of Harvard College.*

to Beroea and attempt more violence (Acts 17:13). Then, in the Jerusalem temple, Judeans from the Diaspora get people in the temple to turn on Paul with violence (Acts 21:27), and their attempt to get the crowd to attempt vigilante justice is successful (Acts 21:30-31). Paul is rescued by a Roman commander. Later on, we are told that the Roman tribune feared Judean group violence against Paul (Acts 23:10), so he put Paul in protective custody.

By any reading, this was a violent society, with frequent public violence and unsure and explosive crowd reaction. Ordinary persons did not have any rights. There was no universalism in the sense that all human beings were equally human, bearing common human endowments, common human rights independent of individual ethnic origin and social status. Tolerance was an idea whose time would come some seventeen hundred years later! Furthermore, the idea of a plurality of nations endowed with equal rights in the forum of nations was totally absent since there were no "nations" as yet. Neither ancient Israelites, nor ancient Athenians, nor ancient Romans had any idea of juridical relations among broader ethnic groups. In the first century C.E., Roman statesmen dealt with other ethnic groups in terms of good faith based on patron–client relationships. In Roman perception, Rome was a patron, not a holder of an empire; it wanted persons to behave like clients. To behave otherwise was to be a rebel, an outlaw. Neither persons nor ethnic groups had what we would call "rights."

What modern readers often interpret as rights was political privilege. For example, Roman citizens had preeminence in the *oikoumenē* (the inhabited world). To dishonor one Roman was to dishonor, hence challenge, Rome itself. Consequently, Roman citizens were always to be treated honorably by noncitizens; they were not to be flogged publicly, nor were they answerable to any tribunal but that of their own Caesar. Such were the ramifications of the customary values of honor and shame. Obviously, since persons and ethnic groups had no rights in our sense, any modern reader's perception of "oppression" in the first-century Mediterranean world would be quite anachronistic.

In short, the Mediterranean world was a violent world, and the Israelite tradition hallowed such violence. Philo, an Israelite Hellenistic philosopher of Alexandria, clearly explains this tradition:

> But if any members of the nation betray the honor of the One, they should suffer the utmost penalties . . . all who have zeal for virtue should be permitted to exact the penalties offhand and with no delay, without bringing the offender before jury or council, or any kind of magistrate at all, and give full scope to the feelings which possess them, that hatred of evil and love of God which urges them to inflict punishment without mercy on the impious. They should think that the occasion has made them councilors, jurymen, nome governors, members of assembly, accusers, witnesses, laws, people, everything in fact, so that without fear or hindrance they may champion respect for God in full security. (*Special Laws* 1.54)

Later, he adds:

> Further if anyone cloaking himself under the name and guise of a prophet and claiming to be possessed by inspiration lead us on to the worship of the gods recognized in the different cities, we ought not to listen to him and be deceived by the name of prophet. For such a one is no prophet, but an impostor, since his oracles and pronouncement are falsehoods invented by himself. And if a brother or son or daughter or wife or a housemate or a friend, however true, of anyone else who seems to be kindly disposed, urge us to a like course, bidding us fraternize with the multitude, resort to their Temples and join in their libations and sacrifices, we must punish him as a public and general enemy, taking little thought for the ties which bind us to him; and we must send round a report of his proposals to all lovers of piety, who will rush with a speed which brooks no delay to take vengeance on the unholy man, and deem it a religious duty to seek his death. For we should have one tie of affinity, one accepted sign of goodwill, namely the willingness to serve God and that our every word and deed promotes the cause of piety. But as for these kinships . . . let them all be cast aside if they do not seek earnestly the same goal, namely the honor of God, which is the indissoluble bond of all the affection which makes us one. (*Special Laws* 1.315-17)

Of course, he is simply restating the biblical warrant for establishment violence set out in the book of Deuteronomy (Deut 13:5, 12-16; 17:2-6, 7, 12; 19:19; 21:21; 22:21, 22, 24; 24:7).

Fellowship

The early chapters of Acts frequently describe the fellowship practiced by Jesus group members. The word "fellowship" translates the Greek *koinōnia* and the Latin *societas* (see Acts 2:42, 44; 4:32).

"At the turn of the eras, *societas* was still a legally binding, reciprocal partnership or association between one person and one or more second people with regard to a particular action, thing or person" (Sampley 1977:159). More specifically, *societas* was a bona fide consensual agreement. This agreement depended fully on the mutual trust and faithfulness of the partners, and it had its focus on some shared goal toward which the partners (*socii*) were to contribute their property or work or both in the fulfillment of the shared aim. With regard to the shared goal, all the partners of the association were equal regardless of their social status or factual contribution toward the goal. *Societas* required no formalities—no independent witnesses, no documents or legal papers, no notification of public officials. The association lasted so long as the parties involved remained of the same mind (*in eodem sensu*). Moreover, it could be dissolved by the attainment of the contracted goal, by the death of a partner unless provisions for its survival were otherwise made, by fraud or deceit on the part of a partner, or when a partner was no longer "of the same mind." In this last instance, the matter might be taken to court, for *societas* was liable to court action. The guilty or terminating party would be declared *infamis* with appropriate penalties. Finally, a *socius* had to account for the business dealings that he might undertake on behalf of the association, and he was entitled to reimbursement for expenses properly incurred. As a result of their common and reciprocally binding *societas*, partners often regarded themselves as fictive family members, that is, as "brothers," and presumably "sisters" (Sampley 1977:159–63).

Final Words

In Acts 1:7-8, Jesus, who is about to be taken up by God, expresses his final words to the Twelve. These final words concern what is forthcoming for the Twelve. While he does not know when the kingdom will arrive, he does know what their forthcoming task entails. They will be witnesses to what the God of Israel has done to Jesus on Israel's behalf (Acts 2:32; 3:15; 5:32; 10:39, 41; 13:31). Paul similarly expresses his final words as he gives notice of his impending fate to the elders of Ephesus, whom he summoned to Miletus: "And now I know that none of you, among whom I have gone about proclaiming the kingdom, will ever see my face again" (Acts 20:25). And so he imparts his final words to them (see Acts 21:21). In modern times, persons about to die are sometimes said to see their whole life flash before their eyes. Not so in the Mediterranean world. What is distinctive of final words before death in the Mediterranean (and elsewhere) is that the person about to die is believed capable of knowing what is going to happen to persons near and dear to him (or her). Dying persons are prescient because they are closer to the realm of God (or gods), who knows all things, than to the realm of humans, whose knowledge is limited to human experience. Thus Xenophon tells us: "At the advent of death, men become more divine, and hence can foresee the forthcoming" (*Cyropaedia* 7.7.21). In the *Iliad* (16.849-50) the dying Patroclus predicts the death of Hector at the hands of Achilles, and the dying Hector predicts the death of Achilles himself (22.325). Similarly, in Sophocles' play *The Women of Trachis*, the dying Heracles summons Alcmene so that she may learn from his last words "the things I now know by divine inspiration" (*Trachiniae* 1148ff.). Virgil finds it normal to have the dying Orodes predict that his slayer will soon meet retribution (*Aeneid* 10.729-41). Plato, too, reports that Socrates made predictions during his last moments, realizing that "on the point of death, I am now in that condition in which men are most wont to prophesy" (*Apologia* 39c; cf. Xenophon, *Anabasis Apologia* 30). Cicero reports concerning Callanus of India: "As he was about to die and was ascending his funeral pyre, he said: 'What a glorious death! The fate of Hercules is mine. For when this mortal frame is burned the soul will find the light.' When Alexander directed him to speak if he wished to say anything to him, he answered: 'Thank you, nothing, except that I shall see you very soon.' So it turned out, for Alexander died in Babylon a few days later" (*De Divinatione* 1.47).

The Israelite tradition equally shared this belief, as is clear from the final words of Jacob (Genesis 49) and Moses (Deuteronomy 31–34); see also 1 Samuel 12; 1 Kgs 2:1-17; Joshua 23–24. The well-known documents called "Testaments," written around the time of Jesus, offer further witness to this belief (for example, *Testaments of the Twelve Patriarchs, Testament of Moses*; see also *Jub.* 22:10-30; 1 Macc 2:47-70; Josephus, *Antiquities* 12.279-84).

In the United States, with economics as the focal social institution, final words and testaments will deal with the disposition of goods. In Mediterranean antiquity, however, with the kinship institution being focal, final words will deal with concern for the tear in the social fabric that results from the dying person's departure. Hence, the dying person will be deeply concerned about what will happen to his/her kin (or fictive kin) group. Before death, the dying person will impart significant information about what is soon to befall the group in general and individuals in the group. This includes identifying who will hold it together (successor) and giving advice to kin group members on how to keep the group together. Of course, before passing on, the dying person tries to assure the kin group of its well-being, offering abiding good wishes and expressing concern for the well-being of the group. It is within this cultural framework that Paul's final words and actions need to be understood.

Generational Differences

Given the foundational quality of the first few generations of Jesus group development, it is important to understand what happens in groups that emerge from situations of radical change (the disappearance of Jesus) through cataclysm (the destruction of Jerusalem) to a generation that remembers the past in the light of those events. The general pattern that emerges in such situations is called the principle of the third generation, first articulated by the historian Marcus Hansen who wrote:

> Anyone who has the courage to codify the laws of history must include what can be designated "the principle of third generation interest." The principle is applicable in all fields of historical study. It explains the recurrence of movements that seemingly are dead; it is a factor that should be kept in mind particularly in literary or cultural history; it makes it possible for the present to know something about the future. The theory is derived from the almost universal phenomenon that what the son wishes to forget the grandson wishes to remember. The tendency might be illustrated by a hundred examples. (Hansen 1938:9)

Hansen's hypothesis was further developed some fifty years ago by the sociologist Will Herberg (1955). On the basis of Hansen's and Herberg's work, I would describe this "principle of third generation interest" as follows. In the face of significant and irreversible change rooted in some appreciable social innovation (such as radical geographical change, for example, emigration or immigration; transfer into a permanent, new social structure, for example, from slavery to nonslavery; emergence of a new social climate, for example, from colonialism to noncolonialism, from political religion to fictive kinship religion), the second generation seeks to "forget" many dimensions of first-generation experience, while the third generation seeks to "remember" what the second generation sought to forget.

From a generational perspective, the most significant, irreversible social change for Jesus groups was the radical institutional transition from first-generation Jesus group concerns with political religion to emerging second-generation concerns with fictive kinship religion. The theocracy that Jesus proclaimed did not materialize. The groups recruited by and adhering to Jesus during his career were held together by the symbolic values attached to a forthcoming kingdom of God, the burden of Jesus' fundamental proclamation. God's raising Jesus led to the consolidation of first-generation beliefs in a forthcoming theocracy, to which was added a firm conviction of Jesus being Israel's Messiah.

A second generation of Jesus groups emerged through family connections (birth and family networking) as well as recruitment largely if not exclusively among Israelites who had not heard about Jesus being raised by God. Some in this second generation, located largely in Palestine and adjacent territories, continued to entertain first-generation political hopes of a theocracy soon with Jesus as Israel's Messiah. Non-Palestinian Jesus groups largely lost interest in theocratic hopes and developed fictive kin relations "in Christ" or some equivalent.

Many third- and fourth-generation Jesus groups, in turn, were much concerned about Jesus' career and his kingdom proclamation, yet not as vital symbolic values but rather as clarification of "the truth of things about which they had been informed" (Luke 1:4).

Consider Luke's articulation of the four generations that developed from the original experience of Jesus (Luke 1:1-4). The author belongs to a fourth generation, among whom a number of narratives (*diēgēseis*) have emerged describing what Jesus said and did. These were based, he says, on what was handed down (presumably, by a second generation), tracing back to the "eyewitnesses and ministers of the word." To "hand down" (*paradidōmi*) is different from direct attestation. Handing down requires intermediaries, in this case a second generation.

> Inasmuch as many have undertaken to compile a narrative of the things which have been accomplished among us, just as they were delivered to us by those who from the beginning were eyewitnesses and ministers of the word, it seems good to me also, having followed all things closely for some time past, to write an orderly account for you, most excellent Theophilus, that you may know the truth concerning the things of which you have been informed. (Luke 1:1-4)

Luke's "orderly account" presumably stands in contrast to the "narratives" of a previous generation based on a tradition that presumably consisted of lists, collections of sayings, and anecdotes of deeds put together in some unconnected fashion, tracing back to the first-generation witnesses to Jesus.

On the other hand, Luke's interest in telling what he knows of the life of Paul would put him in the third generation after Paul. The perspective he adopts would situate him with such documents as the deuteropauline letters to Timothy and Titus, equally rooted in remembrances of the life of Paul (see Malina 2005).

Group Development

The story of the postresurrection Jesus group in Acts is the story of the re-formation and further development of the faction recruited by Jesus in Luke's Gospel. With the death of Jesus, the faction was on the verge of adjourning and dispersing. However, with the appearance of Jesus to the gathered Jesus coalition members, the group takes on new shape. The pattern of group development described by Luke follows the generally recognized internal workings of small groups. These workings look to both changes over time in the group as a whole and changes in the relationship between the group members (see Tuckman 1965; Moreland and Levine 1988). As researchers have demonstrated, the dimensions of group development include forming, storming, norming, performing, and adjourning, with verifiably predictable behavior at each stage. Consider each of these.

Forming Jesus Groups
The forming stage is the period when the group is put together. **Group Formation.** Groups are formed either to accomplish some extragroup task or for intragroup social support. The faction recruited by Jesus was a group with an extragroup task to perform. The task activity of this group is articulated variously in the Synoptic

tradition. At first it is vague: "fishers of men" (Mark 1:17; Matt 4:19 [Q 10:2 remembers a reference to "harvest"; as does John 4:35]; Rom 1:13). In the so-called "mission" charge, the vague project is expanded: to proclaim God's rule, theocracy, and to require Israelites to get their affairs in order to this end, and to heal those in need of healing. Mark indicates that group members were chosen with healing abilities (Mark 3:15 and 6:7 mention only that Jesus gave the Twelve authority over unclean spirits, yet when they return "they anointed with oil many that were sick and healed them" [6:13]). Matthew 10:6 and Luke 9:1, on the other hand, state that Jesus bestowed this healing ability on his recruits. During the forming stage, group members discuss the nature of their task and how it might be performed.

The post-Jesus group described at the outset of Acts was the re-formed Jesus faction, given a new task to perform by the resurrected Lord. Group members were to bear witness to what the God of Israel had done in the resurrection of Jesus as well as to continue the proclamation of the forthcoming kingdom of God. On the other hand, the new feature in Acts is that those accepting the proclamation of the Twelve formed a social support group. During this re-forming stage, individuals are invited by a central personage (the witness) to join the group, while others seek out this central personage with a view to group affiliation. The forming stage develops group dependence.

At this stage, members of both types of groups, that is, the task-oriented and the social type, are anxious and uncertain about belonging to the group. They exhibit typically cautious behavior. Each member cautiously tries to ascertain whether the group will meet his or her needs. The behavior of group members toward each other is tentative; commitment to the group is low (witness Ananias and Sapphira in Acts 5).

Storming in Jesus Groups
At the storming stage, group joiners jockey for position and ease into interpersonal stances. Members of task activity groups such as the Jesus faction resist the need to work closely with one another. Conflict among members emerges, with emotions getting free expression. In the Synoptics we have many remembrances of this phase: the dispute about who is greatest (Mark 9:33-37; Matt 18:1-5; Luke 9:46-48); a general argument about precedence (Mark 10:41-44; Matt 20:24-27; Luke 22:24-27); concern for sitting next to Jesus in the kingdom (Matt 20:20-23 [the mother asks]; Mark 10:35-40 [disciples ask]; not in Luke); and the general concern about rewards (Mark 10:28-31; Matt 19:27-30; Luke 18:28-30). Peter's rebuking Jesus after talk about suffering and death is an attempt to persuade Jesus to change goals to fit what the group is concerned about (Mark 8:32-33; Matt 16:22-23; not in Luke).

Jesus groups in Acts are social activity groups. Luke describes rather idyllic development, with little, if any, storming. Peter's accession to the role of moral entrepreneur emerges without complaint. On the other hand, in the activity of Paul we learn of group members arguing with one another and heaping criticism on the leader. Paul's letters give eloquent witness to this state. Read, for example, 1 and 2 Corinthians or Galatians from this point of view.

In both types of groups, group members become more assertive, and each tries to change the group to satisfy personal needs. Resentment and hostilities erupt among group members with differing needs. Each member attempts to persuade the others to adopt group goals that will fulfill his or her needs. The behavior of group members toward one another is assertive, and their commitment to the group is higher than it was before.

Norming in Jesus Groups

The norming stage is marked by interpersonal conflict resolution in favor of mutually agreed upon patterns of behavior. This phase is one of exchange in task-activity groups such as the Jesus faction. Everyone in the group shares ideas about how to improve the group's level of performance. The task norms for the Jesus core group are listed in the so-called "mission" discourse (Matt 10:5-16 and expanded with vv. 17-25; Mark 6:7-11; see 3:13-15; Luke 9:1-5).

In social-activity groups such as those described in Acts, members of the Judean political religious party that emerged with the proclamation of the apostles and the leadership of James, the brother of the Lord, acquiesce in emerging norms. For Paul's post-Jesus fictive kin groups, on the other hand, the norming phase is a phase of cohesion. Group members begin to feel more positive about their membership in their particular group.

In both cases, norming involves group members in the attempt to resolve earlier conflicts, often by negotiating clearer guidelines for group behavior.

Performing in Jesus' Group

With the performing stage, group participants carry out the program for which the group was assembled. Performing marks the problem-solving stage of task-activity groups. Members solve their performance problems and work together productively. From the evidence provided in the New Testament documents, it is clear that the Jesus faction moved into a performing stage (return from successful task performance: Mark 6:12-13; Luke 9:6; no report in Matthew). The sending of the seventy (-two) and their success (Luke 10:1-20) point to enlarged activity. This implies further recruitment or forming, with subsequent storming and norming to lead to greater performing. Thus, what the performing consisted of, by all accounts, was proclamation and healing. Healing took place in a context of political religion, hence readily threatened those in authority. The purpose of healing was to restore the ill person to his/her station in society. Jesus himself had healing abilities, as did his core group members. They likewise knew how to enter altered states of consciousness (transfiguration). Jesus' own ASC experiences (at baptism, walking on the sea, transfiguration) made it easy for his core group and his fellow Galileans to consider him a holy man (shaman) and a prophet.

The social-activity groups described in Acts depict certain members moving into the performing stage by role-taking: Peter as moral entrepreneur; the rest of the Twelve as witnesses; Philip, Stephen, and others as deacons; and the like. Members take social roles that make the group more rewarding to all. They work together cooperatively to achieve mutual goals.

On the other hand, there is little, if any, evidence for a performing stage in Pauline post-Jesus groups. The problems addressed in the Pauline corpus look to storming and norming. The same seems true of the several letters written in Paul's name that postdate the apostle. The desiderata listed in the Pastorals concerning group leadership still look like items desired and not yet realized.

Jesus' Group Adjourns

The Gospel stories indicate that the Jesus faction was on the verge of adjourning. With adjourning, group members gradually disengage from task activities in a way that reflects their efforts to cope with the approaching end of the group. Of course, the event that precipitated the adjourning of the Jesus group was Jesus' crucifixion. The motive for Jesus' being put to death was reported as envy (Mark 15:10; Matt 27:18)—a motive that perfectly fits the general Mediterranean culture area, the perception of limited good, and concern for honor. It seems to be certainly the motive of the collectivistic persons who had Jesus put to death. As regards Jesus' core group, the postcrucifixion stories liberally attest to the adjourning phase. Jesus' prediction, "You will all fall away" (Mark 14:27; Matt 26:31; notably Peter in Luke 22:31-34), points up how the disciples all abandoned Jesus. The only ones present at Jesus' death, and this "at a distance," were a group of supporting women (Matt 27:55-56; Mark 15:40-41; Luke 23:49; John 19:25 is quite distinctive).

But with the experience of the appearance of the risen Jesus, a feedback loop enters the process of small group development, with new forming, storming, norming, and subsequent performing, as described telescopically in the final sections of Matthew (28:16-20) and Luke (24:36-53), but at length in the first half of the book of Acts (Acts 1–15).

The new postresurrection group takes its start with the presence of the resurrected Jesus. This is a re-forming of the group with a new agenda: faction members are to bear witness to the acts of God under the guidance of the Holy Spirit. With the presence of the Spirit directing the group, there is no initial storming. Peter's role as moral entrepreneur is accepted by all. Norms for ingroup behavior derive from mutual group attachment ("love") and material group support. In Jerusalem the group continues in the shape of a political religious party with an agenda of expectation of the coming of Jesus as Messiah. Meanwhile, Paul and colleagues begin proclaiming the Word of God to Israelites outside Israelite majority population areas. These groups share the political religious hopes of Jerusalemite Jesus groups, but take on the shape of fictive religious associations, much like the associations of the Mediterranean cities.

Luke is quite explicit in underscoring the growth of membership in Jesus groups both in the land of Israel and in all the Mediterranean region. (He is not concerned with Jesus groups in North Africa, Syria, Mesopotamia, or points farther east.)

Luke's story ends with the Jesus group gatherings relatively at peace and with Paul in Rome, interacting with Israelites in that city, as per his commission (Acts 23:11).

Group Formation

The story of Acts is the story of the subsequent development of the group recruited by Jesus. We call this assembly the Jesus group. A group refers to any collection of persons who come together for some purpose. A group stands opposed to a collectivity, a random gathering of people. According to our sources, Jesus and his initial following as well as clusters of post-Jesus followers formed groups that were essentially small, face-to-face groups. Why were these groups formed at all?

All groups derive from some person who sees the need for change. In the New Testament, for example, Jesus in his context as well as the change agents of Acts saw the need for change. Change here means the desire for social satisfaction. The social satisfaction Jesus sought was a forthcoming theocracy for Israelites ("the kingdom of heaven"). The change agents in Acts affirmed the proximity of this social satisfaction as evidenced by the God of Israel raising Jesus from the dead, thus indicating that he would be Israel's forthcoming Messiah. A motive for change is a person's capacity to find satisfaction in some envisioned state of affairs and a disposition to seek that satisfaction. Jesus and the following he recruited obviously found satisfaction in their belief that the God of Israel was on the verge of launching such a new political arrangement. The change agents of Acts with their experience of the resurrected Jesus assured them of the new state of affairs that they proclaimed.

On the other hand, not every instance of awareness of the need for change results in a group. Rather, the person aware of the need for change must share this awareness with others. Peter and John in Jerusalem and vicinity, and Paul, Silas, and Barnabas among Israelites in non-Israelite regions shared their awareness of God's intentions for Israel by means of proclamation among assemblies of Israelites. For Israelite synagogue members to hear the word of God, they would have to compare existing situations, options, obstacles, and the like. Should they agree with the shared awareness after comparing alternatives, they would join local Jesus groups and declare its purposes to others. Hence, at the bottom of every group is this sequence: aware–share–compare–declare.

The positive response of those to whom the change agents who took up the task of proclaiming the word of God points to some societal trigger state. The trigger state arouses individuals to join a group and work to maintain it. A trigger state converts a social situation into motivational material, for example, the appearance of Jesus to the Twelve, some alternate state of consciousness experience like that of Paul and others in the Acts story. The trigger state behind Jesus' proclamation of theocracy seems to have been the fact that Israel's aristocratic landowners refused their role of patron for their fellow Israelites. Instead they collaborated with the monarchy and Roman authorities to amass the lands of small holders, leaving them "poor" and "meek." In the face of this tragic situation, the God of Israel would institute a new political order and thus "save" his people.

In the first part of Luke's story, Jesus shared the awareness of John the Baptist as both proclaimed the need for "getting one's affairs in order" and the onset of a distinctive theocracy (Luke 3:8; 5:32). The existence of the faction recruited by Jesus indicated that Jesus himself believed a specific situation should be changed and that one person acting alone could not create that change. Individuals joined the core group of the Jesus faction by invitation. Invitation was required by the culture in deference to the honor of those asked to join. And since they did in fact join, they too believed some specific situation should be changed and that Jesus acting alone could not bring about that change.

After Jesus' crucifixion, it seems that the awareness of the need for change derived from "experiencing the risen Lord." All traditions that mention the point trace the rise of post-Jesus groups to the experience of the risen Lord (Luke's final vision of Jesus in Acts 1:6-11; Paul's personal insistence on his being invited to his task as a result of having seen the risen Lord in Gal 1:16; 1 Cor 15:8, and his knowledge of five-hundred-plus group members who saw the risen Lord also in 1 Cor 15:3-6). For these persons, it was an experience of Jesus interpreted through a shared story of Jesus that led them to believe that some specific situation should be changed. The situation to be changed was that divine, cosmic rescue called "salvation." The change sought was something that would guarantee God's salvation for Israel, and the guarantee was accepting God's invitation to join the group rooted in Jesus as Israel's Messiah to come.

For a small group to emerge, however, there must be (1) conditions favorable for change, along with (2) a vision of a new situation coupled with (3) hope concerning the successful implementation of the new situation, and all this in (4) a social system that has problem-solving groups. These are facilitating circumstances for the creation of any group. Since groups emerged as a result of the activity of change agents proclaiming the word of God, obviously all four of these dimensions were present. Consider each in turn:

1. *Presence of conditions for change.* Conditions in the social environment or in the behavior of influential persons were satisfactory and offered an opportunity for favorable change. The formation of any group is always rooted in some person's desire for change perceived as feasible because of the presence of conditions favorable for change. Potential organizers such as Peter, John, and Philip in Roman Palestine, and Paul, Barnabas, and Silas in Greco-Roman cities obviously realized that the existing Israelite situation was not what it might be and that something ought to be done about it, largely because of their experience of the risen Jesus and what this implied for a theocracy for Israelites. In Jerusalem, the formation of the main Jesus group looked political; its strategy was to provide social support, hence family-like groupings, "naturing" appropriate individuals through recruitment and nurturing through group attachment and assistance.

2. *Vision of a new situation.* Some subsequent satisfactory state of affairs was described by change agents as they proclaimed the word of God. A potential group organizer does not simply perceive something to be wrong, hence a potential need for change. Rather, a group developer foresees how things could be improved and successfully transmits this vision to others. These better possibilities were envisioned by Jesus and shared by him with his Twelve. We are told of Jesus' plan in

the course of Luke's first volume. Those invited to be witnesses and proclaimers of the world of God believed not only that something was amiss with Israel and the cosmos but also that something could readily be done to improve matters. Their assessment was rooted in the resurrection of Jesus. The New Testament documents portray these organizers as developing their vision of the new situation while they recruited group members as fictive kin, prior to formulating the group's charter, its creeds.

3. *Hope for success.* Luke is quite attentive to noting the growth of Jesus group membership thanks to the activity of change agents. Members actually joined because they believed that they would soon achieve a satisfactory state of affairs. The organizers' efforts will be empty unless they trust that the group's activities will create the desired end and get adherents to believe the same. Peter's activities as holy man working on behalf of others and Paul's and Barnabas's holy-men activities, along with the Jesus group's witnessing to a range of alternate states of consciousness experiences (notably prophecy and healings), enforced confidence in the achievement of the group's purposes of naturing and nurturing one another (1 Corinthians 12). Participants then developed confidence in their group by their active participation and success in realizing the group's objectives.

4. *Cultural context.* Societies must offer their members the option of group formation if groups are to be formed. Societal conditions favoring group formation are called promoters. Conditions in Greco-Roman society encouraged persons to establish groups (synagogue assemblies, burial associations, deity-specific associations) and to take part in their activities. Persons are more likely to form a group if sources of influence foster such a move or, at the least, offer little resistance to it. Given the presence of the preceding three conditions, interest in creating and joining a group tended to be greatest if the social context was stimulating, that is, if people lived in a society where groups were common and valued. For Galilee and Judea of Jesus' day, the presence of Pharisee, Sadducee, Herodian, Essene, and other groups points to such an environment. Similarly, the widespread formation of philosophical schools and clubs (*collegia*) as well as Israelite assemblies in the Hellenistic world would account for a founder-friendly climate for Jesus group formation. Among Israelites living in Greco-Roman cities, some of these circumstances included frequent contact among potential members, similarity among members, personal preference for working with others rather than working alone, more benefits available to members than otherwise, existing legal requirements for the creation of groups (for example, Roman *societas*), and the way of life in a given place being supportive of group activity. Conflict would occur in those societies where such circumstances did not exist. Thus, the situation described by the early-second-century Roman official Pliny the Younger was not triggered by a desire to "persecute" post-Jesus groups. Pliny wrote to the emperor concerning what to do with Jesus groups in his jurisdiction. His problem, it seems, was based on Roman legal requirements that were hostile to the creation of enduring groups. Roman history indicates that it was not only Jesus groups that were involved in that situation.

From the viewpoint of social psychology, groups develop when people in the society are willing (1) to join groups, (2) to tolerate ambiguity during the early days of a group's life, (3) to favor values in the culture that support a particular group, (4) to forgo interest in keeping things just as they are, and (5) to develop the knowledge and skill needed for being a member.

In contrast, persons who are aware of a need for change do not create a group (1) if they cannot conceive of a better state of affairs (hence no vision), (2) if they do not think a group can attain such a state (hence no hope of success), (3) if people are not willing to join groups in their society, (4) if they have no skills in being group members, (5) if they have values opposed to those of potential members, or have no tradition that fosters formation of groups (hence no cultural context). It was perhaps this lack of cultural preparedness as well as the lack of Israelites that limited the spread of Jesus groups among the rural villagers (*pagani*), who formed the majority of residents in the Greco-Roman world.

For the Jesus groups we read of in Acts, the prevailing purpose was awaiting the forthcoming Israelite theocracy, which would result in the transformation of the present situation by the God of Israel, with Jesus as Israel's Messiah. Their organizations consisted of those called by the God of Israel to attain God's rescue by enduring, persevering, and waiting "in Christ." Their problem, given this purpose, was to inform fellow Israelites summoned by God about the word of God and the forthcoming theocracy. The goal was characteristic of fictive kin groups. When religion is embedded in kinship, then kinship concerns and religious concerns are scarcely perceived as different.

In sum, groups are organized when some person(s) is not satisfied with a situation, has enough social standing to define the undesirable state of affairs, envisions a successful alternative, gives others hope for success, and lives a culture that prepares people for group roles. The envisioned better state of affairs is the group's purpose or objective.

Holy Man

Although they are not labeled as such, Elijah and Elisha were typical prophets and holy men (1 Kings 17—2 Kings 13). In the Synoptics, Jesus is called a holy man of God by a possessing spirit (Mark 1:24; Luke 4:34; see John 6:69). And in Acts, both Peter (Acts 3:1-11, 16; 5:1-11; 9:32-35) and Paul (13:6; 14:9-10; 16:16-18; 27:9-11, 21-26, 31, 33-36; 28:2-6, 8-9), among others, perform feats of healing typical of holy men.

A holy man is a person who has direct contact or communication with the realm of God by means of alternate states of consciousness. **Alternate States of Consciousness.** The activity of holy men usually is directed toward the benefit of people in their society. Such persons heal the sick, exorcise the possessed, and know what is going on in the unseen realm of spirits, demons, and angels. In their encounter with spirits, holy men can interact with them without fear of being possessed. They can travel through the spirit/demon world, and they can readily make contact with the realm of God.

Cultures that identify a holy man/woman ("shaman") describe two characteristics: easy access to the realm of the deity and the ability to broker gifts (information, healing) from that realm to this world. There is sufficient information reported by

Herakles Gate at Ephesus. The name was given on the basis of two Herakles reliefs on pillars that flank the street. There was a column with an Ionic capital in the middle of the street and an architrave that spanned the three. From Cities of Paul © 2004 The President and Fellows of Harvard College.

Luke to rank Peter (Acts 3:1-11, 16; 5:1-11; 9:32-35) and Paul (Acts 9:3-19; 22:6-16; 26:12-18) in this category.

Although it is difficult to offer an all-embracing definition of a holy man, there are several typical characteristics. All holy persons have the first five:

1. Holy men have direct contact or communication with spirits. For the holy men in the story of Acts, this is mainly the God of Israel and other entities from the divine realm: the Spirit of God, the resurrected Jesus, angelic beings, and also other spirits in the divine realm.

2. Holy men have control of or power over the spirit. These holy men are never actually controlled by any spirits but do attribute some reversals to Satan, an Israelite specific personification of a hostile force testing loyalty to God.

3. Holy men are in control during alternate state of consciousness experiences, through which they have contact with the unseen world.

4. Holy men possess a "this-worldly" focus on the material world. Their gifts are for the benefit of the group they serve.

5. Holy men often take sky journeys ("soul flight") to the realm of God and throughout that realm (as in the book of Revelation). While this feature is not mentioned in Acts, Paul does mention such a trip fourteen years earlier in a section of 2 Corinthians (12:2).

6. Holy men do not fear spirits in encountering them.

7. Holy men remember their trance experiences.

8. Healing is a major focus. Acts highlights Peter and Paul.

The reports in the summaries and anecdotes of Acts underscore the role of holy men of God among Jesus group change agents. In Hellenism, such holy men were called divine men and were often given the title "son of a god." The experience of Paul and Barnabas (Acts 9:19b-20) is not very surprising.

Holy Spirit (see Three Zones of Personality)

In the two-volume work called Luke-Acts, the writer highlights the role of God's spirit throughout the narrative. Spirit concretely refers to breath, breeze, or wind (Hebrew *rûaḥ*, Greek *pneuma*, Latin *spiritus*). Since human beings breathe as living beings, their breath or spirit is a sort of shorthand for "I, self, myself" (Luke 1:17, 47, 80; 8:55; 23:46). "Spirit" or wind is used as an analogy for the actions of humanlike unseen, unpredictable, and powerful forces, the presence of which is experienced through effects on human beings. A spirit's presence is always known by unforeseen and unexpected effects. Spirits, like angels, can speak and direct people (Acts 23:9). When such effects are negative, the spirit is said to be an "evil" or "unclean spirit" (Luke 4:33, 36; 6:18; 7:21; 8:2, 29; 9:39, 42; 10:20; 11:24, 26; 13:11; Acts 5:16; 8:7; 19:12, 13, 15, 16). When such effects are positive, they are ascribed to the spirit of God, often called the Holy Spirit, meaning the spirit exclusive to God, a divine spirit. In Luke's Gospel, the spirit is quite active, up to Jesus' statement of being anointed by the spirit (Luke 1:15, 35, 41, 67; 2:25, 26, 27; 3:16, 22; 4:1, 14, 18). After that point, Jesus is God's agent, acting in God's name, while the Holy Spirit is a topic of Jesus' teaching (Luke 10:21; 11:13; 12:10, 12). In Acts, the Holy Spirit directs the activities in a sort of hands-on technique (Acts 1:2, 5, 8, 16; 2:4, 33, 38; 4:8, 25, 31; 5:3, 32; 6:4; 7:51, 55; 8:15, 17, 19; 9:17, 31; 10:38, 44, 45, 47; 11:15, 16, 24; 13:2, 4, 9, 52; 15:8, 28; 16:6; 19:2, 6; 20:23, 28; 21:11; 28:21), to the point that Paul is "captive to the Spirit" taking him to Jerusalem (Acts 20:22). It was God's Spirit that spoke through the prophets (Acts 1:16 and 4:25 refer to David; Acts 28:25 to Isaiah).

As with the wind, the presence of God's positive power is known by its effects. Spirit is always an active force. God acts just like the wind: unpredictably, invisibly, effectively, powerfully.

In the physics of antiquity, wind (spirit), like fire, was liquid. Hence, God's spirit could be poured out, poured in, drunk, and the like. God's spirit, the Holy Spirit, thus becomes a shorthand term for God's power.

Hospitality

Hospitality in the ancient Mediterranean world might be defined as the process by means of which an outsider's status is changed from stranger to guest. It is quite

Terrace houses, peristyle of House A, first century C.E. *Location: Ephesus, Turkey. Photo © Vanni / Art Resource, N.Y.*

different from entertaining ingroup members (friends, family, fellow villagers). In hospitality (Greek: *xenia*) the outsider is "received" and socially transformed from stranger to guest. The process of hospitality is crucial, given the human tendency to treat outsiders as simply nonhuman (the social basis for torture, war, unconcern for distributive justice, racism, genocide, and so on). If strangers are not to be eliminated, either physically or socially (see Matt 10:14-23), they have to be "received," or shown hospitality. The process has three stages:

1. *Evaluating the stranger.* This is usually done with some test about whether guest status is possible. Since the stranger is potentially anything, he must be tested as to whether he can subscribe to the rules of the new culture. Officials (Josh 2:2) or concerned citizenry (Gen 19:5) might conduct such tests. On the other hand, invasion from the outside might simply be repelled (see Mark 5:17, where the Gerasenes ask the stranger, Jesus, to leave; or Luke 9:53, where the Samaritans "would not receive him," perhaps because he would not be a proper guest "because his face was set toward Jerusalem"). An invitation to speak can be a test (Acts 13:14-15), while letters of recommendation can excuse one from a test, although sometimes not (see, for example, 2 and 3 John; Rom 16:3-16; 1 Thess 5:12-13). Frequently the ritual of foot washing marks the movement from stranger to guest (see Gen 18:4; 19:2; 24:32; notably lacking in Luke 7:36-50).

2. *The stranger as guest.* In the process of hospitality, this is the transitional or liminal phase. A range of amenities may follow, concluding with a meal and an offer

of an overnight stay. To fulfill the role of guest, the stranger must at least understand and follow the conventions that relate to hospitality and define the behavior expected of him/her. S/he must know how to play the role of guest—thus the Greek distinction between: *xenoi* (strangers who know how to behave as Greek guests) and *barbaroi* (strangers who know nothing at all, not even the language—hence who are totally uncivilized). The appearance of a stranger in a community where he had neither kin nor friends serves as a challenge to the community. A person willing to show hospitality takes in ("receives") the stranger and serves as patron in whom the stranger is socially embedded. Any male accepting hospitality in the ancient Mediterranean places himself in a non-male (actually quasi-female) situation in the household of the host. The stranger is embedded in the honor of the host, just as females in the household are embedded in the honor of the patriarch. Any attack on the stranger's honor is an attack on the patron, who must defend his guest (as Lot in Genesis 19). In the Synoptic tradition, when Jesus sends the Twelve he expects his core disciples to be "received" by honorable persons (Mark 6:11 par.). Should no hospitality be offered, they are to perform the symbolic (and insulting) action of "shaking off the dust on your feet" (Luke 9:5; 10:11; Acts 13:51; 18:6; see also 22:23). After all, honor is gained by all in the community through the visit of an honorable person. On the other hand, a shameful community is not worthy of the presence of honorable guests.

3. *From guest to transformed stranger*. This transition sometimes involves another test. At the end of the process of hospitality, the guest is now known to the host. The guest may depart as a friend, having incurred a debt of gratitude toward the host and his/her ingroup, or as an enemy, in which case the honor of the host requires the attempt at satisfaction. (For more information, see Malina 1986; Arterbury 2005).

Kingdom of God

"Kingdom of God" means a political order marked by God's rule. In Judean usage (not evidenced in Luke-Acts) this political order was called the "kingdom of heaven," the word "heaven" being a substitute word for "God," which was not to be used. Modern social scientists call this type of political order "theocracy" (as in contemporary Iran). The proclamation of a forthcoming Israelite theocracy was the burden of the prophetic proclamation of both Jesus and his mentor, John the Baptist, although Luke passes over this aspect of John's prophetic activity. Rather, in Luke Jesus was fully involved in proclaiming a new political order—hence in proclaiming an innovation. To this end, Jesus recruited a faction to assist him in this task. Of course, such behavior was not very acceptable to the Israelite elites in power—largely forming the Sadducee party—and was criticized by the conservative Pharisee party. Yet in Luke's story, Jesus' political party grew, only to explode in its expansion in the narrative of Acts.

In the Lukan story, what motivates Jesus to proclaim the kingdom of God is a command of the God of Israel (Luke 4:43). The audience that would be attracted by his proclamation of a forthcoming Israelite theocracy were the many Israelites who lost their social standing thanks to the expanding land-grabbing of Israelite elites. For the prophet from Galilee, the advent of the kingdom of God, Israelite theocracy, entailed the God of Israel taking over the country—hence a new political system. For peasants in the region, the collapse of Israel's patronage system meant tragedy in the face of recurrent peasant ills such as disease, accident, natural disasters, and early death, as well as in the face of mounting social ills due to peasant vulnerability, misfortune, and land deprivation. Thus, it is no surprise that in Jesus' proclamation, the role that the God of Israel would play on behalf of the people was not that of monarch but of "Father." In a political register, "father" was a designation for patron in a patronage system. The coming of the kingdom of God marked the advent of a patron for all Israel, the heavenly Father (Luke 11:13).

The story of Acts opens with the resurrected Jesus speaking with the core group of his Israelite political party, his disciples, and some others. The topic of this conversation was the kingdom of God (Acts 1:3), which these disciples were to continue proclaiming. Yet Jesus claims no knowledge about when this Israelite theocracy might be inaugurated (Acts 1:8). Note that in the very last line of Acts, Luke tells of Paul in Rome proclaiming the kingdom of God (Acts 28:31). The phrase "kingdom of God" serves as a sort of literary inclusion, marking the beginning and end of Acts.

This Israelite theocracy that both Jesus and his disciples proclaimed was meant for Israelites, of course. In the first half of Acts, Peter and associates proclaim the forthcoming kingdom to Judeans in Jerusalem, Judea, Samaria, and along the adjacent Mediterranean seashore. For this population, the attraction to the innovation of God's kingdom in Judea was much like that felt by the Galilean audiences of Jesus.

In the second half of Acts, it was the task of Paul (along with a number of others) to make known this news of a forthcoming Israelite theocracy to Israelites living as minorities in the non-Israelite cities of the northeastern segment of the Mediterranean. The concerns of these Israelites were not those of Judeans, Galileans, and Pereans, but rather concerns distinctive to Israelites whose presence in non-Israelite regions traced back to centuries. They understood the proclamation of an Israelite kingdom of God as a restoration of Israel's honor among the nations, for which the non-Israelites (ethnocentrically translated "Gentiles") would applaud the God of Israel for the way he treated his chosen people. Thus, while Paul (and others) proclaimed a new, forthcoming political order in Judea, his activity was focused on forming fictive kinship groups centered on the resurrected Jesus. These Jesus groups were small Israelite groupings in non-Israelite regions.

Was the forthcoming kingdom of God to be merely political, political and religious, or totally religious? This is a misleading question, because in the world of the period of Acts, the only focal social institutions were politics and kinship. Kinship and political norms determined how economic and religious perceptions and behaviors were conceived and articulated. In other words, the writers of biblical documents were inculturated in societies in which the social institutions of kinship and politics were the exclusive arenas of life. Biblical documents come from a world where there was domestic religion and political religion, as well as domestic economy and political economy. Biblical writers never wrote of economics purely and simply; their language was never used to express systems of meaning deriving from a complexified and technologically oriented society. This was not because their language could not be used to speak of economics and religion, of technology and science. Modern Hebrew and Greek speakers do in fact speak of these matters. Rather, the reason for this absence is that the social systems of the period simply did not focus on freestanding economic and freestanding religious institutional concerns. Technology was boring and low-status, best left to anonymous manual workers and slaves. Consequently, the vocabulary and system of distinctions in the various ideologies expressed in the Bible worked in kinship and political frameworks. Conceptions of the henotheistic "God of Israel" are expressed in kinship and political terms. The language of covenant and law derived from politics, just as the language of worship and ritual derived from kinship and political forms of behavior.

Limited Good

In the economic systems of the West, we make the assumption that goods are, in principle, in unlimited supply. If a shortage exists, we can produce more. If one person gets more of something, it does not automatically mean someone else gets less. It may just mean the factory worked overtime and more became available. But in the ancient Mediterranean, the perception was the opposite: all goods existed in finite, limited supply and were already distributed. This included not only material goods, but also honor, friendship, love, power, security, and status as well—literally everything in life. Because the pie could not grow larger, a larger piece for anyone automatically meant a smaller piece for someone else.

An honorable man would thus be interested only in what was rightfully his and would have no desire to gain anything more, that is, to take what was another's. Acquisition was, by its very nature, understood as stealing. The ancient Mediterranean attitude was that every rich person is either unjust or the heir of an unjust person (St. Jerome: "Every rich person is a thief or the heir of a thief" [*In Hieremiam* 2.5.2; Corpus Christianorum Series Latina, 74:61]). Profit making and the acquisition of wealth were automatically assumed to be the result of extortion or fraud. The notion of an honest rich man was a first-century oxymoron. There never was a middle class in antiquity. Attempts to read the middle-class experience of modern societies back into the New Testament are simply anachronistic.

To be labeled "rich" was therefore a social and moral statement as much as an economic one. It meant the power or capacity to take from someone weaker what was rightfully not yours. Being rich was synonymous with being greedy. By the same token, being "poor" was to be unable to defend what was yours. It meant falling below the status at which one was born. It was to be defenseless, without recourse.

Note how often in the New Testament poverty is associated with a condition of powerlessness or misfortune. In Matt 5:3 the poor "in spirit" are associated with "those who mourn," that is, those who protest the presence of social evil (for "mourn," see 1 Cor 5:1), as well as "the meek," people who have had their inherited lands stolen and protest the fact (see Psalm 37). Luke 14:13, 21 list the poor with the maimed, the lame, and the blind. In Luke 16:19-31 the rich man is contrasted with poor Lazarus, a beggar full of sores. In the Jesus group of Jerusalem, the needy are supported by those who had more (Acts 4:45). Revelation 3:17 describes the poor as wretched, pitiable, blind, and naked.

In a society in which power brought wealth (in our society it is the opposite: wealth "buys" power), being powerless meant being vulnerable to the greedy, who prey on the weak. The terms "rich" and "poor," therefore, are better translated "greedy" and "socially unfortunate." Fundamentally the words describe a social condition relative to one's neighbors. The poor are those who cannot be given a grant of honor, who are hence socially weak, while the rich are the greedy, the shamelessly strong.

Along with the palace, the other focal source of power (hence wealth) in Israel was the temple. Those priestly families in charge of the temple were rich, a term that, as noted above, could equally well be translated "greedy" and "vicious." Given a limited-good view of the world, if the Jerusalem temple personnel and their supporters were amassing wealth stored in the "den of thieves" (Luke 19:46), then large numbers of persons were simultaneously becoming poor and unable to maintain their honor as "sons of Israel."

Magi-Magician

The Greek *magos* in its noun and verb forms is translated as "magician" in Acts 13:6, 8; 8:9. The same word, in the plural, is translated "magi" (Greek: *magoi*) in Matt 2:1, 7, 16. Why the difference? The persons described in Matthew are perceived as members of a category of Persian fire-priests of Medean origin responsible for political religious worship and purity ceremonies. They espoused Zoroastrian traditions and theology. Their ideology embraced universalism, a supreme deity (Ahura Mazda) opposed by an evil cosmic entity, concern for purity rules, angelology, a final savior who would come to establish a kingdom of righteousness, and beliefs in afterlife. All these features except universalism were adopted and adapted by the Israelite Pharisee (Parsee = Persian) party that was part of the Persian colonial foundation of Jerusalem in Yehud (Judea). The Zoroastrian fire-priests were significant in the administrative center of Babylon (Chaldea) and moved westward with the Persian armies in the sixth century B.C.E. By the Hellenistic period they could be found in a number of regions in Asia Minor (Cappadocia, Phrygia, Pontus, Commagene, Lydia) as well as in Egypt, Parthia, and Medea.

We know of these magi in the Hellenistic period from Greek observers. However, it has been noted that Greeks were seldom good observers of strange religions, prone as they were to hasty conclusions and identifications and to a contempt or a veneration that was equally uncritical. It seems that it was on the basis of their widely observed but little understood ritual practices and cryptic incantations (in Avestan) that Greek authors described the magi as persons who had powerful words and procedures to control the gods, demons and humans along with phenomena within the purview of those entities: wind, rain, stars, and the like. In the Hellenistic period people composed and collected various incantations that were ascribed to the magi, hence "magical papyri." As a result, by the Hellenistic period, the word "magi" had two meanings that existed side by side: Persian fire-priests, and (Chaldean) magicians or sorcerers.

In the Septuagint, magi as Chaldeans or magicians are noted in Daniel (2:2, 10; 5:15; and more frequently in Theodotion's version: 1:20; 2:2, 20, 27; 4:7; 5:7, 11, 15), where they compete with God's holy man in the king's court. What magicians did was to use words and rituals to compel a greater or lesser deity or demon to comply with their wishes. For Israelites, such behavior looked to controlling God, something quite sacrilegious and insulting to the God of Israel. Yet there were Israelite magicians as well.

Magi as magicians are found in two passages in the book of Acts. First there is the incident of the Samaritan magician, Simon (Acts 8:9-24). He accepted the gospel when he heard the deacon Philip's proclamation; he was duly baptized, amazed at the wonders wrought by Philip. Then Peter and John came to Samaria to lay on hands and give the Spirit. After experiencing the effects of the Spirit's presence, Simon wished to buy from Peter the ability to impart the Spirit of God, an ability that would be a fine thing to a magical repertoire.

Then there is the Israelite magician Bar-Jesus, whom Paul, Barnabas, and John Mark met at Paphos on Cyprus (Acts 13:4-12). Bar-Jesus (son of Jesus), also known as Elymas, proved no match for Saul, also known as Paul, who cursed him as son of the devil and left him blinded for a time.

What is curious is that in Acts, the abilities of the Jesus group change agents and the power they wielded were far stronger than those of successful and socially well-placed magi-magicians. There can be little doubt that in the eyes of contemporaries, those who effectively proclaimed the gospel were perceived by outgroup observers as belonging to the same category as magi-magicians (see Acts 14:11).

Many Gods and Many Lords

There is a general cognitive principle that states that all theology is analogy. This means that human beings can describe the deity, "God," the ultimate all of the universe, only by comparisons with some dimension of human experience. This is rather obvious, since the only thing human beings know immediately and directly is their human experience. Knowledge of everything else, including puppies, guppies, and molecules, is by analogy with the human or in the realm of human experience.

Hence, for a fundamental perspective about God to permeate a society, there has to be some social structure to serve as an analogy for expressing and articulating that perspective. For example, take a society with the social structure of "lordship"

The inscription at Corinth reads ["Sacred] to the deified Julius Caesar." This inscription was the first epigraphic monument found at Corinth that mentions Julius Caesar. From Cities of Paul © 2004 *The President and Fellows of Harvard College.*

and the social role of "lord." A first-century Mediterranean "lord" was a male with total authority over and control of all persons, animals, and objects within his purview. To call the God of Israel "Lord," as so frequently in the Greek version of the Hebrew Bible, requires the existence and experience of the role of "lord." Given the social reality labeled by the word "lord," it can now serve as a meaningful analogy for what the God of Israel was believed to be like. The same is true of the word "lord" applied to the resurrected Jesus.

In their Scriptures, ancient Israelites found a theological image of God rooted in the social structure of monarchy, especially Persian monarchy. While the Persian monarch might be king of kings, there were also many other kings. Israelite kings in the period before and during the New Testament period were confined to a single ethnic group or region. The image of God as king based on that experience was one of henotheism rather than monotheism. Henotheism means "one-God-ism," whereas monotheism means "only-one-God-ism." Henotheism refers to loyalty to one God from among a large number of gods, like loyalty to one king from a large number of kings. It means that each ethnic group or even each subgroup gave allegiance to its own supreme god, while not denying the existence of other groups and their gods. The king of Israel is one king among many other kings; so too the God of Israel is one god among the many gods of other nations. The label "chosen people," in turn, replicates a henotheistic conception of God: one God with preeminence over other gods with one people with preeminence over other peoples. In this case, the God of Israel is named Yʜᴡʜ or Elohim or Adonai (Lord) Yʜᴡʜ/Elohim. The commandment "You shall have no other gods before me" (Exod 20:3; Deut 5:7) insists on precedence and preeminence for the God of Israel, not uniqueness. Similarly, the creed of Israel underscored this henotheism in a polytheistic world: "Hear, O Israel, the Lord *our* God is one Lord; and you shall love the Lord *your* God with all your heart and with all your soul and with all your might!" (Deut 6:4-5; Matt 22:37; Luke 10:27). Paul, in turn, states: "Indeed, even though there may be so-called gods in heaven or on earth—as in fact there are many "gods" and many "lords"—yet for us there is one God, the Father, from whom are all things and for whom we exist, and one Lord, Jesus Christ, through whom are all things and through whom we exist" (1 Cor 8:5-6).

Perhaps the first social structure to serve as an analogy for a monotheistic God was the Persian empire. The Persian monarch as king of all other kings might serve as an analogy for a supreme God among other gods. The way monotheism, both as a practical political-religious orientation and as an abstract philosophical system, came to permeate the awareness of some Middle Eastern persons was through a monarchy that embraced the whole known world. The first monarchy to have this impact over the ancient world seems to have been the Persian. Like Zoroaster, Israel's prophets too were helped to see the oneness and uniqueness of God thanks to the Persian experience. With the collapse of the Persian empire and with the Greek "catholic" experience of Alexander, the result was an eventual fragmentation that left only another set of "henotheistic" monarchies and a reversion to henotheism.

From the foundation of Yehud by the Persians onward, there was no social structure to serve as an analogy for a monotheistic God until the Roman Empire gradually emerged at the beginning of the first century c.e. This empire eventually came to serve as the all-embracing social structure in the circum-Mediterranean. And the individual control of the whole known world by a single emperor could serve as an analogy for a monotheistic deity. It is difficult to say whether, at the time the Jesus movement emerged, its context was traditional Israelite henotheism or some incipient monotheism. The former seems historically more likely. In the second generation, which included Paul, the gospel of God revealed to him was the gospel of the God of Israel who raised Israel's Messiah from death with a view to a forthcoming Israelite theocracy. And in third-generation Matthew, Jesus' final edict to "make disciples of all nations" in context means Israelites dwelling among all nations (Matt 28:16-20). This is similar to fourth-generation Luke, where at the close of the Gospel we read of Jesus explaining Israel's henotheistic Scriptures dealing with the God of Moses and the prophets. "Repentance and the forgiveness of sin" against the God of Israel are for those in covenant with that God (Luke 24:44-49). In the book of Acts, Luke notes how this discipleship spread among Israelites living amidst all nations, "to the ends of the earth." Yet Luke also notes how God calls presumably non-Israelites (Acts 13:46ff.) who seek out Jesus groups, to the dismay of some Jesus group members.

The profound significance of the spread of faith in Jesus as Israel's Messiah designated by the God of Israel in the first century is intimately bound up with the eventual realization of monotheism. With the diffusion of Jesus groups in the Roman Empire, with the proclamation of Jesus (Christ) as unique mediator, "the man Christ Jesus," and with the proclamation of one God in the Roman imperial setting (see 1 Tim 2:5), monotheistic Jesus group traditions begin to develop. By the time of emperor Constantine (early fourth century), this monotheism was perhaps the radical way in which the Christian tradition differed from that other development of Israelite Yahwism, the traditional henotheism that eventually took the shape of Jewish kinship religion (fifth century C.E.).

Moral Entrepreneur (Peter)

An entrepreneur is a person who organizes, manages, and assumes the risks of an enterprise, defined as a project that is difficult, complicated, or risky. A moral entrepreneur is an entrepreneur whose risky and complicated project is one of supporting social values and persons who embody those values. In the gospel tradition, the person embodying Israelite social values focused on a forthcoming Israelite theocracy is Jesus of Nazareth. Thus, Jesus is the value bearer in this instance. And in this story, Peter takes the initiative and the risk of acknowledging Jesus as Israel's Messiah and publicly supporting Jesus' project of proclaiming the forthcoming theocracy in Israel. All the Synoptics record this point (Mark 8:27-30; Matt 16:13-20; Luke 9:18-20). In Luke's second volume, as the Jesus group is reconstituted, Peter again comes to the fore as moral entrepreneur (Acts 1:15-26).

The moral entrepreneur is a person privy to the making and enforcing of societal rules. Rule making is a moral enterprise—a process of constructing and applying meanings that define persons and their behaviors as morally adequate or not. The moral enterprise is an interpretation of a person requiring both the making of rules (rule creator) and the application of rules to specific persons (rule enforcer). The moral entrepreneur is the person likely to initiate a deviance process and to mobilize the forces necessary to make it successful. All right-minded people will be expected to subscribe to the culturally specific and highly emotionally charged goals selected by the entrepreneur. And it is specifically these sorts of goals that the moral entrepreneur espouses. The moral entrepreneur becomes socially unassailable, unless opponents can redefine the situation by neutralizing the constraint unassailability produces. As rule creators, moral entrepreneurs and their followers wish to interpret some behavior as deviant for the purpose of obviating, preventing, or correcting interferences in their interests. They wish to change, enforce, or establish rules to these ends. They do so by defining both certain conditions and those who engage in those conditions as inimical to their values and interests—personal, group, and societal (Malina and Neyrey 1988:43-44).

Numbers in Acts

A number is a word that describes a quantity; in this usage a number answers the question "How many?" At times, such quantity words describe a quality, and in this sense it answers the question "Of what sort?" A numeral is a symbol or figure that stands for a number. In American society, we generally use Hindu-Arabic numerals, and rarely, Roman numerals. In the New Testament there are no numerals at all. The numerals available in that period were either pictures of fingers and hands (Roman numerals), or letters of the alphabet with a mark indicating that the letter stands for a numeral. Such numerals were not readily manipulable (for example, for simple arithmetic) since there was no zero and no decimal points.

Further, since most people in antiquity could not read, they could not make sense of alphabetic numbers or digits and hand symbols used as Roman numerals. In ancient New Testament manuscripts, all number words are written in full, including the quality number six hundred sixty-six. They tell "of what sort" something is. Moreover, since American society has as one of its major features quantity orientation requiring more or less precise calculations, it is difficult for U.S. readers to realize that, for the most part, numbers in the Bible stand for qualities, not quantities. For example, in Luke's Gospel, three and a half years stands for the duration of terrible evil (Luke 4:25). This number is common in Revelation as well, expressed as forty-two months (Rev 11:2; 13:5), or one thousand, two hundred and sixty days (Rev 11:3; 12:6). In Acts, the main qualitative numerals are seven (the number of deacons in Acts 6:5; Paul's entourage in Acts 20:4) and twelve (the number of Jesus' core group; see Acts 2:14 reconstituted; Acts 6:2). The numeral seven stands for the quality of totality, completeness. It is rooted in the celestial seven planets: the sun, the star of the god of the same name; the moon, likewise the star of a like-named god; then the wandering stars designated as the stars of Jupiter, Saturn, Mars, Mercury, and Venus. Babylonian astral traditions would account for the rise in the concern for sevens in Israelite tradition. Jesus' choice of the Twelve (Luke 6:1; 22:30) derives from the number of the tribes of Israel (Acts 7:8; 26:7), which derived, in turn from the Babylonian zodiac, a set of twelve celestial constellations marking the pathway of the sun. This zodiac twelve accounts for the division of mythical Israel into twelve tribal sectors governed by twelve chieftains.

To take these numbers quantitatively is simply a historical and cultural mistake. It is like refusing to get off an elevator on the thirteenth floor of a building. A floor is a floor. But culturally thirteen refers to the quality of bad luck, just as seven culturally stands for good luck. Seven and thirteen do not have these qualities in most other societies.

The writer of Acts narrates the story of the inexorable growth of Jesus groups, a growth impelled by God's spirit. This growth, of course, is quantitative. Consider the development described in Acts:

1:15   about one hundred twenty persons
2:41   about three thousand persons were added
2:47   the Lord added to their number day by day those who were being
        saved
4:4   the number of the men came to about five thousand

5:14   believers were added to the Lord, great numbers of both men and women

6:1   the disciples were increasing in number

6:7   the word of God increased; and the number of the disciples multiplied greatly in Jerusalem, and a great many of the priests were obedient to the faith

9:31   the church throughout Judea, Galilee, and Samaria . . . increased in numbers

9:42   throughout all Joppa . . . many believed in the Lord

11:21   a great number that believed turned to the Lord

13:43   many Judeans . . . followed Paul and Barnabas

13:48   as many as were ordained to eternal life believed

14:1   in Iconium, a great number of both Judeans and Hellenists became believers

14:21   they had preached the gospel to that city and had made many disciples

16:5   so the churches were strengthened in the faith, and they increased in numbers daily

17:4   and some of them were persuaded . . . as did a great many of the devout Hellenists and not a few of the leading women

17:12   many of them therefore believed, with not a few Hellenistic women of high standing as well as men

18:8   Crispus, the ruler of the synagogue, believed in the Lord, together with all his household; and many of the Corinthians hearing Paul believed and were baptized

19:26   in Ephesus and in almost the whole of Asia this Paul has persuaded and drawn away a considerable number of people

21:20   and they said to him, "You see, brother, how many thousands there are among the Jews of those who have believed; they are all zealous for the law

28:23   when they had appointed a day for him, they came to him at his lodging in great numbers

---

Opening in the Sky

In Acts 1:11, two sky beings tell the Eleven that the resurrected Jesus, who was taken by God to the other side of the vault of the sky through the access point over Jerusalem, will return through that access point. Since Jesus is Israel's Messiah and Lord, presently with God in the sky, he would come from the sky. And the opening in the sky to the celestial realm of the God of Israel is over Jerusalem. This opening in the sky is well attested in the Bible (1 Kgs 22:19; 2 Chr 18:18; Ezek 1:1; Mark 1:10; Matt 3:16; Rev 4:1). According to Mesopotamian lore, appropriated so well by Israel, to get to a deity's real home in his celestial temple and its attendant city, a person had to pass through the opening in the firmament that led to the other side of the vault of the sky where the deity in question was enthroned. This opening was to be found directly over the deity's earthly temple. In Acts, for example, the sky opens above Jerusalem to allow the resurrected Jesus to ascend to God, of course, through the opening in the firmament (Acts 1:2-9). Likewise because of a sky opening, Stephen in Jerusalem can see the exalted Jesus standing by the throne of God (Acts 7:56). And in Revelation, John frequently mentions this opening through which one can see the celestial altar (Rev 8:3; 9:13; 14:18) and the ark of the covenant in the celestial temple (Rev 11:19). The celestial Jerusalem descends through this opening ultimately to come to rest where the earthly Jerusalem is located (Rev 21:2, 10). This is consonant with Israel's tradition according to which certain people saw God's presence in the sky from earthly Jerusalem. God's "holy habitation," his "dwelling place," is in the sky (Deut 26:15; 1 Kgs 8:43; 2 Chr 30:27), high in the sky (Job 22:12). The prophet Micaiah "saw the LORD sitting on his throne, and all the host of heaven standing on his right hand and on his left" (1 Kgs 22:19; 2 Chr 18:18). Clearly, his holy temple, his throne, is in the sky (Ps 11:4), although he does have a house below in Jerusalem (2 Chr 36:23; Ezra 1:2).

This was such common knowledge that even those Jesus group members expecting the *parousia* of the Lord knew that "the signs of truth will appear: first the sign of an opening in the sky, then the sign of the sound of the trumpet, and thirdly the resurrection of the dead . . ." (*Didache* 16:6).

Pains of Death

Archaeological evidence and later scribal Pharisaic documents disclose to us the meaning of Israelite burial customs at the time of Jesus. Israelites regarded death as a lengthy process, not a moment in time. In elite circles in Judea, between the last breath and sundown, the body would be laid out on a shelf in a tomb carved into limestone bedrock outside Jerusalem. Mourning rites would commence, continuing throughout the year as the body underwent decomposition. The rotting of the flesh was regarded as painful but also expiatory for the dead person. One's evil deeds were thought to be embedded in the flesh and to dissolve along with it.

After a year, the mourning ritual concluded. In the first century, people thought that the bones retained the personality, and that God would use them to support new flesh for the resurrection. After this year of purification and putrefaction, the bones of the deceased were often collected and placed in an ossuary or "bone box," which was in fact a second burial casket. This process was called the *ossilegium*, "the collection of bones." The ossuary was designed like a box for scrolls, just long enough for the thigh bones to be laid in like scroll spindles awaiting a new hide and new inscription by the divine hand. In an alternate image, the bones could also be regarded as loom posts made ready for God to weave a new body. In keeping with these views on the character of resurrection, inkwells and spindle whorls have been found in excavated tombs.

This day of second burial marked the end of the family's mourning and its turn toward the hope of reunion and resurrection. Obviously, then, the disappearance or loss of a body after death would be experienced as a greater calamity than the death itself because the family would be unable to prepare the bones for resurrection.

Legally, even the bones of an executed criminal were supposed to be returned to the family after being held in custody of the Sanhedrin during the year-long period of atoning putrefaction. In effect, capital punishment included the loss of life, the suppression of mourning, and the imposition of supposedly painful but purifying disintegration of the flesh overseen by the court in a special tomb maintained for that purpose. When the flesh was gone, the sentence was completed, the debt was paid and the bones became eligible for resurrection.

These cultural beliefs and practices provide the context for understanding the claims of the first generations of Jesus' followers about the resurrected Jesus. In John's account, Jesus dies condemned by the Judean populace, leaders and crowds alike (although at the hands of the Romans). Then a ranking Judean, Joseph of Arimathea, takes his body into custody. It is laid in a separate tomb, to begin to serve the sentence of decay in order to atone for its sins.

It is precisely this penal/atonement process that is interrupted if the tomb is suddenly discovered to be empty. To say that Jesus was raised is to say that God overturned the judgment of Israel's chief priests and the Judean populace, the judgment that Jesus needed to rot to prepare for resurrection. Instead, God supposedly took Jesus directly from last breath to resurrection because there had been no guilt in his flesh. God intervened before the rotting started; hence, God overturned the death sentence.

The claim that Jesus is raised by God is a claim of divine vindication for the deeds and words of Jesus. His life has been that of the Word made flesh in Israel, and God preserves its fleshly record intact.

Taken in its cultural context, the claim of resurrection for Jesus asserts that his death was wrong and has been overturned by a higher judge. This cultural interpretation of the death of Jesus contrasts sharply with the theological one: that Jesus' death was right and necessary and required by God "to take away the sin of the world." The Synoptics juxtapose the two interpretations in a smooth narrative sequence, with Jesus even predicting three times that he will die and be raised. But John has none of this. Thus he spares us the dissonance between the two interpretations, or the artistry of the Gospel author who blended them. This dissonance is generally not recognized by Synoptic readers, who often read the Synoptic perspective into John, who does not share these two strands, cultural and theological, in his presentation of Jesus' exaltation. Only one view makes sense and is definitive for the faith of his anti-society. For John, Jesus calamitously died as a result of the intransigence of the Judeans, but God rescued and vindicated him because Jesus was in fact the mediator of life itself. The other tradition, that Jesus died deliberately because God wanted him dead for the benefit of others, is not in John. (For further information on Israelite burial customs, see L. Y. Rahmani, "Ancient Jerusalem's Funerary Customs and Tombs," part 1, *Biblical Archaeologist* 44 [Summer 1981]: 171-77; part 2, *Biblical Archaeologist* 44 [Fall 1981]: 229-35; part 3, *Biblical Archaeologist* 45 [Winter 1981]: 43-53; part 4, *Biblical Archaeologist* 45 [Spring 1982]: 109-19.)

Patronage

Patron–client systems are socially fixed relations of generalized reciprocity between social unequals in which a lower-status person in need (called a client) has his needs met by having recourse for favors to a higher-status, well-situated person (called a patron). By being granted the favor, the client implicitly promises to pay back the patron whenever and however the patron determines. By granting the favor, the patron, in turn, implicitly promises to be open for further requests at unspecified later times. Such open-ended relations of generalized reciprocity are typical of the relation between the head of a family and his dependents: wife, children, and slaves. By entering a patron–client arrangement, the client relates to the patron as to a superior and more powerful kinsman, while the patron sees to his clients as to his dependents.

While patron–client relations existed throughout the Mediterranean, the Roman version of the system, for example, was as follows. From the earliest years of the Roman Republic, the people who settled on the hills along the Tiber had, as a part of their families, freeborn retainers called "clients." These clients tended flocks, produced a variety of needed goods and helped farm the land. In return, they were afforded the protection and largesse of their patrician patrons. Such clients had no political rights and were considered inferior to citizens, though they did share in the increase of herds or goods they helped to produce. The mutual obligations between patron and client were considered sacred and often became hereditary. Virgil tells of special punishments in the underworld for patrons who defrauded clients (*Aeneid* 6.60). Great houses boasted of the number of their clients and sought to increase them from generation to generation.

By the late years of the Republic the flood of conquered peoples had overwhelmed the formal institution of patronage among the Romans. A large population torn from previous patronage relations now sought similar ties with the great Roman patrician families. Consequently, patronage spread rapidly into the outer reaches of the Roman world, even if in a much less structured form. By the early years of the empire, especially in the provinces, we hear of the newly rich competing for the honor/status considered to derive from a long train of client dependents. These were mostly the urban poor or village peasants who sought favors from those who controlled the economic and political resources of the society.

In his *Epigrams*, Martial gives us many of the details of a Roman client's life. In the more formalized institution in Rome itself, the first duty of a client was the *salutatio*—the early morning call at the patron's house. Proper dress was important. At this meeting, clients could be called on to serve the patron's needs and thereby eat up much of the day. Menial duties were expected, though public praise of the patron was considered fundamental. In return, clients were due one meal a day and might receive a variety of other petty favors. Humiliation of clients was frequent and little recourse was available. Patrons who provided more were considered gracious.

As the Roman style of patronage behavior spread to provinces such as Syria (Palestine), its formal and hereditary character changed. The newly rich, seeking to aggrandize family position, competed to add dependent clients. Formal, mutual obligations degenerated into petty favor seeking and manipulation. Clients competed for patrons just as patrons competed for clients in an often desperate struggle to gain economic or political advantage.

A second institution that complemented the patronage system was the *hospitium*, the relation of host and guest. Such covenants were only between social equals and were often formalized in contractual agreements for mutual aid and protection that became hereditary. So long as a party remained in the city of the host, protection, legal assistance, lodging, medical services, and even an honorable burial were his due. Tokens of friendship and obligation were exchanged, which sealed the contractual arrangement and could be used to identify parties to such covenants who had never met (for example, descendants). Such agreements were considered sacred in the highest degree.

Patrons, then, were powerful individuals who controlled resources and were expected to use their positions to hand out favors to inferiors based on "friendship," personal knowledge, and favoritism. Benefactor patrons were expected to support city, village, or client generously. The Roman emperor related to major public officials this way, and they in turn related to those beneath them in similar fashion. Cities related to towns and towns to villages in the same way. A pervasive social network of patron–client relations thus arose in which connections meant everything. Having few connections was shameful.

Brokers mediated between patrons above and clients below. First-order resources—land, jobs, goods, funds, and power—were all controlled by patrons. Second-order resources—strategic contact with or access to patrons—were controlled by brokers who mediated the goods and services a patron had to offer. City officials served as brokers of imperial resources. Holy men or prophets could also act as brokers on occasion. In the Gospel, Jesus often acted as the broker for God, the one through whom clients obtained access to God's favor. An example is Matt 8:13, where Jesus acts as broker to bring the benefits of the Patron (God) to the centurion's servant.

Clients were those dependent on the largesse of patrons or brokers to survive well in their society. They owed loyalty and public acknowledgment of honor in return. Patronage was voluntary but ideally lifelong. Having only one patron to whom one owed total loyalty had been the pattern in Rome from the earliest times. But in the more chaotic competition for clients/patrons in the outlying provinces, playing patrons off against each other became commonplace. Note that according to Matthew and Luke, one cannot be client of both God and the wealth system (Matt 6:24; Luke 16:13).

While clients boasted of being "friends" of their patrons (for example, Pilate as a "friend of Caesar" [John 19:12]), friends were normally social equals, and having few friends was likewise shameful. Bound by reciprocal relations, friends were obligated to help each other on an ongoing basis, whereas patrons (or brokers) were not. Patrons had to be cultivated. Jesus' enemies call him a "friend" of tax collectors and sinners (Matt 11:19; Luke 7:34).

All of these players appear frequently in the Gospels. A good example is Luke 7:1-10, where the centurion, a high-ranking officer representing Rome, acts as a patron for the local population. Even though a man used to commanding clients, he signals to Jesus that he does not intend to make Jesus a client ("I am not worthy to have you come under my roof"), but considers him a superior. Surprised, Jesus acknowledges that the centurion has placed faith in him as broker of the resources of God and hence heals the servant.

For examples in the Gospel of Mark, see the notes on 1:40-45; 2:5; 2:10; 3:13-19; 5:6-7; 5:18-20; 5:24b-34; 6:10-13; 7:24-30; 10:13-16; 10:26-30; 10:35-45; 10:47; 11:9-10.

In the New Testament, the language of grace is the language of patronage. God is the ultimate patron whose resources are graciously given, often mediated through Jesus as broker; note the frequent comment that Jesus spoke with the authority of his Patron (for example, Mark 1:22). By proclaiming that the "kingdom of God has come near" (Mark 1:15), Jesus in effect is announcing the forthcoming theocracy for Israel along with the ready presence of divine patronage. Jesus thus sets himself up as a broker or mediator of God's patronage and proceeds to broker the favor of God with healings and driving away of unclean spirits (essentially in Israel: see Mark 7:27, where Gentile "dogs" come second). He also sends out a core group of his faction, the Twelve, to function as brokers of divine grace (Mark 6:7-13). When they are unsuccessful, people come directly to Jesus (Mark 9:17-18).

Pentecosts

Pentecost is a transliteration of the Greek: *pentēkostē hēmera* meaning "fiftieth day," with the word for "day" being dropped. In Lev 23:15-16, Pentecost is the fiftieth day from the morrow of the Sabbath of Passover, the Feast of New Grain. In Tob 2:1, Pentecost is called the feast or festival of the seven weeks; the feast of Weeks (see 2 Macc 12:32). From the Qumran writings, we know that Judeans had a number of Pentecosts. According to the *Temple Scroll* from cave 11, the Qumranites celebrated three pentecostal feasts, and one of them may shed some light on Luke's story of the first Jesus group Pentecost. (See Rev 6:6, which alludes to the products of these three feasts. These products were sacrificial elements in the temple especially for the daily burnt offerings. See Josephus, *Jewish War* 5.565, who mentions how Titus took the temple wine and oil "which the priests kept for pouring upon burnt-offerings and which stood in the inner temple, and distributed these to his horde, who without horror anointed themselves and drank therefrom.") The *Temple Scroll* texts reads as follows:

Feast of Weeks (New Grain), third month, fifteenth day (18:10–13):

You will count [for yourselves] seven Sabbaths complete from the day you bring the sheaf [of waving]; you will count until the morrow of the seventh Sabbath; you will count [fifty] days and you will bring a new meal-offering to Yahweh . . . .

Feast of New Wine, fifth month, third day (19:11–14):

You [will count] for yourselves from the day you bring the new meal-offering to Yahweh, [the] bread as the first fruit, seven weeks; seven Sabbaths complete [they will be un]til the morrow of the seventh Sabbath; you will count fifty days, and [will bring] new wine for a libation . . . .

Feast of New Oil, sixth month, twenty-second day (21:12–16):

You w[ill] count for y[ourselves] from this day seven weeks, seven times (seven), forty-nine days, seven Sabbaths complete they will be until the morrow of the seventh Sabbath; you will count fifty days, and you will offer new oil from the dwelling-places of [the] tribes of the Is[rael]ites, a half hin from each tribe, new oil crushed [ ] fresh oil upon the altar of holocaust as fresh-fruits before Yahweh.

In other words, fifty days from the morrow of the Sabbath of the Passover octave was the Pentecost of New Grain; fifty days from the morrow of the Pentecost of New Grain, the Pentecost of New Wine; and fifty days from the morrow of the Pentecost of New Wine, the Pentecost of New Oil.

Given this evidence of three Pentecosts, one of which was of New Wine, one understands more clearly the mockery expressed in Acts 2:13, "They have just had too much new wine" (cf. Acts 2:15). It has always been a puzzle why "sweet new wine" would be mentioned in connection with the Feast of Weeks, because new grain and new wine were not harvested together. So the *Temple Scroll* shows how "new wine" could be associated with a Pentecost. Luke may have known of such multiple Pentecosts in contemporary Judea and alluded to the Pentecost of New Wine, when speaking more properly of the Pentecost of New Grain.

The Israelite feast of Pentecost, then, provides the occasion when the Twelve and other early Jesus group members were endowed with the Spirit of the God of Israel. This is their baptism. It is the moment when God's Spirit moves them to take up the task of proclaiming the "word of God," what the God of Israel has done in the resurrection of Jesus and with a view to a forthcoming Israelite theocracy. In the Gospel of Luke, after Jesus' anointing with the Spirit (noted in Luke 4:18), Jesus himself directs what is going on in the story. But in Acts, from this point, all that Jesus group members will do is under the direction of the Spirit.

Sacrifice

In the period during which the book of Acts was written, everyone knew what the word "sacrifice" referred to in the daily experience of people of the time. In the social systems of the day, there were two forms of sacrifice, political and domestic. We say this because there were only two focal social institutions at the time, the political and the domestic. Social institutions are fixed forms of phases of social life. Since the separation of church and state, and of market/bank and state, occurred in the eighteenth century C.E., we can safely say that in the world of Jesus there were only two focal or formal social institutions, politics and kinship. Economics and religion were embedded—hence, the roles, statuses, and values of kinship and politics were used to express and understand economics and religion. The outcome, from our point of view, was a social system with a political institution along with political religion and political economy, as well as a kinship institution along with domestic religion and domestic economy.

Consequently, there were two forms of sacrifice, political and domestic. Consider the following examples, and notice that writers have no need to describe sacrifice. Describing the attitude of worshipers at the Israelite temple of Jerusalem, the priest Flavius Josephus noted the following:

> Our sacrifices are not occasions for drunken self-indulgence—such practices are abhorrent to God—but for sobriety. At these sacrifices prayers for the welfare of the community must take precedence over those for ourselves; for we are born for fellowship, and he who sets its claims above his private interests is specially acceptable to God. (*Against Apion* 2.195-96)

In antiquity, religious behavior that focused on the "welfare of the community" was political religion. Josephus insists that it was Israel's political religion alone that counted, although we know from the rules of Leviticus that there were sacrifices for individuals.

In Ps.-Aristotle's *Rhetoric to Alexander* (1423b), the *politēs* ("citizen" of a polis) is to learn how to address his fellows concerning "the performance of sacrifices in the ancestral manner," something essential to living in a polis. As a matter of fact, we are told that "all the oracles enjoin on mankind the performance of their sacrifices" (ibid.). "Oracles" is a frequent designation for sacred writings. Both Josephus and Ps.-Aristotle point to the importance of sacrifice for societal well-being, the focus of the political religions of antiquity.

What did a sacrifice look like? Lucian, in his treatise *On Sacrifices*, describes how

> the priest himself stands there all bloody, just like the Cyclops of old, cutting up the victim, removing the entrails, plucking out the heart, pouring the blood about the altar, and doing everything possible in the way of piety. To crown it all, he lights a fire and puts upon it the goat, skin and all, and the sheep, wool and all, and the smoke, divine and holy, mounts upward and gradually dissipates into Heaven itself. (*On Sacrifices* 13 Loeb 3:169)

These passages describe public sacrifices, the sacrifices of political religion. There were also similar domestic religious sacrifices, performed at home usually by the father of the extended family.

What were the main features of a sacrifice? First, there was the victim or offering; then the sacrificer called a priest or priestess. The place where sacrifice took place was an altar along with fire. Finally, there were the offerers, the group or persons who present the offering and on whose behalf the victim was offered. What was the expected outcome of a sacrifice? All sacrifice was concerned with some life effect: life maintenance with continued well-being, or life restoration for persons or groups worthy of life-threatening punishments. Sacrifice was a procedure that everyone in the first-century Mediterranean knew and experienced in a range of variations: Roman, Greek, Egyptian, and Semitic.

The law of any god's cult provided that worship be conducted, frequently under the supervision of a special priesthood, by sacrifices, which were often strikingly similar from one country to another, and with the observation of taboos that varied from place to place but show a general similarity of attitude toward the divine. The similarities of ancient codes of civil law are too well known to need description, and their practical independence is well recognized. But it should be noticed that everywhere the civil law, like the cult law, is the god's law, and an offender against either is an offender against the god.

Now—since the gods were like humans—it was expected everywhere that a god would punish humans who offended him and would reward those who did what he wanted; this, moreover, was what he was for. And since he was everywhere thought to want sacrifices, it was also by sacrifices that humans sought to placate the god when they thought they had offended him or to secure his good will when they wanted special favors. The *do ut abeas* (I give that you not interfere) and *do ut des* (I give that you might give in return) relationships are found in all countries of the ancient Near East (Smith 1952:143–44).

Given the range of behaviors labeled "sacrifice," how might one define the term? We propose the following definition: Sacrifice is a ritual in which an offering is rendered humanly irretrievable and ingestible and then directed to some controlling deity by a mediating sacrificer in order to have some life effect for the persons on whose behalf the sacrifice is offered. An animal victim is made humanly irretrievable by killing and burning it; when cakes or incense are offered, they too are burned. Irretrievable means the offerer cannot take back the offering. Ingestible means that by burning, the animal can become edible and can be shared among offerers or burned up entirely and thus left for the deity alone. Furthermore, flour cakes and especially incense are ingested by inhaling. The mediating sacrificer is a priest: in Israel a male member of the lineage of Aaron, but outside Israel there were both priests and priestesses. Public, political religious sacrifices were performed in temples by public officials called priests, both on behalf of the larger group and on behalf of individuals. Private domestic religious sacrifices were performed at home by the head of the family. Sacrifices were always about life: to maintain and celebrate life (communion sacrifices) or to restore life (expiation sacrifices).

In Acts, references to Israel's priests (noted in Acts 4 and 5, for example) are those with the role of sacrificing in the Jerusalem temple (as described and directed in the book of Leviticus). Further, Acts variously mentions sacrifice in other places: Acts 7:41-42 in the wilderness by Aaron; 14:13, 18 at Lystra by priests of Zeus, to Paul and Barnabas perceived as "deities; 15:29; 21:25 on offering sacrifice to non-Israelite deities. (For further details, see Malina 1996a).

Temple Personnel

The temple of Jerusalem marked the centripetal focal point of Israelite exclusivity in the entire world. Israel was the chosen, hence exclusive, people of the God of Israel, the creator of heaven and earth. And Jerusalem was the central and exclusive point where Israelites were able to have direct and immediate contact with the God of Israel. It was in the temple of Jerusalem that such contact took place, and it was through the intermediary of the divinely chosen personnel of the Jerusalem temple that such contact happened. The divinely chosen personnel of the temple were hereditary priests and Levites, structured socially in terms of a divinely constituted, vertical social order of divinely appointed persons chosen for the service of God and endowed with authority by God. This social structure is called a hierarchy (from the Greek for "sacred rule"), and this hierarchy expressed Israelite theocracy, the rule or "kingdom" of God on earth, at present, here and now.

At the head of this hierarchy was the high priest. Next in rank were chief priests (captain of the temple, temple overseers, temple treasurers) who performed a variety of temple services on a more or less daily basis. This group of priests had to be resident in Jerusalem to perform their required functions. Next were directors of ordinary priests who served in the temple for a short time annually (a weekly director and a daily director), usually not residents of Jerusalem. Priests traced their pedigree to Aaron, of the tribe of Levi. Non-Aaron sons of Levi formed the class of Levites, who likewise served in the temple in a number of functions ranging from temple singers to doorkeepers and temple police.

The high priest replicated in his person the whole significance of the temple system. While relationship with God did entail praise and thanksgiving, the main obstacle to any relationship with God was actions that dishonored God, called sin. Since God was Israelite specific—the God of Israel—to dishonor God meant to besmirch his honor and standing both within Israel and in the eyes of all other nations. To restore his honor, God had to exact satisfaction from those who dishonored him, which undoubtedly included those permitting such dishonor. The main duty of the high priest was to dissuade God from taking such satisfaction by means of sacrifices offered in the temple. He was the one authorized by the God of Israel to make atonement for the dishonoring acts (sins) of the whole Israelite community. This office endowed the person holding it even for a short time with lifelong holiness. His death had the power to atone for sins as well. He was the only human being allowed to enter the Holy of Holies on the Day of Atonement. And he presided over the political religious court called the Sanhedrin.

Although according to Israel's Scriptures (Exod 29:7ff.; 30:22ff.) the high priest was to be anointed ("oiled") into office, the practice ceased in the Herod-Roman period. The same is true of the length of office, which used to be lifelong and hereditary (that is, open to sons of high priests, not any priest). Persons from the proper priestly families, chosen by other priests, took office by being robed (investiture) with the sacred robes of office (often kept by kings and Romans to control selection of high priests).

After the high priest came a number of chief priests: one "captain" of the temple (see Acts 4:1; 5:24, 26), who was the right hand of the high priest and was in charge of temple operations. Then came seven temple overseers of various operations, and, next, at least three treasurers. All had to be residents of Jerusalem to fulfill these functions. Furthermore, nonresidents included the directors assigning ordinary priests to their weekly course and the directors of the daily course, Then came ordinary priests, followed by a large number of Levites, some of whom had permanent tasks to perform in the temple. (For details, see Jeremias 1969:147-221.)

Three Zones of Personality

Whereas some philosophically oriented persons in the Greco-Roman world thought of the human person in terms of body and soul, the Mediterranean world traditionally thought in terms of what anthropologists have called "zones of interaction" with the world around. Three such zones make up the human person and all appear repeatedly in the Gospels:

1. The zone of emotion-fused thought includes will, intellect, judgment, personality, and feeling all rolled together. It is the activity of the eyes and heart (sight, insight, understanding, choosing, loving, thinking, valuing, and so on).

2. The zone of self-expressive speech includes communication, particularly that which is self-revealing. It is listening and responding. It is the activity of the mouth, ears, tongue, lips, throat and teeth (speaking, hearing, singing, swearing, cursing, listening, eloquence, silence, crying, and so on).

3. The zone of purposeful action is the zone of external behavior or interaction with the environment. It is the activity of the hands, feet, fingers, and legs (walking, sitting, standing, touching, accomplishing, and so on).

Human activity can be described in terms of any particular zone or all three. In Matt 5:27-32 two zones come into play. Both committing an action such as adultery and using the "right hand" refer to the zone of purposeful action, to activity. Looking, of course, is a function of the "eye," while the "lustful" aspect derives from the heart, together or singly metaphors for the zone of emotion-fused thought. In Mark 8:17-19 all three zones are in play. Thus, in v. 17 Jesus uses his heart to become aware and his mouth to speak. He asks about "hardened hearts," that is, an inability to think and perceive and assess properly. Hard hearts are hearts that malfunction, largely due to ill will. In v. 18 Jesus asks about the eyes that get information for the heart, the ears that learn of others as persons and the heart that is supposed to remember. Verse 19 mentions breaking bread, the hands-feet zone of action.

When a writer refers to all three zones, we can assume that comment is being made about complete human experience. Thus, John writes, "What was from the beginning, what we have heard, what we have seen with our eyes, what we have looked at and touched with our hands, concerning the word of life . . ." (1 John 1:1). The statement is a Semitic expression of total involvement, "body and soul" as we would say. All three zones are likewise given special attention in the latter part of the Sermon on the Mount: eyes–heart (Matt 6:19—7:6), mouth–ears (7:7-11) and hands–feet (7:13-27). The same is true of the interpretation of the parable of the sower in Luke 8:11-15. For additional examples, see Exod 21:24; Prov 6:16-19; 2 Kgs 4:34; Dan 10:6.

The Twelve

The expression "the Twelve" refers to the faction founded and selected by Jesus to assist him in the task of proclaiming the forthcoming Israelite theocracy (Luke 6:12-13; 22:14; and elsewhere in the Synoptics). Thus, in the Synoptic tradition, the Twelve are Jesus' collaborators, working in the communication of the innovation of the kingdom of God. But in Acts their role changes to that of witnesses to all that Jesus said and did, and to what the God of Israel did to Jesus (Acts 1). They make their proclamation in Acts as witnesses to the resurrection. Earlier, Paul mentions the Twelve [sic] in this role, as he lists them in his list of witnesses to Jesus' resurrection (1 Cor 15:5).

Why Twelve? By choosing the Twelve, Jesus sought continuity with the past and the constitution of ancient Israel (twelve tribes), and he looked forward to the kingdom of God, which would embrace all Israel, that is, all twelve tribes. In this way Jesus laid claim to Israel, not a part of it but the whole people in all its divisions. Thus, in the Lukan tradition (22:30), the Twelve would share Jesus' table and "sit on thrones judging the twelve tribes of Israel" (see Matt 19:28). During the period from the death of Jesus to the election of Matthias (Acts 1:15-16) the tradition speaks of the Eleven (Matt 28:16; Mark 16:14; Luke 24:9, 33; Acts 1:26). And Luke notes the urgency of having the number Twelve restored to this group of witnesses in the discussion of filling Judas's place (Acts 1:12-26). Yet in the course of the story of Acts, when one of the Twelve, James the son of Zebedee, is murdered by Herod Agrippa I, grandson of Herod the Great, no one is chosen to take his place, as in the case of Judas (Acts 12:1-3). A good reason for not filling his place is that there were no more living reliable witnesses to events "from the beginning." After all, witnesses cannot have successors.

Witness and Witnessing

From the viewpoint of verifying some event, a person who observes the event is called a witness. There are eyewitnesses and earwitnesses (see Acts 9:7). In this sense, a witness is a person present at the occurrence of some event. Should this person be called upon to attest to the occurrence of some event at which he was or was not present, that person is also called a witness, for example, in court or in a group that questions him/her about some event. Persons who attest to their inner beliefs, for example, to their faith in Jesus, are not witnesses but confessors or professors of some belief.

The writer of Luke-Acts is interested in writing his "orderly account" so that his audience "may know the truth concerning the things about which you [they]

The theater at Ephesus is located on the west slope of ancient Mt. Pion. The theater is one of the best preserved from antiquity and in an excellent example of a very large Hellenistic theater. From Cities of Paul *© 2004 The President and Fellows of Harvard College.*

had been instructed" (Luke 1:4). In the service of this truth, the writer lists the assistance of witnesses. At the opening of Acts, the resurrected Jesus himself states to the Eleven: "you will be my witnesses" (Acts 1:8). Thus, Luke's main witnesses are the Eleven, soon to be the restored Twelve. **Twelve.** On the occasion of searching for a successor to Judas, Luke reports the required qualifications of such a witness. He must be one of "the men who have accompanied us during all the time that the Lord Jesus went in and out among us, beginning from the baptism of John until the day when he was taken from us—one of these must become a witness with us to the resurrection" (Acts 1:21-22). As Acts unfolds, the story is frequently punctuated with the mention of this role (Acts 2:32; 3:15; 5:32; 20:41; 13:31).

Yet the writer knows of another type of Jesus group witness, a person who actually did not accompany Jesus from the time of John's baptism to the resurrection. Rather these witnesses attest to the resurrection of Jesus through an alternate state of conscious experience. **Alternate States of Consciousness (ASC).** The first such witness mentioned in Acts is the Hellenistic deacon Stephen, "who gazed into the sky and saw the glory of God and Jesus standing at the right hand of God" (Acts 7:55). His witness: "Look, I see the heavens opened and the Son of Man standing at the right hand of God" (Acts 7:56). Stephen's audience did not like his witness, so they killed him (Acts 7:57-58). **Establishment Violence.** Later in the story, Paul himself characterizes Stephen as Jesus' witness, as he reports his conversation with the resurrected Jesus: "And while the blood of your witness Stephen was shed, I myself was standing by, approving and keeping the coats of those who killed him" (Acts 22:22).

From Luke's perspective, the highly significant witness to the resurrected Jesus through an alternate state of consciousness experience was Paul. In Acts 22, Paul reports the vision of the Jesus group prophet Ananias, who tells Paul of the significance of his vision of the resurrected Jesus: "The God of our ancestors has chosen you to know his will, to see the Righteous One and to hear his own voice; for you will be his witness to all the world of what you have seen and heard" (Acts 22:14-15). Finally, Paul has a vision in which the exalted Lord notes that just as Paul bore witness to him in Jerusalem (Acts 23:1-10), so now he must do in Rome (Acts 23:11). Paul, then, is not a witness to all that Jesus said and did while "among us," but a witness to his vision of the resurrected Jesus and to what this exalted Jesus said to him.

From these instances, we see that Jesus group witnesses present at the occurrence of some event and the event in question covered consensual reality and alternate reality. Obviously, both count as witnessing to the truth concerning the things about which Jesus group members have been instructed. Both types of event count as real events according to first-century Mediterranean criteria. And according to twenty-first-century neuroscience, both realities (the distinctions are ours) are perceived in the same part of the brain. The assessment of the value of such observations, whether consensual reality or alternate reality, is based not on objective criteria but on social criteria by which cerebral percepts are various evaluated.

Bibliography

Arnaiz-Villena, Antonio, Nagah Elaiwa, Carlos Silvera, Ahmed Rosom, Juan Moscoso, Eduardo Gómez-Casado, Luis Allende, Pilar Varela, and Jorge Martínez-Laso. 2001. "The Origin of Palestinians and Their Genetic Relatedness with Other Mediterranean Populations." *Human Immunology* 62:889–900.

Arterbury, Andrew. 2005. *Entertaining Angels: Early Christian Hospitality in its Mediterranean Setting.* New Testament Monographs 8. Sheffield: Sheffield Phoenix Press.

Aujac, Germaine. 1966. *Strabon et la science de son temps: Les sciences du monde.* Paris: Belles Lettres.

Bagatti, Belarmino, O.F.M. 1971. *The Church from the Circumcision: History and Archaeology of the Judaeo-Christians.* Publications of the Studium Biblicum Franciscanum, Smaller Series 2. Jerusalem: Franciscan Printing Press.

Barna, George. 2002. *The State of the Church, 2002.* Ventura, Calif.: Issachar Resources.

Bartchy, S. Scott. 1991. "Community of Goods in Acts: Idealization or Social Reality?" In *The Future of Early Christianity: Essays in Honor of Helmut Koester,* ed. Birger Pearson et al., 309–18. Minneapolis: Fortress Press.

———. 1995a. "The Credibility Factor: How Christian Practice Affected the Persuasiveness of Early Christian Preaching." In *Faith in Practice: Studies in the Books of Acts,* ed. David A. Fiensy and William D. Howden, 151–81. Joplin, Mo.: College Press.

———. 1995b. "'Agnostos Theos': Luke's Message to the 'Nations' about Israel's God." In *Society of Biblical Literature 1995 Seminar Papers,* ed. Eugene J. Lovering, Jr., 304–20. Atlanta: Scholars Press.

———. 1997. "Narrative Criticism." In *Dictionary of the Later New Testament and Its Developments,* ed. Ralph P. Martin and Peter H. Davids, 787A-792A. Downers Grove, Ill. InterVarsity Press.

———. 2002. "Divine Power, Community Formation, and Leadership in the Acts of the Apostles." In *Community Formation in the Early Church and in the Church Today,* ed. Richard N. Longenecker, 89–104. Peabody, Mass.: Hendrickson.

Brook, Kevin Alan. 1999. *The Jews of Khazaria.* Northvale, N.J.: J. Aronson.

Cohen, Shaye J. D. 1999. *The Beginnings of Jewishness: Boundaries, Varieties, Uncertainties.* Hellenistic Culture and Society 31. Berkeley, Calif.: University of California Press.

De Vos, Craig. 1999. "Finding a Charge that Fits: The Accusation against Paul and Silas at Philippi (Acts 16.19-21)." *Journal for the Study of the New Testament* 74:51–63.

Elliott, John J. 1991. "Household & Meals vs. Temple Purity: Replication Patterns in Luke-Acts." *Biblical Theology Bulletin* 21:102–8. Published also as "Household and meals versus the Temple purity system: Patterns of Replication in Luke-Acts." *Hervormde teologiese studies* 47 (1991): 386–99.

Esler, Philip F. 1987. *Community and Gospel in Luke-Acts: The Social and Political Motivations of Lucan Theology.* Society for New Testament Studies Monograph Series 57. Cambridge: Cambridge University Press; reprinted 1990 and 1994.

———. 1990. "Acts of the Apostles." In *A Dictionary of Biblical Theology,* ed. R. J. Coggins and J. L. Houlden, 2–5. Philadelphia: Trinity Press International.

———. 1992. "Glossolalia and the Admission of the Gentiles into the Early Christian Community." *Biblical Theology Bulletin* 22:136–42.

Goodman, D. Felicitas. 2001. *Maya Apocalypse: Seventeen Years with the Women of a Yucatan Village.* Bloomington, Ind.: Indiana University Press.

Hagedorn, Anselm, and Jerome H. Neyrey. 1998. "'It Was Out of Envy that They Handed Jesus Over' (Mark 15.10): The Anatomy of Envy and the Gospel of Mark." *Journal for the Study of the New Testament* 69:15–56.

Hansen, M. L. 1938. *The Problem of the Third Generation Immigrant.* Augustana Historical Society Publications 8. Rock Island, Ill.: Augustana Historical Society.

Herberg, Will. 1955. *Protestant-Catholic-Jews: An Essay in American Religious Sociology.* Garden City, N.Y.: Doubleday.

Hollenbach, Paul W. 1982. "Jesus, Demoniacs, and Public Authorities: A Socio-Historical Study." *Journal of the American Academy of Religion* 49:567–88.

Hsu, Francis L. K. 1983. "Variations in Ancestor Worship Beliefs and Their Relation to Kinship." In *Rugged Individualism Reconsidered: Essays in Psychological Anthropology,* 248–62. Knoxville, Tenn.: University of Tennessee Press.

Jeremias, Joachim. 1969. *Jerusalem in the Time of Jesus: An Investigation into Economic and Social Conditions during the New Testament Period.* Philadelphia: Fortress Press.

Judah, ha-Levi. 1998. *The Kuzari: In Defense of the Despised Faith* [Kitāb al-hujjah. English & Hebrew]. Translated and annotated by N. Daniel Korobkin. Northvalc, N.J.: J. Aronson.

Krueger, J. 2001. "Psychology of Social Categorization." In *International Encyclopedia of the Social and Behavioral Sciences,* ed. Neil J. Smelser and Paul B. Baltes, 21:142ff. Amsterdam: Elsevier.

Malina, Bruce J. 1986. "The Received View and What It Cannot Do: III John and Hospitality." In *Social-scientific Criticism of the New Testament and Its Social World,* ed. John H. Elliott, 171–94. *Semeia* 35. Decatur, Ga.: Scholars Press.

———. 1996a. "Mediterranean Sacrifice: Dimensions of Domestic and Political Religion." *Biblical Theology Bulletin* 26:26–44.

———. 1996b. *The Social World of Jesus and the Gospels*. London and New York: Routledge.

———. 2001. *The New Testament World: Insights from Cultural Anthropology*. Third ed., rev. and updated. Louisville: Westminster John Knox.

———. 2005. "From the Jesus Faction to the Synoptic Gospels: The Synoptic Gospels and the Third Generation Phenomenon." In *Kontexte der Schrift, Band 2, Kultur, Politik, Religion, Sprache–Text; Für Wolfgang Stegemann zum 60. Geburtstag*, ed. Christian Strecker, 61–74. Stuttgart: Kohlhammer.

Malina, Bruce J., and Jerome H. Neyrey. 1988. *Calling Jesus Names: The Social Value of Labels in Matthew*. Foundations and Facets: Social Facets. Sonoma, Calif.: Polebridge.

Malina, Bruce J., and John J. Pilch. 2000. *Social Science Commentary on Revelation*. Minneapolis: Fortress Press.

———. 2006. *Social Science Commentary on the Letters of Paul*. Minneapolis: Fortress Press.

Malina, Bruce J., and Richard L. Rohrbaugh. 1998. *Social Science Commentary on the Gospel of John*. Minneapolis: Fortress Press.

Moreland, Richard L., and John M. Levine. 1988. "Group Dynamics Over Time: Development and Socialization in Small Groups." In *The Social Psychology of Time: New Perspectives*, ed. Joseph E. McGrath, 151–81. Newbury Park et al.: Sage Publications.

Moxnes, Halvor. 1995. "'He saw that the city was full of idols' (Acts 17:16): Visualizing the World of the First Christians." In *Mighty Minorities? Minorities in Early Christianity—Positions and Strategies: Essays in Honour of Jacob Jervell on His 70th Birthday, 21. May 1995*, ed. David Hellholm, Halvor Moxnes, Turid Karlsen Seim. Oslo: Scandinavian University Press.

Nader, Laura, and Harry F. Todd, Jr., eds. 1978. *The Disputing Process—Law in Ten Societies*. New York: Columbia University Press. See "Introduction," pp. 1–40.

Neyrey, Jerome H. 1984. "The Forensic Defense Speech and Paul's Trial Speeches in Acts 22–26: Form and Function." In *Luke-Acts: New Perspectives from the Society of Biblical Literature Seminar*, ed. Charles H. Talbert, 210–24. New York: Crossroad.

———. 1990. "Acts 17, Epicureans and Theodicy: A Study in Stereotypes." In *Greeks, Romans, and Christians. Essays in Honor of Abraham J. Malherbe*, ed. David Balch and Wayne Meeks, 118–34. Minneapolis: Fortress Press.

———. 1991. "The Symbolic Universe of Luke-Acts: 'They turn the world upside down.'" In *The Social World of Luke-Acts: Models for Interpretation*, ed. Jerome H. Neyrey, 271–304. Peabody, Mass.: Hendrickson.

———. 1996. "Luke's Social Location of Paul: Cultural Anthropology and the Status of Paul in Acts." In *History, Literature, and Society in the Book of Acts*, ed. Ben Witherington III, 251–79. Cambridge: Cambridge University Press.

———. 1998. *Honor and Shame in the Gospel of Matthew*. Louisville: Westminster John Knox.

———. 2003a. "'Teaching You in Public and from House to House' (Acts 20:20): Unpacking a Cultural Stereotype." *Journal for the Study of the New Testament* 26:69–102.

———. 2003b. "The Social Location of Paul: How Paul Was Educated and What He Could Compose as Indices of His Social Location." In *Fabrics of Discourse: Essays in Honor of Vernon K. Robbins*, ed. David B. Gowler et al., 126–64. Harrisburg, Penn.: Trinity Press International.

———. 2005. "God, Benefactor and Patron: The Major Cultural Model for Interpreting the Deity in Greco-Roman Antiquity." *Journal for the Study of the New Testament* 27:465–92.

———, ed. 1991. *The Social World of Luke-Acts: Models for Interpretation.* Peabody, Mass.: Hendrickson.

Oporto, Santiago Guijarro. 2004. "La Articulación literaria del libro de los Hechos." *Estudios Bíblicos* 62:185–204.

Pilch, John J. 1993. "Visions in Revelation and Alternate Consciousness: A Perspective from Cultural Anthropology." *Listening: Journal of Religion and Culture* 28:231–44.

———. 1994. "The Transfiguration of Jesus: An Experience of Alternate Reality." In *Modelling Early Christianity: Social Scientific Studies of the New Testament in Its Context*, ed. Philip F. Esler, 47–64. London and New York: Routledge.

———. 1996. "Altered States of Consciousness: A 'Kitbashed' Model." *Biblical Theology Bulletin* 26:133–38.

———. 1998. "Appearances of the Risen Jesus in Cultural Context: Experiences of Alternate Reality." *Biblical Theology Bulletin* 28:52–60.

———. 2002a. "Altered States of Consciousness Events in the Synoptics." In *The Social Setting of Jesus and the Gospels*, ed. Bruce J. Malina, Wolfgang Stegemann, and Gerd Theissen, 103–115. Minneapolis: Fortress Press.

———. 2002b. "The Nose and Altered States of Consciousness: Tascodrugites and Ezekiel." *Hervormde teologiese studies* 58:708–20.

———. 2002c. "Paul's Ecstatic Trance Experience near Damascus in Acts of the Apostles." *Hervormde teologiese studies* 58:690–707.

———. 2003. "Becoming Holy Women and Holy Men in the New Testament." *Landas* 17:81–91.

———. 2004. *Visions and Healing in Acts of the Apostles: How the Early Believers Experienced God.* Collegeville: Liturgical Press.

———. 2005a. "The Ascension of Jesus: A Social Scientific Perspective." In *Kontexte der Schrift, Band 2: Kultur, Politik, Religion, Sprache–Text; Für Wolfgang Stegemann zum 60. Geburtstag*, ed. Christian Strecker, 75–82. Stuttgart: Kohlhammer.

———. 2005b. "Holy Men and Their Sky Journeys." *Biblical Theology Bulletin* 35:106–11.

———. 2005c. "Paul's Call to Be a Holy Man (Apostle): In His Own Words and in Other Words." *Hervormde teologiese studies* 61:1–13.

———. 2005d. "A Window into the Biblical World: Paul the Apostle in Cultural Context." *The Bible Today* 43:317–22.

———. 2005e. "A Window into the Biblical World: Jesus' Ascent to the Sky." *The Bible Today* 43:389–93.

Prickett, Stephen. 1996. *Origins of Narrative: The Romantic Appropriation of the Bible.* Cambridge: Cambridge University Press.

Rohrbaugh, Richard. 2001. "Gossip in the New Testament." In *Social Scientific Models for Interpreting the Bible: Essays by the Context Group in Honor of Bruce J. Malina,* ed. John J. Pilch, 239–59. Leiden: Brill.

Rubenstein, Jeffrey L. 2003. *The Culture of the Babylonian Talmud.* Baltimore: Johns Hopkins University Press.

Seland, Torrey. 1995. *Establishment Violence in Philo and Luke: A Study of Nonconformity to the Torah & Jewish Vigilante Reactions.* Biblical Interpretations Series 15. Leiden: Brill.

———. 1998. "Once More—The Hellenists, Hebrews and Stephen: Conflict and Conflict Management in Acts 6–7." In *Recruitment, Conquest, and Conflict: Strategies in Judaism, Early Christianity, and the Greco-Roman World,* ed. P. Borgen, V. K. Robbins, and D. Gowler, 169–207. Emory Studies in Early Christianity. Atlanta: Scholars Press.

———. 2002. "Saul of Tarsus and Early Zealotism: Reading Gal 1.13-14 in Light of Philo's Writings." *Biblica* 83:449–71.

Smith, Morton. 1952. "The Common Theology of the Ancient Near East." *Journal of Biblical Literature* 71:135–48.

Strecker, Christian. 2002. "Jesus and the Demoniacs." In *The Social Setting of Jesus and the Gospels,* ed. Wolfgang Stegemann, Bruce Malina, and Gerd Theissen, 117–33. Minneapolis: Fortress Press.

Strelan, Rick. 2000. "Recognizing the Gods (Acts 14:8-10)." *New Testament Studies* 46:488–503.

———. 2004. *Strange Acts: Studies in the Cultural World of the Acts of the Apostles.* (Beihefte zur Zeitschrift für die neutestamentliche Wissenschaft 126. Berlin and New York: de Gruyter.

Talbert, Charles H. 1974. *Literary Patterns, Theological Themes, and the Genre of Luke-Acts.* Society of Biblical Literature Monograph Series 20. Missoula, Mont.: Society of Biblical Literature and Scholars Press.

———. 1997. *A Literary and Theological Commentary on the Acts of the Apostles.* New York: Crossroad.

Trompf, G. W. 1979. *The Idea of Historical Recurrence in Western Thought: From Antiquity to the Reformation.* Berkeley, Calif.: University of California Press.

Tuckman, B. W. 1965. "Developmental Sequence in Small Groups." *Psychological Bulletin* 63:384–99.

van der Horst, P. W. 1976–77. "Peter's Shadow: The Religio-Historical Background of Acts V.15." *New Testament Studies* 23:204–12.

———. 1979. "Der Schatten im Hellenistischen Volksglauben." In *Studies in Hellenistic Religions,* ed. M. J. Vermaseren, 27–36. Etudes préliminaires aux religions orientales dans l'empire romain 78. Leiden: Brill.

List of Scenarios